KING
OF
THE
NORTH
WIND

◆

THE LIFE OF
HENRY II
IN FIVE ACTS

◆

CLAUDIA GOLD

WILLIAM
COLLINS

William Collins
An imprint of HarperCollins*Publishers*
1 London Bridge Street
London SE1 9GF

www.WilliamCollinsBooks.com

First published in Great Britain in 2018 by William Collins
This William Collins paperback edition published in 2019

1

A catalogue record for this book is
available from the British Library

ISBN 978-0-00-755480-5

Maps and family trees by Martin Brown

Printed and bound in Great Britain by
CPI Group (UK) Ltd, Croydon, CR0 4YY

MIX
Paper from
responsible sources
FSC C007454

This book is produced from independently certified FSC paper
to ensure responsible forest management.

Find out more about HarperCollins and the environment at
www.harpercollins.co.uk/green

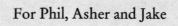

For Phil, Asher and Jake

CONTENTS

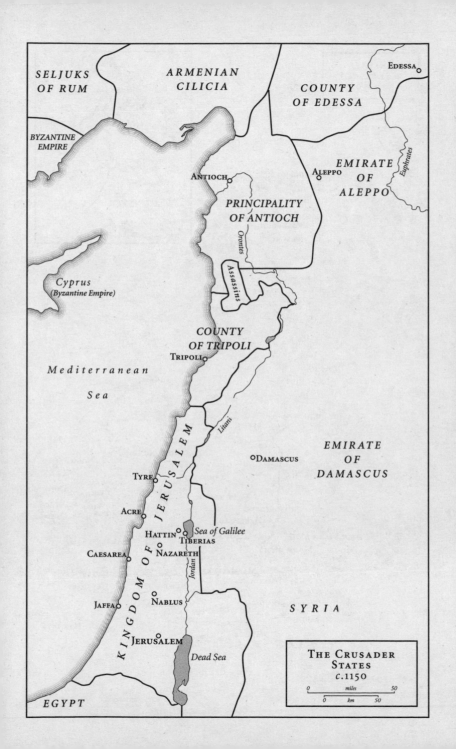

SELJUKS
OF RUM

ARMENIAN
CILICIA

EDESSA

COUNTY
OF EDESSA

BYZANTINE
EMPIRE

EMIRATE
OF
ALEPPO

ALEPPO

ANTIOCH

Euphrates

PRINCIPALITY
OF ANTIOCH

Orontes

Cyprus
(Byzantine Empire)

Assassins

COUNTY
OF TRIPOLI

Mediterranean

TRIPOLI

Sea

Litani

EMIRATE
OF
DAMASCUS

DAMASCUS

TYRE

ACRE

Sea of Galilee

HATTIN
TIBERIAS

CAESAREA

NAZARETH

Jordan

JAFFA

NABLUS

SYRIA

JERUSALEM

Dead Sea

EGYPT

THE CRUSADER
STATES
c.1150

0   miles   50

0   km   50

BRITAIN
& IRELAND
c.1150

ULSTER

CONNACHT
MEATH

LEINSTER

MUNSTER

SCOTLAND

STIRLING
Forth
EDINBURGH
BERWICK
ROXBURGH
JEDBURGH
ALNWICK

CARLISLE
DURHAM

*Irish
Sea*

*North
Sea*

YORK

E
N
G
L
A
N
D

GWYNEDD

CHESTER

POWYS

NOTTINGHAM
Trent

NORWICH

LEICESTER

WARWICK
Severn

HUNTINGDON
ELY
FORNHAM
DUNWICH
CAMBRIDGE
BURY
FRAMLINGHAM
ORFORD

WORCESTER
HEREFORD

DEHEUBARTH

ST DAVID'S

MONMOUTH

CARDIFF

GLOUCESTER
OXFORD
WALLINGFORD

ST ALBANS

LONDON
WESTMINSTER
Thames

MALMESBURY
BRISTOL
BATH
DEVIZES
WINDSOR
NEWBURY

CANTERBURY
DOVER

GLASTONBURY
TAUNTON

SALISBURY

WINCHESTER

ARUNDEL

HASTINGS

EXETER
WAREHAM
SOUTHAMPTON

English Channel

0   *miles*   50

0   *km*   50

ENGLAND

English Channel

BOULOGNE
FLANDERS

BARFLEUR
NORMANDY
BAYEUX
CAEN
LISIEUX
CONCHES
VERNEUIL
PACY
BRETEUIL
SOISSONS
ROUEN
GOURNAY
GISORS
VEXIN
MANTES
St DENIS
PARIS
MONTMIRAIL

FALAISE
ARGENTAN
DOMFRONT
DREUX
SAVIGNY
MONT St MICHEL
DOL
PERCHE
CHARTRES
BELLÊME
ALENÇON
La FERTÉ-BERNARD
BRITTANY
RENNES
Le MANS
FRETEVAL
ORLÉANS
MONTEREAU

Loire

ANGERS
TOURS
BLOIS
SANCERRE
NANTES
SAUMUR
FONTEVRAUD
CHINON
BOURGES
LOUDUN
MIREBEAU
BERRY
POITOU
POITIERS
LUSIGNAN

La ROCHELLE
SAINTES
LIMOGES
ANGOULÊME

*Bay of
Biscay*
AQUITAINE

BORDEAUX
QUERCY
CAHORS

Garonne

GASCONY
TOULOUSE

NAVARRE

*Mediterranean
Sea*

ARAGON

FRANCE
*c.*1170
showing principal
towns and villages

0   miles   100
0   km   100

SCOTLAND

IRELAND

WALES

ENGLAND

York

Oxford

LONDON

Canterbury

Exeter

North Sea

English Channel

FLANDERS

HOLY ROMAN EMPIRE

ROUEN

VEXIN

NORMANDY

Paris

CHAMPAGNE

BRITTANY

MAINE

Le Mans

BLOIS

FRENCH ROYAL DOMAIN

ANJOU

TOURAINE

BURGUNDY

Nantes

Angers

POITOU

Poitiers

BERRY

SAINTONGE

Angoulême

LA MARCHE

Bay of Biscay

LIMOUSIN

PÉRIGORD

AUVERGNE

Bordeaux

AGENAIS

AQUITAINE

GASCONY

TOULOUSE

Toulouse

NAVARRE

Mediterranean Sea

ARAGON

0   miles   100
0   km   100

HENRY II's EMPIRE
*c.*1170

Lands under Henry II's control

French Royal Domain

THE
GREAT REVOLT
1173–4

Lands under
Henry II's control

French Royal
Domain

Revolts/battles

Attacks against
Henry II

miles 100
km 100

IRELAND

SCOTLAND

*William of
Scotland*
BERWICK
WARK
BAMBURGH
BELFORD
ALNWICK
HARBOTTLE
NEWCASTLE
LIDDELL
BURGH
PRUDHOE
CARLISLE
APPLEBY

MALZEARD
YORK

North
Sea

WALES

ENGLAND

TUTBURY
NOTTINGHAM
LEICESTER
NORTHAMPTON
HUNTINGDON
NORWICH
DUNWICH
FORNHAM
FRAMLINGHAM
OXFORD

LONDON
CANTERBURY

*Robert
Blanchmains,
Earl of
Leicester*

EXETER

FLANDERS

English Channel

*Counts of
Flanders &
Boulogne*

ROUEN
GISORS
CAEN
LISIEUX
VEXIN
ST DENIS
PARIS
NORMANDY
AVRANCHES
VERNEUIL
Louis VII
DOL
ARGENTAN
BRITTANY
*Count of
Blois*
MAINE
FRENCH
ROYAL
DOMAIN
*Rebel
Bretons*

BLOIS

ANJOU

Bay of
Biscay

ANGERS

POITOU

The English Succession

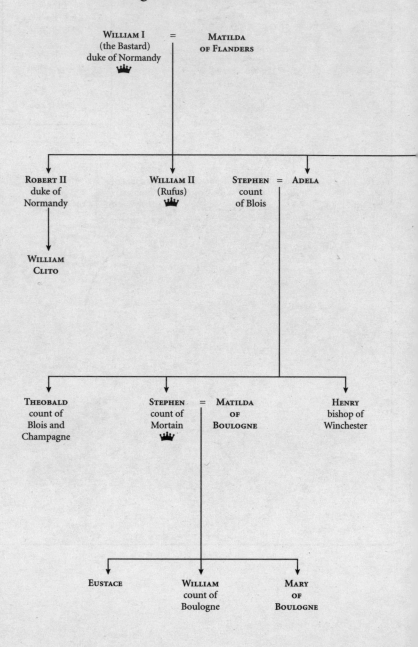

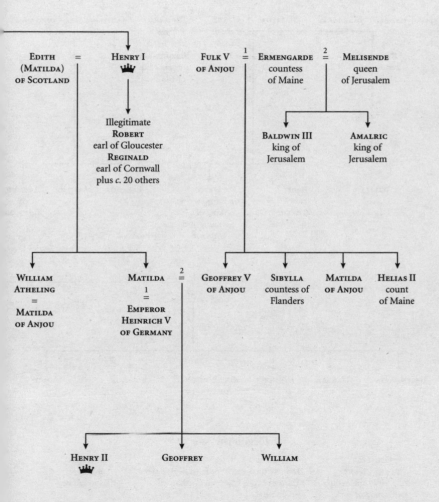

Issue of Henry II

(both legitimate, with Eleanor of Aquitaine, and illegitimate)

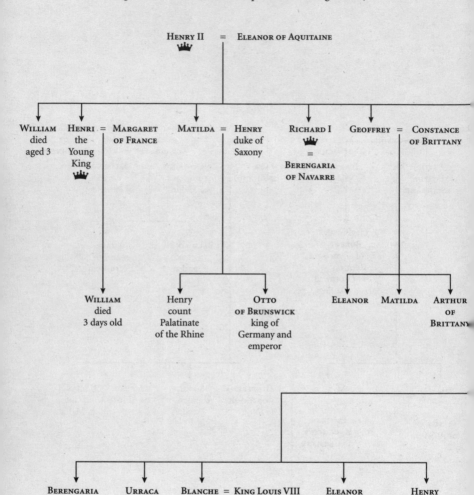

Illegitimate issue

GEOFFREY PLANTAGENET
bishop-elect of Lincoln,
archbishop of York

WILLIAM LONGSWORD
third earl of
Salisbury

MORGAN
provost of Beverley
and bishop-elect
of Durham

MATILDA
abbess of
Barking Abbey

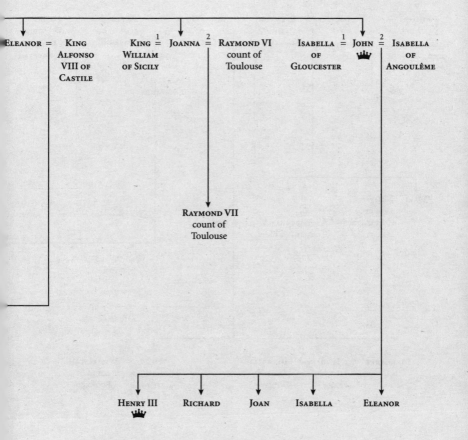

ELEANOR = KING
ALFONSO
VIII OF
CASTILE

KING =¹ JOANNA =² RAYMOND VI
WILLIAM   count of
OF SICILY   Toulouse

ISABELLA =¹ JOHN =² ISABELLA
OF   OF
GLOUCESTER   ANGOULÊME

RAYMOND VII
count of
Toulouse

HENRY III   RICHARD   JOAN   ISABELLA   ELEANOR

The Capetian Family Tree

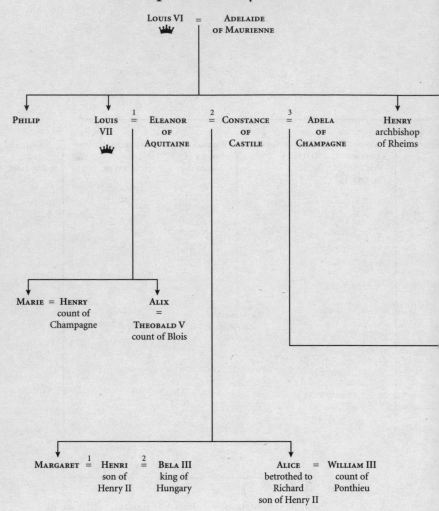

LOUIS VI = ADELAIDE OF MAURIENNE

PHILIP

LOUIS VII 1 = ELEANOR OF AQUITAINE 2 = CONSTANCE OF CASTILE 3 = ADELA OF CHAMPAGNE

HENRY archbishop of Rheims

MARIE = HENRY count of Champagne

ALIX = THEOBALD V count of Blois

MARGARET 1 = HENRI son of Henry II 2 = BELA III king of Hungary

ALICE = WILLIAM III betrothed to count of Richard Ponthieu son of Henry II

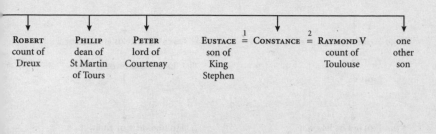

ROBERT	PHILIP	PETER	EUSTACE	1= CONSTANCE =2	RAYMOND V	one
count of	dean of	lord of	son of		count of	other
Dreux	St Martin	Courtenay	King		Toulouse	son
	of Tours		Stephen			

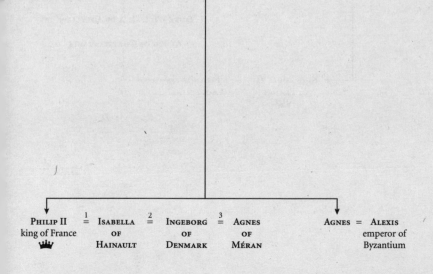

PHILIP II	1= ISABELLA	2= INGEBORG	3= AGNES	AGNES = ALEXIS
king of France	OF	OF	OF	emperor of
♛	HAINAULT	DENMARK	MÉRAN	Byzantium

The Relationship between
Louis VII and Eleanor of Aquitaine

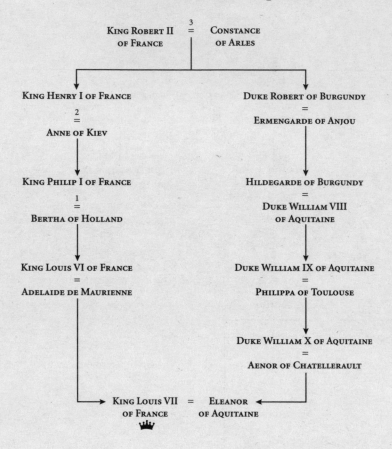

The Relationship between
Eleanor of Aquitaine and Henry II

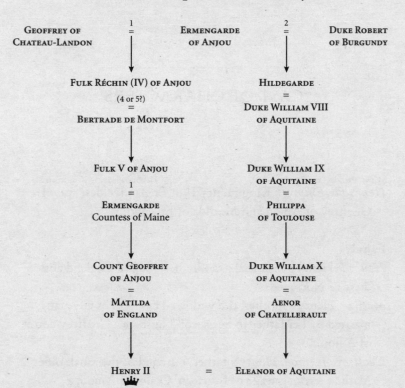

| GEOFFREY OF CHATEAU-LANDON | 1 = | ERMENGARDE OF ANJOU | 2 = | DUKE ROBERT OF BURGUNDY |

FULK RÉCHIN (IV) OF ANJOU
(4 or 5?)
=
BERTRADE DE MONTFORT

HILDEGARDE
=
DUKE WILLIAM VIII OF AQUITAINE

FULK V OF ANJOU
1
=
ERMENGARDE
Countess of Maine

DUKE WILLIAM IX OF AQUITAINE
=
PHILIPPA OF TOULOUSE

COUNT GEOFFREY OF ANJOU
=
MATILDA OF ENGLAND

DUKE WILLIAM X OF AQUITAINE
=
AENOR OF CHATELLERAULT

HENRY II = **ELEANOR OF AQUITAINE**

CAST OF CHARACTERS

Henry FitzEmpress: King Henry II of England, eldest son of Geoffrey of Anjou and Matilda of England.

Family

Henry I: Henry's maternal grandfather; king of England and duke of Normandy.

Matilda: Henry's mother; the widowed empress of Germany, married by her father to her second husband, Geoffrey count of Anjou.

Geoffrey of Anjou: Henry's father; husband of the much older Matilda. From the age of fourteen, Count of Anjou, a principality in northern France.

Geoffrey FitzEmpress: Henry's younger brother, who rebels against Henry as soon as he is able.

William FitzEmpress: Henry's youngest brother; he remains staunchly loyal.

Fulk of Anjou: Henry's paternal grandfather; leaves Anjou to marry Queen Melisende of Jerusalem. Through this second marriage, becomes king of the Latin Kingdom.

Eleanor of Aquitaine: Henry's wife, previously married to Louis VII of France; duchess of Aquitaine, the largest and wealthiest province in France, in her own right. She is about eleven years older than Henry.

William of Poitiers: Henry and Eleanor's eldest son, who dies aged three.

Henri the Young King: Henry and Eleanor's second son; charming, frivolous, the family 'golden boy'. Crowned alongside his father in 1170, but given no authority.

Richard: Henry and Eleanor's third son, destined to rule in Aquitaine.

Geoffrey: Henry and Eleanor's fourth son; duke of Brittany.

John: Henry and Eleanor's fifth son and last child, later known as 'Lackland'; Henry's favourite legitimate son.

Matilda of Saxony: Henry and Eleanor's eldest daughter; married to Henry the Lion, duke of Saxony. Her beauty inspires the troubadour poet Bertran de Born to write scandalous verse about her.

Young Eleanor: Henry and Eleanor's second daughter; married to Alfonso VIII of Castile.

Joanna: Henry and Eleanor's youngest daughter; married to King William 'the good' of Sicily. Later, she is touted as a possible bride for Saladin's younger brother.

Robert, earl of Gloucester: Eldest illegitimate son of Henry I, one of the greatest magnates in England, and Henry's uncle. Robert fought for Henry's rights to rule alongside his half-sister, Matilda.

Reginald, earl of Cornwall: Another illegitimate son of Henry I. Unwavering in his support for his nephew.

Geoffrey Plantagenet: Henry's eldest illegitimate son; probably his favourite and best-liked child.

Matilda, prioress of Barking Abbey: Henry's illegitimate daughter, born before his marriage to Eleanor.

William Longsword, earl of Salisbury: Another of Henry's illegitimate children, born in the 1160s.

Morgan, provost of Beverly, and bishop-elect of Durham: Possibly Henry's youngest illegitimate child, born in the mid-1170s.

Baldwin, 'the leper king': Henry's first cousin, king of Jerusalem. He rules a kingdom riven with byzantine factionalism.

Marie: Eleanor's eldest daughter by Louis, married to the count of Champagne.

Alix: Eleanor's second daughter by Louis. She is married to the count of Blois.

Margaret of France: Louis' eldest daughter by his second wife, Constance of Castile. Margaret is married to Henri, Henry and Eleanor's eldest surviving son.

Alice of France: Margaret's sister; betrothed to Henry's son, Richard. Possibly Henry's mistress.

Friends

Adelard of Bath: One of Henry's four teachers, he brought knowledge of Arabic mathematics to England.

William of Conches: Another of Henry's teachers, and one of Europe's most celebrated scholars.

William Marshal: 'The greatest knight in the world', who served Henry and his family for over fifty years.

Rosamund Clifford: Henry's favourite mistress, 'the love of his life'.

Richard de Lucy: Henry's co-justiciar and one of his great magnates.

Robert, earl of Leicester: Henry's other co-justiciar; an enormously powerful nobleman.

Ranulf de Glanville: Justiciar in the latter part of Henry's reign; possible author of *On the Laws and Customs of England*, which details the reforms under Henry's reign that would become the foundations of English Common Law.

Richard FitzNigel: Henry's treasurer and author of the influential *Dialogue Concerning the Exchequer*.

Brian Fitz Count: Illegitimate son of the duke of Normandy, and one of Matilda's closest allies. They were possibly lovers.

Foes

King Stephen: Matilda's first cousin and mortal enemy. He stole the throne from her.

Matilda of Boulogne: Stephen's queen, a warrior for his cause.

Eustace: Stephen's eldest son and heir, who tries to murder Henry.

William: Stephen's second son; plots to murder Henry, although in secret.

Louis VII of France: Eleanor's first husband and Henry's overlord for his lands in France.

Bernard of Clairvaux: King Louis' closest advisor. Loathes Henry and his Angevin family, believing them to be descended from the Devil.

Thomas Becket: Henry's chancellor, and then archbishop of Canterbury.

Philip of France: A machiavellian boy-king, and Henry's nemesis.

Fairweathers

Philip, count of Flanders: Henry's first cousin, oscillates between fighting Henry and being his ally.

Bishop Henry of Blois: Henry's cousin, the bishop of Winchester; notorious for changing sides during the civil war, Henry never quite trusts him.

Count Raymond V of Toulouse: Henry's slippery adversary in the south, he vacillates in pledging his allegiance to Louis, and to Henry. Nevertheless, it is Raymond who warns Henry of impending disaster.

William the Lion: King of Scotland, and Henry's cousin.

Frederick Barbarossa (Red Beard): The Holy Roman Emperor. Barbarossa's life mirrors Henry's in many ways.

Pope Alexander III: Pope during the Becket crisis, but living in France, Alexander is torn between his host Louis, and Henry, who has pledged to support him against an antipope.

Hugh Bigod: One of Henry's most powerful lords, Hugh virtually controls East Anglia.

Chroniclers

Orderic Vitalis: An Anglo-Norman historian, Benedictine monk and author of the *Ecclesiastical History*.

Robert of Torigni: The librarian of Bec monastery in Normandy, abbot of Mont Saint-Michel. Henry's friend and the godfather of young Eleanor.

Roger of Howden: Court clerk, diplomat and itinerant justice, who spent many years in Henry's company.

William of Newburgh: Historian and Augustinian canon; one of the most balanced writers of Henry's reign.

Jordan Fantosme: Court clerk, historian, and author of an epic Anglo-Norman poem, chronicling Henry's war in the 1170s.

William FitzStephen: One of the biographers of Thomas Becket.

Walter Map: Court clerk and author of *Courtiers' Trifles*.

Gerald of Wales: A luminous and fanciful writer, who hated Henry in part because he believed he deserved a bishopric, which Henry failed to grant him.

Gervase of Canterbury: Historian, and monk of Canterbury Cathedral.

Ralph Diceto: Dean of St Paul's, and historian.

Henry of Huntingdon: Historian and author of the *Historia Anglorum*.

John of Salisbury: One of the greatest writers of his age; a fierce defender of Thomas Becket.

Ralph Niger: A partisan of Thomas Becket; like Gerald of Wales, he detested Henry.

PROLOGUE

They would not let Will leave. The play had finished fifteen minutes earlier. But still 3,000 people roared in delight and begged the players and playwright to remain. They took bow after bow to the din of stamping feet. London's richest – sat in the luxurious gallery – mixed with its poorest, who had paid a penny to stand. Will had made them believe that 'this cockpit' held 'the vasty fields of France' and of England too.

It was May 1599. William Shakespeare's *History of Henry II* was the first play to be staged at the Globe at its new site on the south bank of the river in Elizabeth I's capital city; it offered fantasy by candlelight under a ceiling painted as the heavens.

Shakespeare felt that his subject could not be bettered. He had breathed life into the legend of England's most celebrated king – 'Good' King Henry II.

He told of a duke who had battled to become a king, 'Alexander of the West' and the finest warrior of his age. Henry had forged and held an enormous empire in twelfth-century Europe. England had not had such a king since the days of Arthur. His court was the most cultured in Europe, attracting writers, poets, scholars and mathematicians from across the known world. The king's justice was everywhere, for everyone. He was a scholar-king, sportsman, politician and soldier, and his influence stretched as far as the holy city of Jerusalem.

This king had all the talents and all the gifts – until his family turned against him.

At first, there were only the traditional frustrations of royal sons, close to power but denied any of their own. But soon their mother joined the cause. Perfidy was in the air.

Before long, Henry's sons and wife united with the kings of France and Scotland, and all who bore a grudge against him. Henry was threatened on six fronts: surely an impossible challenge to overcome, even for him.

The audience was enthralled by Henry's rally to his men as they readied to fight at Dol: 'Once more unto the breach, dear friends, once more.' The Globe, for a suspended moment, was a battlefield in north-western France.

Henry could not lose this encounter; if he did, his enemies would take his kingdom. But his skill and cool head won the day.

The victory at Dol spurred Henry to fight on. He put aside his grief as he battled for two hard years across England and France, moving with almost superhuman speed between the fronts.

By the end he had vanquished them all; and, as a mark of his greatness, he forgave them – even his wife. He gave her what he had promised when he stole her from her first husband, the king of France: real power.

He even forced his fractious archbishop, Thomas Becket, into submission. Henry and Becket had been fighting for ten years. Now Becket limped out of his self-imposed exile back to Canterbury, bitter and broken, worn out by fasts and penances. Henry gave him the kiss of peace.

Shakespeare's epilogue completed the hero's life: Henry died the grand old man of Europe, at peace with his wife and his sons, and his empire intact.

The story was brilliant propaganda for Elizabeth, the fairy queen. She was an absolute monarch, just as Henry had been. Shakespeare had not shied from depicting a complex character: Henry sometimes ruled harshly, but he could also be tender. The playwright had shown the audience Henry the king and Henry the man – imperfect to be sure, but remarkable in person and triumphant over adversity.

* * *

This is, of course, not what happened.

William Shakespeare, the genius propagandist of the Tudor and nascent Stuart dynasties, never wrote about Henry II. Instead he scattered his fairy dust over the Lancastrian faction in England's War of the Roses, and the ultimate victors: his masters, the Tudors.

When the Globe theatre was moved across the river, the first play to perform there was most likely *Henry V*. The words I placed in Henry II's mouth before his battle at Dol, Shakespeare placed in the mouth of Henry V on the morning of the battle of Agincourt on St Crispin's Day. Agincourt is one of the most famous battles in English history; Dol is known only to a small band of medieval historians and enthusiasts. And today Henry II, the father of the Plantagenet dynasty that ruled England for 330 years, is largely forgotten.*

Henry was trained for power, but he had to fight for all that he gained. By the mid-1170s he was lord of England, Normandy, Brittany, Anjou, Maine, Touraine and Ireland. The princes of Wales and the kings of Scotland owed allegiance to him. He not only won an empire, but held it all. His lands in France were ten times the size of the French king's.

Besides his conquests, he began a programme of unprecedented reform that set in place the rule of law across England. He was a

---

* 'Plantagenet' was not used by Henry and his contemporaries as a family name. Henry referred to himself as 'FitzEmpress'. It was first used as a surname by Richard duke of York in 1460 when, as 'Richard Plantagenet', he claimed the throne from his mentally unstable cousin, Henry VI.

patron of the arts, a man of letters and he placed England at the very centre of European culture; he was a prince of the twelfth-century renaissance.

By any measure, this is a man who should be celebrated as one of England's greatest kings. And yet he is not. History might have judged and remembered Henry differently, had (as one of his biographers speculates[1]) he died in 1182. It is easy to imagine: a pressing matter of diplomacy that required his presence in Normandy, a sea crossing, a violent storm – and the drowning of the king in the English Channel.

Henry did not die in 1182; he lived for another seven years. These were the worst years of his life. They were blighted by his failure to dominate a new French king, Philip Augustus, and renewed fighting with his sons, who would hound him to his death.

Thomas Becket, Henry's archbishop, did not die in his bed. Henry's men murdered him in his cathedral church at Canterbury in 1170. The murder was the culmination of six years of bitter quarrels over the precedence of church or state. Just days before, Henry had exploded in anger at Becket's behaviour. At his Christmas court he shouted, 'What miserable drones and traitors have I nourished and promoted in my household, who let their lord be treated with such shameful contempt by a low-born clerk!' Four loyal knights, believing Henry wanted rid of Becket, sped across the sea from Normandy to Canterbury. As they entered the cathedral fully armed, they shouted 'King's men, king's men', hacked off the top of Becket's head and left his body awash with blood on the cathedral floor.

It took years for Henry to recover from the propaganda disaster of Becket's death, and this may be a reason why Shakespeare never wrote about him – if he had tackled the thorny issue of Thomas Becket, it is doubtful that the play would ever have been performed. The Elizabethan and Stuart authorities did not take kindly to religious themes in plays.

Henry ended his days, not in the warm embrace of a loving family and peaceful empire, but unloved and alone, a broken man. Even his adored youngest son John betrayed him. England's burning light was reduced to no more than a flicker in the shadows.

Tragic heroes, as Aristotle noted, attract us with their blend of light and shade. Like us, they are neither wholly good nor bad. We empathise with them, in part because the consequences of their mistakes seem to us far more severe than they deserve, echoing Lear's lament, 'I am a man more sinned against than sinning.' We are drawn to them because we see the same frailties and the same capacity to err in judgement that we exhibit ourselves. They hold up a mirror to our own imperfections.

Although we may see fragments of ourselves in them, however, they are ultimately not the same as us. The Aristotelian tragic king plays on a grander stage – and his capacity to do good in the world, or inflict harm on others, is far greater and more wide-reaching as a result.

Henry is in many ways the classic tragic hero. And though an emotionally complex man, the cause of his undoing bears resemblance to that beloved of the Greek dramatists: hubris.

This book tells Henry's true story, and it is a tragedy. It is the story of a great hero whose life traces an arc from ascent, to glory, to defeat, and who is brought down by a tragic flaw in his own character.

Henry II, who forged an empire that matched Charlemagne's – the Alexander the Great of the Middle Ages. This most talented of English kings, who became the most haunted.

Act I
The Bargain

Henry was eighteen when we met, and I was queen of
France. He came down from the North to Paris with a
mind like Aristotle's ... and a form like mortal sin. We
shattered the Commandments on the spot.

James Goldman, *The Lion in Winter*, 1966

The playwright James Goldman imagines a first meeting between
Henry duke of Normandy and Eleanor of Aquitaine, queen of
France, replete with deadly desire and magnetic force. Is there
any truth to this imagined encounter?

Whether Eleanor, aged twenty-nine, thought that the eighteen-
year-old Henry's mind resembled that of Aristotle – the
apotheosis of mid-twelfth-century intellectual aspiration – and
was sufficiently aroused to 'shatter the Commandments' there
and then, we shall never know.

The chronicler Walter Map's Eleanor is a seductress, casting
her 'unchaste eyes' – *oculos incestos* – upon him. 'Unchaste' is the
kindest interpretation; the word has underlying meanings of
impure, immoral, dirty, or even incestuous. Walter accused
Eleanor of not only snaring Henry in Paris, but of sleeping with

his father, which would have made her marriage to Henry incestuous.*

In truth, we know very little about Eleanor. We do know that she was clever, powerful and possibly beautiful – a 'woman without compare'. We also know that Eleanor cared deeply for Aquitaine, the vast lands in the south-west of France that had been bequeathed to her by her father.

Eleanor had brought Louis and the French crown the incredible riches of Aquitaine. And yet married to Louis, she had enjoyed little autonomy. In the few surviving charters, Eleanor rarely acts alone – only jointly with Louis. There was a brief flurry of activity in the period before they departed on crusade, but after their return, when divorce appeared inevitable, Eleanor was further sidelined.

Henry was attractive, clever and bold. He was a soldier, a diplomat, charismatic, educated and ambitious for power; people flocked to him 'even though they had scrutinised him a thousand times before'. Through his mother Matilda, he held the possibility of inheriting the English throne, if he could only overthrow his usurper cousin King Stephen. Through his father, he was heir to much of northern France. In August 1151, Henry was a man with a glittering future.

Sources do not tell us if the bargain they struck at that first meeting in Paris was at Eleanor's or Henry's instigation. Nor do they reveal the precise terms of the bargain, or even whether they were explicit or implicit. But bargain there must have been.

For what if, in return for the advantages he would gain from their marriage, Henry had promised Eleanor something that

---

* Medieval church law stipulated that if you had sexual relations with a relative by marriage, or with someone related to you within the degrees forbidden by the church, you were guilty of incest. It also decreed that if you had already had sexual relations with a close relative of your future husband or wife, you were barred from marrying them as you would be committing incest.

Louis never had, and never would have, given her: the chance to rule her own duchy as she chose, under the loose auspices of Henry's domains?

One thing is for sure: a promise of this potency – a promise made to a woman desperate for the independence that power confers – once given, is best kept.

I

Henry's story began with a drunken party, a dare, and a shipwreck. It was 1120, thirteen years before his birth, and thirty-one years before he met Eleanor. On a bitterly cold day, 25 November, a large party of the Anglo-Norman elite gathered at the town of Barfleur on the coast of northern France. They were led by Henry's grandfather, King Henry I of England and Duke of Normandy, and his only legitimate son, the seventeen-year-old William Atheling. The royal pair were on their way back to England from war with Louis VI (the Fat) of France and King Henry's nephew, William Clito, for control of Normandy. They were in exuberant spirits because they had won.

The party was to sail that night and conditions were perfect. The sky was cloudless, the sea was calm, the moon was in its first quarter but the stars were brilliant.

Prince and king were to travel separately. King Henry had been approached by the owner of a handsome new white ship. His name was Thomas FitzStephen and, during a conversation with the king, Thomas reminded him that it was his father who had carried Henry I's own father, William the Bastard (or Conqueror), from France to England and conquest in 1066. Now he asked for the honour of taking Prince William Atheling across the Channel in his new ship.

William was impressed. The ship was modern and fast, and he was convinced it would outrun his father's older and heavier vessel, the *Esnecca* (the snake, or fast warship).

The ship's fifty oarsmen were delighted to carry William; the young prince, at their request, ordered the entirety of the town's wine to be loaded on board.[1]

Throughout the long winter evening, the 300 or so travellers embarked. They numbered William's bastard half-siblings Richard, and Matilda countess of Perche, most of his aristocratic friends, and many of their parents. William was in a celebratory mood. Not only had he defeated his enemies; just five months before arriving at Barfleur, he had married Matilda of Anjou at Lisieux to form an alliance with Count Fulk V of Anjou, whose territory bordered Normandy to the south.* His victory was secure. With the alcohol on board, the Norman chronicler Orderic Vitalis tells us, the party began. The oarsmen and many of the passengers quickly became drunk. When the priests arrived to bless the ship before its crossing, they were teased and sent away.[2] The mood on the ship was so raucous that some of the passengers got off rather than risk the crossing. Among those who left was William's first cousin, Stephen, son of the king's sister Adela, who pleaded diarrhoea rather than travel with the prince. Henry I had created him, a beloved nephew, count of Mortain.

King Henry's ship departed first. The crossing had to be made at night, in high water, or the boats would not have been able to float. We know that on 25 November 1120 high water was at 10.43 p.m.[3] The *White Ship* left the harbour perhaps an hour later. By now nearly everyone on board, probably including the captain, was drunk. Thomas FitzStephen was persuaded to take a dare from the prince and his friends to out-race King Henry's ship, despite its head start. He was an experienced sailor who had made the journey from Barfleur to England numerous times. He possibly felt himself to be so familiar with the route that extra

---

* William's bride was not on the *White Ship*. She travelled instead with King Henry.

speed, despite the jagged rocks that dotted the outskirts of the harbour, would not matter. Perhaps he was so wine-soaked that all caution was disregarded. Or perhaps he was coerced by his drunken master. The *White Ship* hurtled out of the harbour's mouth and almost immediately hit a rock, probably the Quilleboeuf Rock or Raz de Barfleur, which knifed through its planks.

The sailors desperately tried to free the boat, but it suddenly overturned. The night was freezing and the waters dark. From the shore, the clergymen whose traditional blessing the travellers had drunkenly jeered, heard the petrified screams of the foundering passengers. The bishop of Coutances was among the clerical witnesses. All three of his nephews and his brother were on board.

The situation was ghastly for the hundreds of souls perishing in the bitter winter seas, but it was not yet a disaster for the Norman dynasty. William still might have escaped. He was bundled into a lifeboat and swiftly steered away. But the prince had humanity. William was close to his illegitimate half-brothers and sisters, who had been given lands and titles by their father. He evidently loved his half-sister the countess of Perche and his brother Richard. He ordered his tiny vessel to go back and rescue them. As it reached the wreck, it was engulfed by the scores of panicked people who tried to climb aboard. The boat capsized and they too drowned. William Atheling, heir to England and Normandy, was dead.

It seemed there would be three survivors of the tragedy: Berold, a butcher from Rouen; a son of the nobleman Gilbet l'Aigle; and the captain, Thomas FitzStephen. Berold and l'Aigle's son managed to grab hold of a piece of the wreckage and stay afloat. Thomas fought his way through the freezing waters and asked them for news. When they told him William was dead, unable to face the king, he slipped down into the sea to die. And when l'Aigle's son could hold on no longer, he too drowned.

Only Berold the butcher, kept from freezing in the water by his pelisse and his sheepskin coat, lived to bear witness. In the morning, he was rescued by three fishermen.

No one dared tell the king. The screams of the drowning caught the ears of King Henry and his fellow passengers, but they were bemused by what they had heard. It was not until the following day that the king's nephew, Theobald, persuaded a young boy to break the news.[4] The king collapsed in grief.

Many of the Anglo-Norman nobility were dead too. A generation of aristocrats was obliterated, confounding the lords of England and Normandy who survived. Besides William, the king lost an illegitimate son and daughter, his niece Matilda of Blois, her husband Richard earl of Chester, Richard's half-brother, and members of his household including his scribe Gisulf, William Bigod, Robert Mauduit, Hugh de Moulins, and Geoffrey Ridel.[5] Gilbet l'Aigle lost two sons, both of whom had served in Henry I's household. Eighteen women were among the dead. For the most part their bodies were never recovered, despite the efforts of the families who hired private divers to claw their remains from the sea.

We know so much about the shipwreck because the chroniclers could not make sense of it; so for centuries they picked over the facts. It was an example of what the historian and chronicler William of Malmesbury called 'the mutability of human fortunes'.[6] So senseless did it seem, that a later historian even speculated that the disaster had been the result of a conspiracy to murder.[7]

King Henry I grieved bitterly. The tragedy was both personal, and political. He was the fourth son of William the Bastard and had had no expectation of the throne. But he was ruthless and ambitious for power. When his elder brother King William Rufus was shot in the eye with an arrow and killed in the New Forest in 1100 (some believed Henry was behind his death), he raced to secure the treasury at Winchester; he was crowned within three days at Westminster by Maurice, bishop of London, before his other elder brother, Robert, honeymooning in Italy on his way back from crusade, even heard of Rufus's death. By 1106, Henry I was master of Normandy too; he locked Robert up for nearly thirty years rather than concede power. He successfully battled Robert's son and his own nephew William Clito for lordship of Normandy, and so ruthless was he in pursuit of supremacy that he even ordered the tips of his granddaughters' noses be cut off to avoid appearing weak.[8]

William Atheling's death negated all his efforts. He had no heir, just numerous bastard children, and one legitimate daughter, Matilda, who was married to the emperor of Germany. Even had she been free to return to England, it is doubtful that the nobility would have accepted her as queen. Although no law barred women from the throne of England, there was little precedent in an age when a ruler was expected to lead troops into battle. Matilda was older than her brother, but when William Atheling was born, no one expected her to rule.

King Henry's heartache was such that he never sailed from Barfleur again.[9] But it did not stop him from thinking of the future. The continuation of his 'usurper' Norman dynasty as rulers of England lay in his providing the country with an uncontested heir.

The king was a consummate politician. In August 1100, after stealing the crown from his older brother, he had immediately married Edith (Matilda) of Scotland, just days after William Rufus's death and his own hasty coronation. She was the daughter of the Scottish king Malcolm Canmore, and Margaret, the great-granddaughter of the Saxon king Edmund Ironside. Henry was aware that their children's claim to rule England, with their blood inheritance of both William the Conqueror and the Saxon kings of England, would be far less precarious than his own. The chroniclers noted that their new king had married 'a kinswoman of King Edward, of the true royal family of England ... descended from the stock of King Alfred'.[10]

She had been crowned by Anselm, archbishop of Canterbury; he had ignored objections to the marriage, that Edith had 'taken the veil' (become a nun) while in her aunt Christina's care at Wilton Abbey, where Christina was abbess. Edith strongly repudiated these claims, insisting that her disciplinarian aunt had forced her to wear the veil to protect her from libidinous Normans, including Henry I's brother William Rufus, and that she had never taken vows.[11] She had, she said, 'gone in fear of the rod of my aunt Christina, and she would often make me smart with a good slapping and the most horrible scolding'.[12] The marriage, nevertheless, and therefore her and Henry's heirs, were undisputedly legitimate. Edith's character was unimpeachable; she was the model of queenly piety and devotion. But now William Atheling, Henry's only son by his queen, was dead.

King Henry's contemporaries called him licentious. He had numerous mistresses, and when the *White Ship* sank he was left with many capable although illegitimate sons, as well as nephews. But the king wanted his own legitimate descendant to rule after him. The dual realm of England and Normandy had only been in – albeit sporadic – existence since 1066, and the king, perhaps thinking of his own experiences of purloining the throne from his brother, needed an heir whom all his nobles would accept. Edith died in 1118. Within ten weeks of the tragedy, Henry married again. His bride was Adeliza, daughter of Godfrey, duke of Lotharingia and count of Louvain. She was seventeen, the same age as his dead son. King Henry was fifty-two or fifty-three years old. The chroniclers called the new queen *puella* (girl) at her wedding.[13]

No child arrived. During their fifteen-year marriage the chroniclers did not even hint at a miscarriage or a stillbirth for Adeliza.[14] The problem may well have been the king's. (After his death Adeliza made a love match with William d'Aubigny, the son of

Henry's butler, and they had seven children together.) The king was obviously sensitive about his queen's childless state. During Easter 1124 he brutally punished leaders of a rebellion and meted out the same punishment – blinding – to a knight, Luc de la Barre. This castigation was universally perceived as too harsh for a mere knight. But Luc had composed offensive songs about the king, and some historians have speculated they were about Adeliza's failure to have a child. Luc took his own life, crushing his skull against the walls of his cell, rather than face his awful punishment.[15]

Four years after his second wedding the old king, possibly despairing, was offered a solution to his succession problem when the husband of his only legitimate daughter, Matilda, died.

Matilda was born at the beginning of February 1102. During her early childhood, while her father was fighting for control of Normandy, she and her brother William were placed in the care of Anselm, archbishop of Canterbury. Matilda was extremely fond of him, and they would remain close for the rest of his life. Anselm had been the abbot of Bec in Normandy, and Matilda would show a lifelong devotion to this house, possibly because of her friendship with Anselm.[16]

When she was only eight years old, King Henry sent Matilda away to Germany and a splendid diplomatic marriage with Heinrich V. Heinrich had gained the throne of Germany only two years before his betrothal; it was his bloody prize following years of fighting his own father, Heinrich IV, for the crown. Matilda was formally betrothed to her groom at Westminster, in his absence, on 13 June 1109. Heinrich's envoys arrived in England the following year, to escort her to Germany. He was about seventeen years older than his child bride. For King Henry the match and its association with one of Europe's most powerful princes bolstered his position as a newly crowned king, who had still not been acknowledged duke of Normandy by his overlord, Louis the Fat, over his defeated brother, Robert. Heinrich wanted

Matilda because her father was rich; he desperately needed money to pay for his wars and to aid his campaign to be crowned Holy Roman Emperor by the pope. Matilda's dowry of 10,000 marks* in silver was very attractive.[17]

Eight-year-old Matilda arrived in Heinrich's lands in February 1110, at Liège, and although the couple, because of Matilda's youth, remained unmarried, she was crowned queen at Mainz on 25 July. The day was the feast of St James, whose shrine lay to the west, in northern Spain. St James, one of the twelve apostles, was probably the brother of John the Evangelist – and his hand, looted by Heinrich's father from the archbishop of Hamburg-Bremen on his death in 1072, was a prized relic of the German kingdom. Matilda developed a strong attachment to it.[18] Later, she would steal it, perhaps in memory of her coronation.

Matilda was placed in the care of Bruno, archbishop of Trier, to continue her education, away from Heinrich. We do not know the details of her upbringing, but Heinrich asked 'that she should be nobly brought up and honourably served, and should learn the language and customs and laws of the country, and all that an empress ought to know, now, in the time of her youth'.[19]

It was not until she was nearly twelve, however, in January 1114, that Matilda married Heinrich, now emperor, at Worms Cathedral.[20] The occasion was the most splendid in living memory. An eyewitness, writing in the usual formulaic, adulatory manner reserved for princesses of whom they knew nothing personal, noted Matilda's beauty and lineage. He wrote that:

> the nuptials were attended by such a great concourse of archbishops and bishops, dukes and counts, abbots and provosts and learned clergy, that not even the oldest man present could remember ever having seen or even heard of such a huge assembly of such great persons. For the marriage was attended

---

* A mark was roughly equivalent to two-thirds of a pound.

by five archbishops, thirty bishops and five dukes ... so numerous were the wedding gifts which various kings and primates sent to the emperor, and the gifts which the emperor from his own store gave to the innumerable throngs of jesters and jongleurs and people of all kinds, that not one of his chamberlains who received or distributed them could count them.[21]

Henry I was doubtless immensely gratified to hear of the expense lavished on his daughter's wedding.

Matilda had ability and Heinrich developed her talents. He encouraged her to participate in government, following the German tradition which allowed queens to work alongside their husbands. She was enthusiastic and able, acting as his regent in Italy and Lotharingia. She developed keen diplomatic skills, particularly in her dealings with the papal court. Matilda fulfilled the traditional queenly role of intercessor, and she was popular with her German subjects. Her beauty, vivacity and hard work earned their affections, and they called her 'Matilda the Good'.

Heinrich used Matilda as one of his many instruments of government, just as he used his counsellors. His chief advisor was Adalbert, whom he would create both his chancellor, and then archbishop of the most prestigious diocese in the kingdom – Mainz. This archbishopric held a similar status in Germany to that of Canterbury in England. Ultimately, the combination of the post of chancellor and archbishop in a single individual was a disaster for the crown. It was a lesson that Matilda would never forget, when nearly half a century later she advised her eldest son against the most grievous decision of his life.

The chronicler Orderic Vitalis wrote of how unpopular Heinrich was, particularly for the imperial crowning he forced from Pope Pascal II. When Heinrich entered Rome in 1111 expecting to be crowned Holy Roman Emperor, the pope refused unless he relinquished the privilege of investiture. Heinrich responded by kidnapping and imprisoning the pope until he agreed to crown him, which he did. Orderic wrote that, 'the emperor loved so noble a wife very much but for his sins he lacked an heir worthy of the empire'.[22]

For despite his supposed affection for Matilda, they had no children together. Hermann of Tournai, a near contemporary, hinted at a stillbirth or a child who died soon after birth; whatever the cause, the marriage was childless.[23]

Heinrich had one illegitimate daughter, Bertha, whom he married to Count Ptolemy of Tusculum in 1117, but no legitimate heir.[24] In 1122, he fell ill with cancer, and now he put his mind to deciding the succession. Bertha, illegitimate and a young woman with no military experience, was not a feasible candidate.

It is intriguing to speculate that had Heinrich not contracted a fatal illness, European history might have been very different. After William Atheling drowned in 1120, Heinrich saw a real possibility of inheriting Henry I's domains through right of his wife. She was still young, and it was not impossible to think that they would have an heir who would inherit not only Germany, but the Anglo-Norman realm too. Besides Matilda, Henry I's nearest legitimate heir was his nephew William Clito, son of the imprisoned Robert. Henry did everything in his power to ensure Clito would not succeed him, for William was allied to Louis the Fat, with whom Henry had spent years sparring for Normandy.

William Clito had not seen his father since he was three years old and would spend his entire life fighting his uncle for his birthright, allying himself with Henry's foes; uncle and nephew were enemies, and Henry I would not allow him to succeed, despite his valid blood claim.

In the spring of 1122, probably with a view to discussing the succession of Matilda and Heinrich, Henry and Matilda attempted to meet. Henry was nervous at the number of his nobility who professed to support William Clito as duke of Normandy after his death.[25] The meeting, however, did not take place as Charles, count of Flanders, for fear of offending his French overlord, refused Matilda safe conduct through his lands. Nevertheless, Heinrich and Matilda's father continued as allies against the threat of William Clito and France.

Heinrich may feasibly have expected to add king of England and duke of Normandy to his titles. England and Normandy would have been, in the first part of the twelfth century, subsumed into a greater German empire, ruled from Aachen by the Holy Roman Emperor.

But Heinrich died at Utrecht on 23 May 1125, the last of the Salian kings. He was buried at the Romanesque cathedral of Speyer, on the Rhine, beside the body of the father he had fought for the throne. Matilda, with no child heir to act as regent for, was superfluous. Aged twenty-three, she had lived in Germany all her adult life, yet she had few rights. Now she faced a choice. She could either remain in Germany under the protection of Heinrich's family, married eventually to a candidate of their choice; she could enter a convent, the preference of many widowed noblewomen; or she could answer her father's command and return to England.[26]

With no stake in the German throne, she went back to the land of her birth, carrying with her an enormous amount of treasure, including gold crowns, bolts of silk, and a relic: the hand of St James. She would never give up her title, though, calling herself 'empress' for the rest of her life.

What was to become of Matilda, the redundant empress with an empty title? Despite recalling her from Germany, it is likely that the king had not yet decided what to do with his daughter. King Henry, ever pragmatic, took his time to consider his options.

II

Kingship and inheritance in Europe in the first half of the twelfth century were flexible. Although by the end of the century, primogeniture – succession of the eldest son – was far more established in feudal law, at the beginning the rules were still fluid. In western Europe, the nation state was only just beginning to emerge as a political entity, which meant that inheritance was often precarious.

It was still possible for an illegitimate child to inherit his father's throne or lordship, although it was not always easy; William the Bastard had had to fight for his claim to rule in Normandy. But illegitimacy or being the younger son did not yet automatically bar a strong candidate from the throne: successful kings were often the men who could secure the treasury first, or win in battles against their rivals, frequently close relations. Matilda's own husband Heinrich V had fought his father Heinrich IV for control of Germany. William the Bastard, at war with his eldest son Robert at the time of his death, denied him his full inheritance in favour of his second son William Rufus.[27] And King Henry I took full advantage of William Rufus's death, leaving his brother's dead body in the New Forest as he raced to Winchester to acquire the wealth of England before his elder brother Robert.

What of 'queenship', or a woman's right to rule independently of a father or son? Women were encouraged to pursue the traditional queenly roles of intercessors, helpmates, and even occasionally regents. But there were hardly any examples in the twelfth century of women ruling alone, and King Henry would have been aware of how unusual it was to nominate a woman as his successor.

Although in France, Salic law – where women were barred from the throne – was a development of the fourteenth century (when the death of all of Philip le Bel's male heirs by 1328 precipitated a succession crisis), there was no tradition of female rule in France; the French were, at best, ambivalent about women rulers.[28] England developed no such law, but there was very little precedent for female rule. Many European noblewomen such as Matilda participated in government, although of Matilda's contemporaries, only two ruled as queens in their own right – Urraca, daughter of Alfonso VI of Castile and León, and Melisende, daughter of Baldwin II of Jerusalem. Both found it impossible to rule alone for long. Urraca, after her father's death, swiftly married Alfonso of Aragon, 'the battler', to shore up her regime. Melisende was married off to Count Fulk V of Anjou and never reigned entirely alone, obliged to associate herself first with her father, and then her husband.

With Matilda safely back in England, the king pondered. It was still plausible that his young wife would become pregnant and he kept her constantly at his side. The other possible contenders were his sister Adela's sons, Theobald and Stephen; and his illegitimate son Robert of Gloucester, a man of great intelligence, capability and wealth.

Henry I liked to surround himself with the scions of the Anglo-Norman nobility, partly as companions for William Atheling before his death. At court, Matilda encountered her half-brothers and the king's eldest bastard sons, Robert and Richard, as well as her uncle, David of Scotland. She also met her cousin, Stephen.

Stephen was born in about 1092, the third son of Adela and Étienne VI count of Blois-Chartres. Étienne was a controversial figure. He had answered the pope's call to the first crusade enthusiastically in 1096 but had not, according to contemporaries, behaved well; he failed to bring his men to aid the Christian forces as they besieged Antioch. Perhaps to assuage his conscience, he returned to Jerusalem in 1101, where he was killed the following year, at the battle of Ramlah. Stephen's father was absent during his childhood, and after his death it was Stephen's uncle, now king of England and duke of Normandy, who showed him kindness and favour when he welcomed him at court.

Stephen was charming and liked to please people; he swiftly became a favourite of Henry I. In 1113, when Stephen was about twenty-one years old, Henry gave him lands and created him count of Mortain at his Christmas court.

After William Atheling died, the old king showered honours on his other close male relations, creating powerful and wealthy lords out of those he trusted and loved. By 1125, with Adeliza still not pregnant and with Matilda still married and in Germany, Henry may have briefly considered Stephen to succeed him; he loved him, and respected his skills as a politician and a soldier. Stephen was a very likeable man: 'he had by his good nature and the way he jested, sat and ate in the company even of the humblest, earned an affection that can hardly be imagined'.[29] To strengthen Stephen's hand against William Clito, who had a better claim, the king married him to the heiress Matilda of Boulogne, which made him rich and gave him lands. Stephen was a moral man; his marriage arranged, he left the woman who had been his mistress for at least ten years – Damette (Little Lady) – by whom he had a son, Gervase, and possibly a daughter.[30] He did provide financially for Damette and his illegitimate son: in the 1130s, she was able to put a large sum towards the lease of the manor at Chelsea, and, in 1138, he arranged for Gervase to become abbot of Westminster Abbey. But his relationship with Damette was over. Stephen's marriage to Matilda of Boulogne, although not a love match, would prove an extraordinary partnership.

With his daughter Matilda back in England, Henry I evidently changed his mind about Stephen succeeding him; blood triumphed over gender.

Two years after Matilda's return, her father finally committed to naming her as his successor. What Matilda's feelings were, we do not know. We do know, however, that while in Germany, she had aided Heinrich in government, acting with enthusiasm and diligence. She had not been a lazy consort. She evidently had a talent for diplomacy; later, she would apply the lessons learned with Heinrich and at the papal court to aid her own cause. It is likely that her experiences in Germany had given her a taste for power and that she was happy to comply with her father's plans.

At the end of his Christmas court on 1 January 1127, Henry strong-armed his magnates into accepting her as their future monarch.[31] The nobility of England and Normandy, with Matilda supported by her uncle, David King of Scots, lined up before the empress and swore to uphold her right to the throne of England on her father's death:

> [Henry] bound the nobles of all England, likewise the bishops and abbots, by oath, that if he died without a male heir they would immediately accept his daughter as their lady (*domina*). He said first what a disaster it had been that William, to whom the realm belonged, had been taken away; now there remained only his daughter, to whom alone the succession rightfully belonged because her grandfather, uncle and father had been kings and on her mother's side she was descended from fourteen kings from the time of Egbert. Edward, the last of the race, had arranged the marriage of Malcolm and Margaret, and Matilda, mother of the empress, was their daughter.[32]

Stephen, whatever his personal feelings on the momentous change to his prospects, was the first to promise to be faithful to Matilda as Henry I's chosen successor, even fighting with his cousin Robert of Gloucester for the honour of being first. But Stephen never forgot his uncle's fleeting desire to make him king.

Henry I knew that his plan was precarious, and it may well have included his daughter getting pregnant and producing a son who would eventually rule England and Normandy in her place. Perhaps Hermann of Tournai's account of Matilda giving birth to a dead child in Germany was true; the king evidently trusted in her fertility and now he found a husband for her.

His choice was Geoffrey of Anjou, eldest son of Count Fulk V and brother of William Atheling's widow. Geoffrey was not Matilda's only suitor. William of Malmesbury wrote in the *Historia Novella* that 'some princes of Lotharingia and Lombardy came to England more than once ... to ask for her as their lady, but gained nothing from their efforts, the king being minded to establish peace between himself and the Count of Anjou by his daughter's marriage'.[33]

Matilda may have agreed with her father's plans to make her queen, but she was dismayed at his choice of husband for her, and protested. She had been married to an emperor and was now asked to marry a mere nobleman. She may also have been horrified by the age gap. When marriage negotiations began in the spring of 1127, Matilda was twenty-five and Geoffrey fourteen. Her father's friend Hildebert of Lavardin, possibly at the king's request, wrote to her to 'beg her to set his mind at rest about a report brought to him from England that she was causing distress to her father through her disobedience'.[34]

But despite her age and status as widowed empress, Matilda had no voice in the choosing of her second husband, and she complied. As the chronicler noted, Henry needed to cement relations with Anjou, which bordered Normandy to the south. Her brother William Atheling's death just weeks after his marriage to Geoffrey's sister, also named Matilda, undermined the alliance between Anjou and Normandy that this union had created. Henry had battled Fulk intermittently throughout the 1110s and 1120s for control of Maine. In 1118, a chronicler wrote how:

All this year King Henry stayed in Normandy because of the war with the king of France and the count of Anjou and the count of Flanders. Because of these hostilities the king was very much distressed and lost a great deal both in money and also in land. But those who troubled him most were his own men, who frequently deserted and betrayed him and went over to his enemies and surrendered their castles to them to injure and betray the king. England paid dear for all this because of the various taxes, which never ceased in the course of all this year.[35]

Henry could not afford repeated unrest, both on his lands on the continent and among his barons in England, jostling for position should Henry display any weakness. Now it was useful to him, and far more important than his daughter's desires, that she marry into the Angevin family – the House of Anjou.

Meanwhile William Clito's star was in the ascendant. Louis the Fat not only arranged a brilliant marriage for him to Joanna, daughter of his queen's cousin, Rainer of Montferrat; he also gave him Flanders, after the murder of Count Charles the Good in March at the castle church in Bruges.[36] It was now imperative to Henry I that his nephew not increase his already bloated power base, and be prevented from forming an alliance with the Angevins. Matilda's marriage to Geoffrey was the only way to secure the loyalty of the count of Anjou. She had no choice but to agree.

There was an impediment, however. Fulk V, Geoffrey's father, still ruled in Anjou. It was vital to both Matilda and her father that she marry a count, and not the son of a count. And so to enable Geoffrey's marriage to Matilda, Henry executed a masterstoke of diplomacy. With Louis the Fat, in a brief shifting of alliances, he persuaded Baldwin II of Jerusalem that the widowed Fulk was the ideal candidate to marry his daughter Melisende. Fulk had already been on crusade, in 1120, and had extensive knowledge of the politics of the region. Fulk, they promised, would rule the crusader kingdom jointly with Melisende when Baldwin died. It is doubtful that Melisende in Jerusalem had any more choice than Matilda in England in deciding her future husband.

The promise of Jerusalem was enticement enough for Fulk. In May 1127, Hugh of Payens, the Master of the Knights Templar, set out from Jerusalem for Anjou, to discuss the marriage.[37] Meanwhile Matilda's half-brother, Robert of Gloucester, and her friend, Brian Fitz Count, travelled with her to her formal betrothal to Geoffrey. The wedding was delayed while Fulk settled his plans to take the throne in Jerusalem and waited for the envoys to arrive; they did so in the spring of the following year.

On 10 June 1128, King Henry knighted Geoffrey in Rouen in preparation for his lofty marriage. One week later the wedding was celebrated at the Angevins' lavish Romanesque Cathedral of St Julian at Le Mans, Geoffrey's capital. It had been consecrated when Fulk left for his pilgrimage to Jerusalem in 1120 and now, eight years later, Fulk obligingly departed for Jerusalem for good, enabling Geoffrey to become the new count of Anjou.

Pope Honorius II wrote to King Baldwin, describing the selflessness with which Fulk left his domains to Geoffrey; he 'set aside his barons and the innumerable people under his rule in order to serve God'.[38] Fulk and his children then travelled to Fontevraud Abbey, to allow him to say goodbye to his daughter Matilda too, who had retired there, and he left for his new kingdom. He was married to Melisende as soon as he arrived in the Latin Kingdom. Fulk would never see his son Geoffrey or his other children again.

Just a month after the wedding, Henry I's nephew and enemy, William Clito, obligingly died in battle, at the end of July. For Henry, the succession issue appeared to have passed its crisis.

What was Matilda's new husband like? He was very good-looking – Geoffrey was called 'Le Bel' or 'the Handsome' by his contemporaries. But as he was not a king or churchman, we know little of his personality other than what we can infer from his actions and the sources.

He was one of four legitimate children born to Count Fulk V of Anjou and his wife, Aremburga of Maine. His siblings were

Matilda, William Atheling's widow; Sibylla; and their younger brother, Helias. Geoffrey and his brother were brought up together, in the charge of his father, close friends and allies, and tutors. When he was very young, Fulk began to teach him to govern; he witnessed his first charter when he was only three years old. Once Fulk made his decision to leave Anjou for Jerusalem, he embarked on a period of intensive 'ducal' training for Geoffrey.[39]

We know that Geoffrey became an exceptional military tactician, honed by years of war with his own barons, fighting the Normans, and even his fending off a rebellion by his brother Helias in 1145. We know of his admiration for the classics, of his interest in learning and of his desire to ensure that his sons received the best education available. We know of his loyalty to his closest supporters, above and beyond that of simply furthering his own power base, and that he preferred to surround himself with immensely capable men. We also know that he fulfilled only the conventional notions of piety and was most likely not a religious man.

But these character traits were to reveal themselves only later. In the first year of her marriage, Matilda was unhappy and dissatisfied, probably with Geoffrey's extreme youth and inexperience. He may have treated her with arrogance and disrespect. She is more or less absent from the Angevin charter records. She did not fulfil the role that Geoffrey's mother Aremburga had, witnessing her husband's charters, issuing her own, and acting as his regent.

Matilda did not remain with her husband for long. She waited for Henry I to leave Normandy for England the following summer, and then she fled. She and Geoffrey had been married for little over a year.

We can only speculate as to why the marriage broke down after just thirteen months. The Durham Chronicler said that it was Geoffrey who 'repudiated' Matilda; she presumably would have had the political sense and experience to stay in her marriage, however loathsome.[40] Medieval royal and aristocratic marriages were rarely about love and personal choice, but rather about political and territorial gain.[41] Even modern historians such as Josèphe Chartrou tell us that, as Matilda had a 'detestable' character, the fracture must have been her fault.[42] Matilda's biographer, Marjorie Chibnall, however, believes that it was a youthful and inexperienced Geoffrey who asked Matilda to leave.

The couple were soon forced together again. At a great council held at Northampton on 8 September, it was agreed that Matilda should return to Geoffrey. The dissolution of a marriage with the heiress to England and Normandy would not have been in the interests of the count of Anjou. Now he asked for Matilda to come back to him, and promised to treat her with respect.[43] Before she departed, the king coerced his magnates once again to swear to make her queen on his death.

Matilda and Geoffrey had been made to reconcile; now they determined to make their marriage work, at least politically. Two years later, at Le Mans on 5 March 1133, a son was born. His parents chose 25 March, Lady Day – the feast of the Annunciation of the Virgin – as his christening day. For much of the medieval period Lady Day, one of the four quarter days, was celebrated as the New Year. On this auspicious day at the Cathedral of St Julian in his parents' capital city, Le Mans, he was baptised by Bishop Guy of Ploërmel. Matilda and Geoffrey named the boy after his maternal grandfather: Henry.

III

For a medieval audience, the occasion was drenched in symbolism. It was New Year; but it was also a commemoration of the day narrated in the Nativity, when Mary was told by the Angel Gabriel that Jesus had entered her pure body, just as baby Henry was now entering the pure body of the church. And just as Jesus had a very special mother, so this baby had a special mother too – Matilda. The source of Henry's power would come from both

Geoffrey and Matilda's inheritance to him. But its mystique would not be through his father, a count, but through his mother, an empress and daughter and named successor of a king. Henry would style himself 'FitzEmpress' (son of the empress) for the rest of his life.

Henry's birth meant everything to his maternal grandfather. Thirteen years after William Atheling had drowned, taking with him Henry I's desires for the succession of England and Normandy, a legitimate male child was born into the family. Both Matilda and her father gave gifts and money to the church to mark their thankfulness and their joy.[44]

Matilda kept Henry with her during his infancy. In August 1133 she left Geoffrey in Anjou, taking five-month-old Henry with her to Rouen, to join the old king when he returned to Normandy. Now she devoted herself to learning statecraft from her father to prepare for her accession. Matilda's experience in Germany had been limited to the duties required of a queen consort of a regent. Her father meant to teach her to rule.

King Henry I had another reason for keeping Matilda with him. The chronicler Roger of Howden tells us that the king once again demanded that his reluctant nobles and the archbishops swear to uphold not only Matilda's claim, but young Henry's claim too.[45] Living in her father's court meant that Matilda, her baby son and the Anglo-Norman nobility got to know one another better, presumably – in the king's mind – smoothing the way to her future succession. Matilda may have met some of them when she was a child, but as she had left England when she was only eight years old, strong relationships and loyalties had not been formed. Now the king determined to rectify this.

Matilda had arrived in Normandy pregnant. Her second child, Geoffrey, was born in Rouen at the beginning of the summer of 1134. It was a difficult birth, and Matilda did not expect to survive; she even wrote her will. King Henry showed his daughter tenderness throughout her illness. He delayed his plans to leave and stayed with her until she was well, 'rejoicing in his grandsons'.[46] Henry I no longer had any doubts about the succession. He had his daughter and his grandsons close, and may even have asked his nobles and churchmen to swear allegiance to her yet again.[47]

By September of the following year, however, father and daughter's relationship had deteriorated. Matilda's dowry had included the castles of Exmes, Argentan and Domfront, which lay on the border between Normandy and Anjou, but the king, anxious to retain power, refused to hand them over. Now Matilda and Geoffrey demanded them with immediate effect: Geoffrey argued that he would need them to secure Normandy after Henry I's death and wanted to take possession as quickly as possible. It is likely that the old king's refusal to give them up had rankled with Geoffrey for some time. He already faced intermittent threats from his own bellicose barons, and it made sound military sense to hold these castles sooner rather than later. Matilda and Geoffrey also urged Henry I to return to William Talvas, one of Geoffrey's vassals, his father's castles in Maine.

Talvas was the son of a notoriously barbarous and seditious Anglo-Norman lord, Robert of Bellême, who had briefly harboured William Clito. Even in an age of warfare and violence, Robert's savagery attracted note: Orderic Vitalis called him 'unequalled for his iniquity in the whole Christian era'. Henry I, however, had locked him away not for his cruelty, but for his continuous rebellion. The king captured him in 1112, and he remained his prisoner until Robert died nearly twenty years later, in about 1130. Urged by Geoffrey, Talvas asked the old king for his castles of Sées, Almenêches and Alençon back. Geoffrey and Matilda pushed their luck with an outrageous demand that King Henry swear an oath of fealty to them for the castles in Matilda's dowry – Henry, furious, refused both requests.[48] He exiled William Talvas from Normandy, and went to war with his daughter and son-in-law.

The chroniclers, either eyewitnesses or relying on eyewitness accounts, charged Matilda with causing the war that erupted between her husband and father. Robert of Torigni accused her of deliberately causing trouble, of artfulness, and of detaining the king 'with various disagreements, from which arose several rounds for argument between the king and the count of Anjou'.[49] The chronicler and historian Henry of Huntingdon placed the fault entirely with Matilda for stoking the argument; but Henry I and Geoffrey were hardly blameless. The old king had refused to hand over Matilda's dowry, while Orderic Vitalis accused Geoffrey of avarice, claiming that he 'aspired to the great riches of his father-in-law and demanded castles in Normandy, asserting that the king had covenanted with him to hand them over when he married his daughter'.[50]

We do not know how much pressure Geoffrey put on Matilda to side with him against her father. Nevertheless she was forced to choose, and she chose her husband. It is possible that Matilda had softened towards Geoffrey when she was so ill following the birth of her second son. Instead of giving gifts to a Norman foundation as she lay in fear for her life, she chose an Angevin one – Le Mans – and donated costly curtains and tapestries.[51] She may have decided between her husband and father already. Now, she left Normandy with her baby sons to join Geoffrey in Angers.

The border war was vicious. Orderic Vitalis, giving us a human and sympathetic portrait of the old king, wrote that Henry 'took it very hard' when Geoffrey besieged another of Henry's sons-in-law, Roscelin, viscount of Sainte-Suzanne, husband of Henry's illegitimate daughter Constance.[52]

The war showed that this was not a normal, loving family. Personal relationships were sacrificed to territorial ambitions, and Matilda and Geoffrey were not prepared to wait until the king's death to claim Matilda's dowry.

By late autumn the king and his daughter were still not speaking. Perhaps to alleviate his anger and disappointment, King

Henry went hunting at one of his favourite spots, Lyons-la-Forêt. On 25 November at supper he ate too many lampreys, a jawless fish and delicacy which his doctor had advised him not to touch. He became mortally ill. Although the sources differ as to what he actually said over the following days, all agree that he was lucid and aware that death was coming.

Three days later he sent for his confessor Hugh, archbishop of Rouen, and arranged for his burial in Reading Cathedral. The king also had his most powerful magnates and protégés, including William of Warenne earl of Surrey, the Beaumont twins – Robert of Leicester and Waleran of Meulan – and his eldest and beloved bastard son, Robert of Gloucester, at his bedside. He made them promise not to desert his body, but to accompany it to burial. But during his final bleak days, did he discuss the succession?

As far as we are aware, nothing was written down at this time. The historian William of Malmesbury claimed that, 'when he was asked … about his successor he assigned all his lands on both sides of the sea to his daughter in lawful and lasting succession, being somewhat angry with her husband because he had vexed the king by not a few threats and insults'.[53] Matilda's biographer Marjorie Chibnall speculates that before their argument, perhaps the king had intended Geoffrey and Matilda to rule together. But now he reserved his bile for his son-in-law. His wishes were clear: Matilda would rule alone.[54]

But the anonymous author of the *Gesta Stephani* ('The Deeds of Stephen') claimed that during his final hours, the king performed a volte-face. He was so incensed with Matilda and Geoffrey for their audacious request that Henry pay them homage, and for the war, that he freed his magnates from their oaths of loyalty to his daughter, and repented 'the forcible imposition of the oath on his barons'.[55] John of Salisbury, the brilliant cleric, polymath, diplomat and writer, made a similar claim; he repeated the story told by Hugh Bigod, Henry I's steward, of a deathbed change of heart.[56] The tale appeared in other trustworthy sources.

If this is true, and the king was lucid during his final days as the sources claim, he would have been fully aware of the implications of his actions. The result, he knew, would be a perilous dash for the treasury and the throne.

A clue to the truth may lie with Orderic Vitalis, whose account in his *Deeds of the Dukes of Normandy* contains intricate details of the king's illness and the heated discussion of the succession among the Norman magnates surrounding their dying lord, but says absolutely nothing about who old King Henry nominated during his final hours. It is likely that the king never withdrew support for his daughter, but was still so angry that he chose not to reiterate his wishes. Henry I died on 1 December 1135. He was about sixty-seven years old and had been king for thirty-five years.

If he did withdraw support from Matilda, either tacitly or implicitly, who were her likely rivals?

The *Gesta Stephani* reported that Robert of Gloucester proposed Matilda's son, young Henry, as England's monarch. But as he was only two, his claims were in abeyance.[57]

Robert himself, Matilda's half-brother and the eldest of the king's bastard sons, was with his father throughout his illness. It was to Robert that the king entrusted the payment of his debts on his death. Robert was born sometime before 1100 at Caen in northern France, before his father became king. The chroniclers did not name his mother, although an early source claimed she was Henry's mistress, Nest, the grandmother of the chronicler Gerald of Wales. Gerald documented his family history so carefully that had Robert of Gloucester, the uncle of his king, been related to him, he would doubtless have used the family connection to promote his own interests, for the chronicler 'lived every day an existence of dramatic egotism'.[58] It is more likely that Robert's mother came from Oxfordshire, although we know nothing more about her.[59]

When William Atheling died, their father sought to boost the power of this son who had already proved so loyal. Robert had fought both with and for his father; against Louis the Fat at the battle of Brémule in 1119, and he went on to aid him in suppressing an uprising of Norman barons in 1123. Later in the 1120s, he had custody of his uncle, Robert Curthose, at his castle at Cardiff. Henry I ensured he received an impeccable education, made him wealthy by marrying him to Mabel, the stupendously rich daughter of Robert Fitz Haimon (a very close friend and possibly lover of William Rufus), and created an earldom for him – Gloucester. Robert was an excellent soldier, clever and capable, and his father evidently loved and trusted him completely. He relied on him and sought his advice, in matters both military and financial.[60] Robert was one of his father's chief advisors, and was even consulted on his half-sister Matilda's marriage to Geoffrey.

Was he a realistic contender? Even Henry I thought Robert's illegitimacy a barrier to power, however far he bolstered him with his trust, a title and money. The author of the *Gesta Stephani* thought him capable of taking the throne, but that, burdened by the impediment of his illegitimacy, Robert chose not to assert a claim.

The more viable candidates were the king's nephews by his sister Adela, Theobald and Stephen. Adela's youngest and by far most impressive and able son, Henry, was not eligible as he was a Cluniac monk who had been consecrated bishop of Winchester by his uncle the king in 1129.

Robert of Torigni told how Theobald was asked by the Norman nobility to take control of the duchy. On 21 December, at Lisieux, they approached him formally, and Robert of Gloucester lent his support too. But although Theobald was the elder, it was his brother, the affable and popular Stephen who flabbergasted the Anglo-Norman world by his swift seizure of the English throne.

There is little doubt that had Matilda not quarrelled with her father, she would have been queen. The magnates surrounding the king would have been forced to recognise her. But as she was not there, and the nobility was already apprehensive at the thought of her taking the throne, the succession became a matter of speed.

Despite his oaths to honour her claim, Stephen barely waited for confirmation of his uncle's death before he set sail for England. This must have been a premeditated act, long in the planning. The seeds were sown a decade earlier; Stephen could not forget Henry I's brief flirtation with making him king. This dangled promise, however ephemeral or half-hearted, inculcated in Stephen a desire for the throne that would lead him to perjure himself and forsake loyalties to his family as he stampeded over the rights of his first cousin and elder brother. It was Henry I's 'promise' that justified, in Stephen's mind, the neglect of his uncle in those last days, and his race to England to steal Matilda's crown.

It is possible too that Stephen may have felt providence was on his side: he had, after all, disembarked the *White Ship* before its short, fateful voyage. Had he been spared for this moment?

Stephen was not with Henry as he lay dying, but in his wife's county of Boulogne – Stephen's marriage to Matilda of Boulogne in 1125 gave him access to the wealth garnered from her vast estates in Flanders and south-east England. Stephen was evidently kept informed of his uncle's illness – Lyons-la-Forêt was only two days' hard riding away – which allowed him to plan.[61]

Stephen grabbed the opportunity. Most of the political elite were still with the dead king's body in Normandy. He took advantage of the uncertainty to sail from his wife's Channel port of Wissant to Kent on 3 or 4 December and was welcomed in London; he carried on to Winchester where he claimed the treasury, aided by his politically adept younger brother Bishop Henry of Winchester who helped mastermind the coup. Stephen was crowned at Westminster on 22 December by William de Corbeil, archbishop of Canterbury. The archbishop's initial concern at breaking his oath to Matilda was swept aside by Hugh Bigod, who must have travelled with the furies at his back to give his solemn testimony of the old king's deathbed change of heart.

Perhaps most importantly, Stephen had brought Roger, bishop of Salisbury, over to his side. During Henry I's reign, the chronicler Henry of Huntingdon wrote of Roger that 'he was second only to the king.'[62] Roger may have been nursing a festering grudge that Henry I had not listened to his protests when he married Matilda to Geoffrey, preferring instead to consult his bastard son Robert, and Brian Fitz Count. The chronicler William of Malmesbury wrote: 'I myself have often heard Roger bishop of Salisbury say that he was released from the oath he had taken to the empress because he had sworn only on condition that the king should not give his daughter in marriage to anyone outside the kingdom without consulting himself and the other chief men, and that no one had recommended that marriage or been aware that it would take place except Robert earl of Gloucester, and Brian Fitz Count, and the bishop of Lisieux.'[63]

No one outside Stephen's immediate circle, least of all Matilda, guessed that Stephen would secure the throne a mere three weeks after the old king's death. Stephen was now an anointed king. Although only a small number of the nobility had attended his crowning, such was the mystique surrounding the coronation ceremony that it would be very difficult to dislodge him. Life pivoted around religion in twelfth-century Christendom, and the commandment in Chronicles not to 'touch my anointed ones' was taken seriously.[64]

Matilda's claims were dust; she, and by implication her eldest son Henry, had been forsaken by those magnates who had promised to uphold them.

How did Stephen do it? Despite their solemn oaths, most of the aristocracy were appalled at the idea of Matilda as queen. She was disliked, she was married to the count of Anjou who was unpopular among the Anglo-Norman nobility, and she was a woman. She was thrice damned. Conversely, her cousin Stephen had an easy and appealing manner, was rich and was a respected soldier. He had been a favourite of Henry I and bathed in the residual glory.

And there were the convincing rumours among loyalists to Stephen that Henry I had changed his mind. Those struggling with the moral implications of relinquishing their oaths to Matilda could feel reassured that, if they looked hard enough, the old king had released them from their obligations to a woman.

Stephen had been crowned. Even the pope had given his tacit support. Rather than risk the financial insecurity of civil war, the Anglo-Norman nobility flocked to the new king. 'All the barons immediately determined, with Theobald's consent, to serve under one lord on account of the honours which they held in both provinces.'[65] For Stephen had bought his elder brother's loyalty – or at least his silence – with money; he gave him an annual pension of 2,000 marks. In return, Theobald relinquished any claim to the throne of England or the dukedom of Normandy.

Matilda's claim was abandoned by the nobility, even by her half-brother Robert of Gloucester, putting pragmatism above family loyalty – at least for the time being. In April 1136, he acknowledged Stephen as his king. He was the last to do so and his support for the new king remained at best lukewarm. Robert stayed in Normandy, living quietly on his estates, watching and waiting.

Matilda, as soon as she heard of her father's death, raced to claim her dowry castles on the Normandy–Anjou borders.[66] We have no way of knowing if she mourned, or regretted her argument with her father so close to his death, but she must have lamented the ramifications. For the moment, at least, there was nothing Matilda could do about her English inheritance. She seems to have remained in Normandy, probably in Argentan, holding on to her Norman border. It is probable that Henry and his younger brother Geoffrey remained with her. Her third and last child, William, was born in the summer of 1136.[67]

Matilda could do nothing but cling on to the tiny part of the Norman inheritance she had managed to secure, while Geoffrey gradually made inroads into the conquest of her duchy, forever watching his back against his own Angevin border lords.

By 1139 – only three years later – everything had changed. Walter Map, with a typical acidity of tongue, pronounced Stephen 'a man distinguished for skill in arms, but in other respects almost a fool'.[68] Stephen had had no success in Normandy. He made the only crossing of his reign in 1137, where he bought off his brother and paid homage for the duchy to Louis the Fat. But he recognised Geoffrey's superior military force and negotiated a short truce with him, agreeing to an annual payment of 2,000 marks (the truce only lasted for a year). Despite his homage, Stephen had no power in Normandy and would never return again.

In England, within the same three years, he had alienated the bishops and much of his nobility who descended swiftly into factionalism. They had no respect for their king-duke, who had failed in Normandy and was now short of funds, having partially drained his uncle's enormous treasury.

In the summer of 1139, taking advantage of Stephen's weakness, Robert of Gloucester used the excuse of rumours that Stephen had tried to have him murdered to put his money and his influence firmly behind his sister's cause. Matilda had been preparing for war for at least a year, keeping warriors with her such as Alexander of Bohon, a Cotentin nobleman described as 'the foremost among the countess's military retinue'.[69] Now she and her brother set sail for England together.

Matilda styled herself 'empress', and 'daughter of the king of the English' to enhance her right to rule. In the coming years, Matilda and Geoffrey would work in tandem, pursuing two separate claims: Matilda's responsibilities lay with the conquest of England, and Geoffrey's, with that of Normandy.

The pragmatic Robert's decision was influenced by the stunning military successes that Geoffrey achieved in Normandy.

When Robert declared for Matilda, Geoffrey had made extensive inroads into the duchy. Matilda left Normandy in a much surer position, as she sailed off to England to fight Stephen for her inheritance. She left Henry and his two younger brothers, Geoffrey and William, with their father.

Matilda landed in Sussex on 30 September with her brother Robert and 140 knights, and sought refuge with her step-mother Adeliza, now married to William d'Aubigny, earl of Arundel. Robert, accompanied by only twelve men, left Matilda for his stronghold at Bristol to garner support across the West Country.[70]

Stephen, in a typical and naive display of chivalry – many of his contemporaries thought it his greatest weakness – did not capture and imprison his first cousin who had come to take the crown from him, but granted her safe passage to join Robert at Bristol. Their cause was joined by their half-brother Reginald of Dunstanville; Matilda's uncle, now David King of Scots, who fought on Matilda's behalf in the north; Brian Fitz Count, lord of Wallingford and Abergavenny; and Miles of Gloucester. She received their homage, and it is likely that she set up her court at Gloucester Castle on the banks of the River Severn, while Robert stayed at Bristol.

Matilda's greatest champion throughout the war would be Brian Fitz Count. He was an illegitimate son of Alan Fergant, count of Brittany. He was at court when Matilda returned from Germany, and over the years he would put all his lands and possessions at Matilda's disposal.[71]

He had been one of Henry I's chief advisors, and owed his king all he had – wealth, lands, and a rich wife. He recalled his time at Matilda's father's court as 'the good and golden days', grateful that the king had given him 'arms and an honour'.[72]

Brian believed in Matilda completely; at least one novelist supposed them to be in love, and the author of the *Gesta Stephani* noted their 'affection' for one another, and his 'delight' when she came to England.[73] In 1144, Matilda, in public recognition of his unwavering support, issued a grant to Reading Abbey 'for the love and loyal service of Brian Fitz Count, which he has rendered me'.[74] Whether Matilda and Brian Fitz Count were in love, or whether it was the absolute loyalty Brian believed he owed Henry I – and then after his death, his daughter and chosen successor – we will never be sure.

Matilda combined her military campaign with an appeal to the pope to challenge Stephen's claim to be king. On 4 April 1139, her case was heard before the Second Lateran Council; Matilda's advocates argued that Stephen had seized the throne illegally, and that he had lied to do so. But although the pope found for Stephen, and 'confirmed his occupation of the kingdom of England and the duchy of Normandy', she never ceased to hope that he would change his mind.[75]

Stephen's wife, Matilda of Boulogne, joined him in defending England. He still had enough money left in his depleted treasury to employ mercenaries, also known as *routiers* or 'ravagers', and much of the country, besides the borderlands of Wales and the west of England, remained in royal hands.[76]

Matilda's friends were tenacious in fighting her cause. Her half-brother Reginald of Dunstanville won in Cornwall, and their grateful brother, Robert, granted him the earldom.[77] But one year into the war, the country was feeling its ravages. William of Malmesbury wrote: 'The whole year [1140] was troubled by the brutalities of war. There were many castles all over England, each defending its own district, or, to be more truthful, plundering it. The war, indeed, was one of sieges. Some of the castellans wavered in their allegiance, hesitating which side to support, and sometimes working entirely for their own profit.'[78]

The situation had reached a stalemate, with neither side able to gain a decisive advantage. But unexpectedly, everything changed in Matilda's favour. On 2 February 1141 at Lincoln, in a stellar coup engineered by her half-brother Robert and his son-in-law,

Ranulf earl of Chester, who brought with them 'a dreadful and unendurable number of Welsh', Stephen was captured and imprisoned at Bristol Castle.[79] (It was one of the very few pitched battles of the war – battles were dangerous and their outcomes uncertain; most of the fighting was marked instead by castle sieges.) Stephen had fought bravely, deserted by many of his supporters, with a double-headed axe. But he had lost. Robert placed him in the care of his wife Mabel, at Bristol Castle. It was not a comfortable imprisonment; Stephen would eventually be shackled in irons in his cell.

It looked like the endgame. Matilda was recognised by the church as 'Lady of England and Normandy', took possession of the treasury and was given the crown – although as yet she remained uncrowned. She embarked on a progress around the country and was recognised as queen at Winchester. Meanwhile Stephen's wife, Matilda of Boulogne, frantically attempted to secure her husband's release, promising he would leave the country and live quietly. Matilda however refused, as she refused Matilda of Boulogne's pleas to grant their son, Eustace, his inheritance – the lands Stephen had owned before he stole her crown.[80] She carried on to London, expecting to be crowned. She was even joined by Stephen's disaffected brother Henry, bishop of Winchester and now papal legate, who had welcomed her at his cathedral. The bishop had tired of his brother's hollow promises to uphold the integrity of church freedoms, and was bitter that Stephen had not created him archbishop of Canterbury after William de Corbeil, Stephen's advocate and the man who had placed the crown upon his head, died in 1136. Stephen dithered for two years, while Bishop Henry lobbied the pope for it. Ultimately however, fearing his brother's increasing power, Stephen ignored his requests, and instead invited Theobald, prior of Bec in Normandy, to England. It was Theobald, and not Henry, who was consecrated archbishop on 8 January 1139.

But in the capital, Matilda antagonised Londoners, who resented her appointment of earls and levying of taxes. She was heavy-handed where she could have been conciliatory. Meanwhile Stephen's wife, losing patience with the fruitless negotiations, raised an army and camped on the south bank of the River Thames, just outside the city of London. Londoners, besieged by two Matildas – one threatening pernicious taxes and assaults on their unique rights, and the other threatening them with battle – now decided for Stephen's queen instead of their 'Lady of the English'. On 24 June, while Matilda and her followers were celebrating with a feast at Westminster, Londoners declared for Stephen's queen and attacked. They rang the city's bells which notified its citizens to strike, and the queen presumptive abandoned her banquet and fled for her life to Oxford. Gerald of Wales left us with a damning comment on her failure: 'She was swollen with insufferable pride by her success in war, and alienated the affections of nearly everyone. She was driven out of London.' She was condemned for her pursuit of independent female power, no longer 'Matilda the Good'.

Meanwhile Bishop Henry oscillated, disgusted at Matilda's harsh treatment of Eustace. In the end, he did little to win the pope over for Matilda. When Innocent II ordered him to return to his erstwhile support for his brother, he deserted Matilda for Stephen's queen.

Matilda retaliated with an army, which she took to Winchester, to besiege the bishop's castle. But she was defeated. She fled, riding astride for speed, with her half-brother Reginald and Brian Fitz Count, while Robert stayed to cover her flight. Disaster ensued; Robert was caught by Flemish mercenaries loyal to the royalist William of Warenne, earl of Surrey, and was sent, a prisoner, by Stephen's wife to Rochester Castle.

Had Matilda not estranged Londoners, but instead mollified them, pressing the claim of her young son, she might have been queen. Now, however, she was in a dreadful predicament. She had lost her most powerful ally.

Matilda determined to get him back, and although Robert begged his sister not to make a bargain, she insisted on swapping prisoners. On 1 November Stephen was released, in exchange for Robert's freedom two days later. He hurried to his sister at Oxford where she had, once more, established her court.

Stephen's capture at Lincoln, although it ultimately did nothing for Matilda in England, had an enormous impact on Geoffrey's war to conquer Normandy. Orderic Vitalis wrote 'when he had news that his wife had won the day', Geoffrey and his armies hurled themselves into Normandy once more. This time, they would win.

But the war in England, with Stephen's release, was yet again at a stalemate. Matilda begged Geoffrey to come to her aid, reminding him that it was 'his duty to maintain the inheritance of his wife and children in England'.[81] But he refused: he had nothing to offer her. All his resources were concentrated on the subjugation of Normandy, where he was in the process of triumphing through a combination of force and diplomacy, luring the magnates over to his side. He insisted, instead, that Robert of Gloucester join him in Normandy to aid his fight there: 'If the earl would cross the sea and come to him he would meet his wishes as far as he could; if not, it would merely be a waste of time for anyone else to come and go.'[82] Robert was reluctant to leave Matilda – he was aware how integral he was to her campaign – but he answered Geoffrey's summons.

Around 24 June 1142, Robert left England for Normandy, from the port of Wareham, held by his son William, on the Dorset coast. When they met, Robert tried to convince Geoffrey to send aid to Matilda, but he refused, claiming that 'he feared the rebellion of the Angevins and his other men'.[83] Nevertheless, William of Malmesbury recorded that Robert's visit was successful, and that together he and Geoffrey captured ten castles in the north-west of Normandy. However, perhaps aided by discussion with Geoffrey, Robert had a change of heart over the direction of the war for England. Matilda, he believed, had no hope of becoming queen. It was time to bring in her eldest son, Henry.

Robert returned to England in September with between 300 and 400 men, fifty-two ships, and the nine-year-old Henry.[84]

He immediately set out to save Matilda from disaster. Stephen's forces had surrounded her at Oxford Castle that month; Robert did not have the men to bring an army to confront the king directly, so instead he attacked Wareham, which Stephen had captured earlier, hoping to draw the king away from Matilda. Stephen did not respond to the ruse, and Matilda found herself in terrible personal danger. After a three-month siege, the castle was about to fall, and Matilda's capture and imprisonment seemed certain. The weather, and her bravery, saved her.

At the beginning of December, the land covered with snow and ice, Matilda escaped. She and the four men who accompanied her camouflaged themselves in white cloaks which made them invisible against the snow, and escaped, walking across the frozen Thames. She fled to Brian Fitz Count at Wallingford, fifteen miles to the south, who took her on to Devizes.

Matilda had not yet seen her son. Sometime before Christmas, while Brian Fitz Count offered her refuge at Wallingford, Robert was able to bring Henry to her there, where they were 'delighted' to be reunited. In her joy at seeing her firstborn, Matilda had a brief respite from the hopelessness of her situation.[85] It was from this point, when Matilda saw Henry, that she realised the futility of her pursuit of the crown of England. By 1144, while Geoffrey had achieved complete success with the conquest of Normandy, Matilda had failed. Even Robert, having spent three years and a vast amount of money on his sister's campaign, realised she could never be queen. It was Robert who fashioned the move to bring young Henry from Anjou as the new figurehead of the Angevin party.

IV

While Matilda fought in England, Henry had remained in Anjou, studying with his tutors and learning knightly skills. It is possible that his paternal uncle, Helias, played a part in Henry's education, acting as his mentor.[86]

His parents were clever and inquisitive, both were well educated (Matilda received the greater part of her education at her first husband's German court rather than in England), and they took great care over the young Henry's schooling. Matilda and Geoffrey had a plan. They would provide their eldest son not only with an exemplary military and political education, but with the tools to enable him to become the Platonic archetype of a philosopher-prince. Walter Map's claim that Henry 'had a knowledge of all the tongues used from the French sea to the Jordan' is undoubtedly an exaggeration; but it gives a hint as to the breadth of his learning. The languages Henry spoke fluently were French and Latin – Walter Map went on to say that he 'customarily made use' of them, and later he possibly learned some English.

Western Europe had never experienced such an intellectually exciting period as the twelfth century. Later historians dubbed it the 'twelfth-century renaissance' and it defied the Victorian misnomer of the 'Dark Ages'.[87] It was an age that saw the beginnings of humanism, a sense of the importance of the individual, a massive population shift from countryside to town, the rise of the city, the centralisation of government, and the recognition and employment of the greatest intellectuals of the day in the service of the royal administration. It saw an explosion in art, poetry and literature, particularly in the vernacular, as new fiction was explored for the first time since the classical era, and in science, theology and legal reform. It saw the beginnings of the great cathedral schools, the universities and of the soaring Gothic architecture that visually defined the age and fed the medieval Christian soul.

This quest for knowledge was fed by a 'rediscovery' of the classical thinkers of Greece and Rome, particularly Christian Rome after Constantine's conversion, and by increasing contact with the Arab world and the richness of their intellectual traditions, notably in astronomy, medicine and mathematics. Contemporary writers called this movement a *renovatio*, meaning a rebirth or a renewal, with its underlying connotations of redemption through knowledge.

It was expected that a ruler should be well educated. Henry I and Geoffrey of Anjou were admired for their intellects. William of Malmesbury – monk, historian and devotee of Henry's uncle Robert of Gloucester – pronounced that 'a king without letters is [just] an ass with a crown.'[88]

Henry's teachers – he had four that we know of – played an enormous role in shaping his interests. They were important not simply because they were clever, but because of the breadth and internationalism of their knowledge and understanding. Two were celebrated scholars, two we know far less about. But we do know that the experience of Henry's tutors went far beyond the teachings of the church fathers; they had imbibed the wisdom of the philosophers, mathematicians, medics, poets and scholars of Greece, Rome, the Arabs and the Jews.

His first tutor was Peter of Saintes, chosen by Geoffrey because he was 'more learned in Poetry than anyone this side of the Pyrenees'.[89] Peter taught Henry Latin, and told him stories of the Greek and Trojan heroes; he even composed a poem on the Trojan War.[90]

When Henry was brought to England in 1142, he lived in his uncle Robert's household at Bristol, where he continued his education under both Robert's and his mother's direction. Robert was a scholar. In 1138, Geoffrey of Monmouth dedicated his *Historia regum Britanniae* ('History of the Kings of Britain') to the earl, and it was from this text that Henry probably first became aware of the legends of King Arthur. This was the first time that an author collated and wrote down in Latin, a language the educated classes understood, all the legends connected with Britain's most famous king. Geoffrey may even have written the text as a reflection of the civil war. Robert had recently made an alliance with Morgan ap Iorwerth, lord of Usk; the Welsh saw themselves as the proud descendants of Arthur.[91] And Matilda is possibly portrayed in the text as Cordelia, the loyal daughter of Lear. Geoffrey's Cordelia is married to a Frenchman and forced to fight her cousin for her birthright.[92] It is probable that Henry discussed the book with both Geoffrey and Robert.

His mother, meanwhile, having fled from Oxford at the end of the year, set up headquarters at Devizes, roughly thirty miles from Henry. Henry of Huntingdon enthusiastically called its castle 'the most splendid' in Europe.[93] It would be the centre of Matilda's court for the duration of her stay in England.

The chronicler Gervase of Canterbury wrote of the 'joy' Matilda experienced in her son.[94] It was in England that Henry began his training for leadership. He began to sign himself as 'rightful heir of England and Normandy'.[95] And on the occasions when he was with his mother, he received joint homage from their English vassals.[96]

Walter Map, in his gossipy and beautifully written *Courtiers' Trifles* on the machinations of Henry's court, later wrote about Matilda's methods, much of which she had learned from the old king:

I have heard that his [Henry's] mother's teaching was to this effect, that he should spin out the affairs of everyone, hold long in his own hand all posts that fell in, take the revenues of them, and keep the aspirants to them hanging on in hope; and she supported this advice by an unkind analogy: an unruly hawk, if meat is often offered to it and then snatched away or hid, becomes keener and more inclinably obedient and attentive.

He ought also to be much in his own chamber and little in public: he should never confer anything on anyone at the recommendation of any person, unless he had seen and learnt about it.[97]

It is not a great leap to imagine that Matilda began to teach her son when he was still very young the political methods learned from her first husband and her father.

At Bristol, Henry, alongside Robert's younger sons, was taught by Master Matthew.[98] Historians are uncertain as to Matthew's identity. Some believe that he was Robert's appointment as Henry was living in Robert's household; however, it would seem that Matthew had been in Geoffrey's service for years, teaching his two sisters – Henry's aunts.[99] It is likely therefore that Geoffrey sent Matthew to England as part of Henry's retinue, in consultation with Robert. Both Peter of Saintes and Master Matthew probably initiated Henry into the intricacies of government, working alongside his parents and uncle to teach him the theory as the young boy observed the practice. Henry witnessed his first charter, issued by Geoffrey in June 1138, when he was only five years old.[100]

Robert undoubtedly had an influence on the young Henry's education. Robert, who has been called 'a happy compound of warrior, statesman, and scholar', had studied enough to attract the admiration of William of Malmesbury.[101] Henry I ensured this adored son was well educated, and his library was reputedly vast. It was probably at Robert's invitation that the renowned scholar Adelard of Bath visited young Henry at Bristol.

Two years later, in January 1144, Henry was recalled to Normandy. It was at about this time that Geoffrey heard of his own father's death in a riding accident in Acre, in November 1143.[102] Fulk and Melisende had two sons together, Baldwin and Almaric; Geoffrey's brothers were destined to occupy the throne of Jerusalem.

Geoffrey had captured Rouen, Normandy's capital city. He had never been popular in England, but after his spectacular victories in Normandy and in recognition of his superb military skill, in Angevin and Norman sources he was a hero, 'a second Mars ... a powerful knight ... a philosopher in his knowledge'.[103]

Soon afterwards he began styling himself 'duke'. His seal at this time was double-sided, reflecting his conquest. One side depicted him on horseback, as duke of Anjou, and the other, holding a sword and shield, as duke of Normandy.[104] Geoffrey, having established himself, recalled his son to continue his education and training in Normandy.

In Rouen, Geoffrey employed the remarkable William, 'the grammarian' of Conches, as Henry's tutor. He taught him for three years, and probably taught his younger brothers too.[105]

William was one of Europe's great scholars. He possibly taught at the great cathedral school of Chartres in northern France, was either a physician or a physicist (he is described as a *'physicus'* which meant both), and had a passion for the natural sciences. William wrote commentaries on the works of Plato, Boethius and the Latin grammarian Priscian. When he quarrelled with a bishop, he sought sanctuary with Geoffrey. William approved of Geoffrey's attitude to education. He dedicated his magnificent work *Dragmaticon philosophiae* ('Dialogue on Natural Philosophy') – the culmination of his studies in natural philosophy and observations of the physical universe, written for Henry – to Geoffrey, praising him for encouraging his children to study rather than playing the popular game of hazard.[106] This became one of the most important texts of the twelfth-century renaissance. The work ranged over subjects such as medicine and astronomy, and took the form of a 'dialogue' between a philosopher and a duke – that is, between William and Henry. One particular episode may have been based on the recollection of a conversation that took place between them:

Duke: 'There is one thing that still puzzles me about hearing. If I emit a sound in a cave or a high forest, someone repeats and returns my word to me.'

Philosopher: 'Do you not know, then, that this is performed by "Echo, the resounding nymph"?'

Duke: 'I am not Narcissus to be pursued by her. I ask for a physical explanation.'

The philosopher goes on to explain the science to his pupil, and the duke replies, 'I do not know if what you are saying is true, but I do know that it pleases me a great deal. And so I am waiting all the more keenly for what remains to be said about the other senses.'

Philosopher: 'It pleases me that such explanations please you.'[107]

William had taught John of Salisbury – himself among the greatest writers and thinkers of the twelfth century, who wrote on the intellectual energy of the age, and the debt owed to the past:

> Our own generation enjoys the legacy bequeathed to it by that which preceded it. We frequently know more, not because we have moved ahead by our own natural ability, but because we are supported by the menial strength of others, and possess riches that we have inherited from our forefathers. Bernard of Clairvaux used to compare us to punt dwarfs perched on the shoulders of giants. He pointed out that we see more and farther than our predecessors, not because we have keener vision or greater height, but because we are lifted up and borne aloft on their gigantic stature.[108]

The linguist and scientist Adelard of Bath, at the forefront of this renaissance, also had a profound impact on Henry's education. Adelard probably taught Henry when he was at Bristol. He was famed for his knowledge of Arabic and his translations into Latin of Arabic treatises on mathematics and astronomy. It was Adelard who introduced Arabic innovations in mathematics into England and France. He had travelled for seven years in Italy, Sicily, Antioch and Cilicia (the southern coast of Turkey), dedicating himself to the 'studies of the Arabs'.[109]

The twelfth century saw an explosion in knowledge and cultural exchange from as far afield as the icy western fringes of northern Europe to the Middle East. Crusaders had established a Latin Kingdom in Jerusalem in 1099, and it would not fall until nearly two centuries later.

In 1130 in Sicily, a Norman mercenary – Count Roger de Hauteville – founded a dynasty, conquering the island and much of southern Italy. He and his successors presided over a society of remarkable cultural and religious tolerance, marked by an exchange of ideas between Christians, Muslims and Jews. It was a place where all scholars, regardless of faith, were welcomed. From the ninth century, Spain's Christian kings began their slow conquest of the Iberian Peninsula from its Muslim rulers, leading to a 'rediscovery' of the ideas of Greece and Rome, and Arabic intellectual developments, in western Europe. It was in this exceptional atmosphere of intellectual curiosity and achievement that we find tolerant and humanitarian scholars such as Adelard bringing the ideas and teachings of the Greeks, the Muslims and the Jews to the cathedral schools and the burgeoning European universities. Henry learned from among their finest.

In 1150, Adelard dedicated his work *De opera astrolapsus* ('The Workings of the Astrolabe') to Henry. Here he laid out his understanding of the cosmos, gave detailed instructions on how to use the astrolabe, a device used to track the path of the sun and the stars, and even included a section on hawking as light relief for the scholar. It was the apotheosis of his career.

Adelard's dedication to Henry sets out the aspirations he held for his able pupil:

I thoroughly approve of the fact that the nobility of a royal race applies itself to the study of the liberal arts. But I find it all the more remarkable that preoccupation in the affairs of government does not distract the mind from that study. Thus I understand that you, Henry, since you are the grandson of a king, have understood with the complete attention of your mind, what is said by Philosophy: that states are blest either if they are handed over for philosophers to rule, or if their rulers adhere to philosophy ... Since your childhood was once imbued with the scent of this reasoning, your mind preserves it for a long time, and the more heavily it is weighed down by outside occupations, the more diligently it withdraws itself from them. Hence it happens that you not only read carefully and with understanding those things that the writings of the Latins contain, but you also dare to wish to understand the opinions of the Arabs concerning the sphere, and the circles and movements of the planets. For you say that whoever lives in a house, if he is ignorant of its material or composition, its size or kind, its position or parts, is not worthy of such a dwelling ...[110]

The love of learning and spirit of inquiry Henry imbibed from these exemplary scholars would last all his life. His parents had provided him with the tools to be anything he wanted. His teachers (or masters, *magistri*), tolerant and inquisitive, had opened Henry's mind; many chroniclers tell of his passion for books, learning and discourse. He would aspire to be a philosopher-prince in the Platonic mould.[111]

V

The first war on English soil since the Conquest was a war of attrition, bitter and vindictive, with the rule of law sporadic. Although the fighting was mostly confined to the south-east and south-west of England, Stephen's leadership was inadequate. Contemporaries called it 'the anarchy', a time when they believed themselves abandoned by Christ. The author of *The Anglo-Saxon Chronicle* wrote in despair, 'The earth bore no corn, for the land was all laid waste ... and people said openly, that Christ and his saints slept.'

When he was fourteen Henry, imbued with loyalty to his parents and belief in his own right to rule, decided to fight alongside his mother for their birthright. At the beginning of 1147, he hired mercenaries on credit and sailed to England with a few companions to aid her. He led an attack against his first cousin, Philip of Gloucester, at Cricklade, just over thirty miles west of Oxford. Philip, Robert's son, had deserted Matilda for Stephen, 'seeing that at that time the king had the upper hand, [he] entered into a pact of peace and concord with him, and after being lavishly endowed with castles and lands, he gave hostages and paid him homage'.[112] Philip's defection was a reminder of the extent to which this war left families bitterly divided. But it is likely that Geoffrey knew nothing about his eldest son's trip to England, for Henry had no money to pay his men, and had arrived in England with virtually nothing; once they realised, they deserted. Henry, desperate, asked his mother for money but she had none to spare. His uncle, Robert, gave him a similar answer.

When Stephen's forces routed him nearby, at Bampton in Oxfordshire, Henry persuaded his cousin to give him money to pay for his journey home. Unwisely, Stephen agreed; he was, according to the author of the *Gesta Stephani*, 'always full of pity and compassion'. But whether it was because, as his detractors claimed, chivalry was his undoing, or because he wanted Henry and his troublesome mercenaries out of England as quickly as possible, we may only speculate.[113] By Ascension Day, 29 May 1147, Henry was back in Normandy.

For Henry, the moment marked the passing of the first chapter of his life. It was the last time he would see the uncle who had not only been responsible for shaping so much of his education but who had also made his and Matilda's cause in England possible. Robert of Gloucester died on 31 October at Bristol. He was buried in the Benedictine priory church of St James, which he had founded.

Matilda left England less than four months after her brother's death, in mid-February 1148, defeated and exhausted. Gervase of Canterbury wrote that she was 'worn down by the trials of the English hostilities ... preferring to retire to the haven of her husband's protection than endure so many troubles in England'. She may have stomached the pitiful stalemate for so long because she was waiting for Henry to come of age. And it is possible that she felt unable to continue her cause without the leadership that her half-brother had provided. Robert's son and heir, William, was not up to taking his father's place; he was judged 'effeminate and a lover of bedchambers more than of war'.[114] Matilda made her home at Le Pré, near Rouen. She would never return to England.

Matilda was once again cast as a failure. Her biographer Marjorie Chibnall calls her 'almost a queen'.[115] But Matilda's mission was doomed from the start. She was castigated for her character, her fiery temper – she 'drove [her enemies] from her presence in fury after insulting and threatening them' – and for her lack of femininity: 'The countess of Anjou ... was always above feminine softness and had a mind steeled and unbroken in adversity.'[116] She was a 'virago', who 'put on an extremely arrogant demeanour instead of the modest gait and bearing proper to the gentle sex'.[117]

For not even clever, ambitious, determined Matilda could overcome the 'problem' of her sex. Her father had foreseen the difficulties of his magnates accepting female rule, which is why he had induced them to swear their oaths to her three times. The very few women who did rule independently were encouraged to disregard their femininity altogether and to behave as kings. When Geoffrey's father Fulk died in Jerusalem in 1143, the powerful Cistercian abbot Bernard of Clairvaux urged his widow Queen Melisende to 'show the man in the woman; order all things ... so that those who see you will judge your works to be those of a king rather than a queen'.[118] Urraca of the Spanish kingdom of León and Castile pretended to be a man, signing her documents as a king rather than a queen.

Matilda's hopes would now rest in Henry, her heir. As the coming man and despite his youth, Henry was already attracting support in England to add to those nobles who had staunchly championed the Angevin cause. This allegiance was motivated at least in part by economic interests. As soon as Geoffrey was recognised as duke of Normandy by Louis VII in 1145, it was clear to those magnates who held land on both sides of the Channel that Stephen would never reunite Normandy and England. But once Stephen died, should they offer their allegiance to Henry, and not Eustace, the problem would be solved.

Geoffrey always contended that he conquered Normandy on behalf of his son. His charters, after becoming duke, often read 'with the advice and consent of Henry my son'.[119] The intention was that there should be no impediment to Henry inheriting Normandy. Gilbert Foliot, when consecrated bishop of Hereford in September 1148, swore allegiance to Henry, and not to Stephen. And in mid-1148 William of Gloucester swore to aid Roger of Hereford against all men 'saving the person of their lord Henry'.[120] At this stage, it was more to do with Henry's lineage, as the grandson of Henry I and the descendant of the Norman conquerors and the Anglo-Saxon kings, than his abilities. That was all about to change.

In October 1148, Henry's immediate family – Matilda, Geoffrey, and his two younger brothers – met at Rouen to decide their strategy. Normandy was theirs, won both by diplomacy and by military action, and they had a good shot at England. To claim his entire birthright, Henry would return to England where his uncle, David King of Scots, would knight him. The knighting ceremony, very important as a passage to power, would mark the beginning of Henry's manhood. And as he turned sixteen, it was an apt time to hold the ceremony. On Whit Sunday 1149, David knighted his nephew with the belt and garter in a magnificent ceremony at Carlisle Castle, followed by a lavish party. Henry now began to call himself 'duke'; the bishop of Lisieux wrote to his friend Robert, bishop of Lincoln, to 'favour as much as you can the cause of our duke.'[121]

Many of Matilda's staunchest supporters – Miles of Gloucester, Brian Fitz Count, her brother Robert – were either dead or retired. With Henry's return, a new body of men began to coalesce around the freshly anointed scion of Anjou and Normandy. These men included his uncle Reginald of Cornwall, who remained true to his sister's cause; Robert Fitz Harding of Bristol; Ranulf earl of Chester, married to Robert's daughter but whose allegiance throughout the past ten years had been in flux; Ranulf's brother the earl of Lincoln; and the earl of Hereford. Henry was their acknowledged leader – not so much for his qualities, but more as a result of their bitter experience that Stephen could be duplicitous and capricious. Stephen, after Matilda left for Normandy, had courted the earls of Chester and Essex with lands; he had then, without warning or cause, imprisoned them.[122] These Anglo-Norman magnates yearned for stability, and they looked to the as yet unproven Henry to provide it.

But just as in the previous generation when William Atheling's greatest foe had been his first cousin William Clito, so Henry's biggest danger lay with his cousin Eustace, Stephen's eldest son. Eustace was as determined to be king of England as Henry was. He had paid homage to Louis for Normandy in 1137, and had been married to Louis' sister, Constance, as putative heir to England and Normandy. He was knighted a year or so before Henry, at the end of 1147.

Stephen, fearing Henry's growing importance, and to ensure his son's succession, appealed to Rome to have Eustace crowned alongside him. But Pope Eugenius III refused. Stephen was anointed king before Rome could approve it. If the pope had given his tacit support to an anointed King Stephen (made holy by the anointing ceremony) over Matilda, that support would not necessarily be extended to Eustace. Even the anonymous author of the *Gesta Stephani*, until now firmly in the king's camp, switched sides and proclaimed Henry over Stephen as the coming man, calling him 'the right heir of England'.[123]

Henry made his way south from Carlisle, possibly bound directly for Normandy, possibly intending to fight Stephen and Eustace. But whatever Henry's intentions, Stephen and Eustace were determined to obliterate him. Henry at sixteen – knighted and head of the Angevin party – was a far greater threat than the fourteen-year-old boy who had sailed to England to help his mother. The chronicler John of Hexham captured the spirit of exactly what was at stake: 'There was between [Henry] and Eustace … a contest of arms, for they were rivals for the same crown.'[124] It would be a fight to death.

Henry evaded capture, taking back roads to Bristol, despite Eustace's dogged quest. The *Gesta Stephani* recorded the devastation of Eustace's campaign: 'They took and plundered everything they came upon, set fire to houses and churches, and, what was more cruel and inhuman to behold, fired the crops which had been reaped and stoked all over the fields, and consumed or destroyed everything edible they found.'[125] This bitter civil war had terrible consequences for ordinary men and women, particularly those who lived in the path of battles. The period was peppered with crop failure, famine, wanton destruction, crime and disorder.

Atrocities were committed on both sides; when Matilda's ally Miles of Gloucester sacked Worcester in 1139, he burned the city; his army (made up of domestic forces, not foreign mercenaries), 'rabid and debauched, took those citizens who were not killed in the pillaging and led them away, coupled like dogs, into wretched captivity'.[126] In revenge, Stephen saw nothing amiss when he attacked the countryside rather than Hereford or Bristol castles, destroying everything in his path that could feed the population; he left 'nothing at all, as far as it lay in his power, that could serve his enemies for food or any purpose'.[127] It was commonplace to kill all the livestock and burn the crops, to prevent them falling into enemy hands. Livestock levels would still not return to normal even by the middle of the 1150s.[128]

In the West Country, scene of some of the bitterest fighting, the author of the *Gesta* wrote of famine, the death of the local peasant population, with no one alive or able to bring in the harvest. Stephen's domains were 'reduced to a desert'.[129] Henry of Huntingdon wrote despairingly in 1140: 'Gaunt famine, following, wastes away, whom murder spares, with slow decay.'[130] Neither side left anything for the general population to live on. Those people who survived the path of the marauding armies often starved to death.

In the counties beleaguered by war, acts of generosity and kindness were considered unusual enough by the chroniclers to record them. A local landlord in Gloucestershire, the Angevin stronghold, paid for a chapel to be built at Winchcombe Abbey, 'so that both he and his men could have some refuge there from the incursions of robbers and the ruthless machinations of evil men'.[131] Similarly, Waleran of Meulan was considered kind when he freed those prisoners he had taken hostage after he attacked Tewkesbury.[132]

It was not just Stephen's and Matilda's forces who ravaged the land; some opportunists took it upon themselves to establish their own armies in areas with little rule of law. The author of the *Gesta* wrote bitterly of the atrocities carried out by the Caldret brothers, who he thought were Flemish.[133] The author of the Peterborough Chronicle, meanwhile, recorded that 'both men and women [were] put in prison for their gold and silver, and tortured with pains unspeakable', captured by local lords and held in their dungeons.[134] It was generally not the nobility who suffered during this dreadful war, but the innocent local population who stood in the way of their sieges, occasional battles and devastation of the countryside.

The chroniclers recorded tales of torture and ransom to appropriate wealth, the fear engendered by Stephen's Flemish mercenaries, and the lack of respect for church property. These sacred places were stripped of their valuables and graves were desecrated, often to build more castles upon. Some local lords even extorted money from villages in the form of a 'protection' tax, treating the chaos in those areas riven with fighting as a money-making opportunity.[135]

Oxfordshire experienced some of the bitterest fighting of the civil war, owing to Matilda's presence after Londoners threw her out in 1141, and then her close proximity at Devizes. Both sides had held the county at various points during the war. Oxford, the county's most important town, was the scene of an annual fair, and its central location made it a magnet for trade. It was a wealthy town, about the sixth richest in the kingdom.[136] But Stephen partially burned and sacked it, and besieged the castle in an attempt to capture Matilda in 1142. Local people fled for their lives, leaving all their possessions behind. Matilda had eluded Stephen; but for the people of the town, the burning of Oxford and the loss of their possessions and income were catastrophic. Oxfordshire, one of the most agriculturally prosperous counties in England, suffered regular crop burnings and pillagings, with peasants conscripted into local armies and communities attacked, leaving widows and orphans unprotected. Oxford had still not completely recovered economically by 1155.

In many large towns, however, trade, markets and annual fairs tended to continue as usual, as did the inhabitants' pleasures – their cockfighting, their wrestling matches, and their football matches where, if the town was large enough, members of the trades and the schools would align themselves into teams, cheered on by their friends and relatives.[137]

Chroniclers who recorded the woes of the civil war were for the most part from the areas affected by the fighting. If you lived in Essex, firmly in royal hands throughout the period, you would hardly have known that a war was happening at all.

Peasants continued to till their land and bring in the harvest, unimpeded by either army. Villagers went to church on Sundays and feast days, where they would stand for services presided over by a priest speaking Latin, which they did not understand. Churches were a riot of brilliant colour, from the lurid wall paintings depicting the horrors or joys of the Day of Judgement, to the effigies, tombs and carvings of saints decorated with the congregants' favourite baubles and trinkets.

Community activities held in churches continued too – they were not just a place of prayer, baptism, weddings and funerals, but also the scene of festivals and plays. 'Church-ales' would be held here, effectively fundraisers for the church, which elicited money by selling ale.

Anarchy did not therefore exist in all areas, all of the time. Some form of government was exercised nearly everywhere – whether controlled by Stephen, Matilda, or the great magnates such as Ranulf of Chester, Robert's son-in-law, who acted more or less independently. And each party of power minted coins and collected taxes.

* * *

Henry left England in January 1150. He would not return for three years, although Eustace continued to pursue him obsessively. Only one of them could be king.

He returned to Normandy to great acclaim, where his father officially pronounced him 'duke'. As Henry's star rose, Eustace's declined. Although Henry was absent from England, he was now taken seriously as one of two contenders for the throne. Many believed he would be England's next king, and as such his favour was frequently courted more than Stephen's by the self-interested magnates whose lands straddled the English Channel.

In Normandy, Geoffrey finally captured Gerard Berlai, Louis' friend and seneschal for the county of Poitou, in June 1150 after a year-long siege. Geoffrey, inspired by his reading of the Roman writer Vegetius, had bombarded Gerard's seemingly impregnable double-walled castle with 'Greek Fire', a feared incendiary device of the ancient world.[138]

A desperate Eustace joined his brother-in-law Louis to attempt to annihilate Henry on the continent. Louis was pious. In 1147 he and his wife, Eleanor of Aquitaine, had left their kingdom for two years for Jerusalem with the Second Crusade. Militarily it was a disaster, an utter humiliation for Louis. On his return he was dismayed not only at Henry's and Geoffrey's victories in Normandy, but also at the stupendous progress Henry had made during his absence in pursuing his claim to the English throne.

Louis feared such a powerful neighbour on his north-western border and joined Eustace to rout father and son. But the new duke and his father were untouchable; Normandy's defences remained impregnable.

Louis, badgered by his adored advisor Abbot Suger, and then on Suger's death in January 1151 by his new chief advisor, the cadaverous Cistercian monk Bernard of Clairvaux, was persuaded to pragmatism. He abandoned Eustace's cause and reluctantly invited Henry and Geoffrey to Paris, to accept Henry's homage for Normandy. And so, in August Henry and Geoffrey brought their prisoner Gerard Berlai to Paris, that mosquito-infested, unpaved city of mud and marsh, to meet their pious and tedious overlord, the king of France. It would be Henry's first encounter with Louis' queen, Eleanor of Aquitaine.

No one was prepared for the upheaval that was to follow.

VI

The encounter did not begin well. The great hall of Louis' old palace, squatting at the end of the tiny Île de la Cité in the middle of the River Seine, reverberated with screams of rage. Bernard of Clairvaux, Louis, his brother and advisors, and Count Geoffrey of Anjou all competed to be heard. The noise of their frenzy echoed around the chamber.

When they saw Gerard Berlai presented to them, shackled, Louis and Bernard were furious. They demanded Gerard's immediate release, and the return of the Vexin, a small territory midway between the Norman city of Rouen and the Capetian city of Paris. Whoever controlled this borderland of castles and rivers, whether the Norman dukes or the kings of France, held the advantage. Louis wanted it; Henry and Geoffrey were not prepared to give it up.

Bernard of Clairvaux loathed and distrusted the House of Anjou. He believed they were rogue counts, descended from the devilish fairy Melusine. He had called Geoffrey 'that hammer of good men, and destroyer of the peace and liberty of the Church', and in 1147 he had induced Pope Eugenius III to excommunicate Geoffrey for his besiegement of Berlai.[139] Furthermore, Geoffrey had been noticeably absent from the Second Crusade, when nearly every other French nobleman had responded to Bernard's call to take the cross.[140] When Henry and Geoffrey walked into the great hall of Louis' palace with their prisoner, tempers flared.

Louis took Geoffrey's imprisonment of Gerard as a personal

offence; he was incensed.[141] He ranted that he would only accept Henry's homage for Normandy (the ceremony where Henry would become Louis' man and hold Normandy only by right of Louis) and arrange for the lifting of Geoffrey's excommunication, if they released Gerard immediately. He demanded that they also cede the Vexin. Geoffrey, equally maddened, stormed out of the meeting, 'tormented by vapours of black bile', followed by Henry.[142] They would not give up the Vexin, and they would not release Gerard. Geoffrey, in ferocious temper, cared nothing for his excommunication.

But almost immediately Henry and Geoffrey came back and ceded to both of Louis' demands. Louis kept his word and bypassed his brother-in-law; Henry paid homage for Normandy where he was officially pronounced 'duke'. Eustace's claims were denied, by both Louis and the pope, who refused Stephen's request to guarantee Eustace's succession.[143] Geoffrey, though, still smarting, refused to ask Bernard to lift his excommunication. In a fit of prophetic vengeance, Bernard pronounced that Geoffrey would be dead within two weeks.

Unperturbed by the prophecy, Henry and Geoffrey 'joyfully' left Paris.[144] Henry went to Lisieux to meet his Norman barons, while Geoffrey travelled on to his castle of Château-du-Loir in Sarthe, near his capital, Le Mans. The late summer weather was extremely hot and Geoffrey took an evening swim in the river. He caught a fever, and by 7 September he was dead. He was thirty-eight years old.

In August, Henry had been a young man with enormous expectations, but only one dukedom in his hand. One month on, his father's untimely death made him lord of Anjou and Maine, as well as duke of Normandy. He now controlled a vast swathe of northern France.

But in Paris in high summer, why did Henry and Geoffrey, having stormed out of the talks with Louis, return and give him everything he wanted?

The likeliest reason is that the new young duke of Normandy had made a bargain with Eleanor, Louis' queen. Within a few months of meeting Henry, Eleanor and Louis would divorce; in May 1152, she would secretly marry Henry in her capital, Poitiers.

VII

Henry was eighteen years old when he and Eleanor met in Paris in 1151 and made their bargain. He was tall with a stocky, muscled body and a compelling face. He was charismatic, athletic, clever, educated, empathetic and ambitious. He was already known as a skilful (and lucky) commander of armies. He possessed a restlessness, an unquiet energy that kept his body in perpetual motion. Henry could not sit still.

More stories have been invented about Eleanor of Aquitaine than any other medieval woman. Her life has been imagined by chroniclers, historians, playwrights, poets, romantic novelists and film-makers for over 800 years. She has been portrayed as a vixen, a sexual predator and deviant; as the poisoner of her husband's mistress; as a desperately unhappy woman in a desperately unhappy marriage; as Shakespeare's 'canker'd grandam'; as a model of erudition, beauty and queenly virtue; as the leader of an army of bare-breasted crusader women; a feisty adventuress; a feminist prototype; an intellectual powerhouse and influential patron of the arts; and as the initiator of the famous troubadour courts of love. Although Eleanor undoubtedly grew up at Poitiers among the troubadours, and was the recipient of the unrequited passion of the poet Bernart de Ventadorn – who would follow her to England and Henry's court, proclaiming, 'When the cold wind blows from the direction of your country, it seems to me that I felt a breeze from paradise, for love of the lady' – almost everything that has been written about Eleanor is either a half-truth, wrong, or ultimately unknowable.[145]

The real Eleanor is a chimera, as illusive and fleeting as quicksilver. Such is her fame, we desire to possess her, yet we know almost nothing about her. The historian Richard Barber notes that 'to print out all of the records and chronicle entries about Eleanor would take less than a hundred pages'.[146] The written record is notably small for one of the most famous figures in European history. And that written record for the most part relates to the last fifteen years of her life – she died in her early eighties. Eleanor's earlier life remains in the shadows.

What, then, do we know of Eleanor? She was the daughter of William X of Aquitaine and Aénor of Châtellerault, and was born in about 1122 in or near Poitiers; some rumours put her birthplace at Château de Belin, near Bordeaux.[147] If we take this as the year of her birth (the records are not exact), she was twenty-nine years old when the eighteen-year-old Henry rode into Paris.

Aquitaine was the largest and the richest of the duchies that owed nominal allegiance to the French crown, although its rulers refused to pay homage to the French kings.[148] To the north its border was the River Loire, and to the south the mountains of the Pyrenees. It stretched west to east from the Atlantic to the Massif Central. The territory of its dukes, consisting of several different counties, dwarfed that of the French kings. They resided in their palace at Poitiers, closer to Paris than their southern border, and their subjects treated them as kings.[149] Their palace, a Merovingian fortress, sat at the top of a hill encircled by the River Clain. They certainly behaved as kings, encouraging ties of friendship between themselves and their nobility, taking clerical advice to increase their religious authority, and even acquiring relics. Relics held a cult status in the medieval world, a tangible expression of the story of Christ and his promise. Eleanor's ancestor Duke William V, or the Great, gained the gory prize of the head of John the Baptist for the church of Saint-Jean-d'Angély.[150] This duke was apparently called 'Augustus' by the pope in recognition of his power.

During the tenth century, the counts of Poitou had expanded their lands and became so powerful that they exercised quasi-royal authority. The relatively weak Frankish kings to the north rarely ventured south, except on their way to shrines such as St James's at Compostela, or to Rome.[151] They were obliged to grant Aquitaine's rulers the title 'duke' towards the end of the tenth century. These dukes expanded their power in the eleventh century, to incorporate all the territory Eleanor brought Louis as her marriage portion. They paid lip service only to their royal overlords. They were rich, their wealth buttressed by fertile vineyards, timber from the vast forests, fish, salt, and trade from Aquitaine's sea ports, La Rochelle and Bordeaux, on the Atlantic coast.

Eleanor's family was colourful. We assume that she would have been brought up with the tales of her strong ancestresses, wielding power in their own right – Agnes of Burgundy, her grandmother Philippa of Toulouse – or as regents or wives, and sharing in inheritance, unlike their sisters to the north, where primogeniture was slowly but inexorably becoming commonplace

She would also likely have known of her grandfather William IX, 'the troubadour duke', who had died soon after Eleanor's birth, in 1126. This lotus-eating duke was famous for his poetry, his affairs, his defiance of the church, his crusading expeditions, his success as a warrior, and even of occasional friendship with Muslims allied to Christians. If Eleanor was born in 1122, and not 1124 as some historians contend, she may even have had memories of him. It was about his love life, however, that the most scurrilous stories of the troubadour duke were told. In 1094 he married Philippa, daughter of the count of Toulouse. This was Philippa's second marriage; she was the widow of the king of Aragon. Philippa's decision to marry William was political – she wanted him to pursue her claim to rule in Toulouse. And he did, fighting on her behalf, for over thirty years.[152] William IX ultimately lost, although Eleanor would later take up her grandmother's claim.

Philippa silently tolerated William's numerous affairs. The most notorious was with the married viscountess of Châtellerault, called 'Dangereuse'. She and Eleanor's grandfather lived openly together at his palace at Poitiers, Dangereuse residing in the Maubergeon Tower there. We do not know what became of Philippa. She either retired to Fontevraud, that extraordinary foundation on the borders of Poitou and Anjou where the community of men and women lived under the direction of the abbess, or she outlived William quietly and anonymously, away from him and his mistress.[153]

Dangereuse was Eleanor's maternal grandmother. Before she began her affair with the duke, she had a daughter, Aénor, with her husband the viscount of Châtellerault. The duke arranged for the marriage of his son, also William, to Aénor, probably at the instigation of his mistress while she still resided with her husband. Philippa's feelings on the choice of bride for her son are unrecorded.

William was damned by churchmen for this affair; to live with a married woman, particularly while still married, was an affront to God. The bishop of Poitiers excommunicated him, and a monk from the Limousin explained away the duke's disastrous expedition on crusade, suffering the death of most of his army at the hands of the Turks in Anatolia, as punishment for his adultery: 'In truth he bore nothing of the name Christian; he was, as everyone knows, an ardent lover of women, and therefore unstable in all his actions.'[154]

Contemporaries were ambivalent in their attitudes towards him. Although to many churchmen he was damned, to some, this duke, the first of the troubadours, was worthy of praise for his wit and his wondrous (albeit often obscene) poetry. A thirteenth-century source described him as 'one of the greatest courtiers of the world and one of the greatest deceivers of women ... And he knew well how to compose and sing.'[155]

He died in 1126, although his influence was still felt in the reign of his son Duke William X. This duke was educated at the cathedral school in Poitiers. Yet although he encouraged the troubadours to frequent his court, he was not a poet like his father. He seems to have been rather in his father's shadow, as the children of able and famous parents often are. His greatest military success was capturing the area around the seaport of La Rochelle. He fell victim to Bernard of Clairvaux's wrath when he supported the contentious antipope, Anacletus II, in 1130. Anacletus' ancestry was too much for Bernard to bear, for he had a Jewish great-grandfather, who had converted to Christianity in the middle of the eleventh century, and changed his name from Baruch to Benedict. Voltaire would call him 'the Jewish Pope'. For this travesty, Duke William X's lands were placed under papal interdict, and the sainted Bernard denounced him with his typical incandescent rancour.

Nevertheless, William X capitulated to Bernard's demands that he give up support for Anacletus. In 1135, he agreed to go on pilgrimage to the shrine of St James at Compostela. He left Eleanor and her younger sister Petronilla in Bordeaux, at the castle of l'Ombrière.

We know nothing of Eleanor's family life, or her early education. Her father had one brother, Raymond, who would seek his fortune as prince of Antioch. She also had five paternal aunts, but frustratingly we know practically nothing about them, or the extent of any interaction with, or influence over, Eleanor. One became abbess of the convent of Notre-Dame at Saintes, and another, Agnes, was married in 1134 to King Ramiro II of Aragon.

Eleanor's mother, Aénor, for whom she was named (Eleanor means 'another Aénor' in Latin) died in 1130, when Eleanor was about eight years old. Her elder brother, Aigret, died in the same year.

Eleanor was close to Petronilla, who would stay with her, and to her mother's family, particularly her uncle, Raoul de Faye. He would be extremely important to her later in her life.

The men in her family were well educated, with a good knowledge of Latin, but we know little about how the women were educated. We do know, however, that it was commonplace for tutors to be attached to courts, and there is no reason to suppose that Eleanor was not educated. She probably learned to read and she knew Latin. She was not born to rule and did not even appear in a document until July 1129.[156] What is much better known is the fame of the cathedral schools of Poitiers and Saint-Hilaire, and the cultural sophistication of the court, with its songs of courtly love written and performed by both the nobility and poor poets.

Eleanor, on her brother's death, became her father's heir. William X was still young and intended to marry again in the hope of having more sons. Even in the more liberal south, female rule was problematic, and it was in his interests to shore up the succession with a male heir. In 1136, he had attempted to marry the widow of the lord of Cognac, but she was forced instead to marry the count of Angoulême. For this was a period where it was not uncommon for heiresses to be kidnapped and coerced into marriage for their inheritances.

Eleanor's father would never return from his pilgrimage to Compostela. He died suddenly on Good Friday 1137, a scant two days away from his destination. He was thirty-eight years old. His death catapulted the fifteen-year-old Eleanor to the position of duchess of Aquitaine in her own right.

Before he left, although he had made no plans for her marriage, Duke William had entrusted his daughter, the richest heiress in Christendom, to the guardianship of his nominal overlord, Louis the Fat. On William's death, Louis promptly denied any claim that could have been made by Eleanor's paternal uncle, Raymond, far away in Antioch, and instead betrothed Eleanor to his son, also named Louis. Eleanor's sister Petronilla had no share of their father's inheritance. All was subsumed by the French crown; a Capetian king had never been so closely involved in the affairs of Aquitaine.[157]

Louis VI, although his size had earned him the soubriquet 'the Fat', was an impressive and able king. He was, according to a contemporary source, 'huge in body, but no smaller in act and thought'.[158] For such a wily ruler, the marriage of his son and heir to the heiress to the greatest duchy in France was an obvious and necessary step.

Louis was seventeen. He was his father's second son, and like Eleanor it had not been intended that he rule. But in October 1131 his older brother Philip died when his horse fell over a 'devilish' pig in the rutted and unpaved streets of a Parisian suburb. A source describing the prince's demise paints an uglier picture, of the young man chasing a squire for fun through Paris's streets, when he fell and died.[159] Young Louis reluctantly left the peace of the cloister, where he had been preparing for a career in the church, to learn statecraft. In October 1131, he was anointed king at Reims Cathedral in his father's lifetime, a not uncommon practice of the Frankish kings.

Young Louis, his marriage arranged, promptly left Paris in the summer of 1137 and travelled south to Bordeaux with his mentor Abbot Suger of Saint-Denis, where he and Eleanor were married on 25 July at Saint-André Cathedral. Eleanor was crowned alongside Louis, 'with the diadem of the kingdom'.[160] Eleanor gave Louis a wedding gift – a beautiful pear-shaped vase of rock crystal. At least one historian believes it may have been a christening gift to Eleanor from her grandfather, William IX,[161] most probably gifted to him by the Muslim King Imad al-dawla of Saragossa in Spain.[162] This vase is one of the few objects associated with Eleanor that survives today; it sits in the Louvre in Paris.

What do we know of Louis? His seal in 1137 shows a long-haired young man, but we know little else of his appearance.[163] He had now spent six years, since the death of his elder brother, preparing for rule, yet the aura of piety never left him. Unusually, there was no contemporary gossip of Louis having a mistress. Much later, when he was married to his third wife, Adela of Champagne, it was suggested that a prostitute be sent to him, to hasten his recovery from an illness. The chronicler Gerald of Wales noted this religious man's response: 'If nothing else will cure me, let the Lord do his will by me, since it is better to die ill and chaste than to live as an adulterer.'[164]

Eleanor and Louis began their journey to Paris almost immediately after their marriage. They stopped at Poitiers on the way, where Louis was invested duke of Aquitaine. But Louis' father, meanwhile, was on his deathbed. Louis the Fat died just days after his son's marriage, on 1 August. Louis and Eleanor, France's new king and queen, remained in Poitiers, where they received the news just after Louis' ducal investiture, and were crowned on 8 August.

What did Louis, now king of France, inherit in the summer of 1137? The French kingdom had emerged out of the remnants of the mighty Carolingian Empire. In 751, Pepin the Short, the mayor of the palace in the service of the last Merovingian king Childeric III, seized the throne from his master. Pope Stephen II countenanced his appropriation of the throne in return for a donation of land in central Italy, known as 'the Donation of Pepin', to the papacy.* Pepin was duly crowned king of the Franks; he was the first of the Carolingian kings.

Pepin followed the common practice of the Frankish kings, and at his death he divided his lands between his two sons, Charlemagne (the Great Charles), and Carloman. When

---

* These lands, known as the Papal States, were ruled over directly by the papacy for over 1,000 years, until 1870.

Carloman died in 771, his famous brother become sole master of a vast Frankish Empire. Charlemagne reached the apotheosis of his empire-building when Pope Leo III crowned him emperor of the Romans on Christmas Day 800, accompanied by the words 'Most pious Augustus, crowned by God, the great and peace-giving Emperor'.[165] Charlemagne ruled, either directly or indirectly, lands that encompassed modern-day France, the Spanish March, Germany, Flanders, much of Italy and central Europe. It was the largest land mass in Europe held in a single hand since the fall of Rome in the West.

But Charlemagne's empire did not long survive his death; his descendants did not possess his extraordinary abilities. His only surviving son, Louis the Pious, held his father's domains, but when he died in 840, the lands were divided among his three sons – Charles the Bald, Louis the German and Lothair I – at the Treaty of Verdun of 843.[166] Lothair took a conglomerate of territory (the 'Middle Kingdom') including the lands that would become known as 'Lotharingia' – Lorraine, Provence, Burgundy and Charlemagne's territories in Italy. He kept his grandfather's imperial capital, Aachen, and the title. This 'Middle Kingdom', however, would not survive, and its lands were eventually absorbed into the east and the west Frankish kingdoms.

Louis the German took the eastern part of Charlemagne's empire, lands which would eventually form Germany. Their half-brother Charles the Bald took the west, uniting Aquitaine, Gascony, Septimania, and an area that encompassed most of the rest of modern France. It was from the remains of the western part of the Frankish Empire that Louis would, nearly 300 years later, inherit his kingdom.

The western Frankish Empire, however, began to disintegrate. By the beginning of the tenth century, Aquitaine, Brittany and Flanders, under their ever more powerful dukes and counts, acted independently of the Crown. In 911, Henry's ancestor Rollo, a Viking raider most probably from Norway, was given all the lands from the River Epte to the sea by a weak King Charles III (the Simple), in return for his homage and conversion to Christianity. These lands would become known as Normandy (land of the Northmen).

When Hugh Capet, a count of Paris, was elected king by the Frankish magnates after the death of the last Carolingian monarch in 987, Louis VII's house emerged. Hugh Capet gave his name to the dynasty – the Capetians – which would rule France until 1328, when the throne passed to their Valois cousins. Yet Hugh Capet's and his descendants' grasp on their lordships was minimal, as even such relatively small counties as Blois and Anjou paid their monarch little heed.[167]

Louis the Fat had done more than any of his predecessors to increase the power of the French crown, gradually extending their influence outside the region around Paris and the Île de France. But his success was limited, and the territory inherited by his son, Louis VII, was only a tiny area surrounded by over-mighty vassals – the count of Flanders, the count of Champagne, the duke of Burgundy, the duke of Brittany, the count of Blois, the count of Anjou and the duke of Normandy.

With his marriage to Eleanor, Louis immediately appropriated the enormous riches of his new wife for the French crown, and called himself duke of Aquitaine. Orderic Vitalis noted that 'Louis obtained the kingdom of the Franks and the duchy of Aquitaine, which none of his ancestors had held.'[168] In theory, through his fabulous marriage, his power was already greater than his father's.

There was, however, a problem with the marriage; according to the church, it was incestuous, or consanguineous. Eleanor and Louis shared a common ancestor, King Robert II of France, which made them third cousins once removed. Church law would not allow couples to marry if they were related within seven degrees, or if they shared one great-great-great-great-great-grand-parent.[169]

Mutterings about the irregularity of their marriage began almost immediately. Bernard was never an advocate, and wrote to Bishop Stephen of Palestrina to complain about it in 1143, accusing Louis of sanctimoniously haranguing other couples about problematic marriages while his also violated the law.[170]

But it would seem that in Bordeaux in 1137, although Eleanor may have been aware that she was marrying against church law, Louis was not. And even had Louis the Fat known of the problem as he took advantage of the death of William X of Aquitaine to marry off his son to its wealthy new duchess, Eleanor was far too rich for him to care. Aquitaine was roughly a third of the size of modern France, and its acquisition was irresistible to a king in need of a kingdom.

Louis VII adored his wife – John of Salisbury says he loved her 'almost beyond reason' – but Eleanor was unhappy.[171] The early years of her marriage to Louis were marred with disappointment, war and heartbreak, marked by a jostling for power with Louis' formidable mother, Adelaide of Maurienne, his mentor, Abbot Suger, and his powerful advisors.

Louis had spent his early life in the cloisters and had fully imbibed the teaching of the church fathers as to the dangers of sexual desire to the immortal soul. We may assume that their sex life was not particularly fulfilling for Eleanor, and she had limited success in influencing her husband from the privacy of their bedchamber.

Although at the very beginning, Eleanor's new position by Louis' side caused her jealous mother-in-law to flounce from court to retire to her estates – she accused Eleanor of spending too much money – and Abbot Suger to devote himself more and more to the rebuilding of Saint-Denis in a magnificent Gothic style, there was little room for her to exercise power; she was soon marginalised. She certainly did not wield the sort of power Adelaide had done as Louis the Fat's consort, constantly at his side. Louis listened instead to his powerful advisors, particularly Raoul de Vermandois, his cousin and seneschal of France.

Eleanor did not enjoy an easy relationship with Louis' other close advisors. She loathed some of her husband's inner circle, particularly Thierry Galeran, who had been an advisor of Louis' father. John of Salisbury wrote that he was 'a eunuch whom the queen had always hated and mocked'.[172]

Louis' military ineptitude was disappointing to Eleanor. He failed to put down a rebellion in Poitiers, and his campaign in Toulouse to conquer territories she claimed through her paternal grandmother Philippa also ended in failure.

There was another strain on the relationship, one which had unforeseen and dreadful consequences. Eleanor's sister Petronilla appears to have fallen in love with Count Raoul de Vermandois. Although Raoul was much older than Petronilla, blind in one eye, and already married to the sister of King Stephen, Eleanor pushed hard for a divorce so that he and Petronilla could marry. She had no effective power base, and her sister's marriage to Raoul would feasibly be a way of clawing out influence for herself with Louis and his inner circle.

Catastrophe followed; Raoul was branded an 'adulterous tyrant' by Bernard, and the newly-weds were excommunicated by the pope, who placed France under an interdict. In an age where religion was all-pervasive, a papal interdict meant that no religious rites could be performed – no baptisms, no marriages, no burials. It was a dreadful punishment. The pope described the king as 'a boy who must be instructed' in how to behave, and Stephen's brother, Theobald IV of Blois-Champagne, promptly went to war with Louis over their repudiated sister. This war resulted in a massacre at Vitry, where Louis ordered the burning of the church where 1,300 people had sought sanctuary. All were burned alive and the town became known as Vitry-le-Brûlé – Vitry the Burned.[173] In a strange accident of history, the town's Jews, who had not sought sanctuary in the church, survived, and

Louis spared them. For some time after the horrific slaughter, this small town in Champagne hosted a largely Jewish population.

Louis' delayed horror at his own behaviour led to feelings of enormous guilt and grief. He turned once more to his old mentor, Abbot Suger. On 11 June 1144, Suger's magnum opus, the marvellous cathedral of Saint-Denis, was complete. At the dedication ceremony, Louis gave away Eleanor's wedding present, the rock crystal vase, to his old friend. Eleanor may well have taken this as a sign that her marriage was in trouble. Suger, though, was delighted and commissioned an inscription for the base of the vase. It read: 'As a bride, Eleanor gave this vase to King Louis, the king to me, and Suger to the saints ... as a tribute of his great love.'[174]

But despite war, lost battles and family discord, Eleanor's greatest problem was her inability to conceive. The marriage was under strain, and the chronicler Robert of Torigni tells us that as early as 1143 'a dislike had sprung up' between Eleanor and Louis.[175]

The failure to produce an heir was a disaster for any medieval queen. Eleanor's primary purpose was to bear sons to succeed their father. When Bernard of Clairvaux promised her she would conceive if she helped bring about a peace between Louis, the pope and Theobald of Champagne, a desperate Eleanor agreed. Within a year Bernard's saintly intercession and the queen's prayers appeared to have worked – or at least partially – when she gave birth to a daughter, and not the wanted son and heir, in 1145. She was named Marie, possibly in tribute to the Virgin Mary, to whom Bernard and Eleanor had prayed for a child.[176]

At the first Christmas court after Marie's birth, Louis, in an uncharacteristically ebullient mood fired by religious fervour and the hope of absolution for the slaughter at Vitry, proposed a crusade. A year earlier, in late December 1144, Christendom had watched in horror as the emir Imad ad-Din Zengi (or Nur-ad-Din, meaning light of the religion), Muslim ruler of Aleppo, seized the crusader state of Edessa, based around the city of Şanlıurfa in southern Turkey. An appalled pope and the Christian kings of western Europe demanded 'infidel' blood. Now Louis determined to take back the city for Christendom.

It was Bernard, however, who pushed the initiative as the uncharismatic and weak Louis was unable to fire up his nobility for a crusade. Four months later at Easter, in March 1146, the spiritually irresistible Bernard preached the Second Crusade at Vézelay Abbey, appearing before a massive crowd and crying, 'Hasten then to expiate your sins by victories over the Infidels, and let the deliverance of the holy places be the reward of your repentance.' Louis, inspired as always by his powerful mentor, vowed to take the cross to protect the Holy Land for Christianity.

Eleanor would accompany him. She was the first queen of France or England to venture on crusade.

Why did Eleanor choose to go? The journey, she knew, would be hazardous. She may well have preferred to stay behind in France. Despite later entirely false claims that Eleanor was thirsty for battle, leading a battalion of bare-breasted women into war, dressed as the Amazonian Queen Penthesilea, it is doubtful that Eleanor wanted to travel thousands of miles from home. It would be hot, uncomfortable and dangerous. But she had no choice. As queen, Eleanor's primary role was to conceive, and now in her mid-twenties and with only a daughter, she could not afford to be parted from Louis for the two or more years he would be away from France.

William of Newburgh lamented Eleanor's presence on crusade as providing the opportunity to 'sin': 'The king, whose love for his young wife was a jealous one, thought he should not leave her behind and decided to take her to war. Many other nobles did likewise and brought their wives along. And as the wives could not do without their serving women, a whole host of women found their way into that Christian camp where chastity should have reigned. And this was an occasion for sin in our army.'[181] Nevertheless, at the great church of Saint-Denis on 11 June 1147, both Eleanor and Louis received the papal blessing and departed overland for Constantinople.

Their journey would irrevocably change her attitude to her marriage, and fix in the popular imagination for evermore the 'black legend' of Eleanor of Aquitaine – the image of the queen of France as incestuous, a nymphomaniac, an adulteress, a 'jezebel' and a 'whore'.[178] The legend endures; as late as 2002, a French historian accused Eleanor of being 'a real bitch who could think about nothing but power and sex.'[179]

VIII

It took Eleanor, Louis and their army of crusaders four months to reach Constantinople. They arrived on 4 October 1147, where they were welcomed by the emperor, Manuel Komnenos, who offered Eleanor and Louis the use of his hunting lodge, the Philopatium.[180] They stayed for a week and a half, sightseeing and attending banquets, and departed on 15 October.

Meanwhile the army of Louis' crusading partner, Conrad III of Germany, had been devastated by attacks from the Seljuk Turks. The German crusaders were overwhelmed by completely unknown warfare – exceptionally swift horses, whose riders quickly deployed bows and arrows – and unable to retaliate effectively as they were encumbered by their heavy armour, typically consisting of a chain-mail hauberk and helmet.

Louis now joined his army to the remains of Conrad's, and the pair departed along the coast, bound for Ephesus. They arrived on 20 December, where they were warned by Manuel Komnenos's ambassadors that a huge force of Turks awaited them, and advised them not to continue.

Conrad, who had suffered injuries in the attacks on his army, chose to accompany the ambassadors back to Constantinople. Louis, however, insisted on pressing on, 'forewarned in vain', along the coast of Anatolia.[181] He and his army were not lucky. They were relentlessly harassed by the Seljuk Turks, the terrain was hostile, supplies were scarce, and they suffered attack after attack. The first was on Christmas Eve. The most severe was a few days later, on 6 January 1148, while they attempted to cross Mount Cadmus. This was an enormous army of thousands of soldiers and pilgrims, reaching up to six miles in length, snaking its way through the Anatolian mountains.[182] Louis brought up the rear with his guard. The baggage train and foot soldiers were in the middle; presumably Eleanor was here, the safest place from attack, together with the unarmed pilgrims and the other women. The cavalry were at the front. One of Eleanor's vassals, Geoffrey of Rancon, led the army with Louis' maternal uncle, Count Amadeus II of Maurienne. But the different parts of the army, as a result of poor communication and poor leadership, became separated as Geoffrey and Amadeus continued on without waiting. The Turks then ambushed, and they struck at the most vulnerable part of the crusader army – the baggage train. Hundreds fled, and many hurtled down the cliffs to their deaths; the Turks slaughtered those they caught. Louis and his guard rushed to defend the baggage train, but the Turks murdered Louis' personal guard, forcing him to scramble up a rock and defend himself.

Louis survived, and the remnants of his army gradually came together again. But he was humiliated, and William of Tyre wrote: 'That day the glorious reputation of the Franks was lost through a misfortune most fatal and disastrous for the Christians; their valour, up to this time formidable to the nations, was crushed to the earth. Henceforth, it was as a mockery in the eyes of those unclean races to whom it had formerly been a terror.'[183]

Now, however, Louis realised the imperative for discipline, although those whom the majority believed had led them to disaster – Eleanor's vassal and Louis' uncle – went unpunished. Louis would not reprimand his own uncle, but all the Poitevins, including the queen, were tarnished by association, and Odo of Deuil wrote that Geoffrey of Rancon 'earned our everlasting hatred'.[184] The small force of about 130 men brought by the Knights Templar were the most effective part of his army, and now Louis ceded control and allowed them to lead.

Supplies were scarce and the army was starving. It was bitterly cold as they picked their way across the mountains in mid-winter. The army limped on. Battered and demoralised, it took them nearly a month to reach Attalia, where they hoped to replenish their supplies. But the town was poor and there was nothing to buy – no horses, little food, no clothes, and certainly no ships to take them to the Latin Kingdom. Louis and Eleanor decided to set sail for Antioch with a small force, leaving the army to travel by land to meet them. Less than half the army they left behind would make it, and most of the pilgrims starved to death or were murdered by the Turks. Thousands died.[185]

Finally, on 19 March 1148, Eleanor and Louis arrived at the port of Saint-Simeon at Antioch. Here at the court of Eleanor's paternal uncle, Prince Raymond, they stayed for nearly two weeks, recuperating and planning.[186]

Raymond was ruler of Antioch by right of his marriage to Constance, daughter of Bohemund II, a marriage facilitated by Fulk, now king of Jerusalem. Raymond was only a few years older than Eleanor, born in 1115. He welcomed his niece and the French with generosity and hospitality. Antioch must have appeared incredibly exotic to the Franks. Prince Raymond served Middle Eastern dishes, including sugar; hot baths and even soap were available.[187] Eleanor and Raymond were delighted to see one another and spent hours talking privately. The chronicler William of Tyre describes him as 'a lord of noble descent ... the handsomest of the princes of the earth, a man of charming affability and conversation'.

Raymond was keen to impress Eleanor and Louis, hoping the arrival of a French crusader army would help him increase his power in northern Syria. William of Tyre speculated on Raymond's motives: 'he felt a lively hope that with the assistance of the king and his troops he would be able to subjugate the neighbouring cities, namely Aleppo, Shaizar and several others. Nor would this hope have been futile could he have induced the king and his chief men to undertake the work.'[188] The plan was self-serving; but it made sense for both Raymond and the French crusaders. Louis' original intention was, after all, to take back Edessa, which would be made easier by the capture of Aleppo first.[189]

Louis, however, may have feared for the poor state of his army, ravaged and depleted by the months it had taken them to cross Anatolia. He refused to fight alongside Raymond. William of Tyre wrote that he had changed his mind about taking Edessa, deciding he did not want to delay his visit to the Holy Land any longer; he 'ardently desired to go to Jerusalem to fulfil his vows'.[190] But Eleanor disagreed. Speed was now important; Suger, acting as regent in the royal couple's absence, was sending alarming reports of an uprising by Louis' brother, Robert of Dreux, and begged the king to return.

Eleanor's intense conversations with Raymond may well have included discussion as to who would inherit Aquitaine. As she and Louis had no male heir, it is imaginable that Raymond put his own claim to Eleanor. Eleanor and Louis, fundamentally disagreeing on the direction of the crusade and possibly on the inheritance of Eleanor's own duchy, had a vicious fight which ended in Eleanor refusing to accompany Louis to Jerusalem, threatening to withdraw her vassals, and asking for a divorce.

It was Eleanor who first told Louis that their marriage was 'incestuous' during their ferocious argument in Antioch. John of

Salisbury wrote: '[W]hen the King made haste to tear her away, she mentioned their kinship, saying it was not lawful for them to remain together as man and wife, since they were related in the fourth and fifth degrees. At this the king was deeply moved; and although he loved the queen almost beyond reason he consented to divorce her if his counsellors and the French nobility would allow it.'[191] Eleanor, it seems, knew that there had been some problems when they married, but John suggests that Louis did not, and that Eleanor was the first to tell him.

But the sources go further. She was later accused by some contemporary chroniclers of having an adulterous – and incestuous – affair with her uncle Raymond.

These sources are William of Tyre and John of Salisbury. Both were contemporaries, but both wrote about Antioch many years later – John after a period of fifteen years, and William twenty to thirty years later. William was in France when Eleanor and Louis were in Antioch, but he professed to have followed the crusade closely.[192] And although John was with the papal court in Tusculum (Frascati) at the time, he was with the royal pair and their entourage when they stopped at Tusculum on their way back to France, and he must have heard the gossip. John wrote that:

> the most Christian king of the Franks reached Antioch, after the destruction of his armies in the east, and was nobly entertained there by Prince Raymond … He was as it happened the queen's uncle, and owed the king loyalty, affection and respect for many reasons. But whilst they remained there … the attentions paid by the prince to the queen, and his constant, indeed almost continuous conversation with her, aroused the king's suspicions. These were greatly strengthened when the queen wished to remain behind, although the king was preparing to leave, and the prince made every effort to keep her, if the king would give his consent.[193]

William of Tyre claimed that an embittered Raymond was behind Eleanor's anger towards Louis:

> Raymond had conceived the idea that by [Louis'] aid he might be able to enlarge the principality of Antioch ... When Raymond found that he could not induce the king to join him, his attitude changed. Frustrated in his ambitious designs, he began to hate the king's ways; he openly plotted against him and took means to do him injury. He resolved also to deprive him of his wife, either by force or by secret intrigue. The queen readily assented to this design, for she was a foolish woman. Her conduct before and after this time showed her to be, as we have said, far from circumspect. Contrary to her royal dignity, she disregarded her marriage vows and was unfaithful to her husband.[194]

This is a damning portrait of Eleanor. She is parodied as a 'foolish' woman, easily influenced to commit adultery with her uncle. Later writers, taking their cue from William and John, believed that the queen's behaviour had been, at the very least, 'scandalous'. Gervase of Canterbury told of 'discord', and wrote, tantalisingly, that events happened which one should be silent on.[195] Richard of Devizes, although he called Eleanor 'a woman without compare', went on to say in the margin that 'Many know what I would that none of us knew. This same queen, during the time of her first husband, was at Jerusalem [*sic*, Antioch]. Let no one say any more about it. I too know it well. Keep silent.'[196]

We will never know if Eleanor slept with her handsome, clever and charismatic uncle. We do know, however, that they enjoyed one another's company immensely, and that their close relationship in Antioch maddened Louis.

The most compelling evidence of marital discord and Eleanor's 'bad behaviour' comes from the unimpeachable Abbot Suger.

Suger had obviously heard of problems between Eleanor and Louis, for he wrote from France to Louis in 1149: 'Concerning the queen your wife, we venture to congratulate you, if we may upon the extent to which you suppress your anger, if there be anger, until with God's will you return to your own kingdom and see to these matters and others.'[197]

Louis, meanwhile, urged on by his advisor and Eleanor's adversary Thierry Galeran, refused Eleanor a divorce.

Louis may have been ready to agree to it, but Galeran persuaded him that to return to France with a failed crusade and no wife would injure his reputation. And so he slipped away from Raymond's court in the middle of the night, dragging Eleanor away from Antioch and on to Jerusalem. William of Tyre recorded that Louis' 'coming had been attended with glory ... and his departure was ignominious'.[198]

Whether or not Louis believed that Eleanor had committed adultery, there were evidently some in his entourage ready to accuse the queen. It is probable that she and Raymond spoke together in the language of the southern Aquitaine, the *langue d'oc* (*oc* meaning 'yes') or Provençal. It probably sounded similar to modern Italian, and was unfathomable to most northerners, who spoke the completely different dialect of *langue d'oïl*. Although Eleanor spoke the *langue d'oïl* fluently, by choosing to converse with her uncle in the Aquitaine tongue, it may have increased suspicion of her. On their way back to France, on 9 October, the royal couple arrived at the papal court at Tusculum, where they had been invited to stay by Pope Eugenius III. Here, they discussed their marital problems with Eugenius.

John of Salisbury wrote an account of the pope's intercession; evidently neither Eleanor nor Louis was calm. Eleanor had been kidnapped on the way to Italy. Although she was rescued almost immediately, this, added to her violent arguments with Louis, his refusal to divorce her and his ignoring of her military advice, must have made her agitated. She also learned at Tusculum of

Raymond's brutal death in battle, at the end of June 1149. Nur ad-Din defeated Raymond and his allies at the battle of Inab. To celebrate, he decapitated Raymond and sent his head and right arm to the caliph of Baghdad.[199] Raymond had apparently fought valiantly, 'like the high-spirited and courageous warrior he was'.[200] We have no evidence, but Eleanor may have blamed Louis for refusing to help Raymond militarily, and for his bloody death.

It was in this atmosphere that Eleanor and Louis put their cases to Eugenius, who, acting the role of marriage counsellor and friend, sought to heal their relationship.

John recorded that:

> He reconciled the king and queen after hearing severally the accounts each gave of the estrangement begun at Antioch, and forbade any future mention of their consanguinity: confirming their marriage, both orally and in writing, he commanded under pain of anathema that no word should be spoken against it and that it should not be dissolved under any pretext whatever. This ruling plainly delighted the king, for he loved the queen passionately, in an almost childish way. The pope made them sleep in the same bed, which he had had decked with priceless hangings of his own; and daily during their brief visit he strove by friendly converse to restore love between them.[201]

They departed the following day. The pope cried as they left: 'though he was a stern man, he could not hold back his tears'.[202] But he had succeeded. There would be no divorce for the king and queen of France. Eugenius' intervention worked – or at least for the time being.

Eleanor and Louis arrived back in Paris in November 1149, over two years after they had left on their crusade. The experience had been bruising for them both: Eleanor appears to have lost all respect for Louis, and Louis in turn allowed her no power once they returned to France. Yet Eleanor was pregnant again

– she may have conceived at Tusculum in the pope's beautiful bed – and Louis was once more full of hope for a son. She gave birth to another daughter, Alix, in 1150.

Alix's birth finally persuaded Louis that the marriage was incestuous in the eyes of God, and to grant Eleanor a divorce. Ever pious, Louis now believed God would never give them a son. The pair disliked one another, and the prevailing view of the church – following the teachings of Hippocrates – was that a woman who did not enjoy sex would not produce a 'seed', and would therefore not conceive.[203] The marriage was by this point so dreadful that it was difficult to imagine, even for Louis, that she would become pregnant again. The death of Abbot Suger – who had been a strong advocate of the marriage – in January 1151 allowed other voices to be heard, particularly Bernard of Clairvaux's.

Why did Eleanor push so hard for a divorce? She is rumoured to have said that Louis was 'more monk than man', a statement which implies incompatibility, whether sexual or otherwise.[204] But leaving aside any marital discord or a lack of power in her ancestral lands, Eleanor was an aristocratic woman who had lived all her life at a court, whether her father's or her husband's. Although we have very little evidence of her personality for this period in her life, we have a great deal for her last fifteen years. The older Eleanor was intelligent, brave, determined, a capable and respected politician.

Looking at her character in her twenties through the prism of what we know of the woman in her seventies and early eighties, we may make an intelligent guess that the younger Eleanor was pragmatic enough to realise that she had to be married to someone. If Louis granted her a divorce, as duchess of Aquitaine she would become his vassal; he would have the power to marry her to whomever he pleased, probably a court acolyte – anything to hold on to Aquitaine until Marie was old enough to inherit. Eleanor would not be allowed to rule alone.

We can deduce that Eleanor, although queen of France, rich, and with access to her young daughters, was extremely and irrevocably unhappy, and this is why she manoeuvred for Louis to divorce her. She had no guarantees that she would be any happier in a second marriage than in her first, but Eleanor needed to leave Louis.

By August 1151, the matter was not quite decided – Louis may well still have been deliberating. When Henry arrived in Paris in late summer, he must have appeared to Eleanor as a gift. He erupted into her life, and his energy, self-belief and optimism would have been luminous to her.

Everything we know of their characters suggests that Henry was able to persuade Eleanor to marry him by offering her a match of equals and mutual advantage. For Henry, marriage to Eleanor would provide him with wealth, land and heirs enough to gain and secure an empire. For Eleanor, if she took the gamble, this young duke would be her best chance for autonomy. Louis had denied her power in Aquitaine, and she likely envisaged the rest of her life married to him, the mother of daughters, gradually losing every shred of influence. From our knowledge of Eleanor, we may imagine this would have been intolerable to her. Henry appeared at the right moment, promising her heart's desire: *real* power, rather than its trappings – the rightful duchess of Aquitaine, in deed as well as name. Theirs would be far more of a partnership than Louis had ever offered her. It was the best she could hope for from a marriage.

As far as we know, there were no witnesses to any formal agreement between Henry and Eleanor, nor are there any surviving documents that attest to it. Meanwhile, the chroniclers – mostly churchmen – were too consumed with Eleanor's supposed sexual voraciousness to pay it much attention. Walter Map and Gerald of Wales later accused her of sleeping with Henry's father Geoffrey. Walter claimed she 'married Henry despite rumours circulating to the effect that she had already shared Louis' bed with Geoffrey, Henry's father'. Walter went on to speculate that 'this ... is why their progeny, sullied as their origins were, finally came to naught'.[205] If true, it would have made their marriage incestuous in the eyes of the church. The chronicler William of Newburgh believed it was Eleanor who 'longed to be wed to the duke of Normandy as one more congenial to her character', and Gervase of Canterbury wrote that 'people said that it was she who had cleverly brought about that contrived repudiation', as she had grown tired of Louis' 'decrepit Gallic embraces'. Helinand de Froidmont, writing at the beginning of the thirteenth century, went even further, ascribing Eleanor's desire to divorce entirely to her desire for Henry: 'It was on account of her lasciviousness that Louis gave up his wife, who behaved not like a queen but more like a [whore].'[206]

And as late as the early twentieth century, one historian of the counts of Poitou explained Eleanor's pursuit of marriage to Henry thus: she had grown bored of Louis' 'almost effeminate grace', and rather she 'wished to be dominated, and as the vulgar crudely put it, she was among those women who enjoy being beaten'.[207]

Eleanor was far more likely to have been seduced by promises of autonomy rather than Henry's personal charms alone. Henry was a risk-taker and an optimist. His parents and his tutors had imbued him with self-belief since babyhood. Henry – young, arrogant and talented – likely believed that the crown of England was his; despite Eustace's formidable claim, he had only to wait. England, Normandy, Maine and Anjou, together with the cornucopia of Aquitaine offered by marriage to Eleanor, would all eventually be theirs if she chose him as her new husband.

No wonder Henry left Paris 'full of joy'; he had secured a promise of marriage from the wealthiest heiress in the western world. Now he planned to travel to England immediately, to fight Stephen and Eustace.

The historian Kate Norgate, quoting the chronicler Peter Langtoft, says that Matilda was also in Paris with Henry and Geoffrey, and if so it is likely that both parents were party to his plans.[208] But if Matilda was there to help to smooth the negotiations with Louis, she left before Henry and Geoffrey. The worldly Geoffrey, under Bernard's 'curse', could not have imagined he would have so little time to live. On their way to Lisieux to meet with Henry's Norman barons, Geoffrey caught a fever and died. Henry was not with him, although Geoffrey's last thoughts were of his eldest son. He is purported to have left him sound advice: to govern each of his diverse provinces by its own laws, and not as one 'empire'.[209]

Geoffrey's sudden and shocking death meant that Henry immediately doubled his possessions. He was now lord of Normandy, Anjou and Maine and his territories already dwarfed Louis'. But he was unable to travel to England to aid his desperately beleaguered supporters – at least not for now. He buried his father in the Cathedral of St Julian at Le Mans, his own birthplace, and commissioned a splendid tomb effigy, which reputedly contained a portrait of Geoffrey rendered in gold and precious gems.[210] Henry mourned; later, he would pay for two chaplains to say prayers daily for his father.[211] For now, he stayed in Anjou, asserting his authority over his Angevin barons.

As Henry grieved, Louis prepared for divorce. By Christmas he had pulled his forces out of Aquitaine, ready to give the duchy back to Eleanor.[212] Would Louis have ceded nearly half of France so easily had he known of Eleanor's designs? It is doubtful.

He certainly knew nothing of her plans with Henry when, on 18 March 1152 at Beaugency Castle, halfway between Paris (Louis' capital) and Poitiers (Eleanor's), their marriage was dissolved. Eleanor left behind her young daughters Marie and Alix. Even if she had remained in her marriage to be close to her children, one historian has pointed out that the girls left the French court the following year to join their fiancés' households – Louis' troublesome vassals the brothers Henry of Champagne and Theobald of Blois, whom he hoped to appease by the marriages. We have no evidence that Eleanor ever saw them again.[213]

No records survive of the proceedings at Beaugency, but anecdotal evidence tells us that Bishop Geoffrey of Langres nastily suggested an investigation into Eleanor's supposed adultery, which was thwarted by the archbishop of Bordeaux, Eleanor's subject.[214] The archbishop proposed instead that the marriage be dissolved because it was consanguineous. The archbishop of Sens pronounced the marriage annulled, and their daughters legitimate, as Eleanor and Louis had been unaware their marriage was incestuous.[215] Eleanor's property was returned to her in its entirety. After years of wrangling, it was all over within hours. Louis immediately went north, and Eleanor south.

Luck was on Henry's side – and Eleanor's. As she rode towards Poitiers, she was ambushed in two separate attacks, by two noblemen who attempted to kidnap her and force her into marriage, to acquire her wealth and power – the count of Blois (who would later marry her daughter Alix), and Henry's own seventeen-year-old brother Geoffrey, smarting and sulking at his puny inheritance of only four castles. But Eleanor escaped and sent an urgent message to Henry at Lisieux, as he prepared to sail for England. The news that Eleanor was free, however, made him turn around and race to her at Poitiers.

Here, on Whit Sunday, 18 May 1152, a scant eight weeks after her divorce, they were married at the city's cathedral in a secret ceremony, bringing Aquitaine under Henry's control.

Henry and Eleanor were together for nearly a month; Henry then rode for Barfleur, and England.[216] But at Barfleur, on 16 July, he was forced to turn around once more to deal with Louis' reaction to their marriage.

Louis was furious and bellicose. Although the boundaries of allegiance owed by the rulers of Aquitaine to the French kings were still, in the mid-twelfth century, unclear, Eleanor had at best humiliated him.[217] Eleanor's language, in contrast, was respectful and pacific. In a grant to Fontevraud Abbey she made at this time, she referred to her divorce from Louis in the following way: 'separating from my lord Louis, the very illustrious king of the Franks, because we were related'.[218] But to Louis, two of his vassals had flouted his authority and married without his permission. Eleanor's stupendous inheritance had turned his erstwhile relatively minor vassal into one of the most powerful princes in Europe.

Now Louis declared Henry's lands in France forfeit and went to war, joined in an unholy trinity with Eustace, the thwarted count of Blois, and Henry's brother Geoffrey.

First, Henry dealt with Louis. He surprised and confused him with a devastating attack on the lands of his brother, Robert of Dreux, and laid waste to the Vexin. Then, in August, he moved against his brother Geoffrey, taking his castles away – its castellans surrendered completely to him. He besieged Montsoreau, stronghold of the rebels, where Geoffrey was forced, humiliatingly, to yield. Henry clearly would not be able to rely on his brother to help him fulfil his ambitions.

Henry's military training had been exceptional; now he showed himself to be a level-headed general, fighting tenaciously, with cool and excellent judgement, on many fronts. Speed, one of the defining traits of his warfare, was key to Henry's success. As he marched his armies along at a lightning pace (far beyond the seventeen and a half miles per day averaged by a medieval army) he would soon become known as the 'King of the North Wind'.[219] Henry's father, Geoffrey, had reputedly studied the fifth-century AD Roman military author, Vegetius. Henry too may have remembered Vegetius' lesson: 'Courage is worth more than numbers, and speed is worth more than courage.'[220] In 1152, at Barfleur, forced to abandon his plan to sail to England as he turned to defend Normandy instead, he moved his army along at such a breakneck pace that Robert of Torigni and Gerald of Wales noted that horses died.[221]

Louis, unable to fend off Henry's whirlwind attacks, developed a fever and sought peace. Louis' allies, including an apoplectic Eustace, who had only remained in France to murder Henry, were forced to comply. By the autumn, Henry had routed them all, as swiftly as Hermes. Louis, Henry's overlord for his lands in France, had failed utterly to bring his rebellious vassal to heel.

Henry was now free to return to Eleanor in Aquitaine, where they embarked on a progress of her lands. Henry made known what sort of a duke he would be; at Limoges, the abbot of Saint-Martial withheld money, and the people of the town attacked his men. Henry's brutal response was to raze the walls of the town, his instinct in Aquitaine being to keep the local lords under his control with a heavy hand.

While Henry had been preoccupied with marrying Eleanor and fighting Louis and his allies, the Angevin party in England was desperately fending off Stephen's attacks. When Stephen's men captured Wallingford on the banks of the Thames, not strategically important in itself but a potent symbol of Angevin strength, its defenders begged Henry to help them.

As far as Stephen and Louis were concerned, England was lost to Henry; it would be impossible for him to leave France. Eustace continued his relentless pursuit, and Louis, Henry knew, would stick to their truce only to resume his attack in the spring.

But they had underestimated Henry FitzEmpress. He was a gambler, trusting his intuition that Eustace would follow him, and that Louis and Geoffrey would not be overly troublesome in their harassment of his lands. He left a now pregnant Eleanor in Rouen with his mother, gave Normandy over to Matilda's charge, and sailed from Barfleur during a storm, two weeks after Christmas, at the beginning of 1153. No one but a madman or Henry would have sailed in such conditions, and no one expected him in England. He sailed with a mercenary force of 140 knights and 3,000 foot soldiers in thirty-six vessels, paid for with borrowed money, ready to seize his birthright.[222]

A new man, the 'King of the North Wind', was about to storm Stephen's world.

Act II
Triumph

Henry was drawn 'as much to the business of arms
as to the toga; to war as much as to books'.

Gerald of Wales,
On the Instruction of Princes

I

Henry was poised on the threshold of unimaginable power. But
he would have to work for it.

He sailed to England through a tempest to relieve his friends
and claim his crown. Once again, luck was with him. He and
his mercenaries landed safely, probably at Wareham in Dorset, on
6 January. This time, Stephen took the threat of Henry
seriously.

Eustace, obsessed with Henry, followed his prey from
France across the winter seas. Both sides expected this to be
the final bloody battle between enemies whose camps had been
fighting for nearly twenty years, and Eustace did not want to
miss his victory. Only one man could be crowned king of
England. The pope had refused Eustace; now only Henry's
murder would enable him to inherit the throne on Stephen's
death.

The chroniclers talked of Henry's coming in almost messianic terms. The author of the *Gesta* had England 'shaking' at Henry's arrival; Henry of Huntingdon wrote of England, 'That wretched country, before reduced to ruin, but now regaining new life by the prospect of his coming to her assistance', where Henry is cast as the saviour of a battered land.[1] Henry of Huntingdon positioned the young duke as inheritor of all that had been his namesake grandfather's, Henry I:

> Heir to thy grandsire's name and high renown,
> Thy England calls thee, Henry, to her throne:
> Now, fallen from her once imperial state,
> Exhausted, helpless, ruined, desolate,
> She sighs her griefs, and fainting scarcely lives:
> One solitary hope alone survives.
> 'Save me, oh save me! Henry; or I die ...'[2]

But this was retrospective propaganda. These dazzling words aside, Henry had not yet won.

He did not go directly to the aid of his friends at Wallingford; it was firmly royalist territory where Stephen had erected at least two additional castles and, together with Eustace, had gathered his army. Henry did not yet feel strong enough to be so far from towns loyal to his cause – Bristol, Gloucester and Devizes – and their supplies. Instead he marched his men sixty miles or so north of his landing place to Malmesbury in Wiltshire, to besiege the castle, ensuring Stephen's appearance. Stephen duly dashed his men westwards to fend off the attack.

Henry 'threw himself straight into the siege, for delay was not his way, and soon took it'.[3] He stormed the town and took the castle; these tactics would form Henry's distinctive movements in defensive warfare – swift, decisive, brutal and nearly always effective. But disappointingly there was no battle. Numbed by freezing rain and hungry – famine had ravaged the area – Stephen's army refused to engage; Henry was forced to agree to a truce. Malmesbury's castellan handed the fortress over to him without a fight.

Stephen's men slowly turned to Henry, not least because a number of the most influential magnates felt that in doing so, they would end the civil war. Stephen was evidently 'gloomy and downcast' by the defections; the author of the *Gesta* records that the king was dispirited and 'noticed that some of his leading barons were slack and very casual in their service and had already sent envoys by stealth and made a compact with the duke'.[4]

By early spring, many of the country's leading magnates stood firmly behind Henry – his uncle, Reginald earl of Cornwall, William earl of Gloucester, John the Marshal, and Robert of Dunstanville. Henry had a stunning coup when the powerful and respected magnate Robert earl of Leicester, one of the Beaumont twins, came over to his side. Robert, close to Henry I, had been at the old king's bedside as he died. Although previously, if only nominally, loyal to Stephen, he now saw England's future with Duke Henry rather than a weakened Stephen, or Eustace. Gervase of Canterbury wrote that by April, 'he began to take the duke's part and for some time ministered to his needs'.[5] The Anglo-Norman nobility looked to Robert; he was level-headed and seen as a natural leader. With his newly pledged loyalty, and the thirty castles he brought, the campaign was turning in Henry's favour.[6]

The freezing weather had brought Henry a truce. Now, he spent the next few months making huge territorial gains throughout the Midlands, taking castle after castle, including Warwick and Tutbury, by force or negotiation. He held court wherever he went, behaving as if he were already king. It was a spectacular display of strength, pomp and showmanship, and it painted a picture for the nobility of what his rule would look like.

At Easter, Henry held a lavish court at Gloucester, and called himself 'duke of Aquitaine' for the first time. He granted charters and lands; unlike Stephen, he had the power to grant lands in

Normandy, enticing to the nobility. Henry could now assert his right to rule through succession, including a standard clause in his charters confirming rights, by granting beneficiaries, 'everything that King Henry my grandfather gave him'. This representation of himself as restorer and regenerator of his grandfather's government was a theme Henry would return to again and again throughout his own reign.

Henry knew that the game was not yet won, in spite of his successes over the spring and early summer. Wallingford would change that; for Stephen, it marked the beginning of the end.

In July or August 1153, Henry was finally in a strong enough position to relieve his supporters besieged at Wallingford Castle. Stephen and Eustace arrived with 'an inexpressibly large army from every part of England'.[7] Again, Henry was to be disappointed – there was no battle between the enemies. Stephen's men did not want to fight the man who it now seemed inevitable would be king. The *Gesta Stephani* recorded how the barons on both sides offered irresistible arguments for a peace to save the kingdom: 'Wherefore the leading men of each army ... were greatly grieved and shrank, on both sides, from a conflict that was not merely between fellow countrymen but meant the desolation of the whole kingdom.'[8]

Men who knew the politics and the country better than Henry advocated a negotiated peace rather than the uncertainty and loss of life of a battle.

Henry was 'very angry; he complained of the loyalty of those of his friends who had accepted such terms; but rather than break the agreement he accepted them'.[9] He evidently bucked against the advice of his companions who argued for a truce; it was far from the decisive victory he sought. But instead of ignoring the level heads – the bishops and magnates who had tired of a long, bitter and expensive war – Henry was willing to listen to their advice and pursue victory by means other than battle.

If Henry kept his temper, Eustace did not. His father had provided for his illegitimate son, Gervase, in 1138 when he made him abbot of Westminster; as far as Eustace was concerned, he had made no provision for him – his father's legitimate heir. He realised that the terms of peace did not include his succession to the throne of England. He was furious; now, 'greatly vexed and angry', he stormed out of his father's court to Cambridge, to coerce funds from the monks of Bury St Edmunds to fuel his vendetta.[10] When the monks refused, he devastated the abbey's lands. On 10 August, Eustace dined at Cambridge Castle. By the time he had swallowed his first mouthful he was gravely ill, his body racked with a violent seizure.[11] He died about a week later, probably of food poisoning contracted at Wallingford, although some believed it was divine retribution for his brutal attack on the abbey. He was buried at Faversham Abbey next to his mother, Matilda of Boulogne. For Henry, it was another stroke of luck.

The chroniclers offered mixed opinions of Eustace. To Henry of Huntingdon, he was 'a good soldier, but an ungodly man, who dealt harshly with the rulers of the church, being their determined persecutor'. To William of Newburgh, however, he was, 'a most courageous youth'. Eustace forever had a grievance. His mother, his greatest proponent, had died in May 1152. With her death, an apathetic and grieving Stephen stopped petitioning the pope to allow him to have Eustace crowned in his lifetime. To Eustace, it seemed that his father was no longer on his side. He died as he had lived: angry, bitter and entitled.

Now Henry, his main adversary removed, became God's 'beloved'.[12]

Stephen was 'agonised beyond measure' at Eustace's death. The blow was doubly hard, as he still grieved for the wife who had been his staunchest champion.[13] But for Henry, Eustace's death was the single most important factor that determined his victory. His rival's claim was null, and compromise was inevitable.

The removal of his most dogged enemy cleared the way for him to succeed Stephen as king of England. It had not required a dramatic and decisive battle, which disappointed Henry, but his ends were achieved. It allowed him and Stephen to strike a bargain that named Henry as his successor.

Stephen had another legitimate son, William. In late summer following Eustace's death, Henry went to Colchester to meet him and to neutralise him. Here, they enjoyed a 'day of peace and accord', with Theobald, archbishop of Canterbury, mediating.[14] Henry was generous to a fault. William would have not only all his mother's lands in England, but all the lands granted to his father by Henry I, and the lands of the earls of Warenne besides. There was more, in the form of other castles of the honour of Mortain in Normandy and towns throughout England.[15]

William was less belligerent and more pragmatic than Eustace. He was younger than Henry and must have felt unequal to a struggle to wrest England from the battle-proven duke of Normandy. He had seen how his brother's relentless pursuit of Henry had eventually killed him. Stephen was evidently satisfied that his heir was now richly provided for. Granting William titles and vast territories which made him one of the wealthiest barons in the Anglo-Norman world, Henry bribed and charmed him out of his inheritance.

II

On 6 November, at Winchester Cathedral, the magnates and bishops of the kingdom gathered.[16] Two superb diplomats, Theobald archbishop of Canterbury, and Henry bishop of Winchester (Stephen's brother), had brought them to this point and place. They had been negotiating furiously behind the scenes for months. Stephen, sitting opposite the choir, told the twenty-year-old Henry, seated in the bishop's chair, and the assembled gathering, 'Know that I, King Stephen, appoint Henry duke of

Normandy after me as my successor in the kingdom of England and my heir by hereditary right, and thus I give and confirm to him and his heirs the kingdom of England.'[17]

Stephen agreed to dismantle some of his new castles – the instruments of his war against Matilda and Henry – 'so that the duke at my death may not in respect of these suffer loss or hindrance in his acquisition of the kingdom'.[18] It was a beginning.

At Christmas at Westminster, Stephen adopted Henry and named him 'his son and heir'. He promised to govern 'in all the affairs of the kingdom' with Henry's advice. But he would continue to rule. The *Gesta Stephani* noted that he 'consented to the duke's inheriting England after his death provided that he, himself, as long as he lived, retained the majesty of the king's lofty position'.[19]

Henry then paid homage to Stephen, and received homage from William in turn. John of Hexham wrote how a proclamation went throughout the kingdom to extol the accord. Violence was suppressed, foreign mercenaries forced out of England; 'any fortifications built by individuals on their own possessions after the death of King Henry [I] were to be destroyed'.[20]

Over the next four months Henry and Stephen embarked on a mini-progress around the Midlands and the south-east, where they held several courts. At Oxford in January, 'at the king's command, the English magnates paid to the duke the homage and fealty due to their lord'.[21]

It was done – or so, at least, it seemed. Henry had conquered England, through a diplomatic resolution that left Stephen on the throne for the rest of his life – and it was feasible that Stephen would live for many years yet. Signs of discord between the two men, however, with their very different personalities and leadership styles, were already visible just months after their agreement, particularly over the achingly slow pace at which Stephen ordered the demolition of castles erected unlawfully during his reign.

Stephen had been Henry's enemy since Henry was two years old. It must have been a strain for him to be civil to the new heir apparent. Yet to ensure a smooth transition, they remained in each other's company for several months, travelling around the country while Henry received homage. At Dover at the end of February 1154, Henry discovered that William's and Stephen's Flemish mercenaries were plotting to kill him.[22] These mercenaries, led by Stephen's ally, the notorious William of Ypres, were a plague of the civil war. The chroniclers wrote of them bitterly: 'Flemings were called to England by the king, and they, envying the longtime inhabitants of the land, having left behind their native soil and their job of weaving, flocked into England in troops, and like hungry wolves proceeded energetically to reduce the fecundity of England to nothing. One of these men was William of Ypres, to whom the king gave the custody of all of Kent.'[23]

It is unlikely that Stephen was involved in the plot – instead, his son William, despite the lands and titles that Henry had heaped upon him, was probably making a late grab for power. It was an impetuous move, with little planning involved. Henry said nothing to Stephen, but left England as swiftly as possible, at the beginning of March.

Matilda needed Henry to return to Normandy, to subdue some of the duchy's minor barons. Henry had done as much as he could in England. It was still possible that Stephen would have a change of heart – it would not have been out of character – and would choose to champion his surviving son, despite his oaths to Henry. He had, after all, broken his vows to Matilda so easily. But for the time being, Henry left his uncle Reginald of Cornwall in charge of his affairs in England and departed for Normandy.

He was eager to see his new son, born to Eleanor, possibly at Angers, on the day that Eustace died. The boy was christened William after the dukes of Aquitaine; Henry's friend Robert of Torigni, the abbot of Mont Saint-Michel, wrote that his name was, 'almost the distinctive attribute of the counts of Poitou and dukes of Aquitaine'.[24] William was probably in remembrance too of the great-grandfather who had made Henry's bid for England possible: William the Bastard, duke of Normandy.

In Normandy, Henry and Eleanor celebrated Easter at Rouen with their baby son and Matilda. The chroniclers left no record of what Henry's mother and wife thought of one another. They may have recognised similar traits in each other and got on well, or they may have detested one another; we simply do not know. In any event, they would spend very little time together: Matilda would remain in Normandy for the rest of her life, and Eleanor would travel a great deal. Over the next few years, they seldom met, and neither would loom large in the other's life.

Henry, typically, was unable to rest. He went south to suppress a rebellion in Aquitaine, centred around Limousin and Périgord, and returned to Normandy by the end of June. He also made peace with Louis – who finally gave up the title duke of Aquitaine – to the extent that in early October, Henry provided him with military aid. Louis had married again; in his quest for a son, he let his famous piety slip and married a woman even more closely related to him than Eleanor: Constance of Castile. While Eleanor and Louis shared a common ancestor, King Robert II, and were related in the fourth degree on Louis' side and in the fifth degree on Eleanor's, Constance and Louis were second cousins. But Louis was shrewd in his marriage choice; in forging an alliance with Castile, he found new allies to bolster himself against Henry's formidable power base in the south.

In England, Stephen travelled to the north, 'showing himself off as if he were a new king'. It is possible that, for Stephen, it was not yet played out – he could remain king, and ensure his surviving son took his place when he died. According to Henry of Huntingdon, some of Stephen's men 'sought to sow the seeds of discord between the king who was present and the duke at a distance. The king could hardly resist their persuasions, and some thought he was already yielding to them, and that he listened to their evil counsels with a secret pleasure.'[25] It did not bode well that Henry's appointed deputy in England, his uncle Reginald of Cornwall, was ignored by Stephen and not welcomed at his court.[26]

But on 25 October, at Dover Priory, Stephen suffered crippling stomach pains. It was apparently not the first time. Gervase of Canterbury wrote that 'the king was suddenly seized with a violent pain in his gut, accompanied by a flow of blood (as had happened to him before), and after he had taken to his bed in the monks' lodgings'. Stephen did not recover from this illness; he died. He was about sixty-two years old.

William of Malmesbury wrote of Stephen's contrary nature: 'He was a man of energy but little judgement; active in war, of extraordinary spirit in undertaking any difficult task, he was lenient to his enemies and easily appeased.'[27]

Henry would not be so naive. He was fortune's darling once more; the struggle was finally over.

III

Henry heard of Stephen's death at the beginning of November, as he besieged the castle at Torigni in Normandy. He did not hurry back to England. For the first time in nearly a century, there was no one effectively to contest the succession to the throne of England. Henry determined to take his time, despite appeals for him to 'come over without delay, and receive the crown of England'.[28]

When pressed by friends, fearful that his former enemies would take the opportunity to seize power and to travel to England as quickly as possible, Henry refused: 'he replied ... that they durst not make the attempt to do so; and, though his friends were extremely urgent with him, yet would he not abandon the siege, till he had completed his purpose against the castle, during which time England waited anxiously for him, and no disturbance in the meanwhile arose'.[29] He knew he was secure.

He successfully completed his siege, placed Matilda in charge of Normandy once more, and prepared to sail for England with his brothers Geoffrey and William, many of his friends, and Eleanor, who was pregnant again.

Henry was twenty-one years old. He was master of nearly a third of modern-day France and was about to be crowned king of England. No western European prince since Charlemagne at the beginning of the ninth century had held that much territory. Schooled since infancy for kingship, Henry took it as his birthright.

England, for six weeks, was a land without a king. But, 'by God's providence it was in perfect tranquillity, the love or the fear of the expected king securing it'.[30] Archbishop Theobald of Canterbury easily maintained peace as England waited for Henry.

Violent storms delayed Henry, but the weather on 7 December was calm enough for him to sail from Barfleur. In the tradition of his Norman predecessors, Henry went straight to Winchester to secure the kingdom's treasury, and then on to Westminster, the church rebuilt by his ancestor Edward the Confessor in the Norman Romanesque style, to be crowned, on 19 December, by Archbishop Theobald.[31] The author of the *Gesta Stephani*, now firmly in Henry's camp, recorded that 'the duke, returning gloriously to England, was crowned for sovereignty with all honour and the applause of all'.[32] And John of Salisbury, in a letter drafted for Archbishop Theobald, anticipated the return of a 'golden age'.[33]

Henry's gold crown studded with jewels was an imperial one, part of the treasure brought by Matilda from Germany when she was widowed for the first time.[34] It was magnificent, but so cumbersome it had to be held up by two silver rods.[35] Eleanor was crowned too, although she may not have been anointed.[36]

Henry swore to restore the government of his grandfather, Henry I.[37] He proclaimed himself 'king in his own land, papal legate, patriarch, emperor, and everything he wished'.

William FitzStephen, a cleric and one of Thomas Becket's lawyers and biographers, wrote rhapsodically of a land made whole again by this king from over the water:

> All the Flemish were on their way to the sea with their arms and baggage. All their castles in England were destroyed. Those who had been despoiled were restored to their hereditary rights. The bandits left their hideouts in the forest and entered the villages. They melted their swords into ploughshares; their spears into sickles. Terrified by the sight of the gallows, thieves were glad to exercise the art of farming. Man could now travel in security from town or camp. The kingdom was rich; there was abundance everywhere: the hills were cultivated; the valleys were covered with harvest; the pastures were dotted with herds; the folds packed with bleating sheep.

To establish strong kingship, Henry would need to heal the fractures of Stephen's reign, marked by the poverty and brutality of civil war. His first act was purely military – to demolish the castles illegally erected during the civil war, and expel the mercenaries from the realm. William of Newburgh wrote that the Flemings 'glided away in a moment, as quickly as a phantom vanishes; while numbers wondered at their instantaneous disappearance'.[38]

Henry repaired the battle-scarred Tower of London, the fortress of his great-grandfather William I, with incredible speed; the work was completed between Easter and Pentecost. 'There were so many carpenters and other artisans employed that they had the hardest time to speak to one another ... amidst the din and noise.' The beginning of Henry's reign was characterised by building works in his capital. Westminster Palace too was repaired, under the close eye of Henry's new chancellor, Thomas Becket.

Stephen had reigned for nineteen years, yet Henry quickly obliterated him from the historical record of exemplary rule. Henry, in this narrative, was the saviour, the restorer of the good government of his grandfather, Henry I. His coronation charter promised:

> For the honour of God and holy Church, and for the common restoration of my whole realm, I have granted and restored … to God and holy Church, to all my earls, barons, and vassals, all concessions, gifts, privileges, and free customs, which King Henry my grandfather granted and conceded to them. Likewise all evil customs which he abolished and mitigated, I also grant to be mitigated and abolished in my name and in that of my heirs.[39]

Stephen's rule had depleted the treasury, while English magnates held enormous power – far more than Henry was comfortable with. Yet Henry's problems were not as great as the friendly chroniclers suggested. Henrician propaganda would deliberately exaggerate the anarchy of Stephen's reign, so that the peace enjoyed under Henry I, and now under his grandson Henry II, was all the more perfect by contrast.

Henry's propaganda machine was contrived, and effective throughout his reign; he knew the importance of creating a dazzling public face for his regime. The glory of Henry's court, its wealth, the brilliance of the writing, the numerous building works that Henry commissioned throughout his lands, the pilgrimages and the saints' cults he promoted were all in the service of his dynasty.

He often used saints' relics to strengthen his claim to be God's anointed. He petitioned Pope Alexander III to canonise his ancestor Edward the Confessor, and in February 1161, the pope granted it. Stephen had unsuccessfully lobbied to have Edward canonised in 1139 to glorify *his* regime with the creation of a new saint. He used as his ambassadors to Rome the prior of Westminster, Osbert de Clare, and his illegitimate son Gervase, abbot of Westminster. But he had failed. Once again it was Henry who triumphed. St Edward's body was translated within Westminster on 13 October 1163, in the presence of Henry and his eldest surviving son, Henri,* as a potent symbol of the continuation of the new line. Edward's biographer, Ailred of Rievaulx, duly wrote of Henry as the embodiment of the Norman and the English royal lines.

Similarly, he was delighted to receive the finger bone of Bernard of Clairvaux, now a saint – he was canonised in 1174 – in return for payment of a roof for the new church at Clairvaux.[40] And when Frederick Barbarossa (Red Beard) asked for the hand of St James – purloined by Matilda – to be returned to the Holy Roman Empire, Henry firmly, although diplomatically, refused.

Henry often sent for the hand of St James before crossing the Channel. His sailings were frequent; during his thirty-five-year reign, he made the journey twenty-eight times.[41] Sea crossings were dangerous – the tragedy of the *White Ship* was still in living memory – and disasters at sea were common. Henry, superstitious as the mood took him, adopted the notion of being on the side of caution.

When Frederick asked for the hand back in 1157, Henry was not prepared to let it go.[42] Instead he sent the emperor an elegant letter pledging his friendship, and ambassadors to refuse his request:

---

* Henry's and Eleanor's second child Henry was known, from his coronation during Henry II's lifetime in 1170, as 'Henry the Young King'. I refer him as 'Henri' throughout this book in order to avoid confusion with Henry II.

Let there be then between us and between our peoples an indivisible unity of peace and love and of safe commerce, yet in such a way that the authority to command shall go to you who holds the higher rank and we shall not be found wanting in willingness to obey. And as the bestowal of your gifts keeps our remembrance of your highness fresh so we wish that you remember us as we send you the most beautiful things we had and such as would most likely please you. Pay heed therefore to the fondness of the giver and not to the things given and accept them in the spirit in which they are given. As to the hand of St James about which you wrote to us, we have charged master Heribert and our clerk William to reply for us by word of mouth. Witnessed by Thomas the chancellor at Northampton.[43]

Henry, to mollify the emperor, sent a present close to his own heart: an enormous and gorgeous tent operated by pulleys, evidently big enough to stage a coronation in. Henry often carried a tent in his own retinue, and employed a 'tent-keeper'. This present to Barbarossa was 'a tent worthy of admiration in the splendour of its decoration'.[44] It was a gift from one great king to another.

IV

Henry crafted an administration of exceptional and diverse talent to enrich his kingship.

He had been thinking about it for months, and now he put the players into place. Some of his father's trusted men were in his entourage, as were several men 'new' to England, although they had faithfully served Henry as duke of Normandy. Richard du Hommet (Henry's cousin, a descendant of William the Bastard's brother Odo) was his constable in Normandy, Warin Fitz Gerald his chamberlain, and Manasser Biset his steward. They all came to England with Henry and would form the solid core of his court in the 1160s, 1170s and even into the 1180s when they began to die, still in service, and new loyalists took their place. Henry appointed the ambitious and exceptionally able Arnulf, bishop of Lisieux, as his justiciar of Normandy.[45] Arnulf was a devoted supporter of Henry's. Having served both Stephen and Louis VII, when he met Henry in 1150, he found a prince to whom he thought he could be of service. William d'Aubigny, earl of Arundel, the widower of Matilda's stepmother Adeliza, and notwithstanding his former loyalty to Stephen, was another close advisor.

Henry used his grandfather's loyalists where he could. Nigel, bishop of Ely, the old king's treasurer, became Henry's treasurer in turn; he was extraordinarily successful, bringing the Exchequer back to the strength it had enjoyed under Henry I. Henry was obliged to charm him back into royal service – Nigel was elderly, and did not want to work with his erstwhile foes, particularly Robert of Leicester.[46] Later, Nigel bought the position of treasurer for his illegitimate son, Richard, for £400.[47] Even with Richard's talents, however, Henry was desperate for funds for his Toulouse campaign at the time.[48]

Richard built upon his father's work at the Exchequer. In the late 1170s, he began writing one of the two most important books of Henry's reign, examining the seismic change to the administration of the realm: his *Dialogus de scaccario* ('Dialogue Concerning the Exchequer'). It told the story, in the form of a dialogue between master and pupil, of the beginnings of a massive cultural shift, 'from memory to written record'.[49] The Exchequer, originally a large table housed at Westminster, recorded all income that came in, and everything that went out. It was most likely an invention of Henry I's time, by his able clerks and administrators. The clerks of the Exchequer had long memories and always pursued a debt, even if it took years for the debtor to pay it off.[50] It was not particularly impressive to look at; Gerald of Wales called it 'a sort of square table in London where royal dues are collected and accounted for'.[51] The cloth covering this table over which much of the revenue of the kingdom passed, resembled a chessboard. It was from its appearance that the Exchequer derived its name: *scaccarium*, the Latin word for chess or chequers.[52] (The treasury, meanwhile, was housed at Winchester, along with the Domesday Book, and the royal crown and sceptre.) In Normandy, Caen acted as Henry's financial and administrative centre.[53]

Henry, a respecter of talent from whatever its source, placed former 'enemies' in his inner circle. He chose Richard de Lucy as his first justiciar in England.[54] Although Richard, from an Anglo-Norman family, may have served Henry's grandfather, Henry I, by 1136 he was very much Stephen's man, becoming indispensable to the king. He had even led a raid against Henry in 1153. However, Henry recognised his ability, his loyalty – albeit not previously to him – and his unsurpassed knowledge of the administration of England. Richard would remain loyal to Henry for the rest of his life, and Henry would reward him well.

Henry created Robert earl of Leicester, also recently come over from Stephen's camp, co-justiciar with Richard de Lucy.

Churchmen, alongside those whose reward for loyal service as a clerk or a scribe would be lucrative and prestigious posts in the church, also joined Henry's entourage. They included Theobald archbishop of Canterbury, Rotrou archbishop of Rouen, Richard of Ilchester (later archdeacon of Poitiers and then bishop of Winchester) and Geoffrey Ridel, who would later be appointed archdeacon of Canterbury.

Henry believed in institutional memory – one reason that the talented men from the past two regimes were harnessed into his service. They were loyal to Henry now and most would remain so, until death. If any faltered in their loyalty, however, he simply crushed them; when Henry of Blois, so seminal to the forging of a peace between Henry and Stephen, yet nervous of his standing with Henry now he was king, ran away with his treasure to Cluny in 1155, Henry demolished his castles.

Eleanor acted as Henry's regent several times; in these early years of his reign, she appears to have exercised a great deal of authority.

Henry needed Eleanor. He spent not quite thirteen of his thirty-five years as king in England, and he required, in his absence, strong governance and a sense of continuity for his kingship. Eleanor, working with Henry's most trusted advisors – particularly Robert earl of Leicester, Richard de Lucy, Henry's uncle, Reginald of Cornwall, Archbishop Theobald of Canterbury, and the young Thomas Becket – provided this. John of Salisbury bemoaned that she appointed bishops during her regency, fully dispensing royal power.[55] John also complained that he needed Eleanor's permission to leave the country. Henry placed her where he needed her. While he was away, she interceded in legal disputes, and allowed suits to come before the king's court. It was Eleanor who gave permission for Richard of Anstey to bring his suit before Henry, in what would become known as one of the most famous legal cases of the twelfth century.[56]

She presided over magnificent courts which showcased Henry's wealth – and therefore power – and in the tradition of Henry's Anglo-Norman ancestresses, she issued writs (or instructions for her royal orders to be carried out) and she governed. Henry and Eleanor's court became the largest in Europe, and Eleanor, at Henry's behest, saw to it that the display of pomp and wealth was suitably majestic.

The court had a large number of staff, from those who provided a guard for the king and queen, to bakers, water carriers, clerks, knights, chaplains, almoners (who distributed charity on behalf of Henry and Eleanor), physicians, butlers (responsible for the distribution of wine), and even doorkeepers. Eleanor had her own chancellor and, at the beginning of Henry's reign, the post was held for a while by his former tutor, Master Matthew.

Another member of Eleanor's household had held a place in Matilda's – Jocelin de Balliol, an Anglo-Norman baron; and a Norman loyalist, William Fitz Hamo, who had served Henry's father, also served Eleanor at Henry's behest.[57] Henry evidently placed men he trusted in his mother's and his wife's households, although whether or not in consultation with them, we do not know.

John of Salisbury thought Eleanor's authority equal to Henry's, and her writs reflected this. One, to the sheriff of Suffolk, threatened that, 'if you do not wish [to carry it out] the king's justice will be made to be done'.[58] During the 1150s, Eleanor held more power than Henry's co-justiciars, on one occasion acting to protect the abbot of St Albans, when the earl of Leicester had failed to do so.[59]

Matilda, although she still retained influence, deferred to Henry; she acted frequently as his regent in Normandy. When, in 1155, Henry suggested conquering Ireland and making his brother William FitzEmpress king there, it was Matilda who advised him against the idea. Henry listened, and would not go to Ireland until 1171.

Being a family member did not necessarily guarantee a place at the table. Henry prized talent above all else. He made his natural brother, Hamelin (Geoffrey's illegitimate son) and William FitzEmpress extremely wealthy, but although they fought alongside Henry during his campaigns, they were kept on the periphery of the inner circle.

Who flourished at Henry's court? The witness lists – the names of those who witnessed Henry's charters – show Henry's preference for the Anglo-Norman nobility, as distinct from the Norman, English, Angevin or Aquitainian. They or their families held lands on both sides of the English Channel: Richard du Hommet, Manasser Biset, Henry's uncle Reginald of Cornwall, Geoffrey Ridel, Richard de Lucy, Warin Fitz Gerald, Richard of Ilchester, John of Oxford and Ranulf de Glanville. These men formed Henry's inner circle, and were his closest friends and advisors.[60]

They were not always barons. Richard of Ilchester, for example, did not have an illustrious ancestry. Henry liked and trusted him, and he rose high: 'By the king's order he exercised the greatest power throughout England.'[61] As a reward for his loyalty, Henry made him bishop of Winchester, issuing an infamous writ to the electors of Winchester: 'I order you to hold a free election, but forbid you to elect anyone but Richard my clerk.' Passionate about the law, Henry nevertheless saw himself as sitting above it.

Henry valued his friends, his *amici*. Many of their names are now lost to us.

Henry looked for loyalty, and he would reward those he favoured with riches, bishoprics, sinecures, or marriages to wealthy heiresses. He wanted to keep money and land in his own hands, and as such he created hardly any new nobles. The exception was a limited number from his own family, notably his half-brother, Hamelin, whom he married to the Warenne heiress Isabella, and his sons Richard and Geoffrey. He confirmed some titles granted by Matilda and Stephen: the de Veres, the Aubignys and Bigods, and the Mandevilles.[62]

Talented and ambitious men could rise in administrative service at court.[63] Henry scoured wide for talent, even from overseas. In 1154 he offered a post at the Exchequer to a Thomas Brown.[64] Thomas, whose family had worked in Henry I's administration, went to Sicily after the old king's death to serve King Roger II. He spoke and wrote fluent Arabic, and had held high office in Sicily, as a judge and a chaplain; but when Roger died he chose to travel to England to work for Henry, whose court offered attractive and lucrative opportunities. In 1160 Henry, to reward Thomas's service, gave him the enormous sum of £42 14s, besides an annuity.[65] Henry had great faith in Thomas: between 1164 and 1175 he held the office of almoner, and he may well have been one of Henry's close friends. He served Henry until his death in 1180.

Similarly, the lawyer Simon of Apulia, born in southern Italy, sought his fortune in England. By 1186, he was canon of York Cathedral.[66]

Intellectual talent travelled both ways. In the 1180s, Gervase of Tilbury, who served as chaplain to Henri, travelled to Sicily where he was given a post by Henry's son-in-law, King William II. And Peter of Blois, perhaps the most talented and vivid writer of Henry's reign, and who would come into Henry's orbit towards the end of the 1160s, also served the young King William II in Sicily, acting as his tutor when he first came to the throne. Two Englishmen were leading ecclesiastics in Sicily – Richard Palmer became bishop of Syracuse in 1157, and in 1169 Herbert of Middlesex was appointed archbishop of Conza.

Friendships and mutually beneficial relationships were forged between Henry's closest advisors and friends. The author of the Chronicle of Battle Abbey noted that Henry's uncle Reginald of Cornwall, Richard du Hommet, Richard de Lucy (du Hommet's brother), and Abbot Walter of Coutances had 'joined together in a pact of friendship'.[67] John of Salisbury, however, thought them superficial and a target for satire: 'From this the disgrace of the kingdom is thrown away; from this comes its glory!'[68]

The chroniclers tell us repeatedly that Henry was willing to listen to advice from his inner circle. They were, for the most part, not the great magnates, but the clerks and the minor aristocracy. He was rarely without the company of learned *magistri* – masters – such as Walter of Coutances. Even after Walter became archbishop of Rouen in 1184, Henry continued to send him on diplomatic missions all over Europe, as he did with many of his trusted intimates.

To the great magnates themselves, Henry was generous in his gifts and reaffirmation of grants, and won them over. He led the regular council meetings at which the nobility gathered, and he allowed them to believe they were intrinsic to his decision-making.

Henry could not afford for his nobility to challenge his authority, and he went to war against any who defied him. In 1138, Stephen had created William le Gros earl of York. He was 'more truly a king there than his master'.[69] If Stephen was prepared to tolerate his behaviour, Henry was not; one of the first actions of his reign was to advance north to deal with William. Henry's reputation preceded him: when William le Gros heard the king was coming, he immediately relinquished all his properties. Henry did not create a new earl of York.[70]

Henry moved too against Roger earl of Hereford and Hugh Mortimer, two men who had been loyal to the Angevin party. Roger was the son of Miles of Gloucester, a fierce advocate of Matilda's. Nevertheless, Henry wanted their castles in his hands, and Roger was persuaded to give up Gloucester and Hereford to the king. Hugh, however, would not relinquish his, but instead fortified them. Henry took Cleobury, Wigmore and Bridgnorth, and by the summer, Hugh too acknowledged the king's full authority.[71]

Besides the appointment of his co-justiciars Richard de Lucy and Robert of Leicester, the most important post in the realm was that of chancellor. The position was significant, not least because its holder had unfettered access to the king; he disseminated the king's will in the form of writs, letters and charters; he controlled Henry's secretariat; and he was master of the royal chapel.[72] In 1154 Henry prudently sought advice on the appointment from Archbishop Theobald, doubtless soothing Theobald's concerns regarding a government in transition. Theobald duly recommended one of his own clerks, Thomas Becket, archdeacon of Canterbury, for the post. Becket was about thirty-four years old.

Henry had come to know Thomas during the diplomatic negotiations of 1153. Theobald may have thought he was placing his own man at court, to protect the church against any anticlerical tendencies of Henry's. When the archbishop proposed Thomas as chancellor to the king, Henry accepted.

As chancellor, Becket worked intimately with Henry over the next decade; his meteoric rise was the best example of how those from modest backgrounds could do well at Henry's court. It was peopled, not only with the aristocracy, but also those new men 'raised from the dust'.[73] Henry valued clever people and this preference was reflected in his entourage. He was holding an empire in his hands. He needed them.

V

Henry's court was large, glittering, and more international than any that had gone before it. His wife was Eleanor of Aquitaine; many of his ambitious clerks had studied at the great schools of Paris, Chartres, or Bologna, before entering Henry's service; many were lawyers. One historian judges Henry's courtiers as being 'better trained than any other in the West'.[74] They went on diplomatic missions throughout Europe, and his daughters' marriages into the royal families of Castile, Sicily and Saxony gave Henry access to an even broader stage.

England had a population of about 2.5 million people. The capital, London, by far the largest city in the kingdom with a population of over 20,000, became a magnet for the import of the exotic. Among the goods found at the docks were scarlet silks from China, gold from Arabia, gemstones from Egypt, French wines, sable from Russia, and almonds from the Middle East.[75] William FitzStephen wrote of London as an international city, to which merchants from all over the world brought their goods. It was a bustling, thriving centre of commerce, dotted with palaces of the wealthy magnates who flocked to court, and where apparently all tastes could be satisfied: 'Whatever evil or malicious thing can be found anywhere in the world can also be found in that city … The number of parasites is infinite. Actors, jesters, smooth-skinned lads, Moors, flatterers, pretty boys, effeminates, pederasts, singing and dancing girls, quacks, belly-dancers, sorcerers, extortioners, night-wanderers, magicians, mimes, beggars, buffoons.'[76]

In November 1176, Henry held court at Westminster. Here, he was visited and lauded by ambassadors from the very edges of his spheres of influence; visitors to Westminster in the winter of 1176 would have found themselves in the company of ambassadors from the courts of Frederick Barbarossa, from Manuel Comnenus, the emperor of the Eastern Roman Empire, from the king of Sicily, from the duke of Savoy and the count of Flanders, and from the archbishop of Rheims. Henry also received delegations from the kings of Navarre and Castile.[77]

Henry was, according to Richard FitzNigel, 'the greatest of the illustrious rulers of the world'. His court and the ambassadors it attracted reflected this. For Henry was a man of enormous influence and power, a prince at the very centre of the intellectual life of the twelfth-century renaissance.

The boundaries of Henry's world went far beyond England and France, although he never travelled outside his lands. Through his grandfather Fulk's second marriage to Melisende, Henry's cousins occupied the throne of Jerusalem. And on his mother's side, the Normans too were conquerors, and not only through William the Bastard's victory in 1066. The First Crusade led to the establishment of a Norman-ruled crusader state at Antioch, and a princedom in Galilee.

In 1130, Count Roger de Hauteville, a Norman mercenary, led his army to overthrow Sicily's Arab rulers and found a dynasty there. They not only ruled the island, but most of southern Italy below the Papal States, and much of North Africa too. It would endure until 1194, when it fell to the forces of the Holy Roman Emperor. These astute Norman rulers made Sicily into a world power, one whose monarch could successfully ask Henry II,

Fourteenth-century manuscript showing Henry I on his throne, grieving for the loss of his only legitimate son, and the hundreds besides him who died on the *White Ship* in 1120. The death of the king's heir threw the English and Norman succession into a crisis that would be resolved only when his grandson, Henry II, took the throne over thirty years later.

Enamel effigy of Henry's father, Geoffrey Plantagenet, Count of Anjou. Henry spared no expense commemorating a father he admired and loved.

Matilda, Henry's mother, from the late-fourteenth-century *Golden Book of St Albans*. She was accused of being a 'virago'. Failing to win the English crown for herself, Matilda devoted herself to her son's cause.

The hand of St James, one of the twelve apostles, on display at St Peter's Church, Marlow. Matilda was crowned in Germany on the day of the Feast of St James. She stole the hand when she returned to England, possibly in remembrance of the occasion.

Eleanor of Aquitaine's wedding to Louis VII of France. The marriage was a disaster, and she later complained that Louis was 'more monk than man'.

King Stephen, the charming and chivalrous favourite of his uncle, Henry I. He stole the throne from his first cousin Matilda – in spite of his pledges of loyalty to her. This portrait hangs in the National Portrait Gallery in London.

Henry's face on a coin, curly hair topped by a crown made up of five pearls, issued after 1180.

Henry and Eleanor's eldest surviving son, Henri – the Young King. He was crowned alongside his father in 1170, but he had absolutely no power. Henry did not think his son capable of ruling his empire when he died.

Pilgrims at Edward the Confessor's shrine. Henry successfully petitioned the pope to have his ancestor canonised, to glorify his own regime.

Fascinated by design, Henry himself commissioned the intriguing octagonal Byzantine-Romanesque-style kitchen, or smokehouse, at Fontevraud Abbey.

In an impressive display of wealth and power, Henry and Eleanor rebuilt Poitiers Cathedral, some time after John was born in 1166. Here, they may be seen offering up the window; their four sons are in the background.

King Henry II seated on his throne, arguing with Thomas Becket. Henry created his friend and chancellor archbishop of Canterbury. It was the first great mistake of his reign.

Murder of Thomas Becket, from the fifteenth-century *St Albans Chronicle*. An unarmed Becket is hacked to death in his own cathedral at Canterbury by four knights loyal to Henry, thinking they would please their king. Did Henry secretly desire Becket's death?

from the mid-1170s the most powerful ruler in Europe, for his daughter's hand in marriage.

The court of the Hauteville kings, with its links to the Christian Eastern Roman Empire of Constantinople, attracted multilingual scholars, translating those Greek and Roman texts 'lost' to European scholarship in the chaos that followed the disintegration of the Western Roman Empire in the fifth century. These writers – Cicero, Aristotle, Plato, Euclid – were Bernard of Clairvaux's 'giants', whose knowledge of algebra, dialectic, mathematics and medicine would be so influential in the West for centuries to come.

Sicily, poised in the middle of the Mediterranean (the Mid-earth Sea), between East and West, was vital in disseminating these ideas to the West. Many Greek texts had been preserved in the Basilian monasteries of the Eastern Roman Empire. Sicily's trilingual scriptorium, a magnet for international scholarship, became a centre where the works of classical scholars, many of them translated into Arabic from the original Greek, were in turn translated into Latin. It was through Sicily that mathematical and medical innovations too became known to European scholars. Sicily had been conquered by the Greeks, the Romans, the Vandals, the Goths, the Byzantines and the Arabs, and her intellectual and physical treasures were vast.

The atmosphere was, for the most part, one of religious tolerance of the Christian kings to their Arab and Jewish populations. Al-Idrisi, a geographer and an advisor to King Roger II, praised Sicily as: 'the pearl of this century ... Since old times, travelers from the most far away countries ... boast of its merits, praise its territory, rave about its extraordinary beauty, and highlight its strength ... because it brings together the best aspect from every other country.'

For a short period in time, it was a perfect fusion of cultures and religious tolerance, and today we have a glimpse of the co-operation of this society through the artefacts people left behind.

Two small pieces of work are particularly striking. The first is an ivory casket, created by Muslim craftsmen, depicting Christian saints.[78] It was typical of the period. And then there is the remarkable funerary inscription of a woman called Anna, who died there in 1149. Her son, a Christian priest, wrote her eulogy in four different languages – in Latin, Greek, Arabic and Judaeo-Arabic (Arabic written in Hebrew script). It was dated giving the Islamic year of 544, the Hebrew year of 4909, and the Byzantine year of 6657.[79]

Henry, educated by some of the greatest teachers of the century, among them Adelard of Bath and William of Conches, added lustre to this renaissance.

The cathedral schools in England were not as developed as those of France, Italy and Spain, and so English scholars continued their education abroad. But many came back and some found a home within Henry's administration. By studying at the great European schools, in Sicily, Constantinople and the Latin Kingdom, those who returned brought their newly acquired knowledge back to England, wrote their books and laid the foundations for the great intellectual achievements of subsequent centuries.

Henry, typically building on existing tradition, did several things. He encouraged the continuation of cultural links throughout his areas of influence, from the Hebrides to the Levant, ensuring his diplomats were at all the courts of note; he offered a welcome to roving scholars, fostering their influx into his realms and at his court, and thus disseminating the new knowledge in science, the law, art and architecture, and theology; and it was under Henry's patronage that we see an explosion of spectacular literature written in the vernacular, taking tales ancient and new beyond their dusty Latin purview.

By the time Henry came to the throne of England, there was already a long-established tradition of the roving scholar. Henry's grandfather, Henry I, had employed Petrus Alfonsi as his doctor.

Petrus was a Jewish scholar from northern Spain who converted to Christianity. His major works were the *Dialogi*, where he wrote on faith using the form of a dialogue between his Jewish self, and his newly converted Christian self, and the *Disciplina Clericalis*, a collection of Arabic and Hebrew fables. This was the first time these fables were available in the west, and Henry would have been aware of these works. Like Henry's tutor, William of Conches, Petrus Alfonsi delighted in teaching and the pursuit of knowledge, telling his pupil, 'part of this we transmit for your enjoyment, so that you may both see and know how desirable and how beautiful this art is'.[80] Petrus Alfonsi's example may have been followed by Adelard of Bath, inspired enough by the great Spanish scholar's experience to travel to Spain, and to bring the knowledge he acquired of Arabic developments in mathematics back to northern Europe.[81]

Other texts vital to the development of knowledge in the West came out of the scriptorium in Sicily. Perhaps the most important was the translation into Latin of the Almagest, one of the greatest treatises in the history of science. It was written in about AD 150 by Claudius Ptolemaeus of Alexandria (Ptolemy), was translated from Greek into Arabic in the ninth century, and then in Sicily, from Arabic into Latin. It explains, in thirteen books, the author's study and observations of the heavens, and it allowed astronomers to predict the path of the sun, moon and planets. Scholars disseminated it into the West, where it became the most influential text on astronomy until the seventeenth century.

Robert Cricklade, prior of St Frideswide's in Oxford, not only dedicated his translation of Pliny's *Natural Histories* to Henry, but brought back for his queen, Eleanor, in the 1150s, a copy of the *Gynaecia Cleopatrae* from Sicily via Constantinople, a text on gynaecology which dealt with everything from women's diseases to contraception, abortion and child-rearing, thought to have been written by either Cleopatra or her female doctor, Theodote.[82]

One of Eleanor's biographers argues that the queen, anxious to avoid the horror of losing another child, asked for the text as she mourned her dead son, William.[83] The fact that Eleanor could ask for it shows how widespread the knowledge of Greek and Latin texts was among the educated classes.

Scholars from the Anglo-Norman realm developed an international reputation. John of Salisbury was regarded as the greatest Latinist of his day, and Nicholas Breakspear, an Englishman, was elected Pope Adrian IV in 1154.[84] Breakspear became pope just days before Henry became king, but when England was already his – on 4 December. He remains the only English pope in history. He did not forget his homeland; his greatest service to Henry was his papal bull, *Laudabiliter*, which brought Ireland into Henry's empire, in return for ensuring the inhabitants' conversion to Christianity.[85]

It was Henry's patronage, whether direct or indirect, that enabled a galaxy of talented writers to thrive. They included Walter Map, Peter of Blois, Arnulf of Lisieux, Gerald of Wales, John of Salisbury, Roger of Howden, the unknown author of the influential treatise on English law (traditionally attributed to Henry's chief justiciar, Ranulf de Glanville), Richard FitzNigel (author of *Dialogue Concerning the Exchequer*), Henry of Huntingdon and Robert of Torigni.

Henry's reign saw huge advances in the art of historiography – the last years of his rule having been described as the beginnings of 'the Golden Age of Historical Writing'.[86] He encouraged the rehabilitation of the great Anglo-Saxon saints, particularly the cult of Edward the Confessor. Henry harnessed the Anglo-Saxon past to shore up his, to some, usurper regime, and the historical research that preceded Edward's canonisation is a fine example of this. Osbert of Clare researched Edward's life, which furthered the push to canonise him. This was an extremely important movement in 'historical inquiry'. It was a very English development, as the monks of the English monasteries, with their plethora of ancient documents, researched their saints and their relics, and Henry was pleased to nurture it.

Some of the best history, legend and romance of the day emerged from Henry's court, albeit evidence of the extent of his patronage is patchy. Although dozens of works were dedicated to Henry, the only commissions that we know for certain were Wace's *Roman de Rou*, a history of Henry's Norman ancestors, and Benoît de Sainte-Maure's *Chronique des ducs de Normandie*, the continuation of Wace's work, commissioned to glorify Henry's rule after he nearly lost everything in the 1170s.[87] As a reward for his history, Henry gave Wace a prebend at Bayeux Cathedral.[88] Wace also penned the *Roman de Brut*, a history of Britain which relied heavily on Geoffrey of Monmouth's *History of the Kings of Britain*. It was reportedly dedicated to Eleanor, lauding her as 'generous ... gracious and wise'.[89]

Peter of Blois explained the attraction of Henry's court to a poor man of letters: 'What binds us to the court is more delicate clothing, food more exquisite and more refined, and there I am feared, and not afraid, and can increase the estate my parents left me, and thunder out great words; I am tied there by the counsels of the rich, and the chances of dignities, which the friendship of magnates can bestow.'[90]

As well as these accomplished writers, the environment is believed to have fostered Chrétien de Troys (the author who developed the legend of King Arthur and the Holy Grail), who may even have visited Henry's court – he wrote that 'My heart draws me to these people' – and the poet Marie de France, who some scholars think may also have been Henry's illegitimate half-sister, Mary abbess of Shaftesbury.[91] Marie dedicated her *Lais* for 'your honour, noble king, so worthy and courtly, before whom all joy bows its head and whose heart is the root of all virtue'. If not Henry, the dedicatee could only have been his eldest surviving son, Henri, crowned in 1170 in his father's lifetime.[92]

Despite both his and Eleanor's awareness of Arthurian legend – during the reign of Eleanor's father, there is evidence that two troubadours sang about it – Henry barely used the story of the ancient king of the Britons to bolster his claim to rule.[93] This does not mean that the stories did not fascinate them, and that Henry and Eleanor did not read Wace's *Roman de Brut* with anything other than pleasure. Later, in about 1200, it was contended that Wace 'presented his work to the noble lady Eleanor, Henry II's queen'.[94]

But although Henry felt the need to legitimise his regime, his chroniclers, no doubt directed by Henry, preferred to compare him to the mighty heroes of the classical world. For Walter Map, he was Achilles, and as a young man, Henry had been compared to Hector.[95] To Gerald of Wales, Henry was 'our Alexander of the West'. For the story of Arthur acted as a mirror for the nationalist hopes of the Celtic Bretons and the Welsh far more than it served the cohesion of Henry's empire. Gerald of Wales claimed that it was Henry who told the monks of Glastonbury where to dig on their land to find the bones of the mythical king. Henry reputedly said that 'according to the traditions that he had heard from a singer of ancient British history, the body would be found buried, at least sixteen feet deep, in a hollowed-out oak tree'.[96] Whether or not Henry knew where Arthur's body lay, it was a desire to excise the myth rather than to propagate it – Arthur, lying dead in the ground, was no '*rex quondam, rexque futurus*' (once and future king) who would return to free the Welsh and the Bretons – that prompted Henry to direct the monks. Nonetheless, the body at Glastonbury was not exhumed during Henry's reign, but in the 1190s, when he was already dead. The grave reputedly contained the sword Excalibur, which Richard gave to King Tancred of Sicily on his way to the Latin Kingdom.

The life of the roving scholar was not to everyone's taste. John of Salisbury and Walter Map lamented their fates, while others satirised their predicament. The English cleric Nigel de Longchamps, in his 'A Mirror for Fools', described their 'labours':

> To Paris then my way I'll make,
> A ten years' course in Arts to take;
> I'll start at once, Then if God will,
> I'll come back home, and learning still,
> Become well versed in all the rules,
> By studying in Bologna's schools,
> Of civil law: the Sacred Page
> And the Decreta will engage
> My final labours, if I live.
> Then, then at last I shall receive
> The title and reality
> Of Master; master shall I be,
> And 'Master' shall precede my name.[97]

Yet as a result of their labours, cross-cultural influences could be seen everywhere. At Otranto Cathedral, King Arthur remains immortalised in a mosaic created between 1163 and 1165. The image of this legendary Celtic king captured someone's imagination; a story was told in Sicily towards the end of the century of King Arthur, still alive, living beneath Mount Etna.[98]

In England, the Winchester Bible, probably commissioned in 1160 by Bishop Henry of Blois, is one of the finest examples of an illuminated book of the twelfth century. The costly blue pigment was made from lapis lazuli, which came from the Badakshan mines of Afghanistan. This was an extremely expensive book, and its paintings show that one of the artists was either Sicilian, or had seen Sicilian artefacts, in Sicily or elsewhere.[99] Bishop Henry was acquisitive. John of Salisbury knew he had taken antique statues from Rome, and it is not impossible that he asked for an icon from Sicily, to be copied by an artist at Winchester.[100]

The influences of Arabic architecture could be seen from the great cathedrals to country churches; at Durham, interlaced round arches and star-shaped vaulted ceilings were seen from the 1130s.[101] Durham, particularly the nave, built during the early 1130s, and the Galilee chapel, completed in the latter part of the century, bear a striking resemblance to two Spanish buildings: the great mosque at Cordoba and the Jafiriyya Palace in Saragossa. In 1118, Alfonso of Aragon captured Saragossa and it became one of the great intellectual centres of Christendom, its beauties known to Europeans. The Arabic motifs that appeared at Durham and in English country churches were either carved by people who had visited Sicily or Spain, or copied from the sketches of an artist who had.[102]

Similarly, although it was William the Englishman who replaced the east end of Canterbury Cathedral after it burned down in 1174 and its style is widely known as 'Early English', this was anything but an English church; it was rather a fusion of English and Arabic styles. The stone vaulting shows Arabic influences, as do the enormous striped double columns, made of marble.

The monasteries were producing illuminated manuscripts of exquisite quality, and the twelfth century has been called 'the greatest in the history of English book production'.[103] England's abbeys contained manuscripts of the 'new' learning. In the 1170s and 1180s, at Bury Abbey, could be found Greek and Arabic treatises on chemistry translated into Latin.[104] Not least among these were the legal texts, no doubt commissioned by Henry, such as FitzNigel's *Dialogue Concerning the Exchequer* and *Treatise on Law and Customs of England*, attributed to Glanville. It was only in Henry's domains that such thought was put into the business and management of government. The great historian R. W. Southern wrote that 'nowhere else but in England is there such a large literature so full of the learning of the schools in its reference to the practical life'.[105] It gave unprecedented power to the king.

England was a trilingual society. Anglo-Norman French and Latin were the languages of the court and government business, used by educated people – clerks, lawyers, theologians, scientists and masters (those who had been educated at the cathedral schools). Anyone who benefited from a decent education would have been able to speak them. English merchants too would have spoken French, particularly those living in centres of international trade, such as London, or the great port towns and cities.

If you were not an aristocrat, the closer you lived to London and the court, the more likely you were to use French or Latin rather than English as the language of business. Towns from the middle and across the southern half of England – including Bury St Edmunds, Exeter, Leicester, London, Northampton, Southampton, Taunton and Winchester – used French for their civic regulations, and not Latin. In the north, however, English was more common: French did not generally permeate north of the Midlands.[106]

Although the great treatises of Henry's reign were written in Latin, the language had a disadvantage – it was not a living, breathing language like English or Anglo-Norman French, and so occasionally non-Latin substitutes were made. In one of the pipe rolls for 1159, the author of a particular section was clearly searching for a Latin word for the support structure of a building – its frame. But as no Latin word would suffice, he chose 'frama', not a Latin word, but an English one that he 'Latinised'.[107]

English scholars, or scholars working in England, were pre-eminent in the writing down of legend, often in the vernacular. It is possible that *The Owl and the Nightingale*, a beautiful poem recounting a discussion between the two birds and written in English, was composed during Henry's reign.[108] Jordan Fantosme, in his epic poem detailing Henry's wars in the 1170s, chose to write in French, and not Latin. And Marie de France wrote her Anglo-Norman fables in French. Marie possibly provides the most striking example of cross-cultural influences.

Henry's tolerance of his Jewish community did much to spread the growth of ideas; Rabbi Berechiah ben Natronai ha'Nakdan, who lived in Henry's England and Normandy, translated Marie's *Fables* into Hebrew. They influenced at least one of his works, *Mishlei Shu'alim*, or *Fox Fables*.[109]

Despite Peter of Blois' claim that at Henry's court, 'every day is school, in the constant conversation of the most literate and discussion of questions', Henry was busy governing an empire, probably far too busy for dedicated study.[110]

But he allowed and encouraged the growth of an environment that was receptive to, and encouraged, the spread of ideas. Henry went as far as he could, in the limited time available to him. It was Henry who directly influenced the growth of historiography – second to none in Europe – of government administration, and of his most enduring legacy, the law. And it was on Henry's watch that we see the most significant leaps in the production of books, illuminated manuscripts, Arabic influences in English architecture, literature in the vernacular and the development of legend.

* * *

Although all contemporary courts were itinerant, Henry's was by necessity far more so than most. Its comings and goings certainly confounded Walter Map: 'I am in the court and speak of the court but what the court is God alone knows, I do not.'[111]

No English king had ever ruled over such a vast conglomerate of lands. As such, Henry rarely stayed in one place for more than three days, and when he travelled, his advisors, courtiers, clerks and often his family travelled with him. Some of the clerks, notably Walter Map and Peter of Blois, thought him restless by nature. Herbert of Bosham complained that he was like a 'human chariot dragging all after him'.[112] But wherever Henry went, he took it upon himself to make investigations – into the condition of his houses, the suitability of his judges, the upholding of the unpopular forest laws. He fast acquired a reputation for inhuman speed, and was noted to 'fly rather than travel by horse or ship'.[113] In the execution of a lightning campaign, no one could touch him.

Henry's contemporaries left pen portraits of a court in constant flux, noisy, sometimes argumentative, with many dark deeds done in the middle of the night.[114]

Peter of Blois described the tumult of a court move:

If the king has announced that he will go early next morning to a certain place, the decision is sure to be changed; and so you know he will sleep till midday. You will see pack-animals waiting under their loads, teams of horses standing in silence, heralds sleeping, court traders fretting, and everyone in turn grumbling. One runs to whores and pavilioners of the court to ask them where the king is going. For this breed of courtier often knows the palace secrets. For the king's court has an assiduous following of entertainers, laundresses, dice-players, flatterers, taverners ... actors, barbers – gluttons the whole lot of them![115]

Peter was dismayed by the spectacle, and his part in it: 'I was led by the spirit of ambition and immersed myself entirely in the waves of the world. I put God, the Church and my Order behind me and set myself to gather what riches I could, rather than to take what God sent ... Ambition made me drunk, and the flattering promises of our Prince overthrew me.'[116]

Walter Map, meanwhile, called the court 'a hydra of many heads'. Although he refrained from a direct comparison with 'hell', it was nevertheless for him 'a place of punishment'.[117] He complained of the noisy chaos, and despaired of the erudite forced into close company with the depraved: 'The ripe in years or wisdom were always before lunch in the court with the king, and, by the cry of the herald, there were summoned to them those who desired a hearing in regard to business; after midday and the siesta those were admitted who sought amusement. Hence this king's court was a school of virtue and wisdom all the morning, of courtesy and decorous mirth all the afternoon.'[118]

As with the world, so with the court; it contained the learned and the profane. For his amusement, Henry employed 'Roland le Pettour' – Roland the Farter. On Christmas Day, Roland was expected to perform a 'leap, a whistle and a fart'.[119] Henry employed whoremasters to oversee 'the creatures of the night' who peopled the court. He was reportedly a serial adulterer, ever unfaithful to Eleanor.

Games and gambling were important, particularly chess and dice, and Henry was often described as immersed in a game of chess. The game, which dates from sixth-century India, had arrived in western Europe via Persia, the Islamic world and Spain at the end of the tenth century, and was highly fashionable.

Writers who knew Henry left us other vignettes, and they were not always flattering.

He slept little, preferring to spend his time hunting and playing chess almost daily, and even repairing his own simple clothes. When he did sleep, his courtiers complained he slept until noon. There were moans about Henry's obsession with the hunt, often to escape the tumult of court; the abbot of Battle Abbey grouched that when he went to court to see Henry, 'he could get nothing done that day since the king had gone hunting'.[120] William of Newburgh also believed that Henry 'delighted in the chase, and more than was right'.[121]

For all his affability and approachability, Henry could also be capricious, volatile and fiercely protective of his kingly status. When Bishop Hilary of Chichester attempted to lecture Henry on the need for papal approval for his 'ecclesiastical privileges and exemptions' to churches, Henry, incensed, replied, 'You are plotting to attack the royal prerogatives given to me by God, with your crafty arguments … by your fealty and your binding oath to me, I command that you undergo just legal judgement for presumptuous words against my crown and royal prerogative.'[122]

John of Salisbury called him 'Proteus' after the Greek god of seas and rivers. It was not a compliment; he thought the king an artful operator who did not keep his promises. Henry loved falconry, and was supposed to have written a treatise on it, now lost.[123] He was portrayed as a lotus eater, indifferent to the world, while serenaded with a harp and having his feet rubbed.[124] Critics accused him of being irreverent to the church, even hearing petitioners at Mass.

Henry's rage was an important part of his arsenal to assert kingship. He rowed with his cousin William the Lion of Scotland, and then 'the king, enflamed with his customary fury, threw the cap from his head, untied his belt, hurled his mantle and other garments from him, removed the silk coverlet from the bed with his own hand and began to chew the straw of the bedding'.[125] Gerald of Wales, no lover of Henry because he believed he failed to give him an adequate position, noted that he peppered his speech with oaths: 'By God's eyes, throat or testicles' was one of his favourite phrases. He wrote of his relief when Henry's 'stormy bout of temper subsided into calm and his loud thunderings were not followed by the deadly blow of the thunderbolt'.[126] Henry, or Zeus, had been appeased.

Other writers praised Henry. He made himself available to his people, and despite the propaganda machine that projected his authority, he was not aloof. He could be cajoled out of his anger. Hugh of Lincoln's biographer, Adam of Eynsham, related how Henry, angry with Hugh for excommunicating a royal forester, ordered him to come to him at Woodstock. When he arrived, Henry turned his back on him and busied himself sewing a bandage, to which Hugh commented, 'How you resemble your cousins at Falaise.' The comment referred to William the Conqueror's illegitimate origins, as son of Arlette, a tanner's daughter from

Falaise. Another king might have taken grave offence, but Henry burst into laughter.[127]

In his manners, Henry did not distinguish between high and low rank. Walter Map told a story of a poor Cistercian monk who hurried to get out of the way as Henry approached, leading a large party of knights and clerks. The hapless monk tripped and fell in front of Henry's horse: 'The wind blew the poor man's habit right up over his neck exposing all his private parts. The king, that treasure house of courtesy, pretended to see nothing and said nothing.'[128]

Henry could be extraordinarily generous; if he got what he wanted he was the most affable man in the world. After a tumultuous crossing of the Channel where his entire fleet except his own ship was thrown onto the rocks, Henry reimbursed all the sailors for their losses.[129] In 1179 he gave his fool Roger a post – keeper of the royal otter-hounds – and a house and land in Aylesbury 'by the service of finding straw for the king's bed, and straw or grass for decking his chamber thrice a year, straw if he should come in winter and grass in summer'.[130]

Walter Map spoke of Henry's 'secret' almsgiving and his enormous popularity. 'Whatever way he goes out he is seized upon by the crowds and pulled hither and thither, pushed whither he would not.'[131] Henry was loyal; even Gerald of Wales admitted that 'once he had taken to a man, [he] scarcely ever came to dislike him'.[132]

VI

If Henry was to be a strong ruler, it was imperative that he be rich. He was not particularly greedy or acquisitive, and cared little for money itself; his dress was relatively modest, his diet sparse – certainly in later life when he attempted to keep his weight down. Henry concerned himself with money, because he understood that a strong state required deep financial reserves.

Richard FitzNigel, Henry's treasurer in the latter part of his reign and bishop of London, appreciated this too. He noted in his *Dialogue Concerning the Exchequer* that, 'We are, of course, aware, that kingdoms are governed and laws upheld primarily by prudence, fortitude, moderation, and justice, and the other virtues which rulers must strive to cultivate. But there are times when money can speed on sound and wise policies, and smooth out difficulties, just as skilful negotiation may.'[133]

When Henry became king, his coffers had been depleted by the struggle for Normandy, while Stephen had left very little money in the treasury. To shore up his kingship, Henry would have to ensure the defence of Normandy, suppress rebellion in Anjou, and subdue Wales, Brittany and Toulouse. He needed funds.

How did Henry accumulate his wealth? Crown income came from land, taxation, the forest, and 'the profits of justice'.[134] The accounts for royal revenues for the years 1158–9 list income totalling nearly £30,000 from among the following sources: farms, for England was primarily a rural economy; the proceeds of justice, including pleas, murder fines and reliefs; and taxation, which included Danegeld (an archaic tax) and scutage, a tax paid in lieu of military service. Revenue was also raised from guilds, the Jewish communities and mining.[135]

Henry's unprecedented centralisation of administration increased the Crown's revenue from rents and fees across all his dominions by massive proportions. In 1166, he ordered an inquest into knights' service; with a nationwide list of knights' fees at the Exchequer's disposal, income naturally increased. Henry's successful wars also brought him income from plunder.

Forest covered over a quarter of England, and it all belonged to Henry. The draconian forest laws were instituted by his Norman forebears and Henry did not impose them just because he wanted the hunting ground to himself: they were a tremendous source of income, from minerals, timber, charcoal and hay.[136]

In twelfth-century Europe, society followed strict feudal rules concerning the relationship between lords and their vassals. Men were bound to one another through ties of obligation and promise, the apotheosis of which was the ceremony of 'homage', where a vassal prostrated himself before his lord and promised to be his 'man'. It was perceived to be a sacred oath, theoretically only broken by death, or formal renunciation. Kings were at the apex of this system and they could impose their will. The nobility held their estates from the king (they never really owned them, only held them at the king's pleasure), and in return they and their knights offered military service. Vassals, or tenants, owed allegiance to their local lords, as did peasants, who in addition to doing their lord homage and living on his lands, offered a portion of their farming produce and worked the lord's land for three days a week, as well as their own. In theory, the lord was obliged to protect them militarily.

Henry's tenants-in-chief, the great magnates, averaged an annual income in the region of £200. A wealthy knight might have £50 if he was extremely lucky, a priest £5, and a wealthy peasant between £2 and £3.[137] The valued master craftsman Maurice, who enjoyed Henry's favour, earned one shilling per day at the height of his career.[138]

The king claimed the military service of knights from his tenants in chief, the realm's great magnates. These knights were obliged to serve the king militarily for forty days, and in turn, they were supported by infantry from the general population. Over time, however, Henry increasingly preferred to take a tax – scutage – in lieu of a knight's service, to employ paid armies to fight his wars. This tax was generally levied at two marks per knight's fee, and it raised a good deal of money.[139] In Henry's drive to raise funds for his Toulouse campaign of 1159, he collected the immense sum of just over £9,000 from scutage and associated taxes.[140] Scutage contributed to a gradual shift whereby Henry was raising funds outside the feudal system; and not only through scutage, but also through his taxes on the inhabitants of towns.

Once in a while, Henry was presented with an opportunity that was financially irresistible; one such occasion was Henry of of Essex's error.

Henry of Essex had been loyal to Stephen, although he had transferred his allegiance to Henry when Stephen died. He often travelled with Henry, and held several posts, including royal constable, and sheriff of Buckinghamshire and Bedfordshire. He also held, by hereditary right, the post of royal standard-bearer. It was in a forest in 1157, while campaigning against Owain lord of Gwynedd to assert his control over Wales, that Henry of Essex mistakenly thought the king had died during an ambush. He dropped the royal standard and shouted out to all that Henry was dead. Henry, however, quickly regrouped, led his men out of danger and forced Owain of Gwynedd to sue for peace.

Henry of Essex's career was effectively over, although it staggered on for a while. Six years later, in 1163, he was accused of treason over the incident by Robert de Montfort, who severely injured him in judicial combat. Henry of Essex survived, living out his days in a monastery, his lands forfeited to Henry. Henry never forgot a slight, and was happy to take retribution in a manner that would also enrich himself.

A similar financial penalty awaited the brother of Michael Belet, who held the post of hereditary butler, and served as a judge and sheriff. He witnessed at least twenty of Henry's charters and held high favour. At some point he brought his brother Robert to court. But Robert angered Henry in 1164 by committing an unknown misdemeanour; Henry snatched his estate and fined him £100.[141] Similarly, in 1177 William de Cahagnes was fined 1,000 marks, 'that the king might set aside his anger towards him and confirm his charters'.[142]

There were small fines too that profited Henry. 'Matthew son of William has a debt of half a mark for selling wine contrary to the regulation.' And 'Geoffrey the Fleming owes 20s amercement for bringing a false claim in the king's court.'

These fines were numerous, and they litter the pipe rolls; but every shilling collected added to Henry's coffers.[143]

When his men retired, Henry demanded back any money owed. Reginald de Warenne, when he left court, was obliged to begin paying off his huge debts immediately, in spite of his high standing with Henry.[144] As a rule, Henry exacted repayment of all monies owed, however long it took. A Geoffrey de Neville paid off a debt he had inherited of £9 6s 8d; the Exchequer had been pursuing the money for twenty-four years.[145]

When Henry died, Gerald of Wales wrote that his castles were 'bursting with treasure.'[146]

Henry also prospered from his policies towards England's Jewish communities. He not only taxed them heavily, but used them as a bank. It has been estimated that during a normal year, revenue raised from the Jewish community amounted to a seventh of the total income of the Crown.[147] When Henry levied his Saladin Tithe in 1188 on personal property, Jews had to pay one-quarter rather than the one-tenth paid by the rest of the population on their moveable goods. Henry, although he extracted money from the Jews, also protected them. England's Jewish communities thrived under his rule.

Towards the end of Henry's reign, the Jewish financier Aaron of Lincoln was the richest man in the country. In 1165, Henry repaid a loan to Aaron. When Aaron died, Henry seized his entire estate, purportedly worth as much as £100,000; it was his legal right, although one he rarely exercised. Aaron's fortune was too large to resist. He sent Aaron's treasure to France, but it sank on the way, in February 1187. Aaron's debtors, however, who numbered William the Lion of Scotland, and the archbishop of Canterbury, still owed £15,000. The amount was so enormous that a separate branch of the Exchequer was established to collect the debt – the Scaccarium Aaronis, or Aaron's Exchequer.[148]

The Jews, denounced by Gospel writers as the murderers of Jesus, occupied a nebulous and often dangerous place in Christian society. The entire Jewish population was guilty for evermore, in the medieval Christian mind, of the crime of deicide. They were destined to be outcasts in Europe.

Church law, taking a Jewish law from Leviticus – 'Take no interest from him or profit, but fear your God, that your brother may live beside you' – prohibited Christians from practising usury.[149] Usury tended to be the only occupation open to Jews, who were usually barred from other trades and professions. Christian kings often used the Jews as their moneylenders. But many of the host population resented the debts they owed to the Jews, often resulting in violence and death. The first Norman kings understood how vital Jewish economic activity was to the swift flow of finance; to ensure its continuity, they sought to protect the Jews. Henry did too.

Most of England's Jews came from Rouen following a massacre there in 1096 by knights embarking on the First Crusade. William the Bastard witnessed at first hand the financial boost Jewish communities could give to the wealth of the Crown, and he welcomed them as the country's bankers and merchant class. William Rufus liked them far more than his Christian contemporaries were happy with, and Henry I issued the communities with a charter of protection.[150] Jews settled in all the major towns of England – London, Winchester, York, Cambridge, Oxford, Norwich and Bristol. In London they lived in Jewry Street, and Old Jewry. The one surviving pipe roll for the reign of Henry I notes Jewish economic activity.

Prior to Henry's accession, however, the Jews had endured England's first blood libel, the vicious slander that the Jews killed a Christian child to use its blood for their Passover bread – and its consequences. An English invention of the time – this dark myth still persists in some corners of the world today – it is no accident that the blood libel took place under Stephen's weak rule. It happened at Norwich on the night before Easter in 1144. A twelve-year-old boy, William, was found dead, and the story spread – with no proof or evidence – that the Jews were responsible. Although the local sheriff did his best to protect the Jewish community, a knight who was in debt, murdered his Jewish creditor (by law, a Jew's death cancelled out his borrower's debts).[151]

Two years later, in 1146, Bernard of Clairvaux thought the Jewish community in England in possible peril. During the First Crusade, in 1096, crusading pilgrims had murdered Jews as they passed through Europe on their way to Jerusalem. Over 5,000 people from the communities of Speyer, Worms, Mainz, Cologne, Regensburg, Metz, Prague and other cities lost their lives. Priests and burghers were, for the most part, powerless to save them in the face of an army of zealots. Bernard feared a similar bloodbath as he preached the Second Crusade, and he warned crusaders against harming the Jews of England, France and Germany. Bernard's outcry meant that hundreds, rather than thousands, perished in Germany and central Europe. The Jews of England were left unharmed.

The golden age for English Jewry came with Henry's accession. He not only extended his grandfather's charter of protection, but allowed the Jews autonomy to govern themselves by Talmudic law. The chroniclers were unhappy with the favour they believed Henry showed to the Jews. William of Newburgh blustered, 'By an absurd arrangement they were happy and renowned far more than the Christians, and, swelling very impudently against Christ through their good fortune, did much injury to the Christians.'[152] This was a wild caricature, but it showed that Henry's policy was not a popular one.

Jewish communities were established in new economic centres of activity: Exeter, Bedford, Devizes, Ipswich, Canterbury, and elsewhere.[153] The Jews' international connections meant that scholars from Germany and Spain came to England too. The wandering Spanish scholar Abraham Ibn Ezra visited London in 1158 and northern France. It is possible, in the light of Henry's interest in Arabic learning, that this Jewish poet, scientist and biblical scholar met with the king. Conditions under Henry's rule were so favourable that Jews from other parts of Europe came to settle in England. In 1168, Frederick Barbarossa complained that so many members of his most lucrative community were leaving Germany to settle in England.[154]

* * *

Henry used his vast wealth in the service of power; in England the pipe rolls provide us with the expenditure of Henry's ambitious building programme. The direction for new building came from Henry himself, noting the state of his castles, palaces, bridges, kitchens, hospitals and other structures, and the requirements for new ones as he continued the ceaseless round of his empire. During Henry's reign, there was no Master of the King's Works – the action was performed by the king himself.[155] The similarity of Henry's buildings suggests that he used many of the same craftsmen across his dominions.

He used his money to build, whether a magnificent kitchen at Fontevraud, a leper hospital at Caen, the refurbishment of the cathedral where he married Eleanor at Poitiers, or his showcase castle, Dover. Henry, embarrassed that Dover in the late 1170s did not adequately reflect his great wealth, spent nearly £7,000 refurbishing it. The modern historian John Gillingham has argued that Henry used Dover for entertaining guests after he was caught unawares by Louis' sudden visit in 1179.[156] The works were started in 1180 and completed by Richard in 1191.[157]

Henry's castles were 'the bones of the kingdom', according to William of Newburgh. Whoever held them, held the country. They were fundamental to the security of Henry's lands, and he spent a huge amount on their erection and maintenance. He made them virtually impregnable, at a cost of over £20,000 during the course of his reign.[158] When he was threatened, as in the Great Revolt of 1173–4, he spent more on castles.[159] These, coupled with his innovative siege engines and other groundbreaking machines of war, built for him by his skilled engineers, meant that in siege warfare Henry was virtually unbeatable.[160]

Henry refurbished those castles he chose to keep, and built new ones throughout his dominions; in Normandy, at Gisors; at Ancenis, between Anger and Nantes; and in England at Orford (with its intriguing polygonal design), Nottingham, Scarborough and Newcastle. In 1176, Henry 'took every castle in England into his hand, and removing the castellans of the earls and barons, put in his own custodians; he did not even spare his intimate counsellor, Richard de Lucy, the justiciar of England but took from him his castle of Ongar'.[161] From 1176, Henry was at the height of his power; it was from this period that he began to style himself 'Henry, by the grace of God, king of the English, duke of the Normans, duke of the Aquitanians, and count of the Angevins'.

Henry spent nearly as much on his favourite houses, among them Clarendon (the house he declared 'which I delight in above any other') and Woodstock, as he did on his castles. There was a garden outside his bedchamber at Arundel, dovecots at Nottingham, a fish pond, with wine continuously making its way towards his residences. Henry enjoyed luxury.[162]

He was also interested in hospitals and leper colonies. In his funding of leper colonies, Henry possibly had in mind his cousin, Baldwin 'the leper king' of Jerusalem.[163] Baldwin, when he was a child, contracted leprosy, an extremely painful and debilitating condition which affects the skin and nerve endings. It was Baldwin's tutor, William of Tyre, who first noticed the disease. When he was play-fighting with his friends, he seemed to feel no pain. William wrote that Baldwin 'endured it all patiently, as if he felt nothing ... At first I supposed it proceeded from his endurance, but I discovered that he did not feel pinching or even biting in the least ... we recognised in the process of time, these were the premonitory symptoms of a most serious and incurable disease.'[164] This contagious condition was prevalent throughout Europe and it terrified people, despite the fact that it affected only roughly one in 200.[165]

Henry, superstitious and perhaps as a bid to ward off the disease, built leper hospitals, also called 'lazar houses' after Lazarus in Luke's Gospel who lay down 'covered with sores'. He built them at Fontevraud, Angers, Caen, Bayeux, and Rouen.[166] He also built churches, abbeys, bridges, kitchens, palaces, parks and hunting lodges throughout his empire, in England, Normandy, Aquitaine, Maine, Touraine and Anjou. He even built a dyke thirty miles long on the Loire plain between Tours and Saumur to prevent it from flooding.[167]

There was little that did not interest Henry, both in its detail, and as a show of wealth and power. Henry was fascinated by architectural innovation and design: the unique, octagonal Byzantine-Romanesque-style kitchen, or smokehouse, at Fontevraud Abbey near Chinon, with its painstaking craftsmanship, was built under his direction and patronage. Monastic kitchens were usually square or rectangular, but the building at Fontevraud reflected Henry's interest in construction design, and similar kitchens were built throughout his lands, at Canterbury, Marmoutier and Caen.[168]

In the 1170s, as a part of the penance he owed the pope for his role in Becket's murder, he built abbeys, magnificent structures to promote God's glory – and naturally the man who paid for them. During the 1170s and 1180s, Henry founded an abbey at Waltham, a charterhouse at Witham in Somerset, and a nunnery at Amesbury. And notwithstanding his detractors, beginning with Gerald of Wales, who lamented the paucity of Henry's expenditure on these buildings, he in fact spent huge sums of money.[169]

Inside they were a riot of colour, not only in the stained-glass windows, but on the gorgeously painted walls, often illustrated with scenes from the Bible and the lives of the saints. Similarly Fontevraud Abbey, one of the major recipients of both Henry's and Eleanor's patronage, was not the serene, pale and cavernous space we see today. Instead interior walls abounded, and we can see from the remains of the fresco of Henry's grandson, Count Raymond VII of Toulouse, that the walls would have been covered in brilliant hues of reds and yellows.

VII

In 1163, Henry came back to England after an absence of four years.

When he returned, he was horrified at the lack of punishment for clerks charged and convicted of crimes, theoretically under the jurisdiction of the ecclesiastical courts. William of Newburgh wrote that Henry learned that while he had been away, men in clerical orders had committed a hundred murders; there were also many lesser crimes of violence, assault, and robbery.[170] Henry, when he investigated, found that heinous crimes, such as the sexual assault of a girl and the murder of her father by a clerk in Worcestershire, had gone virtually unpunished.[171] The church courts preferred to mete out acts of penance to punish those convicted of violent crimes; with little retribution, misdemeanours ran high.

Henry called a council at Westminster in October, where he attempted to remedy the problem. He 'demanded that clerks seized or convicted of great crimes should be deprived of the protection of the church and handed over to his officers, adding that they would be more prone to do evil unless after incurring a spiritual penalty they were subjected to physical punishment'.[172]

This desire to bring the crimes of villainous clerks to his own courts would eventually lead to a rupture of such drama that it would almost ruin him; but, in the early 1160s, Henry could not know that. His investigation did, however, bring the law to the king's attention – and from 1163, Henry began to reform the legal system he had inherited.

It is doubtful that he set out with a great programme for change, but by the end of his reign, Henry's reforms had transformed England's legal and judicial landscape. Over a period of twenty years, the changes he wrought would form the foundations upon which the English legal system as we know it today would be built. Henry is 'the one king of England who has most claim to be regarded as the founder of the English Common Law'.[173] His innovations to the practice, procedure and system of justice have arguably done more to establish and embed the rule of law in England than any other monarch before or since.

Henry was not content to entrust the job of reform to others; he involved himself in every aspect, no matter how small. He was said to have stayed up at night pondering judicial language, 'perpetually wakeful and at work'.[174] The author of the Chronicle of Battle Abbey wrote of Henry's involvement in the intimate detail of legal draftsmanship when the monks petitioned the king to have one of their founding charters renewed. Henry, in consultation with his barons, agreed and, in renewing the charter, 'himself dictated another [phrase] never before employed'.[175]

Walter Map, who was a royal justice as well as a clerk and a chronicler, wrote that Henry was the 'subtle inventor of uncustomary and hidden judicial process', and that he had 'discretion in the making of laws and the ordering of all his government, and was a clever deviser of decisions in unusual and dark cases'.[176] Map noted how close Henry could be to the everyday workings of justice:

I had heard a concise and just judgement given against a rich man in favour of a poor one, I said to Lord Ranulf, the chief justiciar: 'Although the poor man's judgement might have been put off by many quirks, you arrived at it by a happy and quick decision.' 'Certainly,' said Ranulf, 'we decide causes here much quicker than your bishops do in their churches.' 'True,' said I, 'but if your king were as far off from you as the pope is from the bishops, I think you would be quite as slow as they.'[177]

Henry called several assizes (meetings between himself and his barons which issued binding decrees) between 1166 and 1184. They numbered the assize of Clarendon, of 1166, which dealt with criminal law; the assize of Northampton, of 1176, which increased the powers of Henry's justices; and the assize of the forest of 1184, which ensured that forest offences were brought within the law. Previously punishment for a forest offence was at the caprice of the king. Roger of Howden – a forest judge as well as a chronicler and diplomat – attended these meetings, and he wrote down the details of Henry's instructions to his judges. Howden's text makes it clear that the orders came directly from Henry: 'This is the assize which King Henry ordered.'[178]

Why did Henry choose to direct his considerable energies into the cause of legal reform? Change was obviously needed: crime was rife and, a decade into his reign, Henry had still not addressed the chaos of those dispossessed of land and property during the civil war. He was alarmed at the power of the ecclesiastical courts. And revenue – never far from his thoughts – from a streamlined legal system would unquestionably be plentiful.

It is likely, however, that for Henry this was more than just a matter of public order and income. It was about the obligations of a prince to dispense justice. Henry, who modelled much of his kingship on that of his grandfather, would have recalled the promise in Henry I's coronation charter of 1100 to 'rule justly'. The grandson would honour this pledge.

Henry's reforms inevitably produced winners and losers, and it is an achievement that his more contentious changes did not spark violent dissent. This owes much to his decision not to graft a form of Roman Law onto the existing system. Instead, he built on what he found when he conquered England, choosing to work with customary law and practice, and improving it little by little. This rooted him to the times of his Anglo-Saxon ancestors – Edward the Confessor, Alfred the Great, and Æthelberht, a deviser of laws dating back to the seventh century. By enriching *English* law and an *English* system of justice, Henry presented himself as the rightful heir not only to his grandfather, but to the hero-kings of Anglo-Saxon England.

Well educated, Henry would also have had the Noahide laws in mind. Before God made his covenant with Abraham, Talmudic legend has it that he gave seven laws to the children of Noah; these were universal laws to be followed by all humanity. Six of the Noahide laws are negative – do not deny God, do not blaspheme, do not murder, do not engage in incestuous, homosexual or adulterous relationships, do not steal, and do not eat a live animal. But the seventh is a positive command: to establish courts and a legal system to ensure the obedience of these laws. Henry's furtherance of the rule of law placed him firmly in the tradition of the judges, prophets and kings of the Bible. In improving the rule of law, he would be seen as a strong and wise king, meting out justice to his people.

Henry's great innovations fall into four areas, each distinctive and yet all interconnected: the role and authority of judges; the organisation of justice; the conduct of cases; and changes to the laws of land and property.

At the beginning of his reign, the number of judges, or justices, were few, and their authority was highly circumscribed. 'The king's justice' still had literal connotations, and it might involve Henry himself issuing writs and judgements, as he did in the case of one Hugh de Neville over a disputed property matter:

I command and order that you shall without delay and justly reseise the monks of St Andrew's Northampton, of their land of Newton and of their men, and justly give back to them their chattels which you have taken thence. And unless you do it my justice of Lincolnshire shall do it. And let me hear no further complaint thereof for want of right. Witness the chancellor. At Northampton.[179]

In practice, this meant the amount of royal justice that could be dispensed was extremely limited: there was after all only one king, however prodigious his work rate may have been.

Access to justice was massively extended when Henry started to appoint judges to travel on circuit courts around the country. He could now take his justice to the people, without having to travel himself. William of Newburgh wrote that Henry was 'most diligent in defending and promoting the peace of the realm ... in appointing judges and legal officials to curb the audacity of wicked men and do justice to litigants'.[180]

He vetted the judges himself, having become close to many of them during the 1160s and his bitter fight with Becket. These were by and large loyal partisans, whom he had known for years. They were exceptionally well educated, some were 'masters' of the cathedral schools, many had ties of friendship and kinship, and these men, his most trusted friends and advisors, were instrumental in aiding Henry to shape the law.

They included his chief justiciars, Robert earl of Leicester and Richard de Lucy. From 1179 Ranulf de Glanville was a judge, as were Richard FitzNigel, Henry's treasurer, and Michael Belet, his butler; Richard of Ilchester, archdeacon of Poitou and then bishop of Winchester, was a justice between 1165 and 1184. Hubert Walter served in the latter part of Henry's reign. Added to their ranks were Henry's faithful servants Geoffrey Ridel, archdeacon of Canterbury and then bishop of Ely, and Geoffrey's great-uncle, who had been a justice of the old king, Henry I.

Geoffrey's cousin, William Basset; John of Oxford, bishop of Norwich, another fierce anti-Becket loyalist; Ranulf of Gedding; Hugh Bardulf; Roger Fitz Reinfrey; Robert of Wheatfield; Godfrey de Lucy, son of Richard de Lucy – who was from 1179 leader of the itinerant justices in the north – also served. Some served for years at a time.[181]

The king's interest in his judges extended well beyond their appointment. Peter of Blois commented on his keen oversight of their performance: 'Truly he does not, like other kings, linger in his palace, but travelling through the provinces he investigates the doings of all, judging powerfully those whom he has made judges of others.'[182]

Henry strengthened the authority of his judges – it became known that if you were sitting before one of Henry's justices, it was as if you were sitting before the king himself. In the latter part of Henry's reign, these justices were empowered by the king to sit in judgement. This took the rendering of justice out of the hands of local landlords, who had been accustomed during Henry's I's reign to preside over the courts themselves. There had been one particularly macabre case in 1124, when forty thieves were tried, six were mutilated and the rest were hanged. It is likely that the pre-eminent landowners in Leicestershire pronounced on this case, rather than the king's justices, who seem to have simply attended.[183] This was far too arbitrary for Henry's liking.

Henry's reforms brought unprecedented change in the protection of free men against their lords. The law began to recognise and protect the individual against landowners by recognising personal status. The regular presence of Henry's justices throughout the country meant that there was a shift from local magnates dispensing arbitrary or corrupt justice, to a system that produced more objective settlements and judgements. Should there be a dispute between a lord and his villein (tenant) as to whether the villein was a freeman, it was Henry's courts who would decide, and not the self-interested local lord.

If Henry provided the impetus for change, it was the tireless and often wearisome work of this small band of judges who travelled around the country on circuit courts, made decisions and meticulously recorded them that truly brought justice to life. They would set out from the 'chief court' at Westminster, and return there when their tour of duty was done. The court at Westminster became a place where circuit judges could meet to compare decisions on similar cases or seek counsel from colleagues on more difficult or complex matters.

Now that cases were heard and decided according to common standards, case decisions could be documented and reviewed by other justices; and once reviewed, they might be used as the basis for future legal precedents. Thus began to emerge the body of English common law as we know it today.

By 1176, Henry's judges were systematically touring the country and offering a recognisably common standard of king's justice. At Henry's assize at Northampton, in January of that year, the country was parcelled into six circuits, to be toured by the king's justices, who would typically stay in a particular shire court for up to three weeks, hearing hundreds of cases. These judges, usually before packed assemblies, were charged with investigating all manner of crimes and misconduct.

They would expect defendants to answer a charge on a named day.[184] If a defendant did not appear when and where required, there were fierce penalties. Henry extended the use of writs to begin legal action – these could only come from Henry, his justices, or his clerks. It is estimated that by the end of the reign, there were roughly thirty standard writs to initiate legal action. This revolutionary process marked 'the routinisation of charisma': the king's word was now everywhere.[185]

* * *

Towards the end of Henry's reign, a book was written that would become one of the most famous in legal history. Its full title is *Tractatus de legibus et consuetudinibus regni Angliæ* ('Treatise on the Laws and Customs of the Realm of England') – and it has been called 'the first textbook on the English common law'.[186]

The treatise opened with a declaration that it was 'composed in the time of King Henry the Second when justice was under the direction of the illustrious Ranulf de Glanville, who of all in that age was the most skilled in the laws of the Realm, and the ancient customs therof, then holding the helm of justice'.

Its authorship has been ascribed to Ranulf de Glanville: sheriff, judge, diplomat and soldier. Ranulf was exceptional, not least because he travelled himself on every circuit court; he was the person 'whose wisdom established the laws which we call English'.[187] Henry trusted him completely, and in 1180, appointed him chief justiciar. He replaced Richard de Lucy who had retired in 1178 or 1179, having served Henry to the last months of his life.

Glanville had seen that reform of the system – the whole organisation and administration of justice – was pressing. He wrote that the courts had been 'so diverse and numerous that they cannot readily be reduced to writing'.[188] Their great number was bewildering to the population – and to add to the confusion, Norman and Anglo-Saxon law ran side by side: William the Bastard never sought to supplant Anglo-Saxon law, but to enable Normans to have Norman law at their disposal too.

There was certainly no shortage of law courts; England had several types which dated back to Anglo-Saxon times, from the tiny village (or vill) court, which upheld the village laws, to the local manorial court, dealing with issues between a lord and his peasants and tenants; the larger hundred courts, which brought together several village courts, and tended to adjudicate on less grievous crime; the shire courts, which generally dealt with more serious offences and matters of tort; borough courts; the king's court, which operated wherever the king was, and acted as the supreme court; and numerous ecclesiastical courts, dispensing justice to the clergy, yet also dealing with matrimonial disputes and the breaking of oaths.[189]

The jurisdictions of these courts were vague: it was unclear, depending on your place in society and where you lived, where you would present your plea – whether to the ecclesiastical courts, the vill courts or the hundred courts.[190] Litigation could be prolonged for years, taken before different courts.

The case of Richard Anstey exemplifies how disjointed the system was before Henry initiated his reforms. When Richard's wealthy maternal uncle William de Sackville died, Richard claimed that he was his heir, rather than William's daughter, Mabel de Francheville. Richard maintained that Mabel was illegitimate, as her parents' marriage had been annulled by Bishop Henry of Winchester, because of an existing pre-contract between her father and another woman; he was therefore his uncle's nearest legitimate heir. Furthermore, Richard claimed that before his death, William had 'instituted' him – acknowledged him formally – as his legal heir.[191] William's wealth was considerable; not only did he own lands on the continent, but also in Essex, Hertfordshire, Suffolk and Norfolk.

To pursue his case, Richard first brought a suit against Mabel in 1158, before Richard de Lucy, Henry's co-justiciar. But as the basis of Richard's claim was Mabel's illegitimacy, it then went before Theobald, archbishop of Canterbury. Theobald referred it to papal judges, who took the case to Rome, where Pope Alexander III finally pronounced Mabel illegitimate. Now, however, Richard was obliged to continue his suit in England and the secular courts. He was duly informed that only Henry could decide the matter. He chased the king around south-west France in order to get a judgement, and Henry finally ruled on the case himself in 1163, in Richard's favour. Justice, it seemed, served the wealthiest and most determined: the case had taken five years and cost Richard the vast sum of nearly £350, not least from expenses incurred in employing three canon lawyers.

Under Henry's gradual systematisation of court standards and procedures, it became the norm that defendants would be summoned by writ to appear at a specified time to answer a charge; that punishment would be meted out for false excuses (false essoins) for absence from court by a litigant; that courts would meet each day and for a full day, instead of at intervals and for only part of the day; and that written records of proceedings were kept.

The introduction of standardised writs was a revolutionary spur to the system. The standard-form writ of 'novel disseisin' – a fast legal remedy for those who had been unlawfully dispossessed of their land – could only be issued from the chancery; its wording was always the same, save for the particulars:

The king to the sheriff, greeting: *N.* has complained to me that *R.* unjustly and without judgement has disseised him of his free tenement in *such-and-such* a vill since *my last journey to Normandy*. I command you, therefore, that if *N.* gives you security for prosecuting his claim, you are to see that the chattels which were taken from the tenement are restored to it, and that the tenement and the chattels remain in peace until *the Sunday after Easter*. And meanwhile you are to see that the tenement is viewed by twelve free and lawful men of the neighbourhood, and that their names are endorsed on this writ. And summon them by good summoners to be before me or my justices on *the Sunday after Easter*, ready to make recognition. And summon *R.*, or his bailiff if he himself cannot be found, on the security of gage and reliable sureties, to be there to hear the recognition. And have there the summoners, and this writ, and the names of the sureties. Witness, etc.[192]

For the first time, every step in the process was thoroughly considered: from the sheriff being ordered to summon the defendant to court at a particular day and time, to his taking the relevant goods into his possession, and to his bringing together twelve men of good character to serve on the jury – these were the essential ingredients for the smooth running of the courts and execution of justice. Towards the end of Henry's reign, another new device would help speed up the process: the 'returnable' writ. This humble innovation, which required the sheriff to return a writ to the court, once served, gave the judge written authority to begin proceedings and to issue further instructions as necessary.

Henry's reforms sought not only to streamline the judicial system, but also to improve its efficiency by rooting out corruption – particularly among the sheriffs. Sheriffs generally came from the families of local lords. In 1170, Henry, briefly back in England, and concerned at reports of corruption in local government, turned their world upside down when he ordered a new commission. It became known as the 'Inquest of the Sheriffs'. He ordered that 'inquiry should be made as to what and how much the sheriffs or their bailiffs have received from each hundred and each village and each man, since the lord king crossed to Normandy ... and let inquiry be made about allegations, their cause, and the evidence for them'.[193]

Most of the sheriffs were dismissed. Of the twenty sheriffs charged with corruption in 1170, by the end of September only six remained, four of whom were from Henry's household. From now on, the post would be held mainly by professional clerks. It was purely administrative, without lustre and therefore without attraction for the ruling classes, subordinate to Henry's judges.

* * *

How was a case prosecuted, prior to Henry's reforms? It was mostly delegated to God, and it could be deadly. Although juries did exist, frequently neither supporting documents were presented nor were witnesses examined properly. Instead, trial took place by oath, or by ordeal.

Trial by oath meant that witnesses would be called by both parties to swear that the plaintiff and the defendant were telling the truth. These witnesses would often be asked to swear on a holy relic; it was assumed that few lied. Otherwise, it was believed, divine retribution would visit them.

Trial by ordeal was either by battle, water or fire. Ordeal by battle required accused and accuser, or their nominated champions, to fight it out.[194]

There were two ordeals by water – hot and cold. By hot, water was brought to boiling point, and the prisoner was made to put their hand in, either up to the wrist or up to his elbow, depending on the nature of the crime, and pick up a stone. They were then bandaged for three days. When the bandages came off, if there was no scalding, they were deemed innocent. If, however, they were scarred, it was assumed they were guilty. By cold, the accused was tied up and tipped into a pond; if they floated, they were guilty, and if they sank, they were innocent. Other tortures included ordeal by fire, where the accused was made to walk three steps holding a red-hot poker, which had been blessed by a priest. Again, if God miraculously healed their scars, they were innocent.

Naturally, there were not many divine interventions, and many died or were maimed in these trials by ordeal. Henry was keen to get away from such practices, preferring to build on the Anglo-Saxon tradition of trial by jury, or a group of men who swore to tell the truth. Nevertheless, ordeal by submersion in water continued to be used in serious criminal cases throughout Henry's reign, perhaps for its perceived value as a deterrent. Trials by ordeal gradually went out of favour and were eventually abolished in 1215.

Under Henry, trial by jury was made available for civil cases that related to land and property. The jury would consist of men who knew the person attempting to establish that a piece of land or property was rightfully his, and their role was primarily to 'fact-find'. In an ideal case, they would remember how he had come into possession of the property, or otherwise they could attest if he had farmed the land, or for how long he had lived there. Their inquiry was limited: the jury were only to establish if he had been unlawfully dispossessed of the property, and not the rights and wrongs of how he had acquired it in the first place.[195] That issue could be addressed by an appeal court.

Criminal matters were treated differently. Henry was apparently concerned about crime, and his treasurer, Richard FitzNigel, wrote of a 'crime wave', linked, he believed, to increased economic prosperity and the ability to buy more alcohol. Serious criminal offences were murder, rape, robbery, arson, treason and forging money or the king's seal.[196] We do not have reliable crime figures for Henry's reign, but the figures in Lincolnshire for 1202 cite 114 murders, eighty-nine robberies, sixty-five woundings and forty-nine rapes.[197]

The courts would use the services of a 'presenting jury' to try criminal offences. Here, men swore an oath to tell the truth, would examine the facts, and advise. They would not, as they do today, pronounce a verdict. This was left to Henry's judges. Minor cases, however, would be tried at the shire court, and would not come before the itinerant judges.

It would seem that by the end of Henry's reign, a presenting jury would name the accused, who would be arrested and imprisoned, and brought to trial before the king's justices when the eyre (roving court) next met. If found guilty, a person could be hanged, or mutilated, with their right hand and foot cut off.[198] Glanville wrote that judges pursued every avenue to give the defendant justice: 'The truth of the matter shall be investigated by many and varied inquiries and interrogations, and arrived at by considering probable facts and possible conjectures both for and against the accused, who must in consequence be either completely absolved or made to purge himself by the ordeal.'[199]

* * *

In twelfth-century England, land meant wealth. From the mid-1160s Henry began the reformation of land law, predominantly inheritance law. His primary motivations were public order and money.

Henry had come to power just over a decade before, after nineteen years of civil war. His victory was not, as he desired, the decisive subjugation of his enemy by battle, but instead a diplomatic compromise. The author of the Chronicle of Battle Abbey noted of the civil war that 'he who was strongest got most, and everyone held on to what he had seized as if by right'.[200] In the aftermath of war, there were many competing claims for land, where rightful owners had been dispossessed and others took the opportunity wrongfully to seize their property, thus sowing the seeds for potential civil strife and public disorder.

Henry was determined to bring land and property ownership into the courts, for his justices to establish legal and binding ownership. The most successful of his land law reforms were those of 'novel disseisin' (whether a tenant had been unlawfully deprived of his land) and 'mort d'ancestor' (whether the claimant's ancestors owned the land, and was the claimant the rightful heir). It is possible that Henry had in mind his own experiences, when developing mort d'ancestor: his rights had, after all, been usurped by Stephen.[201]

Henry's assize in 1176 at Northampton brought a welcome clarity to the resolution of these disputes and an unmistakable warning to anyone minded to defy the court's decision:

If any freeholder has died, his heirs should remain possessed of such seisin as their father had of his fief on the day of his death; and they should have his chattels from which they may execute the dead man's bequests; and afterwards they should seek out the lord and pay him the relief and anything else that is due from the fief ... And if the lord of the fief should deny the heirs the seisin of the said deceased which they claim, the justices of the lord king shall cause an inquiry to be made by twelve lawful men as to what seisin the deceased had on the day of his death; and as that inquiry establishes it, so shall restitution be made to his heirs. And if anyone shall do anything contrary to this and is convicted of it, he shall be at the king's mercy.[202]

By making the inheritance of land more certain, the number of violent incidents fell. Brawls were not uncommon in cases of disputed land or property, and by providing a legal solution Henry diminished this threat to public order.

In ensuring that property disputes were heard in his courts, rather than in the courts of the local lords, Henry also brought more coin to his treasury. The profits of justice were a staggering source of wealth for the Crown. During 1176–7, income from court fees, fines and the forest was in the region of £30,300; to put this in perspective, farm payments that year were only £4,300.[203] (Not all the proceeds of justice reached their rightful destination: the king's judges not only received a salary, but they took bribes too, whether of money, food or other gifts. These kickbacks never appeared in the pipe rolls.)

But it was not all about the money. It is probable that Henry had loftier considerations too; as king, it was his duty to protect his subjects' lawful rights to inherit their land, unmolested.[204] He insisted, for example, on protections for the rights of widows: any widow who had been wrongfully deprived of any portion of her dower on her husband's death could now petition the king's court to remedy the position.[205] Even Gerald of Wales, ever the harsh critic, believed Henry to be 'a fine administrator of justice for the downtrodden'.[206]

As his reign progressed, Henry's influence on the rule of law was felt everywhere – from the thousands of standard-form writs, marked with the king's seal, that began the judicial process, to his assizes, his streamlining of the myriad courts, his investigations into corruption, and his hand-picked itinerant justices, invested with the authority of the king. By the end of Henry's reign, theoretically at least, the king's justice was available to anyone who could afford to pay for it.

VIII

Henry was 'the one who holds England and all the seaboard between Spain and Scotland, from shore to shore'.[207]

The area under Louis' control was slight compared to that of his mighty vassal. When Henry was crowned, Louis accepted the inevitable; he made an accommodation with him and, apart from a small number of battles where the English king easily defeated him, Louis gave Henry little trouble for twenty years. Henry, following his mother's advice, let Louis keep his dignity, when he could.

To compete with the might of Henry FitzEmpress would, for Louis, have been ill-advised. To his contemporaries, Henry 'prospered in everything, as though accompanied by the favour of God'.[208]

Henry had broken the power of any magnate who dissented. Instead, the first threat to his rule came from close to home: his younger brother. Geoffrey was jealous of Henry's power and disappointed in his inheritance of just a few castles, including Chinon, Mirebeau and Loudon. He spread the story that on his deathbed, their father left instructions that should Henry become king of England, he was to relinquish Anjou, Touraine and Maine to Geoffrey.[209]

Geoffrey was an opportunist looking for an inheritance. He had attempted to kidnap Eleanor on her journey to Poitou in 1152, following her divorce from Louis, presumably to force her into marriage and gain Aquitaine. In December 1155 Geoffrey demanded his fictitious inheritance and went to war. The following month, Henry crossed to Normandy to deal with him.

He met with Louis, who recognised him as count of Anjou. By now, Louis had decided to forgive Henry for his marriage to Eleanor, at least publicly. Henry then brought in his immediate family to coerce Geoffrey into submission – at Rouen, Geoffrey was forced to hold peace talks with not only Henry, but also their mother, Matilda, their aunt Sibylla, countess of Flanders, and William, their brother. We can imagine the pressure exerted on Geoffrey by his family. Geoffrey, however, saw this as his only opportunity to gain real power for himself and refused to listen. He left Rouen for Anjou to fortify his castles, but few would join him now Louis had recognised Henry as count.

Geoffrey eventually submitted to Henry in the summer, and settled for an allowance of £3,000 and the county of Nantes in Brittany, which Henry arranged for him.[210] Although Henry was harsh with the viscount of Thouars, who had assisted Geoffrey in his uprising, he was generous and forgiving with his brother. Later, this would be a pattern when those he loved rose up against him; his cup of forgiveness was too deep. But the problem of Geoffrey ever rebelling again was removed when he died suddenly in 1158. He was twenty-four years old.

Henry was rarely defeated. Nantes was given over to him in 1158; he acquired Brittany in 1166, betrothing his legitimate son Geoffrey to its heiress, Constance, and deposing Constance's father, Conan – the duchy was fully subjugated by 1173; and the Welsh princes, Owain of Gwynedd and Rhys ap Gruffudd of Deheubarth, were both forced to pay him homage. The kings of Scotland had taken advantage of Stephen's weak rule to encroach south of the border, taking Northumberland, Cumberland and

Westmorland. Henry, however, drove them back. Although they took every opportunity to harass him, Henry's capture of William the Lion in 1174 left the Scottish kings weak dependants of the English crown.

Henry the victor was magnanimous; on the rare occasions that he faltered in battle – Toulouse in 1159 (his first taste of defeat), and in Wales in 1165 – he was ruthless with himself, and others.

In 1159, Henry attempted to conquer the county of Toulouse in Eleanor's name – she claimed it through her maternal grandmother, Philippa. Whoever held Toulouse had access to the tremendous wealth generated by trade between the Mediterranean and the Atlantic via the River Garonne. Henry already held Bordeaux, where the river flowed into the Atlantic, through his marriage to Eleanor. Toulouse was ruled by Louis' brother-in-law, Count Raymond V: he was married to Louis' sister Constance. As far as Henry and Eleanor were concerned, Count Raymond was not the rightful ruler. Louis had attempted to win Toulouse for Eleanor in 1141, but had failed. Now, Henry left Eleanor in England as regent, and gathered an enormous army. They arrived in July.

The Toulouse expedition was the largest campaign of Henry's career: he threw everything he had at it. Thomas Becket was a particular advocate and had raised taxes for the campaign. (He was later accused of charging the church an excessive amount.) Thomas's retinue alone sported 1,900 cavalry and 4,000 infantry.[211] Henry was joined by his ally Ramon Berenguer IV, count of Barcelona and prince of Aragon. In return for Ramon's military support, Henry agreed to a marriage between Ramon's daughter and his son, Richard. Together, they planned that one day the couple would rule Aquitaine.[212]

Count Raymond placed himself inside Toulouse, preparing for a long siege. Toulouse had access to fresh water inside the city, and it was protected by three sections of seemingly impenetrable walls. The count believed it would be impossible to take by force.

Henry was not, however, disheartened; he had rarely lost a siege.[213] But all hope of success was stymied when Louis decided to support Raymond. Louis feared Henry's power; he knew that if Henry took Toulouse, his own land route to Rome would be severed.[214] He placed himself in the city, making it morally impossible for Henry to attack; Louis, after all, was overlord for his lands in France. Henry attempted to draw Louis out of the city by sending forces north to attack his lands, but Louis would not budge. Henry was forced to retreat.

Just as Louis had failed in 1141, so did Henry. But it was not a complete disaster. Henry lost no territory. He even made some gains in the Vexin. He captured the city of Cahors, roughly seventy miles north of Toulouse, and the region of Quercy.

Henry's burning of the countryside around Toulouse was devastating for the population; but a thwarted Henry was not simply being vindictive. It was a show of power.

In the end, it was not battle that ravaged Henry's army, but sickness. Many of his men succumbed at the end of September. Casualties included William of Boulogne, Stephen's surviving son who had tried to assassinate Henry. William died in October, childless. Henry now broke the remnants of Stephen's family. He ordered Stephen's daughter, Mary of Boulogne, out of her convent at Romsey and forced her into marriage with his cousin, Matthew of Flanders, to strengthen his influence there, and to gain access to its famous men of war. Matthew, on his marriage, became count of Boulogne and a surviving document from 1163 stipulated that Matthew, together with his father Thierry of Flanders, provide Henry with 1,000 knights, as required, in return for £500 per year.[215] William was buried, separated from his family in death, at the Poitevin abbey of Montmorel; his mother, father and Eustace all lay at Faversham Abbey in Kent.

Henry's second difficult campaign was in 1165, against the Welsh princes. Disregarding their homage, they took advantage of Henry's preoccupation, when he was away from England in

Normandy on a diplomatic mission. While Henry attended a conference with Louis and the count of Flanders, and met with ambassadors from the court of Frederick Barbarossa, the princes took up arms against Henry. He had to rush back to England to raise an army against the Welsh, whom he fought in the Vale of Ceiriog.

Henry's army numbered some 3,000 sergeants and many knights.[216] This was a large army by twelfth-century standards. It remains difficult to be exact, particularly when the chroniclers are so vague, mentioning a 'powerful company', but giving no hard numbers.[217]

But the outcome was inconclusive, and Henry withdrew with his hostages. He blinded and hanged twenty-two Welshmen, including five Welsh princes.[218] Henry was magnanimous in victory; but in an indecisive fight, or a loss – as with the burning of the Toulouse countryside – he would show his strength through monstrous acts. He may have looked to his grandfather Henry I not only as an exemplar of strong leadership, but also for lessons in the infliction of cruel punishments.

Long, drawn-out campaigns, in Toulouse, and against the Welsh, were Henry's weakness in war. When he acted as an attacker, his characteristic methods of quick assaults, taking castles with astonishing rapidity, meant there was no one to touch him. But whenever Henry was forced to invest in a protracted campaign, long in the planning, he rarely saw a decisive victory.

IX

Henry and Eleanor had at least eight children together over fourteen years, and Henry loved them with 'extreme tenderness'.[219]

Not only did he love them; they also formed another weapon in Henry's arsenal, the girls to make advantageous marriages, and the boys to aid their father in running his empire – or at least that was the idea. The fact that Henry did not pay sufficient attention to his wife, or effectively train his sons for leadership, was to have lasting consequences.[220]

Nevertheless, during the latter part of the 1150s and the 1160s, Henry and Eleanor's family grew. Louis, who remained without a son until 1165 when his third wife, Adela of Champagne, finally gave birth to a male heir, must have looked on in horror. His most powerful vassal, the man who had taken his wife and formed the biggest threat to Capetian power, produced son after son.

Their eldest child, William, died in 1156 when he was two years old. Henry was not in England. He was on the continent dealing with Geoffrey's insurrection, and he left Eleanor as regent. She buried their infant son at Reading Abbey at the feet of Henry I, his great-grandfather.[221] Henry would not return to England for nearly a year. But he had left Eleanor pregnant, and when he returned she presented him with their third child, a new baby daughter, named Matilda.

Henry and Eleanor's second child, Young Henry (Henri), had been born at the end of February 1155. In 1156, when the toddler William died, one-year-old Henri became heir to the throne. Siblings followed in steady succession – Matilda in 1156, Richard in 1157, Geoffrey in 1158, Eleanor in 1161, Joanna in 1165 and John in 1166. Eleanor spent much of the first fifteen years of her marriage either pregnant or the mother of very young children, which may have been one of the reasons why she was a far less active patron than her sister queens and queen consorts.[222]

But even in her later years, we have little evidence of Eleanor's direct patronage, although one historian wrote, rather curiously, that Eleanor was 'the progenitor of the French "renaissance" of the twelfth century'.[223] Although many historians and novelists have written of Eleanor as the 'queen of the troubadours', presiding with her eldest daughter by Louis, Marie countess of Champagne, over the celebrated courts of love, it is simply untrue.[224] We have little evidence that mother and daughter saw one another again after Eleanor fled her marriage, although the possibility for a meeting was there, firstly at Poitiers sometime between 1170 and 1173, and again in 1191 as Eleanor travelled through Champagne on her way to pay Richard's ransom.[225]

Medieval royal families were not close in the modern sense; Henry and Eleanor did not spend a great deal of time together when their children were young, and the nature of Henry's rule over his vast conglomerate of lands meant that he travelled more than most, seeing his young children rarely.

But this was not unusual. Sons went to live with other aristocrats for their education and military training about the age of seven, and girls were married young. Henri went to live in the household of Thomas Becket when he was seven (or perhaps younger.) John and Joanna spent their early years in the care of the nuns of Fontevraud, and John later went to live in the household of his eldest brother Henri, and then to Henry's justiciar, Ranulf de Glanville. By 1183, Ranulf was his tutor and his education must have been superb.

We know little about the children's education – far less than we do about Henry's. From later evidence, we can deduce that the boys all received some education. Despite his reputation for curiosity and learning, and Peter of Blois' description that he was never without 'weapons or books', we have no concrete evidence that Henry owned a library; it is likely, however, that he did. John built up a formidable library in adulthood, containing works in both Latin and French, and Richard's Latin was good enough for him to correct Archbishop Hubert Walter's.[226] The archbishop of Rouen was evidently concerned that Henri should receive a rounded education, one that extended beyond just chivalry.[227]

We know even less about the girls' education. Henry arranged their marriages when they were still very young, as he wove his diplomatic web throughout the courts of Europe. They all left England for their husbands' courts between the ages of eleven and thirteen – Matilda for Saxony when she was eleven (the husband her father chose for her, Henry the Lion, was twenty-seven years her senior); Eleanor for Castile in 1174, when she was thirteen, promised to King Alfonso to prevent Louis forming an alliance; and Joanna for the Norman kingdom of Sicily in 1176 when she was eleven – and any education they received continued in their new homelands. Henry's aunts had been educated when they were young, and it is likely that Eleanor was educated too. Master Matthew, one of Henry's tutors, had also tutored Geoffrey's sisters; there is no reason to suppose that Henry would not have given an exemplary education to his own daughters.[228]

Because Henry and Eleanor travelled so much, other attachments were formed. Richard had a wet nurse named Hodierna, whom he adored. He gave her a pension and arranged for her son, Alexander Neckham, to became abbot of Cirencester. John was cared for by a woman called Agatha, to whom Eleanor was generous.[229]

It was rare that the whole family was together, except for occasional Christmas courts. They were together at Cherbourg for Christmas 1162, and later in the 1160s, Eleanor had all the children with her at Angers, except for Henri who stayed in England.[230] Henry may have wished to see his children more, but his ceaseless travelling prevented it. He usually tried to see Eleanor at Christmas, despite the dangers of the Channel crossing in winter; at least four of their children were born in September or October. Henry would not allow his punishing schedule to let him neglect the begetting of heirs, and Christmas meetings were the perfect excuse.

That Henry was a loving father is demonstrated by his treatment of his eldest illegitimate son, also called Geoffrey. Henry planned his education with care. When Geoffrey was in his early twenties, he sent him to study at the law schools of Northampton, and he possibly studied in Paris. Later, after 1175, he was at the schools in Tours.[231] As an adult, Geoffrey filled his household with scholars. He counted Peter of Blois a friend; Peter dedicated his life of St Wilfred to Geoffrey.[232]

Henry had this son brought up alongside his legitimate children and he would raise him high. It is likely that Geoffrey was the child Henry liked best.

At the beginning of the 1160s, Henry appeared unstoppable. He was married to an 'incomparable' woman; he had sons to succeed him and daughters to marry into the royal families of Europe; Thomas Becket, an exceptional administrator and soldier, was his chancellor; his court was brilliant; his closest advisors served him well; he had begun the extensive reforms to law and administration throughout his domains; he was rich; he was successful in war and diplomacy, and he was on the brink of becoming the most powerful prince of his generation.

The only thing that could possibly have stopped him was himself.

Act III
Pariah

*Put on the new man, who in the likeness of God has been
created in righteousness and holiness of truth.*

Ephesians 4:24

I

On 18 April 1161, Theobald, archbishop of Canterbury, died at
his palace. He had been archbishop for twenty-two years.

Henry had much to thank him for. It was Theobald, working
with Pope Eugenius III, who refused to crown Eustace during
Stephen's lifetime; Stephen was so furious that Theobald was
forced to flee to Flanders. Theobald was instrumental in the
diplomacy that ensured Henry's bloodless accession, and
crowned him king of England. He had a reputation for being
'noble and honourable', and during the early part of Henry's
reign was one of his chief advisors. Henry respected him and
listened to his advice.

At Theobald's suggestion, Henry appointed the archbishop's
charming and talented clerk, Thomas Becket, his chancellor. The
post of chancellor was the most important in Henry's household,
as the chancellor held the king's seal. The appointment took place
in early 1155, very soon after Henry's accession.

Thomas Becket was born thirteen years earlier than Henry, on 21 December 1120, the feast of St Thomas the Apostle, in a large house in Cheapside in the City of London. He was the son of a wealthy Norman merchant family; his parents were Gilbert and Matilda Becket.

They educated their son well, at the Augustinian priory at Merton, and then a London grammar school, possibly St Paul's.[1] When he was twenty, Thomas studied in Paris for a year or two at most. Paris was an exciting place to be a student in the 1130s and 40s. The brilliant humanist scholar John of Salisbury was his contemporary – the two would become devoted friends – and the legendary philosopher and theologian Peter Abelard may still have been teaching there (he left in 1140).

Thomas, unlike John, was not an academic. He was most probably in Paris to receive just enough education to enable him to try for a position as clerk on his return. When he arrived back in London he was offered a job by a relative, Osbert Huitdeniers, who was probably a moneylender.[2] Soon afterwards, Thomas gained employ as a clerk in the household of Archbishop Theobald, who may have been a distant cousin.

Becket's contemporary Robert of Cricklade, prior of St Frideswide, Oxford, described him at twenty-two, about the time he entered Theobald's household:

> He was extremely tall, a slim man of pale countenance and dark hair, with a long nose and regular features. He was gentle of manner and sharp of intellect, and he was easy-going and amiable in conversation. He was authoritative in speech, if somewhat stammering. He was so keen in discernment and comprehension that he would always solve difficult questions wisely. His memory was so amazing that whatever he heard of scriptures and legal judgements he was able to cite any time he chose.[3]

Although Thomas was probably in minor orders, he was secular in his tastes. He loved to hunt, and he was an excellent swordsman. He was worldly, charming, and often frivolous – he liked to wear sumptuous clothes. The church, for the time being, was to be the tool of his advancement.

Theobald did advance him. Thomas's abilities impressed him; he sent his clerk to the schools of Bologna and Auxerre for a year to study law. When he returned, Thomas became a member of the archbishop's closest circle of friends, which included his fellow clerks, John of Salisbury and Robert de Pont l'Évêque. Thomas acted as a diplomat, and travelled to the papal court in Rome on Theobald's behalf several times. When Robert de Pont l'Évêque became archbishop of York in 1154, the way was clear for Thomas to step into his place as archdeacon. The office came with many lucrative benefices; it made Thomas wealthy.

As an intimate of Theobald's, Thomas was involved with the diplomatic manoeuvres to position Henry FitzEmpress as Stephen's successor. Henry was impressed with Thomas's talents and personality and took an instant liking to him. Henry, on Theobald's recommendation, offered him the position of chancellor. Theobald, regardless of his fond feelings for Thomas, was keen to have his man close to the king. It was a stratospheric promotion for Thomas, now thirty-four years old.

The office of chancellor was potentially the grandest in the land:

The dignity of the chancellor of England is such that he is considered second to the king in the realm; that he seals his own mandates with the other side of the king's seal, which belongs to his charge ... that he is present in all the king's counsels and may attend even without a summons; that all documents are sealed by his clerks, keepers of the royal seal, and all matters arranged according to his service; likewise, if through God's grace the merits of his life allow it, he may, if he wishes, be made archbishop or bishop before he dies. That is why the chancellorship cannot be bought.[4]

Henry raised Thomas high. No chancellor in English history would ever hold so much power again. He was at the heart of Henry's court and kingdom, the most intimate of his friends. The nobility sent their sons to his household to learn, and they paid homage to Henry's powerful right-hand man.

Thomas's responsibilities were vast: as head of Henry's chancery, and with a large role to play in the Exchequer, he had fifty-two clerks working for him. Henry held him in such high esteem that even Theobald was obliged to use his former clerk as an intercessor between himself and the king. In asking Thomas for a favour, Theobald wrote: 'common report and rumour seems to indicate that you [and Henry] are so strongly of one heart and mind'.[5] Theobald was right; Henry had such confidence in him that Thomas alone was not required to produce his accounts, despite his huge expenditure.[6]

Henry and Thomas not only worked together: 'When the serious work was over, the king and his chancellor played together … in the dining-room, in church, assemblies, or when out riding.' They hunted together, they indulged in Henry's passion for hawking, and they played draughts and chess. On occasion, Henry would enter Thomas's dining room still on horseback, 'perhaps an arrow was in his hand as he returned from or went to the chase … two men never lived in closer harmony and friendship'.[7]

In 1158, Henry sent Thomas to Paris to negotiate the spectacular marriage of three-year-old Henri, Henry's eldest surviving legitimate son, to Louis' six-month-old daughter Margaret. Henry ordered Thomas to put his wealth on display to Louis. He led an embassy designed to amaze contemporaries with its riches, ostentation and pomp, and 'to display the splendour of the English kingdom, and to lavish its wealth, in order that the mission might manifest to the whole world the high dignity of both the king and his representative'.[8]

He was accompanied on the road to Paris by 200 soldiers, servants and clerics. He had twenty-four different suits of clothes made from luxurious fabrics, among them silks and furs. His train carried fabulous tapestries, gold and silver furniture, money, hawks, dogs and monkeys, one each perched on a packhorse.

Thomas's lavish train had the desired effect on the French. They marvelled, saying, 'If the Chancellor of England travels in such splendour, what must the king be?'[9] It was exactly the impression Henry wanted to give, and Thomas was the perfect man to give it. The marriage was arranged.

The following year, in 1159, Henry prepared for war to fight for Eleanor's ancestral rights to Toulouse. He believed he would never fully control Aquitaine unless he held the county. Henry was supported by Thomas and Eleanor; both believed passionately in this venture. Thomas was Henry's instrument in raising the punitive taxes throughout his domains to pay for the war. Once in France, Thomas commanded a force of 700 knights and fought alongside Henry in a bloody campaign. When Henry and his army left Toulouse on 4 September and marched north, Thomas alone, dressed in full armour, led an enormous army of 1,900 cavalry and 4,000 foot soldiers to devastate the Vexin.[10]

Thomas fought for Henry again, in the Vexin in 1161, against Louis' forces. He was once more the warrior, leading men into battle. He ravaged Louis' lands 'with fire and sword'.

Not only did he command, but Thomas fought with his men. When a French knight threatened him on horseback, Thomas attacked: 'With lance couched and horse at the gallop [he] cast him off his horse and claimed his charger as a prize'.

Henry's chancellor and friend inhabited each new role to the full; that was his nature. In war, he was a soldier's soldier: 'In all the army of the English king, the chancellor's knights were always first, always the most daring, always performed excellently, for he trained, led, and urged them on, the signal to advance or retreat being sounded on the slender trumpets which he had, peculiar to his soldiers, but well known to rest of the army.'[11]

There was more to Thomas than just the pursuit of excellence: it was something akin to fervour. Despite Henry's best efforts, Thomas was chaste. Henry slept with many women, and he encouraged his chancellor to join him. Thomas's lack of sexuality was evidently perplexing to Henry, and he 'laid plots day and night to seduce him to fall. But devout and predestined by God, he sought to keep his flesh pure ... he never soiled his chastity.'[12]

Thomas was obsessed with sexual purity and he punished the transgressions of others. When one of his clerics, Richard Ambly, seduced the wife of a friend by lying to her that her husband had died abroad, Thomas expelled Richard from his household and locked him up in the Tower of London.

He chastised his body, and received 'the discipline secretly on his bare back'. Thomas even had his preferred punishers; when he was in London, Ralph the prior of St Trinity would whip him, and in Canterbury he visited Thomas, priest of St Martin, for the same purpose.

Henry and Thomas had an intense friendship and they were forever in one another's company. Jean Anouilh's play *Becket* imagined that the relationship between the two was homoerotic: Thomas was not interested in women because he desired his king, and Henry was alive to that desire.[13] Anouilh conjectured that it was this sexually charged relationship between Henry and Thomas that fractured Henry's marriage with Eleanor, who accused her husband of being 'lured away from the duties that you owe me'. We have no evidence that Thomas ever had a liaison with a woman; if it was because he was in love with Henry – and if Henry reciprocated – we will never know.

The relationship was far from perfect, and by the early 1160s, there is even evidence that it was deteriorating. Henry may have blamed Thomas for pushing him so hard to fight for Toulouse and questioned his advice. In Henry's mind, the campaign had been a failure, and Thomas was an easy and close target for reproach. It was Thomas who had raised the taxes for the campaign, and Thomas who fought with such enthusiasm at the head of a mercenary force.

The pair became familiar enough with one another to bicker, and Henry would tease his chancellor; Thomas complained that he bullied him. William FitzStephen wrote of an absurd incident between Henry and Thomas which supposedly showed the intimacy the chancellor enjoyed with his king. As they rode together in London one cold day, they came across a beggar inadequately dressed for the weather. Henry asked the man if he would like a thick cloak and, instead of offering his own, offered Thomas's new one of scarlet and grey. Henry 'tried to remove it but the chancellor resisted and so quite a scuffle ensued ... At last Thomas gave up the struggle in favour of the king ... Then the king told the story to his nobles who laughed loud and long.'[14] Thomas protested; the episode had underlined his inferior status, and did not sit well with him.

Meanwhile, Archbishop Theobald was failing. As he lay dying in the spring of 1161, he begged his former protégé and his king to visit him; they tarried, both busy in Normandy. A dying archbishop had outlived his usefulness, and Theobald was bitter at Thomas's neglect. John of Salisbury alone was with him at the end. Theobald was buried at Canterbury in the chapel of Holy Trinity. His death created a vacancy for the highest ecclesiastical office in England.

Shortly afterwards, by 1162 at the latest, Henry placed his eldest legitimate son Henri in Thomas's household. It was seen by contemporaries as a mark of the king's regard for Thomas. Henry, however, had a grander plan towards which end his chancellor could serve a purpose: he wanted to crown Henri king in his lifetime, and needed an accommodating archbishop of

Canterbury to assist. Theobald too, despite his disenchantment at the end, had thought Thomas a perfect choice. Now, Henry was determined to ensconce his 'yes man', and succeed where Stephen had failed – in crowning his young son alongside him.

II

The history of the three Norman kings of England – William the Bastard, William Rufus and Henry I – and their archbishops was one of accommodation and compromise. These kings had applied flexibility over the delineation of power between church and state, and a delicate balance prevailed. The kings gave their archbishops dignity where they could, and the archbishops, for the most part, sought to please their kings.

The strength of these kings was noted by the monk and historian Eadmer of Canterbury, Archbishop Anselm's biographer. In William Rufus' and Henry I's time, he wrote, the bishops could not 'lay down any ordinance or prohibition unless these were agreeable to the king's wishes and had first been approved from him'. So too was church jurisdiction over errant clerics limited, for they could not, except with the monarch's approval, 'take action against or excommunicate one of his barons or officials for incest or adultery or any other cardinal offence or even when guilt was notorious lay upon him any penalty of ecclesiastical discipline'.[15]

These late eleventh- and early twelfth-century archbishops of Canterbury were loyal to their king. Lanfranc became archbishop of Canterbury in 1070, four years after the Conquest. He was an Italian scholar from Pavia who became a monk, and then the prior, of Bec in Normandy. He was William the Bastard's advisor before he ever conquered England, and he went on diplomatic missions to Rome at William's behest. When in 1070, Stigand, archbishop of Canterbury was deposed by papal legates, William asked Lanfranc to be his new archbishop. Lanfranc was sixty years old, and he was circumspect. But under pressure from his king-duke and the legates, he accepted, and was consecrated on 29 August. He would be a loyal archbishop, to both William, and William Rufus, whom he crowned.

Lanfranc's successor, Anselm, was also an abbot of Bec. Lanfranc had been his teacher and his mentor. He was elected, in turn, by William Rufus in 1097. Anselm's relationship with William Rufus was more fractious than Lanfranc's had been, as he keenly protected his privileges. It was no accident that it was Anselm, and not the more compliant Theobald, who was to become Thomas Becket's hero. When William Rufus refused to let him call a council, and Anselm refused the king's demands for money and knights from the church, the archbishop went into exile. He journeyed to Rome to seek Pope Urban II's advice. Urban considered excommunicating William Rufus, but Anselm, gentler than Becket and keen to avoid such a catastrophe, asked him not to.[16] By the time Anselm arrived back in England, William Rufus was dead, killed in the New Forest.

After William Rufus' death, his brother Henry moved quickly. The barons would only accept his kingship if he granted them certain freedoms. Henry agreed, and in the absence of Anselm – and before he had been able to negotiate with Henry for similar freedoms for the church – had himself crowned by the bishop of London, and had given the archbishopric of Winchester to his friend, William Gifford.

Although Anselm essentially sought no confrontation with Henry I, he was exiled again between 1103 and 1106, over investiture – the knotty issue of whether or not the king had the right to appoint clerics. In the end, king and archbishop reached an accommodation, when Anselm threatened to excommunicate Henry I. The king, to appease the archbishop, agreed to give Anselm back the revenues from Canterbury.[17]

As a consequence, Henry I agreed with the pope a new compromise. Bishops and abbots would go on paying him homage for their lands (they held about a quarter of England from the king), but he would no longer have the right to invest them with the symbols of their office, and neither could he nominate them.[18] This issue of homage mattered, although Pope Pascal II lamented it: 'It is intolerable that a clerk who has been received into the order of God and has advanced beyond the dignity of laymen should do homage to a layman for earthly wealth.'[19] And yet, compromise there was. It made the system work to everyone's advantage. It was a delicate balancing act, to be sure, but one that was generally successful.

The fractures of Stephen's weak reign, however, had resulted in far more power being ceded to Rome and the church than Henry II's forebears had tolerated. Henry was determined to claw it back, and he had been aided by Theobald, a generous and obliging archbishop of Canterbury.

Theobald strove to work with Henry, and Henry did the same, each respecting the ancient rights of the other. In 1159, with the papacy in schism, they acted in tandem. Schism was extremely dangerous, and Theobald wrote about its perils to Henry. He warned that 'Some of us are prepared to approach or visit Alexander, while others are for Victor.'

He continued: 'While the matter is in suspense, we think that it is unlawful in your realm to accept either of them, save with your approval. It is far from desirable that the English church should be torn asunder after the example of the Church of Rome and by so doing give occasion for a conflict of church and state.'[20]

Henry heeded Theobald's advice; king and archbishop worked in respectful harmony. When the time came to choose, Theobald counselled Henry to support Alexander III as pope over the antipope Victor IV, but was at pains to make clear that the final choice was Henry's. Henry followed the archbishop's advice and gave Alexander his backing.

Archbishop Theobald wrote again to Henry, before he died. He talked of his desire that church and state should show mutual respect: 'When the members of the church are united in loyalty and love, when princes show due reverence to priests and priests render faithful service to princes, then do kingdoms enjoy that true peace and tranquillity which must always be the goal of our desire. But if they clash one against the other, in all their might, then the vigour of the secular power will be impaired no less than the ecclesiastical.'[21]

Theobald evidently trusted that his beloved protégé Thomas Becket, who had worked as one with his king, would continue in this tradition when he put on the pallium of archbishop of Canterbury.

But no one, except Henry and his dead archbishop, was enthusiastic about the prospect of Becket becoming archbishop of Canterbury. Thomas himself thought it ludicrous, exclaiming to Henry, 'What a religious and saintly man you wish to appoint to so holy a see, and over so renowned and holy a community of monks!'[22]

He told the prior of Leicester that if he was ever to become an archbishop, it would be a disaster for him. For 'my lord the king and I know for certain that if I am ever promoted to that dignity I will have to forfeit either the king's favour or … my service to God Almighty.'[23] Nevertheless, in Henry's mind Thomas had served him excellently as chancellor. There was no reason to suppose that he would not serve him equally well in the dual post of chancellor-archbishop.

Matilda advised her son against the appointment. She saw nothing in Thomas's character to recommend him as an archbishop. He was already archdeacon of Canterbury and provost of Beverley, yet as chancellor he had neglected these posts. He was extravagant and ostentatious, although Thomas may have argued that his luxurious lifestyle was only to promote the reputation of his master's wealth.

Matilda is likely to have had a particular experience in mind, which prompted her to query her son's choice. In 1111 Matilda's first husband, Heinrich V, had appointed his exceptional chancellor, Adalbert, as archbishop of Mainz. Mainz, like Canterbury in England, was the most important archbishopric in Germany. In raising Adalbert so high, Heinrich created a huge problem for himself: now, his previously compliant chancellor fervently attested the power of the church. Adalbert abused his power to make his own family rich and Heinrich eventually imprisoned him. For Matilda, the whole episode was unsettling: she would have seen the parallels between Adalbert and Thomas Becket. Matilda believed that Henry, fifty years later, was making a grave error. But frustratingly, there was nothing she could do. Henry was bull-headed; he still listened to her, but did not always follow her advice. Matilda's influence over her son was fading.

The bishops of England and Wales, and the monks of Canterbury, were united in not wanting Thomas Becket for their archbishop.[24] It was a mighty and spiritual office, and hardly anyone believed Thomas to be suitable. Henry, however, would hear no objection, even from the candidate himself, and forced his election through.

He sent Richard de Lucy and his brother Walter, abbot of Battle Abbey, to Canterbury to coerce the monks to elect his choice for their archbishop. They took with them Henry's instructions, by writ. It was a naked threat: 'You should know that it is the king's will that you should have a free vote', but, Henry continued, 'if someone is chosen who does not please the king, you will be in schism and discord and experience not refuge but dispersion ... whereas, if you choose one who pleases the king, you will immediately enjoy no small advantage.'[25]

What choice did the monks have? Although they objected to the imposition of a knight as their archbishop, on 23 May 1162 they elected Thomas Becket unanimously. He was consecrated on 3 June at Westminster Abbey.

Contemporaries observed that Thomas Becket 'became a new man', as he diligently studied theology, washed the feet of paupers, gave abundantly to charity, and took his pastoral duties extremely seriously.

The shift in his thinking appears to have coincided with his receiving the pallium from Pope Alexander III on 10 August. The pallium, a piece of white wool embroidered with crosses and resembling a chain, was worn around the neck. It had great spiritual significance, the lamb's wool symbolising the role of its wearer in protecting his flock. Only the pope and archbishops had the right to wear it. As Thomas put it on and recited the holy oath, he must have felt the enormity of his position for the first time. He promised to 'be obedient to St Peter and the Holy Roman Church'.

Ralph of Diceto wrote that as soon as he had made his oath, Thomas resigned the office of chancellor and sent the seal back to Henry in Normandy. Henry was shocked, and furious. He took it personally.

Now a consecrated archbishop, Thomas thought himself imbued with the power of the church and an equal to his king. He had warned Henry that if he persisted in his plan to make him archbishop, he would be forced to choose between upholding the rights of the church or the rights of his king. But Henry had not listened. His mind was on the coronation of young Henri, and he believed wholeheartedly that his loyal friend would officiate.

Perhaps Henry had in mind Roger, bishop of Salisbury, who had served his grandfather Henry I. Roger had risen high in Henry I's service, initially because of the incredible speed at which he said Mass for Henry's soldiers. This worldly cleric, described as the king's 'manager', had combined his office as bishop with administrating England, ensuring the royal revenue flowed and all the while keeping a mistress, Matilda of Ramsbury. If Roger could do this for Henry I, why not Thomas for Henry II? Thomas, though, was a different man. His model was not Roger, nor even Theobald, but the saintly, spiky Anselm.

When Thomas put on the pallium he threw himself zealously into the service of the church he had sworn to protect. Thomas Becket was a cipher inhabiting a new persona – he would be the most perfect archbishop imaginable, a soldier now for Christ rather than a temporal king: 'No prayer, not even of the king, no letter had any influence with him unless it was accompanied with justice.'[26] Justice, presumably, that was determined by Thomas.

No temporal authority, least of all a prince, could touch him. He increasingly cared little for consequences. Henry would rue his failure to listen to those who had guided him well in the past. His appointment of Thomas Becket as archbishop of Canterbury was the first great mistake of his life.

III

Henry had been absent from England for over four years, fighting in Toulouse, and then remaining in his continental domains. When he returned in January 1163, he was still livid with Thomas for resigning the chancellorship. Thomas met him at Southampton, but Henry turned away from him, announcing his displeasure to the world. In April 1163, Thomas left England for Tours in France to meet with the pope at his general council. Although archbishop now, his entourage was apparently as luxurious as the one he had led to France five years earlier. At Tours, he petitioned Alexander III to have his hero, Anselm, canonised; Alexander, engulfed in the papal schism, was not particularly interested, and Thomas failed.

Thomas Becket had undergone a seismic internal shift; as he strove to protect the church, so Henry, in his mind, became the embodiment of tyranny. It was Becket's duty to save the church from this over-reaching despot who would encroach upon the law of the holy institution to which he now wholeheartedly devoted his life. Henry's worldly chancellor and companion was no more. The king faced an enemy, determined and immovable.

Back in England, Thomas's fight with Henry for the authority of the church began in earnest. Intransigent tyrant met intransigent tyrant. They came to blows first in July at Woodstock, over the issue of 'sheriffs' aid', a tax of two shillings per hide payable to the sheriffs by landlords; now Henry wanted it from Canterbury, but Thomas refused to allow it. Thomas proclaimed that 'it was not right that what was freely given by himself and others should be counted as royal income.'[27]

Thomas provoked the king's wrath. Henry ranted, 'By the eyes of God, it shall be given as revenue and entered in the royal rolls: and it is not fit that you should gainsay it, for no one would oppose your men against your will.' Becket replied in kind: 'By the reverence of the eyes by which you have sworn, my lord king, there shall be given from all my land or from the property of the church not a penny.'[28]

Soon afterwards, Henry and Thomas clashed again, this time over which jurisdiction should govern clerics accused of committing crimes. This was a longstanding sore. In 1154, before Henry became king, Archdeacon Osbert of Richmond was accused of killing his archbishop by putting poison into the chalice he used at Mass. Henry, when he took power, wanted the case tried in the secular courts, but it stayed in the clerical courts, although only by a whisker.[29]

Thomas and Henry were already set on a collision course over the fate of 'criminous clerks'. FitzStephen wrote of the first serious case for Thomas the archbishop, which took place before the summer of 1163: 'The first difference between the king and St Thomas occurred on behalf of a certain cleric of Worcestershire who was said to have violated the daughter of an upright man and murdered her father for the sake of the girl. The king wished to examine and try this cleric in the secular court. The archbishop resisted and had his bishop keep the cleric in custody, lest he should be handed over to the king's justices.'[30]

Henry was concerned that a separate court – the ecclesiastical court – operated in parallel to his own. But he was also vexed that punishments meted out by these clerical courts were negligible. Instead of the terrifying trials by battle or ordeal, clerics might instead be submitted to trial by blessed bread. The accused cleric was made to stand in church before the altar, and eat bread that had been sanctified. If he was guilty, God would punish him by closing his throat, and making him choke. This was hardly a deterrent, and crime among the clerical classes was high.

The reach of the ecclesiastical courts was vast, for they did not simply deal with the misdemeanours of priests. In twelfth-century England, the term 'clergy' applied to anyone who was in minor orders – and that included all university students and some grammar school students, along with numerous accountants, doctors, lawyers and clerks, few of whom were fulfilling priestly duties. Many in major orders took wives and had children, despite being prohibited by Rome, and many visited taverns. At the beginning of the thirteenth century, it is estimated that about 4 per cent of the adult male population in England – some 40,000 men – were in major or minor orders.[31] They could all claim that they were members of the clergy, and as such, if they committed a crime, they could invoke the right to be tried in a church court.

In asserting jurisdiction over clerical courts, Henry was, as far as he was concerned, simply asserting the rights and privileges of his grandfather. In the time of both William the Bastard and Henry I, churchmen had traditionally sought to have violent crimes tried in secular rather than clerical courts, or if not tried in secular courts, at least the punishment would be meted out by the king's justices. Becket, however, disagreed.

Henry proposed a compromise, just as his forebears had done: clerks who had committed 'great crimes' should be tried by the church, and then if found guilty, be handed over to the secular authorities for judgement and punishment.[32] He also wished to put a stop to suspected criminals appealing to the pope, taking them out of the jurisdiction of secular courts. In his determination to reform the legal system, Henry felt it was impossible for him to govern a realm with two separate courts of law, one of the church and one of the state. It went against his plans for centralisation under royal control.

Henry put this proposal to the bishops at Westminster on 1 October, shortly after the grand ceremony that marked the translation within the abbey of the body of Edward the Confessor:[33]

> We have been silent awhile and have meekly observed the attitudes you bishops adopt towards our royal authority and the government of this country. And as we have listened to your views, we have been wondering and humbly searching our mind, as to what fault you should find in us that you should deem us less worthy than other kings, our predecessors, to wear a secure crown; for they, each in turn, enjoyed legal powers and royal prerogatives which no learned man hitherto sought to subtract from the honour of the Crown.[34]

Henry felt he was entirely within his rights, asking only for what his grandfather, Henry I, had had. The king, bolstered by the sainthood recently conferred on his ancestor Edward, must have felt assured of success. But Thomas and the bishops, as one, refused him, claiming that all clergy already had a king in Christ, and should not suffer secular rule of law.

Henry attempted a reconciliation with Becket, at Northampton. Herbert of Bosham, one of Thomas's biographers, wrote about the meeting. Henry tried reason, asking him, 'Have I not raised you from the poor and humble to the pinnacle of honour and rank? How can it be that so many favours, so many proofs of my affection for you, which everyone knows about, have so soon passed from your mind, that you are now not only ungrateful but oppose me at every turn.' To which Thomas replied, 'I am not unmindful of the favours which, not simply you, but God ... has deigned to confer on me through you ... You are my liege lord, but He is lord of both of us, and to ignore His will in order to obey yours would benefit neither you nor me.' Thomas concluded with a feint pledge of loyalty: 'I am ready for your honour and good pleasure, saving my order [the honour he owed to God and the church].' Henry refused to accept the caveat.[35]

Henry retaliated; despite the fact that Thomas had warned him what sort of an archbishop he would be, Henry took away Thomas's castles and titles of Berkhamsted and Eye, leaving him with only Canterbury. Henry also removed his son, Henri, from Thomas's household.

Thomas's next move took their quarrel to a more personal level still. It concerned a marriage.

Henry's youngest brother William had fallen in love with Isabella of Warenne, the widow of Stephen's youngest son. Henry wanted the match as it would place Isabella's wealth and title – the earldom of Surrey – into the hands of his brother. But Thomas, avenging himself against Henry for confiscating Berkhamsted and Eye, refused to allow it. He used the cloak of consanguinity as his excuse – William FitzEmpress and Isabella were distant cousins. William was devastated, and sought comfort with his mother in Normandy.

Meanwhile, Henry, at Westminster, was frustrated that the bishops would not obey him and recognise his 'royal customs'.[36] Arnulf of Lisieux counselled him to pick them off one by one. Individually, they were reluctant to oppose Henry, and he gathered Roger of York, Gilbert of London, Robert of Lincoln and Hilary of Chichester to his side, encouraging them to appeal against Becket to the pope.[37] Henry engaged in furious diplomacy with the pope, dispatching Arnulf and Richard of Ilchester to Sens where the pope was in exile, asking him to give his approval to the 'customs of the realm'.[38]

Unexpectedly, a jostling for position between Thomas and Roger de Pont l'Évêque, archbishop of York, now took place. They had both served as clerks in Theobald's household, and together with John of Salisbury, enduring ties of friendship were established between the old archbishop's protégés. It would seem that Theobald and Thomas Becket protected Roger against a charge of homosexuality with a young boy called Walter.[39] When Walter spread the tale of what he and Roger had done, Roger had the boy blinded, and then sentenced to death and hanged, rather than be found out. Thomas had fought for his friend, persuading Hilary, bishop of Chester, and John of Pagham, bishop of Worcester, to defend Roger to Theobald. Roger, as a result of Thomas's intervention, was absolved, and the pope too was persuaded that he was of moral character.[40]

Their relationship may have soured in the wake of Roger's crime, and a naked enmity took hold between the two. Now, Roger saw an opportunity to make the see of York equal to that of Canterbury; he grasped it, despite all that Thomas had done for him.

Thomas wrote to the beleaguered pope, to request his support. He complained about Roger's behaviour, raising a fear that the church was

> beginning to be subjected to servitude by the repeated blows of hostile fortune ... we mean the lord archbishop of York, who is attempting to deprive the church of Canterbury of her ancient honour, although he should show every respect to her. For although we preside with ancient dignity over our whole province [Canterbury], he has raised cross against cross ... taking advantage of a particular opportunity, as he well knows, thereby symbolising that Christ is divided and making the cross into a cause of scandal.[41]

Alexander sought to find some sort of accommodation between Thomas and Henry, and he pleaded with Thomas to make peace, urging him to 'return to the church of Canterbury and travel as little as possible about the country ... We are giving you this particular advice so that you may not be compelled to renounce the rights and dignities of your church by any fear or misfortune which might fall to you.'[42] Alexander also sent emissaries to Thomas, beseeching him to find a way to accommodate the king. He put Henry's side to Thomas, assuring him that he only looked to have his 'customs' acknowledged.

In December 1163 at Woodstock, and persuaded by Alexander, Thomas finally agreed to give a verbal acceptance of England's ancient customs to Henry.

Henry called a great council at Clarendon around 25 January. Here, at the beginning of 1164, he attempted to bring the church under his control, finally reversing the losses made by Stephen during the civil war. The planning had taken place at Thomas's forfeited manor of Berkhamsted during the king's Christmas court – Henry could be petty. And now he went far beyond what Thomas and the other bishops were expecting.

In front of a council of his barons, Henry intended that Thomas and the bishops should formally express their adherence to the customs of the realm. They should swear 'on the word of truth to the lord king and his heirs that these customs should be kept and observed in good faith without evil intent'.[43]

Two clauses were particularly contentious. The first was that there were to be no further appeals to the pope without Henry's permission. The second concerned the matter of jurisdiction over 'criminous clerks', stating that 'Clerks cited and accused of any matter shall, when summoned by the king's justice, come before the king's court to answer there ... And if the clerk shall be convicted or shall confess, the church ought no longer to protect him.'

Henry reminded the assembled bishops that during his grand-father's reign, clerks were tried in the secular courts. He demanded that they submit to his authority over the dispensing of justice, and swear an oath upholding 'the customs and privileges of the realm'.

Thomas and the bishops were locked in for three days while they made their decision. Many, including bishops Jocelin of

Salisbury and William of Norwich, were terrified of Henry. The king's intimates reinforced the image of Henry the tyrant by promising to visit a dreadful vengeance on any bishop who refused to comply. Furthermore, four of the bishops, including Roger of York, told Thomas that if he did not agree to the king's demand, 'he would fall into [Henry's] hands and be condemned as a disturber of the royal majesty and enemy of the Crown, and killed'.[44]

By the third day, there was no option but to agree. The bishops assented to Henry's demand to uphold the named sixteen ancient customs, known as the Constitutions of Clarendon. But to Thomas's and the bishops' horror, Henry then produced his constitutions as a written document, and commanded that they fix their seals to it. These ancient laws of the kingdom had never been written down before; since William's conquest in 1066, they had been upheld through a delicate balancing act between the king, his archbishops and the papacy. Even Henry's mother Matilda expressed her fear that Henry was making a serious and potentially dangerous error.

Although the twelfth century saw a huge shift in the way information was stored and disseminated – in the historian Michael Clanchy's phrase, a passing 'from memory to written record' – Henry's request was a step too far. As far as Thomas was concerned, Henry had betrayed him; he had promised he would only ask for his verbal consent. For with the constitutions written and recorded in triplicate, at Henry's insistence, there would be no room for nuance or flexibility. Henry was intransigent; he would accept nothing less than to be 'everything he wished' in his domains. Although Thomas had assented through coercion to accept Henry's reforms, he refused to put his seal on the document. He distanced himself at the last minute and the other bishops resented him for it. Gilbert Foliot, bishop of London, wrote bitterly: 'It was the general of our army who deserted, the captain of our camp who fled.'[45]

Thomas hated himself for his partial capitulation. He appealed to Pope Alexander for absolution, stopped performing his priestly duties and underwent a self-imposed regime of relentless physical penance. It is possible that in the wake of Clarendon he began to wear a hair shirt beneath his clothes.

Soon after the meeting at Clarendon disbanded, Henry received news that his brother William had died on 30 January; he was twenty-seven years old. Matilda buried him at Rouen Cathedral. Henry, and William's friends and family, believed he died of a broken heart and they blamed the man who had blocked William's marriage to Isabella of Warenne – Thomas Becket. Becket's interference in Henry's family affairs was cruel and vengeful, and Henry would never forgive him. For Henry, their squabble was no longer a matter of business; it was deeply and viscerally personal and, from this point on, Thomas disgusted Henry.

Three months later, in April, Henry married Isabella to his illegitimate brother Hamelin, creating him earl of Surrey and keeping Isabella's wealth in the family. There was no issue of consanguinity for Thomas to object to. Isabella's views are not known.

In October 1164, Henry latched on to Thomas's unique privilege of not declaring his expenditure when chancellor to catch him. Henry charged him with contempt of court and demanded that he account immediately for £30,000 that had passed through his hands. It was an impossible request. Thomas, believing it to be a trap for imprisonment and even death, was frightened; he was threatened by some of Henry's barons, who reminded him how Henry's ancestors had treated their clergy who would not conform. The king's own father, Geoffrey, they whispered, 'had Arnulf elect of Séez and many of his clergy castrated and forced to carry their members before him in a basin, because he [Arnulf] had accepted the election and they had made it without the count's assent'.[46]

Thomas, however, refused even to hear the court's judgement. When Robert of Leicester attempted to speak with him, Thomas snapped back: 'Are you come to judge me? You have no right to do so ... Such as I am, I am your father, and you are magnates of the household, lay powers, secular persons. I will not hear your judgement.'[47]

Thomas then picked up his processional cross and made his way out of the hall, pursued by some of Henry's angry friends. Among them was Hamelin, still incensed over his brother's death – despite his own marriage to the woman William FitzEmpress had loved.

Thomas realised that his breach with the king was irreparable. He fled the country to Flanders, and then on to France, where he told Alexander III in exile that Henry had attempted to destroy the power of the church by his 'evil customs'.

Henry meanwhile issued an order that no one was to harm his archbishop. He then wrote to Louis, telling him that Thomas 'has been publicly judged in my court by the full council of the barons of my realm as a lawless and perjured traitor ... and he has unlawfully withdrawn'. Henry continued, 'I earnestly pray you not to allow a man disgraced for such wickedness and treasons ... in your kingdom.' Thomas, Henry declared, was his 'former archbishop' and his 'enemy'.[48]

Louis, ever pleased with an opportunity to hinder Henry, ignored his letter and offered Thomas sanctuary. Henry would not see his archbishop again for five years.

IV

Louis welcomed Thomas at Soissons, north-east of Paris. Thomas's mission over the next few years was to present his case to the pope. He believed that had he remained in England, Henry would have murdered him. Exile was the only option open to him.

Pope Alexander was in a difficult positon. He had been elected in September 1159, but it was a split election and two popes emerged – Alexander, and Victor IV. The election had been farcical – and violent. Alexander had the support of the majority of the cardinals, who placed the purple mantle of the papacy around his neck. But it was snatched away by his rival, Victor, whose armed men stormed the basilica.[49] Victor was backed by the Holy Roman Emperor, Frederick Barbarossa, and his massive army. In 1162, Barbarossa invaded Italy, and, seizing the moment, antipope Victor IV occupied the papal throne in Rome. Alexander fled, and sought refuge with Louis.

Alexander was grateful to Louis for sanctuary, and dependent on him for money. But he owed much to Henry, too, who had also supported him against the antipope. He could not afford to offend either prince. Although Alexander may have sympathised with Thomas, he was compelled to tread a careful path. For the next few years he would procrastinate, even while agreeing with Thomas that the Clarendon Laws were not 'good'.

Henry's messengers arrived at Sens to meet with Alexander on 24 November 1164, seeking Thomas's deposition as archbishop of Canterbury. They were extremely persuasive and even used bribes to entice the pope to find in Henry's favour. Alexander, however, refused to condemn Becket; indeed he had welcomed Thomas with the words 'Rightly have you come, dear brother', as he listened to Thomas's complaints. The archbishop was bitter: 'They hurled accusations and malicious charges as pretexts for my persecution.'[50]

When news reached Henry that his embassy to Alexander had failed, he retaliated brutally. He confiscated all Thomas's possessions and placed them in the care of Ranulf de Broc, who moved into Saltwood Castle in Kent. Henry then exiled all those associated with his disgraced archbishop – friends, and even distant relatives. The king apparently made 'no distinction of rank, or order, or condition or fortune, or age or sex. For he banished women yet lying in childbed, and children who still were being rocked in the cradle. This fury proceeded yet further, and broke out into cruelties shocking to religious ears.'[51] Henry exiled 400 people, pitilessly forcing them to cross the sea in the middle of winter.[52]

Thomas's supporters approached Henry's mother, thinking she might soften his resolve. Matilda remonstrated that Henry would not listen to her on the issue of church reform, as their views differed so markedly. Henry believed that royal will trumped everything. Matilda, increasingly religious in her old age, did not agree. When a friend of Thomas's, Nicholas of Mont Saint-Jacques, visited her, she agreed to help. Nicholas called her 'a woman of the stock of tyrants' who would, however, 'do all she could'.[53]

Nicholas's letter showed how much Matilda cared for Henry: 'The lady empress is very adroit in the defence of her son, excusing him by pointing out sometimes his zeal for justice, sometimes the malice of the bishops, sometimes his reasonable and shrewd perception of the origin of trouble in the church.' Over the next few years, she offered some help to Thomas and his friends. But any small influence she had was cut off by her death on 10 September 1167.

Matilda was buried at the abbey of Bec-Hellouin, before the altar. Henry was not with her when she died; he was in Brittany, quashing an uprising by Eudo, count of Porhoët, who had taken to calling himself 'duke of Brittany' in right of his dead wife, Bertha, the daughter and heir of Count Conan IV.

Étienne of Rouen was a confidant of Matilda's, and it was probably he who took the news of Matilda's death to Henry. Étienne – also a partisan of Henry's, who defended him vehemently in the quarrel with Becket – was a monk of Bec and author of the epic poem lauding the Normans, the *Draco Normannicus*. In his poem, he described 'a monk of Bec' who told the king of his mother's demise. It is likely that Matilda was his patron.[54] In return for his service, Henry gifted Étienne a staff, with which the poet wished to be buried.[55]

Matilda, in her will, left 30,000 shillings to the monks of the order of Grandemont, and Henry matched the sum.[56] Her funeral was a grand one held by candlelight. It was conducted by Rotrou, archbishop of Rouen, and attended by a huge crowd of clergy. None of the chroniclers record Henry's feelings on the death of his mother. But since his birth, mother and son had been bound together in a struggle for his inheritance. When he was young, she had kept him with her when she could, and chroniclers noted happy reunions between them when they had been apart. Henry had learned invaluable lessons of statecraft from Matilda; and with the notable exception of Thomas Becket, he listened to her and heeded her advice.

Henry had respected his mother; with any charter he signed jointly with her, he always ensured that her name came first. He admired the knowledge she had gleaned of Germany and the papal court from her marriage to Heinrich, and he used this knowledge. He knew he would not have had a chance of the throne of England without his mother's military involvement in the pitiless civil war. Time and again, he relied on her good counsel and subtle understanding of human nature.

Henry owed Matilda far more than his lineage, and we may assume that he mourned her. But whatever his personal feelings, Matilda's memorial was in the service of Henry's dynasty. Henry's own father, Geoffrey, neither a king nor an emperor, was written out of his wife's epitaph. Instead, it was the man who had given Matilda an imperial title – her first husband Heinrich – who appeared. It read: 'Great by origin, greater through her husband, but through childbirth greatest – Here lies the daughter, wife and parent of [a] Henry.'

It was the chronicler Ralph of Diceto, dean of St Paul's, who wrote of Matilda's legacy as a warrior queen to her three young granddaughters, Matilda, Eleanor and Joanna: 'They might have lived in continual terror from the cold barbarism of the Saxons, the uncertain wars against the Saracens, and the fierce tyranny of the Sicilians, had not the nobility of their grandmother the empress, and her masculine courage in a female body, shown her granddaughters an example of fortitude and patience.'[57]

Thomas could no longer count on Matilda. Neither could he expect any support from Eleanor. Jean Bellesmains, bishop of Poitiers, wrote to him in 1165, complaining about Eleanor's uncle Raoul de Faye, one of her closest advisors, and his violations of church privileges. Eleanor, he said, relied on her uncle entirely, and was therefore unlikely to have any sympathy for Becket's cause. Bellesmains went on to accuse Eleanor of adultery and incest: 'Every day many tendencies come to light which make it possible to believe that there is truth in the dishonourable tale we remember mentioning elsewhere.' He probably confused one uncle for another, substituting her maternal uncle Raoul de Faye for her paternal uncle Raymond of Antioch, with whom Eleanor was reputed to have behaved so scandalously twenty years earlier; the rumours of her incest and adultery pursued her relentlessly.[58]

Thomas spent the next few years at Pontigny Abbey, and then from November 1166 at the Benedictine abbey of Columba at Sens. He lived on Louis' charity, his few companions furiously churning out letters in support of his cause against Henry, and continuing his appeal to the pope.

The ever-loyal John of Salisbury accompanied Thomas into exile. He had remained with Theobald until his death, and then served Thomas when he became archbishop. John became one of Thomas's greatest advocates and dedicated his works the *Metalogicon*, a defence of the seven liberal arts, and the *Policraticus*, a groundbreaking work of philosophy and the leadership of princes, to Thomas. John, presciently anticipating trouble with Henry which might lead to Thomas needing to flee England, had left for France in late 1163 or early 1164 to make arrangements. He disagreed with Thomas's intransigent stance, but loyally stayed with him until the end. During their exile John wrote numerous letters describing the wearisome process of continued appeals and stalemates. He despaired of the conflict and thought Henry, for his part in it, wasted his talents:

> Consider how great the king of England was when he seemed of small account in his own eyes ... His arrow turned not back, his shield did not turn aside in battle, and no one dared rouse him. Even a sight of him made his enemies afraid, his neighbours turned to his service, and distant princes sought his friendship; he was cherished by his subjects, respected by foreigners, praised by all. He was loved by good men, but especially by the clergy who cherished him to the top of their bent, did him the fullest reverence they could, and one and all loved him, passing the love of women ... He felt no fear or anxiety; he enjoyed by human standards abundance of everything a man could desire, freed from all fear and anxiety ... But to what end has he brought all these gifts from on high?[59]

Thomas, though, relished the conspiracy, the intrigue and the diplomatic machinations. Lonely and isolated, he became ever more pious.

To Henry, the crisis was a sideshow, albeit a troublesome one. Still, it was a fight that he determined to win. He contented himself with making it clear that should Louis and Alexander push Thomas's case further, he would ally with Frederick Barbarossa and support the antipope.

Henry was not beyond issuing colourful threats. It is doubtful that he meant them seriously, even as he spoke the words. In April or May 1168, John of Salisbury wrote to a friend, describing Henry's latest outburst. Henry had instructed his ambassadors to go to Pope Alexander, now at Benevento near Naples, saying that he would convert to Islam if Alexander continued to prevaricate. Henry, they claimed, 'would sooner accept the errors of Nur-al-din [the sultan of Aleppo] and become an infidel, than suffer Thomas to hold sway in Canterbury Cathedral any longer'.[60]

Despite Alexander's desire to settle the matter, neither Henry nor Thomas would compromise. Thomas demanded that he and his fellow exiles be restored to their lands and positions, and the repudiation of Henry's 'evil' customs of Clarendon which blighted the church. Henry did agree to some limited compromise, but although some of Thomas's friends urged him to make peace, he no longer trusted Henry. He believed that should he return to England, he would be imprisoned and killed. Henry meanwhile referred to the archbishop as 'a certain Thomas, who was our chancellor'. He no longer recognised his religious authority.

At the abbey of Vézelay, on 12 June 1166, Thomas struck back. The symbolism of the place would have been immediately obvious: it was where the holy and venerated Bernard of Clairvaux had preached the Second Crusade.

After celebrating a public Mass, Thomas excommunicated anyone who had anything to do with drawing up the Constitutions of Clarendon, including Ranulf de Broc who held his assets at Canterbury, as well as John of Oxford, Richard of Ilchester and Richard de Lucy – all Henry's men. He sent provocative letters quoting popes and biblical prophets to Henry:

Unless you come to your senses, unless you cease attacking churches and the clergy, unless you keep your hands from causing disorder among men, the Son of the Most High will indeed come in the staff of his fury, in response to the sighs of captives and the voices crying out to him; because it is already time to pass judgement against you in the equity and sternness of his spirit. Truly he knows how to take away the spirit of princes, and is terrible before the kings of the earth.[61]

He addressed a letter to Canterbury, which began, 'Dearest brothers, why do you not rise up with me against the wicked?'[62] 'The wicked' were presumably the king, and his closest advisors.

Henry was incandescent. He would not allow anyone even to speak Becket's name.

No one had ever threatened his royal authority in such a way before, and to Henry, who guarded it jealously, this was beyond the pale. Declaring Thomas his enemy, he forced him out of his refuge at Pontigny by threatening the Cistercian order with the confiscation of their property in his lands if they continued to harbour him.

Henry demanded that all English students studying in Paris return to England; and they did. They flocked to Oxford, where students had been taught since at least the end of the eleventh century. The students' enforced removal from Paris meant the gradual establishment of a university at Oxford. By 1188 there were enough students and teachers for Gerald of Wales to give a lecture.

Thomas moved to a Benedictine monastery in Sens, where he continued his barrage of letters to Henry. He complained bitterly of his diminished authority: 'For it is to my priesthood that God has enjoined the care of the church of Canterbury, and to your rule that he has, for the present, deputed the human affairs of this kingdom.'[63] Thomas the archbishop forever placed himself above Henry the king.

V

Henry had given Thomas Becket the archbishopric to enable the crowning of his son, Henri. Their argument had delayed the ceremony, but by 1170 Henry was prepared to go ahead without him. He wanted an end to his confrontation with Thomas; something had to shift.

In June 1170, in a provocative move that undermined the primacy of Canterbury, Roger de Pont l'Évêque, archbishop of York, eagerly crowned the young king at Westminster. Henry deliberately excluded Henri's wife, the French princess Margaret from the ceremony, detaining her in Normandy. It was both a slight to her father Louis, and a hidden promise of the possibility of Thomas returning to England to crown her, and to re-crown the young king, at a later date.

Thomas and the pope were predictably angry. Henry immediately announced that he was ready to come to terms with Becket.

Thomas faced enormous pressure from Louis and Alexander to reconcile with Henry. On 22 July, at Fréteval, they finally made peace, with Henry's promise that Thomas could crown the young king once more.

They had attempted to do so eight months earlier, at Montmartre in November 1169. The process was stymied, however, when Henry would not carry the pretence so far as to give Thomas the kiss of peace. He even ordered a Mass for the dead to avoid it.[64] Henry – still disgusted by his former friend – claimed that he had taken a vow never to kiss Thomas, and he did not want to break it. Thomas was appalled, and the negotiations broke up.

By the summer, however, the prospect of re-crowning the young king, as was his ancient right as archbishop of Canterbury, brought Thomas back to the table.

Henry, a consummate actor, behaved as if nothing had ever been amiss between them. He held Thomas's stirrup as a symbol of their rapprochement, and according to Thomas seemed pleased to see him. Henry apparently came to Thomas with his head uncovered, 'anticipated our salutation exultantly pouring forth words of greeting ... and, to the amazement of everyone, led us apart and spoke for a long time with such familiarity that it seemed there had never been any discord between us'. He recounted that Henry bid: 'let us restore the old affection between us ... and let us forget the enmity that has gone before'.[65]

Thomas would not return to Canterbury until December, preferring to remain in France until all the practicalities had been arranged. He waited for the return of his lands and his income, as well as the back payment of monies he had lost while in exile. Henry was seriously ill in August, so much so that he made his will. When he recovered he was distracted by yet another military threat by Louis. And so Henry did not, as he had promised, accompany Thomas across the Channel at the end of 1170. Instead he sent John of Oxford, the dean of Salisbury, to escort him. Had Henry been there as pledged, what followed might never have occurred. And whether or not Henry deliberately absented himself, we do not know.

In October, Thomas sent his last letter to Henry, showing the strains in their recent peace:

> It now appears from the clearest signs that the holy church of Canterbury, mother in Christ of the British Isles, is perishing through hatred for our person … we shall expose our person for her … so that she may not perish, but escape, ready by God's favour not only to die for Christ, but to suffer a thousand deaths and every kind of torment, if he deigns by his grace to grant us the strength to endure. I had intended to return to your presence, my lord, but fate is drawing me … to that afflicted Church; by your licence and grace I shall return to her, perhaps to die to prevent her destruction, unless your piety deigns swiftly to offer us some other comfort.[66]

Henry's men were not carrying out his instructions regarding the return of Thomas's estates as quickly as they might have done. Perhaps Henry issued orders which undermined the peace at Fréteval. Thomas felt threatened, despite Henry's assurances. We can only guess at Henry's intentions.

VI

On 1 December 1170, Thomas's ship docked at Sandwich in Kent. Just before embarking at Wissant in Flanders, he excommunicated Archbishop Roger of York, and the bishops of London and Salisbury, for their parts in the coronation of the young king. Thomas, despite his recent peace with Henry, appeared to be determined on vengeance – perhaps unable to help himself.

Thomas's reception was mixed. The nobility was not pleased, and Ranulf de Broc, it seemed, had to be restrained by John of Oxford from doing him physical harm. But the popular support was overwhelming, as thousands turned out to greet him in London.

Thomas intended to visit the young king. They had apparently become fond of one another during the year or more that Henri spent living in his household. Henri, however, acting on the instructions of Geoffrey Ridel bishop of Ely, loyalist of his father, refused to see him. He sent messengers to order him back to Canterbury. The implication was that he was welcome nowhere else in England.

To Thomas, the situation cannot have looked promising. His estates were still not returned, Ranulf de Broc had stolen his wine and his clerks were not allowed to travel across the Channel, presumably to forestall appeals to the pope. Henry's uncle Reginald of Cornwall saw the direction in which events were marching; he feared that 'Before the middle of Lent we shall have committed a terrible deed.'[67]

Thomas, with no other option left open to him, returned to Canterbury for Christmas. On Christmas Day, he excommunicated Ranulf de Broc and his coterie, and sent envoys to the pope to inform him that Henry had broken the peace.

Meanwhile Roger of York, Gilbert of London, Jocelin of Salisbury and Richard of Ilchester arrived in Normandy to complain to Henry of Thomas's actions. They embroidered the truth. As well as Thomas's sentences of excommunication, they told a tale of an archbishop and his soldiers, roaming England intent on disturbing the peace. Henry's response was his usual calculated frenzy.

In the midst of a volley of expletives he is reported to have said, 'What miserable drones and traitors have I nurtured and promoted in my household who let their lord be treated with such shameful contempt by a low-born clerk!'

John of Salisbury gave a more chilling account; he was not an eyewitness, but he heard about it six months later, at Chinon: 'The king complained exceedingly of the archbishop of Canterbury with sighs and groans: as those who were present afterwards reported, he declared with tears that the archbishop would take from him both body and soul. Finally he said they were all traitors who could not summon the zeal and loyalty to rid him of the harassment of one man.'[68]

When Henry calmed down, he was methodical. He ordered the ports to be watched and spies to be sent to Canterbury in case Thomas tried to flee, and he sent the constable of Normandy and Earl William of Mandeville to arrest him.

However, four of Henry's loyal knights – William de Tracy, Reginald Fitz Urse, Hugh de Morville and Richard Brito – had witnessed Henry's tantrum, and they chose to take their king at his word. They were eager to win his favour, and they likely did not wait for his anger to abate, as it always did; we may imagine a whispered and hurried discussion among the four, as Henry raged against the man who had been his most troublesome subject for six weary years.

These men knew one another well. All had lands in the West Country, and Morville and Fitz Urse may have been kinsmen.[69] Three of them – Morville, Fitz Urse and Tracy – had paid homage to Thomas when he was chancellor.[70] Now, joined in a pact they were convinced would please Henry, they left the hunting lodge of Bur-le-Roi near Bayeux on 26 December where the king was celebrating Christmas, and headed for the coast. They crossed the Channel in extremely bad weather and were dispersed. They met, however, at Saltwood Castle on 28 December, where they were welcomed and dined by the recently excommunicated Ranulf de Broc.

Ranulf de Broc, besides his other duties, was one of Henry's whoremasters. He had pilfered from Thomas's lands during his exile, and the two men hated one another. Ranulf willingly aided the four knights who, presumably at this point, intended to arrest Thomas. It was he who let them into Canterbury cathedral – he had the keys and unlocked the gates. They may have been drunk, gorging on wine Ranulf had stolen from Thomas. They did not travel alone, having gathered armed men from the castles of Dover, Rochester and Bletchingly, shouting '*Reaus, reaus*' – 'King's men, king's men!' – as they stormed into the cathedral precinct. It was late afternoon on a dreary midwinter day, already dark.

These men were all dressed in full armour, holding swords and axes in their hands. They would have looked extremely threatening.

John of Salisbury begged Thomas to appease the knights. He replied simply, 'I am resolved. I know what I must do.'[71] Thomas, although not armed himself, did have some armed men at his disposal. But he chose not to use them. Instead he proceeded into the church for vespers, ordering the crowd of monks accompanying him not to lock the doors against the soldiers.

The four knights, led by Fitz Urse, shoved open the heavy oak doors and cried, 'Where is Thomas Becket, traitor to king and kingdom?' Many of the monks surrounding Thomas fled, but he stayed, perfectly still. He replied, in the midst of the candlelit church, 'Here I am, no king's traitor, but a priest; why do you seek me?'

The four attempted to take Thomas out of the church to arrest him, but he refused to move. He pushed Fitz Urse violently, calling him a pimp. He had provoked the knights – perhaps it was deliberate. He bowed his head in prayer, seeming to offer it to the men. He chanted, 'I commend myself and the church's cause to God and St Mary the holy patrons of this church, and to St Denis.'[72] Fitz Urse called to the knights to strike Thomas, but Edward Grim, a clerk from Cambridge who was in the fray, raised his arm to protect the archbishop. William de Tracy struck, nearly severed Grim's arm, and sliced through Thomas's shoulder to the bone.

Then the blows fell furiously on Thomas. He wiped the blood which was flowing from his head. Another blow felled him face down. He appeared to rearrange himself in a position of prayer but swayed on his right side. Richard Brito, who struck the final blow as Thomas lay on the floor, cried, 'Take that, for the love of my lord William, the king's brother!'[73] He sliced off the top of Thomas's head with such force that his sword broke as it crashed to the stone floor. Hugh de Horsea, Ranulf de Broc's clerk, 'full of iniquity', crushed his boot onto the archbishop's neck.

It was over. Thomas Becket was dead, his brains spilling over the cathedral floor, as blood pooled around him.

The monks were frightened and left Thomas's body alone for hours, while the murderers sacked his palace and even took the horses from the stable. It was only after they left that the monks felt brave enough to approach their dead archbishop. They scooped his brains and blood into a basin, and some dipped their clothes in his blood and wiped their eyes with it; 'others eagerly dipped in parts of their clothes they had cut off: later no one seemed happy with themselves unless they had taken something away, however insignificant, from this precious treasure'.[74] They bound Thomas's head in a linen cloth and laid him before the high altar in the choir. Robert of Merton, a monk, found a hair shirt infested with lice beneath Thomas's clothes.

It was not until the following morning, when the Broc family threatened to hang the corpse, that the monks dared to bury

Thomas. They did not wash or embalm his body, as it had been washed in its own blood. He was about fifty years old.

Almost immediately, rumours spread throughout Canterbury of Thomas's saintliness and martyrdom. Reports abounded of miraculous cures; the paralysed could walk, the blind could see, the mute could speak. All were attributed to the power of Thomas the martyr.

VII

Henry was brought the news of Thomas's murder on 1 January 1171 at Argentan.

We cannot know his feelings on hearing of the death, or whether he had covertly ordered four knights to murder Thomas. Nevertheless, for public appearance, Henry did everything right. He immediately

> burst into loud lamentations and exchanged his royal robes for sackcloth and ashes, behaving more like the friend than the sovereign of the dead man. At times he fell into a stupor, after which he would again utter groans and cries louder and more bitter than before. For three whole days he remained shut up in his chamber, and would neither take food nor admit anyone to comfort him, until it seemed from the excess of his grief that he had determined to contrive his own death. The state of affairs was lamentable and the reason for our grief and anxiety was not changed. First we had to bewail the death of the archbishop, now, in consequence, we began to despair of the life of the king ... by the death of the one we feared in our misery that we might lose both.[75]

He then went into the seclusion of the penitent for forty days.

Henry became the pariah of Europe. Gerald of Wales called him 'the hammer of the church'. Pope Alexander refused to speak to an Englishman for three weeks, and Louis, together with his brothers-in-law Theobald of Blois and Archbishop William of Sens, all wrote recriminations damning Henry to the pope. Louis wrote an uncharacteristically incendiary letter: 'Let the sword of St Peter be unleashed to avenge the martyr of Canterbury.'[76] The four murderous knights were 'these dogs of the court, these retainers of the king of England'.

William of Sens was the least cryptic in his message to Alexander. He blamed Henry entirely: 'I have no doubt that the cry of the whole world has already filled your ears of how the king of the English, that enemy to the angels and the whole body of Christ, has wrought his spite on that holy one.'[77]

Thomas, in death, had achieved a far greater status than during the last years of his life. He was no longer a thorn in the side of a king, a dependant in exile, or yet another problem for the pope to deal with. His murder made it simple. Thomas, protecting the holy church, was a sainted martyr. All the difficulties of his character were forgotten in a wave of recriminations against Henry and his killers.

Henry tried to present his own version to the pope, distancing himself and explaining in a missive that it was the mighty enemies Thomas had made who perpetrated the murder. But the eyewitness accounts of the murder overwhelmed his account.

We know so much about the final minutes of Thomas Becket's life because many credible witnesses saw it, and wrote about it very soon afterwards. William FitzStephen and Edward Grim were both beside Thomas throughout his ordeal. Three others – John of Salisbury, William of Canterbury and Benedict of Peterborough – were further away, but still in the cathedral as the attack took place. These men spoke and wrote about the murder, inspiring others who had heard their accounts to write about it. There was, therefore, no lack of information. If when Henry heard about it he planned to place the blame on Thomas, it would have been impossible. FitzStephen wrote that: 'As once Christ suffered in his body, he suffered anew in his champion Thomas.' How could Henry compete?

Pope Alexander, in spite of his personal feelings, could not afford to alienate Henry entirely. Although he was encouraged to lay England under an interdict and to excommunicate Henry, he did not do so. Henry was simply banned from entering a church, until the pope had determined his guilt or otherwise. The archbishop of Sens was not so lenient, and placed an interdict on Henry's lands in France.

The four knights appear to have suffered overwhelming feelings of guilt and remorse, William de Tracy perhaps the most.[78] He went to Rome by the end of 1171 or the very beginning of 1172 to confess to the pope. All made religious donations.

Henry was advised by the prior of Grandmont, who knew him well, to spill the blood of the four knights.[79] He did little to punish them, however, besides curtailing the succession of their children to their estates.[80] He preferred to leave them to the judgement of the church. The pope demanded that they went on pilgrimage to the Holy Land, and all died soon after 1173. They were probably all buried at Jerusalem.

By the time Alexander sent legates from Rome towards the end of 1171, Henry had left the country. He had conveniently gone to Ireland.

Regardless of the timing, the situation in Ireland was perilous, exacerbated by Richard Fitz Gilbert de Clare, the renegade earl of Pembroke (known as Strongbow) who made himself 'nearly a king', and beheaded a rival Irish lord.[81] Now Henry felt compelled to assert his control. He left from Milford Haven on 16 October, with a stupendous army. Contemporary accounts of the size of Henry's force differ, with the most exaggerated claiming that 400 ships carrying up to 10,000 men set sail.[82] It was the first time a king of England had come to Ireland.

The papal legates did not arrive in Henry's lands until December. By the time Henry returned seven months later, in

May 1172, he was forced to face the consequences and answer them. After three days of negotiations at Savigny Abbey, an accord was reached.

On Sunday 21 May, at Avranches Cathedral, Henry fell to his knees and made public penance for his part in Thomas's murder, swearing that he had not commanded the knights to murder Thomas. He did, however, concede that his words may have led to his archbishop's death. He promised to provide 200 knights to serve with the Knights Templar for a year in the Holy Land; he should either take the cross for three years, departing before the following Easter, or fight the Moors in Spain; to return to Canterbury all the property he had confiscated; and to abolish customs detrimental to the church. Henry would not obstruct appeals to Rome, with the legates proclaiming that: 'You shall neither impede appeals in ecclesiastical causes to the Roman Church nor allow them to be impeded, but they are to be made freely, in good faith, without fraud and trickery, so that the Roman pontiff may consider and terminate such cases.'[83]

Henry, having sworn all this on a copy of the Gospels, now at the door of the church, was absolved by the legates, Albert and Theodwin, who took him into the church, newly cleansed.

Henry had no choice but to comply. Thomas's murder had, perhaps irrevocably, damaged his standing. He compromised with good grace, ever the actor. The legates were impressed: 'How he fears God and is obedient to the Church. His actions sufficiently reveal, and will reveal still more in the future, as we have been given hope to believe.'[84] Henry had learned a lesson. From now on he would need to be less intransigent, more flexible and accommodating in his dealings with the church and the princes of Europe. His flexibility would serve him well.

Thomas's reputation as a worker of miracles grew to the point that, after the prior of Canterbury petitioned the pope, Alexander III canonised him on Ash Wednesday 1173. In death, he was St Thomas Becket.

Circumstances would overtake Henry and he did not go to the Latin Kingdom as a penitent. Instead, with the pope's permission, he built glorious structures in England to commemorate a Norman who had become a very English saint – at Waltham, Witham and Amesbury. It was from this point that Henry began to send roughly 2,000 silver marks annually to the Holy Land, which he placed in his 'Eastern' account, under the guardianship of the Knights Templar and the Knights Hospitaller.

Thomas's cult status blossomed almost as his blood congealed on the cool slabs of the cathedral floor. Henry quickly appropriated Thomas in death for his Plantagenet dynasty. Before Thomas died, Henry had been to Canterbury only twice. After his death, he went so often that it was described as 'customary', visiting every time he returned to England. The cult of Thomas spread all over Europe, and became indelibly associated with Henry FitzEmpress, to the glory of his house. The archbishop who had defied him while living, served him well in death.

In 1174, the choir of Canterbury Cathedral burned down. Now the opportunity presented itself to rebuild something worthy of their saint. The project was given to William the Englishman, and he rebuilt Canterbury in the English Gothic style. William was paid ninepence per day for his service, as well as an annual stipend of £5.[85]

It was finished in 1220. Thomas's bones were exhumed and wrapped in silk and moved to his grand new marble tomb. Some 33,000 pilgrims attended festivities that lasted two weeks, while wine flowed through the streets of Canterbury; it was all presided over by Henry's grandson, Henry III.

Thomas's body brought enormous wealth to Canterbury. In the early years after his death, earnings from pilgrims accounted for 28 per cent of the cathedral's income.[86]

Canterbury's riches continued to grow. In 1221 income from pilgrims reached two-thirds of the total, and in the sixteenth century, the Venetian ambassador was taken aback by the wealth of Canterbury, brought by its famous saint: 'The shrine is entirely covered with plates of pure gold. But the gold is scarcely visible beneath a profusion of gems, including sapphires, diamonds, rubies and emeralds ... exquisite designs have been carved all over it and immense gems worked intricately into the patterns.'[87] It was remarkable for a cathedral to have a whole saint – most only had a body part, or a relic identified with Christ. Canterbury exploited it to the full.

Henry's descendant, the eighth Henry, as he broke the wealth and power of the monasteries, ordered Thomas's bones to be burned in 1540. The monks may have hidden their saint's bones, and given over different ones to the king's men. This was not unusual practice during the Reformation; due notice was always given that the king's men were on their way, and many clerics attempted to save their precious relics. The remains of Thomas Becket may still be buried within Canterbury today, secreted away from the agents of Henry VIII, their location long forgotten.

Henry VIII, although he may not have purloined the bones of the man, did however take the fabulous ruby given to Thomas's shrine by Louis in 1179. It was known as the *regale* and he wore it on his index finger.

Act IV
Rebellion

Tell me … where were you [Eleanor] when your eaglets,
flying from the nest, dared to raise their talons against
the King of the North Wind?[1]

Richard le Poitevin

I

Between 1178 and 1179, Henry commissioned the refurbishment
of his living quarters at Winchester Palace. Despite his plain dress
and disregard for the trappings of power – although never power
itself – comfort was important to Henry. He spent a great deal of
money on making his castles, hunting lodges and palaces – among
them Clarendon, Woodstock, Westminster, Windsor, Nottingham,
Chinon, Angers – luxurious.[2]

As part of this grand scheme, Henry commissioned a wall
painting for his private quarters. It was an allegory of his self-
described greatest misfortune. It was not about the murder of
Thomas Becket. By the early 1170s, through a series of brilliant
acts of public penance, Henry had gained absolution. He had
even harnessed the booming Becket miracle industry into the
service of his nascent dynasty. Through Henry's efforts, the

Angevins became linked inexorably to the cult of the newly canonised St Thomas, to the glory of their house.

With the debacle of Becket's death behind him, in 1173 Henry was struck by a disaster that wounded him far more gravely. His three elder legitimate sons – Henri, Richard and Geoffrey – apparently galvanised by Eleanor, banded with Louis and Henry's other enemies to perpetrate a series of violent and, to Henry, astonishing and unforeseen attacks on his lands.

The mural at Winchester, now lost, showed an eagle with his four sons, or 'eaglets'. Three were tearing their parent apart, while the fourth sat on his neck, waiting for the perfect moment to peck out his eyes. Gerald of Wales, albeit writing years after the event, probably in the late 1190s, recorded Henry's own supposed explanation: 'The four eaglets', the king told him, 'are my four sons who cease not to persecute me even unto death. The youngest of them [John], whom I embrace with so much affection, will sometime in the end insult me more grievously and more dangerously than any of the others.'[3]

Henry commissioned the mural at least four years after the rebellion had ended. Its events had made the king wary enough of his immediate family that he felt compelled to have a large and visible reminder in the most intimate quarters of one of his favourite houses. The two years during which his family viciously rose against him had left their scars on Henry. While publicly forgiving his sons, and continuing to love them, he clearly felt in need of an emotional armour. This painting was there to help him, reminding him not to trust his sons again. It would be Henry's tragedy that he failed to heed his own warning.

II

In 1168, after sixteen years of marriage, Henry and Eleanor separated amicably; Eleanor left for more or less permanent residence in Poitou, taking her favourite son Richard with her.

William of Newburgh, typically, ascribed a sexual motive to the separation. He claimed that Henry had tired of Eleanor after she reached the menopause: as he was no longer interested in sleeping with her, he let her go. It was William, however, who had claimed, rather fantastically, that Louis had only taken Eleanor on crusade because he was 'jealous' and that her beauty 'enslaved' him. It was far more likely that Louis' purpose was to get his queen pregnant with a much-needed son. The same William also wrote that it was Eleanor who sought divorce from Louis because she had found Henry so sexually attractive. But Henry and Eleanor's marriage was more political bargain than love match.

Assuming that Henry and Eleanor did reach an accommodation in Paris in the summer of 1151, Henry was fulfilling his part now. Eleanor had borne him at least eight children, five boys and three girls, seven of whom were still living. Now, having produced her last child and being about forty-four years old, she was finally at liberty to pursue autonomy in her own lands.

The new arrangement suited Henry; by 1168, his territories were vast, encompassing not only England, Aquitaine, Anjou, Normandy and Maine, but also Brittany. Aquitaine was the most difficult province in Henry's empire to govern, its magnates frequently rebelling against ducal authority: 'The men of Poitou were always in revolt against their lords', wrote the author of the *History of William Marshal*.[4] Although Normandy and England, and to some extent Anjou, had a strong, centralised form of government, Henry had tried and failed to implement similar measures in Aquitaine, where many of its lords paid, at best, lip service to authority.

Henry's approach had been heavy-handed. He deployed none of the subtlety of Eleanor's ancestors, preferring instead to wage harsh campaigns often fought by his feared Brabanter mercenaries. Preoccupied with other regions in his vast empire, Henry now allowed Eleanor to take the burden of ruling Aquitaine from him. As the province's duchess, she would perhaps fare better in subduing rebellion, providing strong government, and increasing revenue for Henry's coffers from the lucrative trade in Aquitaine's ports.[5]

Eleanor was hardly a political novice. She had intrigued in Louis' government in the early years of her marriage, promoting the union of her younger sister, Petronilla, to Louis' cousin and advisor – the married and much older Raoul de Vermandois – in a bid to increase her influence.

She was Henry's regent in England at the beginning of 1157, and again in 1159 while Henry tried to conquer Toulouse in her name. She was regent in Anjou and Maine in 1165 while Henry campaigned in Wales.[6]

But Eleanor had not actively governed her duchy for ten years. She had barely visited since Henry became king of England, except for her progress around Aquitaine in 1156–7. In the first two years of their marriage, Eleanor took the lead, with Henry confirming her acts; but then her role was swiftly diminished. At their Christmas court at Bordeaux in 1156, Eleanor's barons had sworn allegiance to Henry, and not to her. Henry, duke of Aquitaine in right of his wife, and having established his own right to rule in Eleanor's lands, could now remove his queen.

Henry may have wished to use Eleanor's talents more in the northern reaches of his empire, where she was frequently regent; or her disappearance from her duchy may have been because she was almost constantly pregnant and unable to participate fully in the Angevin Empire's most recalcitrant province. Whatever the reason, between 1157 and 1167, Eleanor is absent from the charter records. 'Not a single act mentions her, either alone or jointly with Henry.'[7]

But by the mid-1160s, it was becoming increasingly evident that Henry needed Eleanor back in Aquitaine. Eleanor's uncle, Raoul de Faye, warned her that the nobility of Aquitaine were planning a revolt against Henry's rule, 'because of his pruning of their liberties'.[8] Some Poitevin clerics, in an attempt to rid themselves of Henry, even called the marriage into question, citing consanguinity.[9] Henry's response was to hold his Christmas court of 1166 at Poitiers with Henri, but without Eleanor.

Some historians have seen Eleanor's failure to join Henry at this Christmas court in her duchy as an indication that relations between them were now cool. But Eleanor was in England, heavily pregnant, and it would have been dangerous for her to risk travel across the Channel in winter. She gave birth on or around Christmas Day. The name given to the baby was John, probably chosen because his birth fell around the time of the feast of St John the Evangelist, on 27 December.[10] He would be her last child.

Eleanor spent the following Christmas 1167 in Argentan with Henry, and then left for Poitou at the beginning of January. She would remain in her homeland for the next five years. She brought the nine-year-old Richard with her, and possibly her second daughter Eleanor, leaving two-year-old Joanna and one-year-old John in the care of the nuns of Fontevraud Abbey, fifty miles north of her capital, and the recipient of much of her and Henry's patronage. It was in her ancestral lands that she would prepare Richard, her favourite son, to be duke. It is possibly because Henry had designated Aquitaine to Richard from a very young age that she allowed herself to think of him as her favourite; this was the child in whom she would invest the most. He would need her help and guidance if he was to rule well in her duchy.

For Eleanor, Aquitaine may have pulled her in as much as the situation in England pushed her out. Henry had increasingly delegated power to his justiciar Richard de Lucy, particularly after the death in 1168 of de Lucy's co-justiciar, Robert earl of Leicester. Such was Henry's confidence in de Lucy that he was known as the most powerful man in England; Eleanor was sidelined. She knew that Henry was thinking of how to divide his lands after his death. Anxious to secure her son Richard's succession to Aquitaine, she determined to keep her duchy autonomous, and not a part of a conglomerate Angevin Empire.

For this, Eleanor would need to be resident there with power.

Power in Aquitaine was Eleanor's *raison d'être*. She placed the duchy above everything and everyone – the king included. Henry failed to understand this, failed to maintain her loyalty, and catastrophically underestimated her will to succeed.

III

Eleanor's revolt can be traced to Henry's departure from Aquitaine in the spring of 1168. It was gradual, to be sure, and was nurtured on seeds sown earlier still.

Eleanor, while in power in Aquitaine, continued to enjoy Henry's confidence. He consulted with her on young Henri's controversial coronation by Roger de Pont l'Évêque, archbishop of York, in June 1170, a stinging rebuke to Thomas Becket, who was denied the right to crown a king of England. The crowning was exclusively within the purview of the archbishop of Canterbury. But the decision was made 'by the counsel of the queen and all her entourage, for such was her duty'.[11] Young Henri's coronation would formally free up his mother from the duty of serving as regent in England, a physical impossibility when she moved south; from 1170 it was Henri who acted as his father's regent, while his mother was busy governing Aquitaine.

Henry crossed to England in violent storms, and Eleanor, at his request, went to Normandy to act as temporary regent there. She was joined by her daughter-in-law Margaret, whom Henry deliberately excluded from the ceremony, using the young French princess as a pawn in his power-play with Becket and Louis.

Here, Eleanor worked with Henry in a double-headed monarchy; she was completely in accord with him, and with the aid of Henry's justiciar in Normandy, Richard de Hommet, she closed the ports to prevent Becket's supporters and messengers travelling to England to stop the ceremony.[12]

Eleanor was with Henry again at the end of the year, at the hunting lodge of Bur-le-Roi for Christmas together, joined by their sons Richard, Geoffrey and John. It was here on Christmas Day that Henry is supposed to have uttered his ill-fated words that led the four knights to commit murder in the cathedral.

Eleanor's feelings on Becket's gruesome demise are not known, but she left Henry soon afterwards for her capital. Did she, like so many others, feel disgust for Henry's perceived part in Becket's murder? It is possible, although she left no record.

Henry issued no charters in Aquitaine for the next five years; instead, Eleanor acted alone. When the fourteen-year-old Richard, her protégé, was invested as duke in June 1172 at the cathedral church of Saint-Hilaire-le-Grand at Poitiers, and given the ring of St Valerie, she associated herself with him – 'I and Richard my son' – and not the other way around.[13] Even as late as the summer of 1172, she was still acting in tandem with him. The momentous decision to invest Richard as duke was, by necessity, taken jointly with Henry: 'King Henry Senior transferred to Richard by the will of his mother Eleanor the duchy of Aquitaine.'[14]

But she had reason to be troubled. Although Henry took only a nominal role in the governance of Aquitaine, he had reduced her income and limited her military authority.[15] As such, in the spring of 1171 the abbot of Saint-Martial, lord of La Souterraine, when faced with an insurrection, appealed to Henry for military aid, and not to Eleanor.[16] And Eleanor may have been concerned at how harsh Henry was with her rebellious nobility. He had razed the walls of Limoges twice, and had ordered the mutinous lord Robert de Seilhac to be treated so brutally that he died in prison. Eleanor, in sympathy with Seilhac's widow and in quiet revolt against Henry, witnessed a grant made by her to Fontevraud Abbey.[17]

These five years, from 1168, marked the slow erosion of Eleanor's trust in her husband. Although Henry denied her supreme authority over the duchy, Eleanor attempted to act independently where she could. In 1168 and 1171, she held Christmas courts with Richard, and not with Henry. She received the kings of Aragon and Navarre herself, as head of her duchy. And in that same year she changed the wording on her charters from 'the king's faithful followers and hers' to 'her faithful followers'.[18] She was attempting to govern alone, although ultimate power still rested with Henry. Her seneschal was her maternal uncle, Raoul de Faye, trusted by Henry, and one of the few of the Poitevin nobility to rise high in his service. He was the only Poitevin to receive an estate in England – Bramley, in Surrey – which Eleanor had procured for him in 1155.[19]

By 1173, therefore, Eleanor could reasonably expect that Henry had given her all the authority he would ever allow her to have – considerable, although by this time she had realised that ultimate power would always rest with him. Even after Richard's investiture, Henry retained the title 'duke of Aquitaine' for himself, while Richard was known as the count of Poitou. In the spring of 1173, Eleanor precipitated the greatest and most painful crisis of Henry's reign. She turned Henri, Richard and Geoffrey against their father to the point where they could betray him to his enemies, seek to deny him his kingship – the very thing that defined him – and obliterate him in battle. Henri particularly, backed by Eleanor, wanted nothing less than his father's total humiliation and capitulation. How could Henry's immediate family, the people he should have been able to trust above all others, have come to desire his extinction?

IV

Henry was an exceedingly fond father, particularly towards his eldest surviving legitimate son Henri, and his youngest, John.[20] Even Gerald of Wales, a brutal critic who loathed Henry for failing to grant him an English bishopric, said that: 'On his legitimate children he lavished in their childhood more than a father's affection.'[21]

Henry spent much of the 1160s pondering how to divide his vast empire on his death. He did not wish to leave any of his boys – Henri, Richard, Geoffrey and John – without significant territories, castles, or money. In January 1169, after two years of skirmishes with Louis, punctuated by truces, the two kings met at Montmirail in Maine to discuss a long-lasting peace. Henry chose the occasion to make known publicly how he wished to manage the succession.

His lands would not pass as a whole to Henri as the eldest son, as Henry's parents' lands had passed to him. Instead Henry decreed that his domains would be divided among the three older boys. Henri would inherit England, Normandy, Anjou and Maine; Richard, Eleanor's duchy of Aquitaine; and Geoffrey would have Brittany. In 1166, Henry had forced Brittany's beleaguered duke, Conan IV, to promise his only legitimate child Constance in marriage to Geoffrey. Conan, exhausted by battle, retired, leaving his duchy to Henry's rule. Now, Henry confirmed that Geoffrey would be duke in Brittany.[22]

Henry revealed too that Richard would pay homage directly to the French king for his southern lands, while Geoffrey would pay homage to his elder brother Henri for Brittany, confirming the duchy as a province of England, and not France. To further seal relations between Henry and Louis, and in a diplomatic coup for Henry, Louis' daughter Alice (Margaret's sister) was to be married to Richard. There was nothing for John, despite his reputed position as Henry's favourite legitimate child, perhaps because he was still so young, just two years old. Doubtless, Henry felt an opportunity would present itself to provide for him.

The following year, Henry believed he was dying. In August 1170, while at La Motte-de-Ger near Domfront, he fell desperately ill, frightening for a man who had always enjoyed such excellent health. For Henry, his age was significant: he was thirty-seven years old, a year off his father's age when he had died after a sudden fever. Superstitious about such matters, Henry may have feared his father's fate awaited him too. He made a will, and ordered that his body be buried at Grandmont Abbey. The will reiterated how his lands were to be divided on his death. As he lay ill, he was obviously concerned for John's future as he had left him no provision. He made a special request to Henri, that he have custody of his youngest son 'that he might advance and maintain him', and asked that Henri grant John the county of Mortain.[23] (Henry did not recover fully until the end of September; rumours spread quickly throughout France that he was already dead.[24])

Henry's will had established his wishes – and when he recovered he probably believed that at his death a smooth succession throughout his lands was guaranteed. He was mistaken. His error was in omitting to take into account his children's characters, their ambitions, their relationships with one another and the influence of their mother.

Henry simply assumed his children would be as loyal, obedient and loving to him as he had been towards his own parents. But Henry's parents, despite their own fractious relationship, were always of the same mind when it came to the future of their eldest son; they worked in harmony to advance his interests. Whatever Henry may have believed, Eleanor did not share his views on the succession. This was to have repercussions for the entire family.

Henry's children hardly knew one another. They had grown up in different households, and there was a large age gap between the eldest and the youngest. Henri and Richard were respectively twelve and ten years older than John. They never lived together and we may presume that during childhood, no real relationship existed between them. (Later, from the mid-1170s, a close friendship would form between Henri and Geoffrey.) Henry believed, however, that through the extraordinary strength of his resolve, he could fashion bonds between his offspring powerful enough to hold his empire together at his death. Henry's plan was premised on a belief that his lands would have to be passed to a generation, not one of whom had inherited his gifts and abilities.

Absolute master of his lands, Henry was a man who was never at rest. He slept for only a few hours a night, and he was a constant magnet for the scores of messengers who carried news to him, and then relayed his orders to the furthest reaches of his empire. Henry placed himself at the centre of a tornado, in absolute command, and it suited him.

How could any one of his children possibly hold all this together? Henry believed that his enormous and diverse empire was ungovernable by any of them; he only held Eleanor's southern barons' loyalty with extreme difficulty. Henry doubted his sons' abilities for leadership. Instead, like King Lear, he envisaged a loose federation, with his three eldest boys each inheriting a part of his empire. But, as with Lear, he failed to bring his children with him in the fashioning of his plans. He ignored their suggestions, and overlooked their resentments. It was an epic leap of faith, for Henry did nothing to prepare them to rule, nor did he attempt to establish strong emotional ties between the brothers. Their separate upbringings led to division and rivalries rather than the forging of fraternal bonds.

Henry's decision to divide his lands among his sons was common practice at the time. He seems to have given the division a good deal of thought; he gave his boys what he believed they could handle, in the hope that they would use their resources to the common benefit of their 'federation'. To Henri, his eldest son, he assigned the lands he had inherited from his parents – England,

Normandy and Anjou. These domains all benefited from Henry's massive expansion of centralised government. Bitter experience had taught him that the rule of Brittany and Aquitaine were problematic; by assigning Brittany to Geoffrey and Aquitaine to Richard, he was doubtless giving over to them what he thought they were capable of ruling.[25] Henry was not confident that any one of his sons would be able to do as he had done, and was loath to hand everything over to Henri.

Henry was a fond and loving parent. But he was an absent father out of necessity, often spending years apart from his offspring and from Eleanor as he moved ceaselessly around his lands. Walter Map famously decried the constant movement of Henry and his court, lamenting bitterly 'those wanderings in which we wear out our clothes, lay waste kingdoms, exhaust ourselves and our mounts, and never have time to see to our sick souls'.[26]

Eleanor travelled too, although to a lesser extent. But when she did, she occasionally took at least one child with her. In the summer of 1156, after her young son William died, she left England for Normandy and Anjou for several months, and took Henri and baby Matilda with her.[27] Perhaps it was William's recent death that led her to want to have her young children close by. But these occasional trips apart, it is unlikely that any of the children enjoyed a close relationship with either parent when they were very young.

For Henry, infrequent contact with his sons when they were young would not necessarily have led to antipathy during their teenage years. During his own childhood, Henry had lived separately from both Geoffrey and Matilda for long periods, but his relationship with each of them was excellent. Eleanor did not see much more of their sons than Henry during their childhood, and if the importance of the position she enjoyed during the reigns of Richard and John is anything to go by, they held their mother in high esteem. But they did not like their father.

V

Little did Henry expect it, but it was Henri, the beloved golden boy destined to inherit the greater part of his realm, who would prove the first great threat to his rule. Henri was the only monarch since the Norman Conquest to be crowned during his father's lifetime; yet although he numbers among the anointed kings and queens of England, he is forgotten. The remarkable feature of his reign was that he had absolutely no power – it all remained in his father's hands.

Henry managed to disregard his son's growing disaffection and unhappiness as he piled on him all the trappings of majesty with none of the substance. For the prince believed his father kept him impoverished and deprived of any real power. His was the empty face of the Angevin monarchy.

Henri was an easy person to love. His chaplain, Gervase of Tilbury, adored him. He even wrote a book for him – a *Liber facetiarum* – on entertainment. Gervase left this glowing portrait:

> Tall in stature, and distinguished in appearance; his face expressed merriment and mature judgement in due measure; fair among the children of men, he was courteous and cheerful. Gracious to all, he was loved by all; amiable to all, he was incapable of making an enemy. He was matchless in warfare, and as he surpassed all others in the grace of his person, so he outstripped them all in valour, cordiality, and the outstanding graciousness of his manner, in his generosity and in his true integrity.[28]

Henri was the second child of Henry and Eleanor and the first of their children born after Henry became king. He was born in London on the last day of February 1155; a heavily pregnant Eleanor had been crowned with Henry at Westminster. With two legitimate young sons, Henry believed the succession was secure and he obliged his magnates to swear an oath to the princes. But William died in April 1156. Henri, only fourteen months old, became his father's heir.

When Henri was three years old, in 1158, his father betrothed him to Margaret of France, the daughter of Louis and his second wife Constance of Castile. Their betrothal marked an accord between Henry and Louis. Margaret's dowry was the much-desired Norman region, the Vexin.

Henry came to Paris himself, in September 1158, to collect his son's betrothed. He travelled in a far less extravagant style than Thomas Becket had when he visited Paris on behalf of his king. Henry took only a few companions with him – this time there was no stupendous baggage train replete with marvels – and Louis played the gracious host.[29] The year 1158 marked the apex of their relationship; after Paris, the kings travelled together to Normandy, and Louis, to Robert of Torigni's 'wonder', declared his admiration for Henry.[30] The terms of the marriage contract were agreed: the Vexin was to be handed over to Henry when the couple married – and Louis imagined, due to their extreme youth, that this was a long way in the future. Margaret, still only six months old, was entrusted to Henry, with the stipulation that Louis' former wife, Eleanor, would not be involved in her upbringing. She was placed instead in the care of Henry's seneschal in Normandy.[31] The Vexin's castles were given over to three Knights Templar for safekeeping, until the children were old enough to marry and Henry might claim his daughter-in-law's dowry, according to the terms of his agreement with Louis.[32]

Margaret would never see her mother again. Two years later, in September 1160, Constance died in childbirth. Louis, in haste, and despite his lamentations, abandoned all protocols of mourning and found himself another wife. He was desperate for a son and heir; only two weeks after Constance's death he arranged to marry Adela of Blois-Champagne, the sister of the betrotheds of his two daughters by Eleanor, Marie and Alix.* The marriage was shocking to contemporaries, not only for its speed: in the eyes of the church, through the betrothals of his two eldest daughters, Louis and Adela were already related. It was deemed an incestuous marriage.

Henry was furious; but his rage was calculated. He was naturally wary of an even closer relationship between Louis and the powerful house of Blois-Champagne. Lambert of Waterlos recorded Henry's outburst, of how 'the English King, having got wind of this marriage, and moved by anger, attempted to counter it by every means'.[33] But more than anything else Henry wanted the Vexin. He was, according to William of Newburgh, 'impatient with delay' to have it back.[34] He took advantage of Louis' marriage plans to get his hands on it immediately.

Louis' wedding was planned for 13 November. Henry moved fast. There were problems with the marriage of Henri and Margaret – they were far too young, and too closely related for the church's liking. Henri was five and Margaret just two years old. They were described as being 'still little children, crying in the cradle'.[35]

Nevertheless, Henry bullied, bribed and lied to get his way. He persuaded two cardinals of the new pope, Alexander III, that he would only support Alexander's claim to the papacy against the antipope Victor IV, if Alexander would grant the children a dispensation to marry. (Henry had already determined to back Alexander. But he gambled on the cardinals panicking and giving him what he wanted.[36]) The dispensation was duly given. Louis, feeling hindered by his own need for a papal dispensation, found himself morally compromised, unable to thwart Henry's plans.

The children were married in haste, at Neubourg, on 2 November, before Louis' puny protests amounted to anything. The Knights Templar who had acted as guardians of the Vexin

---

* Marie married Henry I of Champagne, and Alix, Theobald V of Blois.

castles – Robert of Pirou, Tostes of Saint-Omer and Richard of Hastings – accordingly vacated them, to Louis' horror. Louis, expending his wrath and disappointment on these unfortunate targets, banished them from France, but Henry welcomed them and made them rich.[37]

Henri and his young wife lived separately. By Easter 1162, when he was seven years old, the prince had been entrusted to the household of Henry's chancellor, Thomas Becket, by his parents. It was usual for royal and noble children to leave their parents' nominal care at a young age, to study and to learn knightly skills in a fellow noble's household, and Becket was the best. He was a beguiling role model for the young prince. Becket was clever, learned, an exceptional and proven soldier. William FitzStephen noted that 'The king ... commended his son, the heir to the kingdom to his training, and the chancellor kept him with him among the many nobles' sons of similar age, and their appropriate attendants, masters and servants according to rank.'[38] Becket and his protégé became fond of one another. Henri may well have been impressed by Becket's astonishing and meretricious wealth, displayed far more ostentatiously than his father's.

Henry was plotting. He planned to crown his eldest son in his lifetime to ensure the succession, and as quickly as possible, hoping to avoid another blood-drenched race to the throne when he died, as had happened at the death of every monarch except Stephen since the Norman Conquest. This was not a new idea, at least in the empire before the rules of primogeniture were more firmly established. It was, however, new to England. Stephen had attempted to have Eustace crowned within his lifetime, but had failed. Henry was determined to prevail.

There was another consideration too. Louis still had no son; Philip would not be born until August 1165. In the first half of the 1160s, it seemed entirely plausible that the Capetian throne would pass to their greatest enemies, the Plantagenets, through the as yet unborn issue of Henri and Margaret.

Henry had not kept his promise regarding Margaret's care. Against Louis' explicit request, in 1164 John of Salisbury found her living in Eleanor's household when he went to ask the queen's permission to leave the country. This was a clear indication of Henry's lack of respect for Louis, and his acknowledgement of the French king's weakness in his eyes. John, after meeting with Louis in Paris, told his great friend Thomas Becket of his shocking conversation with the French king: Louis had wished his daughter dead, saying 'that he would be very thankful if she had already been received by the angels in Paradise'. Louis feared the inexorable march of Henry FitzEmpress, and dreaded the prospect that his daughter might give birth to a Plantagenet heir who would inherit France. As John remarked, 'The French fear our king, and hate him.'[39]

Henry, although he granted Henri no formal power, began to associate his son with government while he was still extremely young. Henry was following in a tradition set by his parents; first, Matilda had begun to associate him with government in England from 1141, and later Geoffrey had made it clear that he had conquered and held Normandy safe for Henry, for when he reached adulthood.[40]

And so, when Henry was on the continent, young Henri became the ceremonial face of his father's government in England. Preparing the prince for coronation, Henry sent Becket from Normandy to England in May 1162 with the instruction 'to gain the fealty and subjection of all to his son, then to be crowned and sworn in as king'.[41] In the same month, it was Henri who formally accepted the recommendation of the bishop of Winchester – Henry of Blois – that Becket be appointed archbishop of Canterbury, and was present at Becket's consecration on 3 June in place of his father.

Henry ordered the regalia for the prince's crowning to be prepared, in anticipation of an imminent coronation. But an early ceremony was not to be. By October of the following year Henry, locked in dispute with his new archbishop, punished him by removing his eldest son from Becket's household and establishing him in his own.

The crisis with Becket obliterated the king's hopes for the coronation, at least for now. Henry, determined to have his way, planned to circumnavigate his recalcitrant archbishop. John of Salisbury reported that the king beseeched the pope to crown Henri himself.[42] The pope refused.

Coronation or no coronation, Henry placed his designated heir at the centre of his political machine. Young Henri was present at Henry's propaganda showpiece, the translation of Edward the Confessor's relics at Westminster in October 1163. Henri was most likely also at the consecration of Reading, in April 1164 – his presence a potent symbol of the king's dynastic ambitions, in the great abbey which housed the hand of St James, and the buried remains of his great-grandfather Henry I and his elder brother, William.[43] And Henri, still only eight years old, was placed beside his father at the Council of Clarendon in January 1164, where the king issued his Constitutions.

Henri was finally crowned at Westminster on 14 June 1170. Resplendent in green, he may have been knighted before the ceremony. In anointing and crowning him, Henry afforded his son equal status.

Yet his coronation gave the young king no real power. Henri's role was symbolic only. His father had placed a new master well versed in law, William FitzJohn, in Henri's household, presumably to assist in his training for kingship. But Henry could never bring himself to hand over any genuine responsibility to his principal heir.[44]

Later, in the thirteenth century, a story was circulated by the chronicler Matthew Paris of Henry serving his son at his coronation banquet, demeaning his own kingship in the process; Paris wrote of young Henri's supposed and rather smug remark to his father, that it was proper for the son of a count to serve the son of a king.[45] If the story is true, Henry's act of generosity would have meant no diminishing of his authority. Henry was always willing to give up the superficial and was inclined to be magnanimous, so long as the gesture detracted nothing from his total and absolute grasp of power.

The day after his coronation, the new young king received the homage of William the Lion of Scotland, and his brother, David earl of Huntingdon, and of the chief barons of England and Normandy. But the oath sworn by the king of Scotland and the great magnates of the realm put Henry above his newly crowned son, ending with the words 'stand by my son [Henri] with your might and your aid against all the people in the world, save where my own [Henry II's] overlordship is concerned'.[46]

After the coronation, the king placed the unsurpassably loyal William Marshal as head of Henri's household, to tutor him in chivalry.

William Marshal first came to the attention of the royal family in 1168. When Eleanor returned to Poitiers, he went as part of his uncle Patrick of Salisbury's household; Patrick was charged by Henry to lead his troops there. In April, Earl Patrick and his men, William among them, saved Eleanor from kidnap by the thuggish Lusignan family. Patrick was murdered in the skirmish, but William fought brilliantly and although he was captured and held for several months, Eleanor paid for his release and took him into her service. He would never desert Henry's family, and worked for them until his death in 1219, at the age of about seventy-three.

The chroniclers first wrote of William when he was only five years old. His father, John Marshal, was a staunch advocate of Matilda's during the civil war, and had even lost an eye in her service when an abbey he was sheltering in was set on fire. When his castle at Newbury was besieged by Stephen in 1152, he offered the king his fourth son, five-year-old William, as a hostage to facilitate a truce. But John broke the truce; Stephen, who had taken the boy into his camp, was kind to him and even played a game of 'knights' with him, sent John word that if he disobeyed him, he would execute his child. John's response was to send a message that he had the equipment – 'the anvils and hammers' – to make new and better sons, and did not need this one.

Stephen's supporters urged him to execute young William; luckily for William, Stephen refused, although he did keep him as a comfortable hostage for over a year.

We know so much about this man who was neither royal nor a high-ranking cleric, because William's son, unusually, commissioned a biographical poem of him: *L'Histoire de Guillaume le Maréchal* ('The History of William Marshal').

Although Henri liked and respected William Marshal, he may well have felt that his youth was now over – he was married, an anointed king, and fifteen years old – and had little need for a 'babysitter'. At fifteen his father had already hired soldiers to battle Stephen, and was being groomed for leadership by both his parents. Henri's hopes perhaps rose higher when Henry, decamping for Normandy after the coronation, left him in England with power to dispense justice – *'omnes rectitudines et justicias'* – and ordered a new seal for him.

Just a month after the young king's coronation, Henry fell dangerously ill in Normandy. Rumours spread that he was dead. Before Henri received correct information, he must have reasonably expected that he would now rule alone. We may only speculate on his emotions when he heard that his father still lived – delight, despair – or a little of both?[47]

In Henry's absence the young king asserted his kingship through pomp. While his father campaigned in Ireland, Henri held a lavish Christmas court in Normandy, attended by Geoffrey and his Breton lords; he showed his men what a magnificent and less financially intrusive duke he would be. But it was the most he was allowed to do. Although designated regent, it was Richard de Lucy the justiciar who ruled in practice, and not the young king. Henri was, and increasingly felt himself to be, powerless.

In August 1172 Henri was crowned again at Winchester, this time by Rotrou, archbishop of Rouen. For Henri, who had already been anointed with the sacred oil in 1170, this was a crown-wearing.[48] Margaret, who had been excluded from the first ceremony, was now crowned queen. Although he did not attend, Henry arranged it in part to please Louis, and in part as an act of cleansing, to wash away any smear associated between his son, his first coronation, and Becket's death.[49] It was most likely at this point that the young couple finally consummated their marriage and began to live together. They had been married for twelve years.

Despite his marriage and double-crowning, Henri's status remained ambivalent. Henry granted him neither power nor money to keep his wife and his household, and he kept the leash tight. Henri was allowed no control over Margaret's dower lands. Roger of Howden wrote that Henri 'took it badly that his father did not wish to assign him any territory where he could dwell with his queen'.[50] His financial dependency was a matter of comment by the author of the *Chronicle of the Princes*:

Henry the Younger, his [Henry II's] son, came to him to ask him what he might do or what he ought to do after his being ordained new king. For although he was king with many knights under him, yet he had no means by which he could reward them, unless he obtained it from his father ... And his father replied that he would give him for expenses twenty pounds daily of the money of that land. And the son, when he heard that, said that he had never heard of a king being a paid servant, and that he would not be such.[51]

Henri's surviving acta, or charters, show that even his grants were merely confirmations of his father's grants.[52] William Marshal, although one of the greatest knights in the realm, was called a youth until his forties because Henri had no money or land to give him, despite the longevity and faithfulness of his service.[53] Henri, with no kingdom to rule, was 'at a loss for something to do'.[54]

Henry seems not to have noticed his immediate family's growing alienation from him. He had disregarded Eleanor's craving for autonomy over her lands, refused any compromise with her or their children, and in doing so lost first their affection, and then their loyalty. He behaved like an autocrat towards his sons, contrary to the model set by his own parents that had so benefited him. The early promise was withering as Henry's flaws began to sabotage his rule; the intransigent tyrant emerged.

VI

During the last week of February 1173, Henry, Eleanor, Henri and Richard gathered at Limoges. They were joined by a pantheon of southern European nobility – Count Raymond V of Toulouse, Alfonso II the king of Aragon, Sancho VI the king of Navarre, and the count of Savoy, Humbert III of Maurienne. During that same week, on the 28th, Henri turned eighteen.

For Henry, the week of feasting, celebration, new alliances and new promises was a triumph, particularly after his humiliation before the papal legates at Avranches less than a year before.

The occasion was marred only by a warning from Henry's erstwhile enemy and rebellious vassal, Count Raymond of Toulouse: 'Beware your wife and sons.'[55] It was a bold claim.

Raymond and Henry had never been friends. Eleanor, and therefore Henry too, believed Toulouse belonged to her as duchess of Aquitaine, through right of her grandmother, Philippa.[56] Eleanor's grandfather, William IX of Aquitaine, the troubadour duke, had married Philippa, daughter of Count William IV of Toulouse. On William's death, the lordship had passed to his brother, Raymond IV, and not to his grandson, Eleanor's father, despite William IX's ardent protests. Raymond V, Eleanor's cousin, was therefore, in Henry's and Eleanor's eyes, a usurper.

The counts of Toulouse ruled over a large and mountainous territory, bordered by France, Provence and Spain. As such, they did not look to just the French king for alliances, but also to the German emperor who held Provence as a fief, and to the kings of Aragon-Barcelona. The kings of France had long been anxious over the potential threat of an independent power base represented by the counts of Toulouse. But for Louis, one of the only good things to come out of the luckless Second Crusade was the friendship that developed between him and Count Raymond V. In 1154, Louis gave Raymond his sister Constance, Eustace's widow, in marriage. Raymond and Constance quickly produced three sons, and in the absence of a son of his own, during the 1150s and early 1160s these nephews were Louis' heirs.[57]

Raymond's friendship and allegiance were therefore extremely important to Louis. They remained close: in 1162, Raymond declared to Louis 'I am your man, and all that is ours is yours.'[58] Louis needed Raymond's loyalty as a buffer to Henry. There was nothing that Louis desired more than Henry's destruction, or at the very least, the diminution of his authority.

But by 1166, the friendship had cooled. Raymond repudiated Constance and persuaded the imperial antipope to grant him an annulment on the flimsy pretext of consanguinity. Louis was furious, and nervous as to where Raymond would find new alliances.

When, in 1167 at Grandmont, Louis heard that Henry and Raymond held a conversation – 'the king of England spoke with the count of Toulouse' – he was petrified.[59] Louis picked a fight with Henry over the relatively small issue of raising funds in

France for the Holy Land. Henry, against Louis' wishes, preferred to send money collected in his lands via his own people, whereas Louis required all monies to go through him. Robert of Torigni, abbot of Mont Saint-Michel, tells us that this led to a *'magna discordia'*, a great argument, between the two monarchs. Louis was obviously fearful that Raymond, freed from familial loyalty by the dissolution of his marriage to Constance, was about to forge an alliance with Henry. Louis and Henry began a series of skirmishes interrupted by truces that would last for two years, until the peace made at Montmirail in 1169.

By the time Raymond came to Limoges in February 1173, he had made up his mind to pay homage to Henry and his sons for Toulouse. And he did. He prostrated himself before his new lords, declared himself their man, and promised to deliver ten warhorses, his military service when required, and an annual contribution of a hundred silver marks.[60] This act of homage to Henry and his sons was humiliating for Louis. Ermengarde, viscountess of Narbonne, wrote that it made him a 'shadow king', 'not only in Toulouse but in all our region from the Garonne to the Rhône'.[61] But Raymond alarmed Eleanor by paying homage not just to Richard as the duchy's heir, but to Henry and the young king too. It was becoming clear now to Eleanor that, unless she acted, her precious Aquitaine would be subsumed into the greater Angevin Empire on Henry's death, with Richard fated to hold the duchy from his older brother.

Eleanor already had cause to be angry with Henry; as early as 1168 he had begun siphoning off parts of her duchy, when he promised their second daughter, young Eleanor, in marriage to King Alfonso VIII of Castile. Her dowry was to be Gascony. To Henry, it made perfect sense. The marriage thwarted Louis by severing his ambitions towards Castile (the death of his second wife, Constance of Castile, ended his influence), and it strengthened his own position in the south of France against the hegemony of the counts of Toulouse and the kings of Aragon-Barcelona.

Furthermore the marriage treaty stipulated that the kings of Castile could not claim Gascony until Eleanor's death.

For Henry, the marriage was a victory. The young Princess Eleanor, not quite nine years old, was duly delivered to the Castilian royal family by her mother in September 1170. But Eleanor seethed. Henry had given away part of *her* duchy, not his. Gascony, her southern bloc – one-fifth of her lands – was to be surrendered to Castile. She was left fearful for Richard's inheritance. His would be a fractured duchy.

Salvation was still possible, were Henry only to have repaired his alliance with Eleanor. Instead, he sidelined and neglected her.

Henry had not kept his side of the bargain. He had trampled on his wife's rights to rule in her own lands and now he humiliated her by his acceptance of Raymond's homage for Toulouse, publicly abandoning his queen's claims there. It is unlikely that Henry even discussed the matter with her. Naively he did not envisage any repercussions and doubtless believed that what belonged to Eleanor by birth, was his by marriage. He did just as Louis had done; he failed to appreciate his wife's value to him. He would live to suffer the consequences.

VII

The gathering at Limoges precipitated another fracture within the family.

Henry was acutely aware that he had still not provided for John, now six years old. When Humbert of Maurienne, the count of Savoy and a powerful lord whose territories in the Alps bordered France and Italy, approached Henry to suggest a marriage between John and his daughter and heiress, Henry was delighted. John would be provided for by inheriting Maurienne in right of his wife. Henry, in return for the marriage, promised 5,000 marks to Humbert. Towards the end of the negotiations, Count Humbert asked Henry what else John would bring to the marriage. Henry, in haste, promised away the castles of Chinon, Loudun and Mirebeau in Anjou.

The gift of three castles pleased Humbert. But news of the transaction infuriated Henri, for the castles formed a part of his inheritance, and he did not want them promised away to John, whom he barely knew, certainly not when Richard was starting to exercise real power in Aquitaine, and Geoffrey was now invested as duke of Brittany.

Henri complained to his father that he had given his castles away without consulting him. His anger was probably exacerbated by the proximity of his eighteenth birthday; he was now of age. Yet his father still refused to relinquish any power to him, despite promises to do so more than two years earlier as Henry believed himself dying.

Henri's rage brought to a head years of frustration with his father; for he believed that, in denying him power and money, Henry had treated him appallingly. Even Henri's seal reflected his nebulous status. It was single-sided, and unusually he was depicted without a sword, a cogent symbol of power. It was half a seal, as he was only half a king.[62]

In February 1173 anger made the young king bold. Possibly following heated discussions with his equally angry mother and brother Richard, Henri asked his father to relinquish to him immediately either England, Normandy or Anjou. It was not an unreasonable request, given that Henry had been installed as duke of Normandy when he was eighteen. Henry refused his son. The chronicler Jordan Fantosme understood that it would simply not have been in Henry's nature to accede: Henry would 'choose death rather than life before his son came to that power [England], so long as he could smite with sword and lance'.[63]

Henry heeded Raymond's warning. As the gathering at Limoges disbanded, he secured his fortresses in Aquitaine and Normandy, and took the unhappy and bitter Henri and his companions with him. They travelled north to Henry's castle of

Chinon, one of the three castles Henry had promised away from his eldest son to John. His choice of destination must have stung the young king.

Chinon served as a fortress, an administrative base, and a home. The family residence was rather intimate, not built to a grand scale. It was from this comparatively small house nestled within the castle walls that Henri, on 5 March, made a daring and forbidden dash for his father-in-law's court in the middle of the night, accompanied by just his closest friends.[64]

Henry, as king, naturally exerted enormous control. It was one of the hallmarks of successful monarchy. But Henry's control extended beyond his intimates, his nobility and his subjects to his immediate family. One of the young king's many grievances against his father was that Henry placed his own men in his household, the *familia* who acted as his knights and his most personal servants. The chronicler Robert of Torigni, abbot of Mont Saint-Michel and Henry's friend (he was young Eleanor's godfather), believed it to be, above all, Henry's interference in his son's inner household, his incorporation of his own servants into Henri's household and particularly his dismissal of Henri's close friend Hasculf of Saint-Hilaire and other knights, that led him to revolt, demanding the power and autonomy he felt he deserved.[65] Henry's eldest son had reached his breaking point.

Now, in the middle of the night, he ran away from Henry, and from 'his ministers, whom his father had deputed to his service'.[66]

As soon as he discovered the young king's defection, Henry set off in pursuit. The author of the Melrose Chronicle wrote that 'The father had intended to capture his son, and to put him in a sure and close place of custody.'[67] Perhaps Henri believed this, and perhaps the fear of captivity made him fleet of foot. For once, and despite his legendary reputation for speed, Henry was too late. The young king managed to reach Chartres where Louis was waiting to welcome him, with his father a few miles behind him.

He was out of Henry's reach, safe inside his father-in-law's domain.

Henri's defection was probably planned four months earlier, in November 1172, when he and Margaret had visited Louis in Paris for All Saints' Day. It was on this occasion that his father-in-law inculcated in a willing convert the desire to be king in fact as well as name.

Louis, in Paris, did everything he could to undermine Henry. He manipulated his young son-in-law adroitly, using him as his tool to destroy his greatest foe. He reminded him that he was an anointed king, and encouraged him to demand part of his inheritance immediately, either England or Normandy. Henri trusted him completely. William of Newburgh recorded that he 'confided in his advice in all things'.[68]

Despite Louis' apparent mild manner, his hatred of Henry was constant. Henry had, after all, stolen his wife, and he controlled vast swathes of territory which Louis believed belonged within the domain of the French crown. He had endured numberless slights and machinations by Henry. Louis used the occasion of their visit to exploit Henri; but he gambled on Henry's refusal to hand over territory. This refusal would achieve the French king's desired outcome: Angevin family fracture, and war.

Henry had failed to capture his son. He was mortified, and begged Henri to return, sending 'men of distinction to the king of France, with pacific words, demanding his son by paternal right, and promising that, if anything should appear to require amendment with regard to him, by his advice he would immediately amend it'.

The answer he received stunned him:

The king of France, upon hearing these words, asked, 'Who is it that sends this message to me?' They replied, 'The king of England.' 'It is false,' he answered, 'behold the king of England is here; and he sends no message to me by you – but if, even now, you style his father king, who was formerly king of England, know ye that he, as king, is dead: and though he may still act as king, yet that shall soon be remedied, for he resigned his kingdom to his son, as the world is witness.'[69]

Worse was to follow, as Henry's family defected to Louis and the young king one by one. Even Gerald of Wales was uncharacteristically sympathetic to Henry: 'The enmity of those of the same family is among the worst of human plagues'.[70] Eleanor had stoked the boys' anger towards Henry, founded in his denial of their power. Richard, and then Geoffrey, incited by their mother, joined the young king at Chartres. Rotrou, archbishop of Rouen, wrote to Eleanor, damning her actions. She had 'opened the way for the lord king's, and your own, children to rise up against their father ... You alone are now the guilty one, but your actions will result in ruin for all in the kingdom.'[71]

Sure as Rotrou was of her active role in the revolt, he charged her to return to Henry: 'So before worse befall, return with your sons to the husband whom you should live with and obey. If you do return to him, no suspicion will fall on either you or your sons. We are quite sure that the king will offer you affection and utter safety. Exhort your sons, I pray you, to be obedient and devoted to their father: he has been through so much anxiety on their behalf, so many difficult situations, so much labour.'

The missive bore Rotrou's name, but the silky threats revealed the true author: 'You are one of our flock, as is your husband, but we cannot ignore the demands of justice: either you come back to your husband or we shall be obliged by canon law to lay upon you the censure of the church. We say that reluctantly, but reluctantly, in tears and in anguish, we shall do it, if you fail to come to a better mind.'[72]

Eleanor, however, was not inclined to soothe her sons' disaffection, nor to submit to her husband; she had been pushed too far and for too long to return to Henry. As Henry's men poured south into Aquitaine, she fled north towards her sons and Louis at Chartres, possibly disguised as a man to elude capture. But she was apprehended by her husband's agents and taken as a prisoner to Chinon. The spark she had lit would soon engulf Henry's empire in flames.

It is possible that Eleanor's capture is the subject of a curious wall painting at the underground chapel of Sainte-Radegonde at Chinon. The central crowned figure is plausibly Eleanor, being led by another crowned figure, assumed to be Henry, and saying goodbye to Richard and the young king as Henry leads her to her prison. If it is a painting of Eleanor, it is one of only four contemporary images that survive.[73] She remains as elusive in art as she does in the written record.

VIII

'The king ... was not a little anxious by reason of these unexpected difficulties which were arising to face him on every side. But assiduously reassuring his supporters, and giving an impression of optimism with a cheerful and undismayed countenance, he mustered whatever resources he could from every quarter and by all possible means.'[74]

Gerald of Wales's assessment was an understatement. Ranged against Henry were his wife, three of his sons, the might of the French king's army and their allies. He would have to call upon his vast military experience, and deploy the entire arsenal – diplomacy, siege warfare, pitched battles and mercenary forces. Henry was fighting for his life; he could not afford to lose.

The rebellion was highly incestuous. Besides his three eldest sons and wife, Henry could count among his enemies his son's father-in-law (Louis); his cousins, the brothers Philip of Flanders and Matthew of Boulogne, sons of his paternal aunt Sibylla of Anjou;[75] his maternal cousins the brothers William the Lion of Scotland and David of Huntingdon; his cousin Hugh of

Chester, the grandson of Henry's uncle Robert of Gloucester, who had been so unwavering in his support for his nephew's cause during the dark days of the civil war; and Robert Blanchmains, earl of Leicester, son of Henry's deceased co-justiciar, who had been an intimate not only of Henry, but of his grandfather Henry I too.

These family members and close friends were joined by many others, including Raoul de Fougères, the bellicose Norfolk lord Hugh Bigod, the count of Bar, the earl of Fife, the earl of Angus, the bishop of Durham, the earl of Dunbar, Richard de Morville, constable of Scotland, and Roger de Mowbray.

To gain the loyalty of these great magnates, the young king promised lands, castles and revenue, tantamount to giving away a kingdom. The scale of his gifts to William the Lion of Scotland (vast swathes of the north of England), to Philip of Flanders (money and the key castles of Dover and Rochester), and to Philip's brother Matthew of Boulogne (the county of Mortaine and the honour of Hay), among others, was extraordinary and would almost certainly be impossible to fulfil while holding on to power, should he win.[76]

To add legitimacy to the rebel cause, Louis knighted Richard; and William Marshal knighted Henri – if Henri had been knighted by his father before his first coronation, he now purged himself of the taint by having himself knighted afresh, the very act denying his father's kingship.[77]

At the beginning of April, at Saint-Denis, the players against Henry assembled. It was a menacing force. Many of the chroniclers believed that Becket's death, despite Henry's show of penance, had devastating consequences for the king. By inciting the four knights to murder the archbishop, Henry had brought upon himself the wrath of heaven, culminating in this moment – the greatest personal and political crisis of his reign, as 'the Lord's martyr [Becket] ... seemed to seek vengeance for the innocent blood. For the king, the king's son, rebelled against his father, bent on expelling him from the throne, and many of the great magnates sided with him, and helped him.'[78]

Henry was shocked by the betrayal and the unprecedented scale of the revolt. The affable dictator, Henry had never imagined, even in his wildest nightmares, and despite Raymond's warning, that his children and his wife would turn on him.

The chroniclers wrote in words that dripped with doom and messianic fervour. In 1173, 'the three sons of King Henry rebelled together against their father: the kingdoms of the earth were overthrown, churches laid waste, religion dragged through the mire and peace lost throughout the land'.[79]

Henry's sons, however fierce their anger, were only the token face of the rebellion. They were still young and were largely ineffectual. The real threat came from Louis, and from the many magnates who had long nursed grievances against Henry; now their time had come.

Once Henri's defection was known, and that he had the backing of Louis, several of Henry's nobles surged towards the young king. By June 1173 much of Henry's empire was in revolt.

In England, those earls who came out openly against Henry – Hugh Bigod, Hugh of Chester, Robert Blanchmains of Leicester and William de Ferrers of Derby – all believed that Henry had not handed over the full extent of the lands and grants that were rightfully theirs, denying them power and money. In Normandy and Brittany, the rebels were mainly those whose power Henry had curtailed – in Brittany, since bringing the duchy under his control in 1166. And in Aquitaine, the count of Angoulême and some of the barons in Poitou determined to fight against Henry, each driven by the belief that Henry owed them more, be it land, power, or money.[80]

Ralph of Diceto blamed Henry's poor judgement for the rebellion, citing 'those men ... who joined the party of the son, not because they regarded his as the juster cause, but because the father ... was trampling upon the necks of the proud and haughty, was dismantling or appropriating the castles of the country'.[81]

Henry, as he centralised government to maximise his income and strengthen his regime, had ordered in 1171 'an investigation to be made throughout Normandy as to the lands which King Henry his grandfather had held on the day of his death; and inquiry was also made into what lands, woods, and other property had been occupied by barons and other men since the death of King Henry his grandfather; and by this means he doubled his income'. The attack on baronial wealth infuriated many.[82] Furthermore the Constitutions of Clarendon, made nine years earlier in 1164, curbed the power of the barons as well as the church in the Crown's pursuit of criminals. Many of the rebels believed Henry had gone too far in the erosion of their powers.

Henry never relished warfare. He preferred to seek his ends though diplomacy, 'regarding with horror the shedding of blood and the death of man, he made it his study to seek for peace: with arms ... when he could not do otherwise, but more willingly with money, whenever he was able'.[83] This time, however unwillingly, Henry had to fight.

For over a year Henry battled doggedly in what contemporaries called 'the Great Revolt'. Its scale was horrifying. Roger of Howden wrote that 'immediately after Easter ... the wicked fury of the traitors burst forth. For, raving with diabolical frenzy, they laid waste the territories of the king of England on both sides of the sea with fire and sword in every direction.'[84] More daunting still, Henry or his faithful deputies were forced to fight, often simultaneously, on six fronts – in central England, northern England, Brittany, and three in Normandy – as his enemies arrayed against him.[85] Throughout the Great Revolt, Henry and his allies engaged in nearly forty sieges, skirmishes or battles.

Henri began the fighting by attacking his father's forces in the Vexin, but he failed, and so he went south to Louis, at Verneuil. Philip of Flanders, however, made astonishing early gains.

Aumarle in Normandy fell to him on 29 June, then Drincourt on 21 July. The rebel Matthew of Boulogne, the brother of Philip of Flanders, was fatally wounded here by a stray arrow. His brother took him to Flanders, but he died a few days later. Matthew's death quickly eliminated a major enemy almost before the fight had begun; for Henry, it was a stroke of luck.[86]

The rebels were all familiar with Henry's defining characteristic in battle – his almost superhuman speed in reaching a trouble spot. But Henry was fighting on many fronts, and he was obliged to delegate. He was adroit in his choice of deputies. As Henry dealt with Philip of Flanders, the highly able Hugh de Lacy and Hugh de Beauchamp held out against Louis and Henri at Verneuil.

In England, Henry faced William the Lion of Scotland (William's grandfather David of Scotland had knighted Henry when he was sixteen), and many of his own magnates on his northern borders. The chronicler Jordan Fantosme, in his epic poem describing the war with William the Lion in the north of England, recorded that 40,000 soldiers turned out to fight for William. (William of Newburgh gives the fantastical figure of 80,000 men.[87]) Although the numbers are exaggerated, Henry faced huge danger. We do know that Henry had hired thousands of mercenaries, and was likely able to match his enemies' forces.

William marched into Northumbria towards the end of June, arriving at Wark Castle, where its beleaguered and frightened castellan, Roger de Stuteville, begged William for forty days' grace to appeal to Henry to come to his aid. William, observing the rules of chivalrous warfare, agreed. He left Wark and continued south, but was unable to successfully besiege any castles as he had no siege engines. Instead, frustrated, he laid waste to the countryside around Newcastle in a bloody campaign, and continued on to Carlisle in Cumberland. Here, finally, William began a siege but was unable to take the castle. When news reached him that Richard de Lucy was racing north with an army to fight him,

William left a skeleton force at Carlisle and took flight with the remainder of his men.[88]

Louis and William had a once-in-a-generation opportunity to defeat Henry FitzEmpress; but they had no grand strategy, and their tactics were generally poor. They were up against an enemy of excellent judgement, determination and capability. Henry had put in place good commanders and castellans, he deployed his deadly mercenary forces, which made up the bulk of his armies, very effectively, and he continued to appear when the enemy least expected him. Henry could be observed 'racing through the border country, dashing from one area to another and doing three days' journey or more in a single day; his men thought he must be flying'.[89] This all helped him greatly. Luck helped him too – no invasion from Scotland or Flanders materialised, and Louis was a poor military leader. The historian John Hosler, in his brilliant analysis of Henry's military prowess, calls Louis 'a weak general, much like his ally William the Lion', employing 'haphazard methods of fighting'.[90]

Henry benefited as much from his enemy's weakness as he did from his ability to inspire enormous loyalty, in paying his legion of mercenaries very well, his military cunning and strength, and his renowned inability to lose. Psychologically and physically, his successes created the myth of an unbeatable general.

This war, however, took a huge emotional toll on him. He was devastated that he was obliged to fight his own children for his kingdom. After the war, Jordan Fantosme recorded Henry's anguish: 'Rage seizes my body, I am nearly mad ... To those who hate me to death they have abandoned themselves, to King Louis ... and to my eldest son, who comes disinheriting me of what I possess. He would rob me of my land and fiefs and heritages. I am not so old ... that I should lose land on account of my great age.'[91]

Roger of Howden, clerk, diplomat and Angevin court historian, was with Henry from 1174 until the king's death; praising

Henry's martial skills, he called him an 'adroit and formidable man at arms'.[92] William of Newburgh noted that Henry, realising the mistake he had made in crowning young Henri, galvanised himself to meet the threat. He quickly fortified his castles, and raised money throughout his empire, particularly from the Jewish communities, and from Flemish moneylenders, to pay for the war to come.[93]

Henry also commissioned Brabanter mercenaries whose terror tactics stupified their enemies; they so petrified Rome that they were outlawed at the Third Council of the Lateran in 1179. Henry predominantly used mercenaries from Brabant (a region in the Low Countries) and Wales, occasionally hiring Irish and Scots too. Flemings, rarely found in Henry's armies, were more often in the ranks of his enemies, particularly in Louis' forces. Henry had expelled them from England in 1155; perhaps a distaste for them remained. He used them only very reluctantly.

Mercenary forces formed the bulk of his foot soldiers, and he also used them in his infantry and as archers. Henry trained them and remunerated them well. Despite the hostility of the chroniclers, these men were not always bands of brigands. They were skilled and effective soldiers, and many remained in Henry's service for years, forming bonds of loyalty. Although they could wreak devastation on local populations as they foraged for food, and obeyed their commanders in burning the land, for the most part they were well ordered. They 'served [Henry] faithfully, but not without the great pay which he gave them'. A modern historian has estimated that Henry hired about 6,000 mercenaries to fight the war, although this number is arguably too small.[94]

Throughout the Great Revolt, Henry tried to bring his enemies into open battle, but his adversaries were equally keen to avoid it, fleeing before Henry and his armies. Brittany, however, was a different matter; Henry's rebellious vassals Hugh of Chester and Raoul de Fougères had raised an enormous army. Now, Henry sent William de Hommet (the son of his constable in Normandy) at the head of his Brabanter force to subdue them. Roger of Howden wrote that this army consisted of 20,000 men.

The battle which took place on 20 August at Dol, in Brittany, close to the Norman border, resulted in the complete annihilation of the rebel Breton force. The cavalry led the charge, followed by the infantry. Hundreds, perhaps thousands were massacred; Roger of Howden thought that 1,500 Bretons died.[95] Many of the survivors sought refuge at Dol Castle. Henry was quick to follow from Rouen, 170 miles away, with his famed siege engines, and, 'forgetting both food and sleep, and constantly changing his relays ... arrived so quickly that he seemed to have flown'.[96] Hugh of Chester, when he realised that Henry would take the castle, surrendered on 26 August. Henry, capturing about one hundred of his rebellious nobility, treated them 'with very much more clemency than they deserved'.[97] Henry could not have won at Dol without his Brabanters, a fundamental pillar of his warfare.

The rebels were now a desolate force and they sought a pragmatic peace with Henry. On 25 September 1173, at an uncomfortable meeting at Gisors, Henry met with Henri, Richard, Geoffrey, Louis and their rebel partners. Henry wanted peace and was prepared to be conciliatory.

He could have crushed them, but he did not. Henry's terms were generous. He offered his children castles and money, and to Geoffrey he promised Brittany, if he married the duchy's heiress, Constance. He did not mention Eleanor at all. But although the boys may have been inclined to settle with their father, Louis and his advisors schemed to keep the Angevin royal family at each other's throats. Robert of Leicester, in an outrageous spectacle, screamed at Henry and tried to attack him, reaching to draw his sword on the king. The earl was held back, and Henry walked out, possibly in anger or just disappointment.[98] All hopes of peace were broken.

IX

In England, Henry charged his able justiciar and regent, Richard de Lucy, to protect the country.[99] Richard, working with Humphrey de Bohun, Henry's constable, forged truces, and they bought themselves time. His ability meant that Henry could trust the defence of England to him, while Henry fought for his lands in Normandy. He may have been fighting on six fronts, but he was not alone. As it happened, Henry was hundreds of miles away when the largest battle of his reign was fought. It was Richard de Lucy rather than his king who was forced to face an apoplectic Robert of Leicester, goaded to bring an invasion force to England by Louis and still smarting from his failed personal attack on Henry.

Robert, seeking vengeance and intent on ravaging eastern England, hired Flemish, Hollander and French mercenaries, and landed at Walton in Suffolk on 26 September. He allied with Hugh Bigod, who brought more troops, horses and provisions from his castle, Framlingham; Robert went west to besiege Haughley Castle, near Bury St Edmunds, and it fell after four days.

Meanwhile those loyal to Henry rallied to Richard de Lucy and the constable, Humphrey de Bohun; they numbered Henry's uncle, Reginald of Cornwall, Robert of Gloucester, and William of Arundel. Henry's eldest bastard son, Geoffrey Plantagenet (the son he liked best), now bishop-elect of Lincoln, fought with the royalists. All brought with them more men, and the local peasantry joined the fight on the side of the king.[100] There was no appetite in East Anglia for the rebels: when, at Dunwich, Robert of Leicester and Hugh Bigod tried to persuade the inhabitants to their cause, thereby betraying their king, women and children threw rocks at them.[101]

Robert of Leicester's mercenary force, 'of hundreds, of thousands' consisted mainly of infantry, with some French cavalry.[102]

The exact numbers are not clear, and the chroniclers doubtless exaggerated wildly; Ralph of Diceto had the number of fighting men at 3,000, but even this sum may be too large.[103] It is possible that Richard de Lucy commanded more men, but the enemy had more professional soldiers within their ranks.[104]

The two armies met on 17 October at Fornham in Suffolk, in a chance battle, as Robert of Leicester made his way to the Midlands via Cambridge. Richard de Lucy had the advantage – he happened upon Robert of Leicester's army as they were crossing the River Lark near Bury St Edmunds, apparently heedless of a massive royalist force just miles away. Robert was in a vulnerable position; some of his men were in the river, some were on one side and some on the other. There was no opportunity to bring them together. The Flemings ran away, chased by the peasants who turned out to fight for Henry and who butchered those they caught, massacring them 'in fifteens, in forties, in hundreds, in thousands'.[105] Richard's cavalry destroyed the earl of Leicester's mostly French horsemen. Roger of Howden wrote, with considerable exaggeration, that Richard de Lucy only lost 300 men, while his army slaughtered up to 10,000.

Robert's wife, Petronilla de Grandmesnil, fought alongside him in battle, 'carrying shield and lance'.[106] But when she fell into a ditch and lost her rings, she became hysterical and threatened to drown herself. She was dissuaded by a royalist knight, Simon de Wahull, and captured. Robert, when he saw her predicament and his men being hacked down around him, panicked. He too was easily captured, as was his cousin, Hughes de Châteauneuf. The prisoners were taken to Porchester Castle, and then to Normandy, to answer to Henry. Robert of Leicester was not freed until 1177, and Henry destroyed or confiscated all his castles save for Breteuil in Normandy. He would never trust Robert, nor his wife, again. Hugh Bigod, meanwhile, was allowed to pay for a truce.

The battle at Fornham highlighted the meagre and often shambolic quality of the enemy Henry faced during this war. Richard de Lucy had won, securing England for Henry, at least for the time being. His efforts allowed Henry to stay in Normandy, capturing castles and securing his frontiers.

By the end of 1173, the insurgents in Brittany had been subdued, and the two major rebels in England – Robert of Leicester and Hugh Bigod – were imprisoned or neutralised. Leicester's Flemish mercenaries were dead or captured. But Henry's sons, Louis, and Philip of Flanders fought on. And although Richard de Lucy had agreed a truce with William the Lion, William remained a putative threat on Henry's northern border.

Henri, still intent on defeating his father, joined with his allies Philip of Flanders and Theobald of Blois to attack Sées in Normandy. When they failed, they arranged for yet another truce, to last until the end of March. Henry, meanwhile, continued to shore up his defences in Normandy, Anjou and Poitiers, and prepared to fight after Easter. But England was once again in peril as William the Lion, attracting many anti-royalist rebels in the north of England, began to take castle after castle in a violent campaign in the summer of 1174. Roger of Howden described the atrocities: 'His men ripped asunder pregnant women, and, dragging forth the embryos, tossed them upon the points of lances. Infants, children, youths, aged men, all of both sexes, from the highest to the lowest, they slew alike without mercy or ransom.'[107]

This was a savage war; Henry's enemies wanted him out of his lands on the continent so they could begin to make headway there, and prepare to invade England, which Philip of Flanders had sworn to do.[108] Richard of Ilchester, one of Henry's loyalists, pleaded with him to return to England immediately. He did, trusting his forces in Normandy and Anjou to hold off his sons and their allies. Though he had physically left the continent, his men fought as if he was still alongside them directing operations, and had success after success.

Henry left Barfleur on 7 July for Southampton, to relieve England. It was not the first time he had travelled back to England during the conflict – the year before, in late spring and just after the fighting commenced, he had sailed quietly from Normandy to assess his position.[109] Henry was so successful in keeping this trip a secret, that not one of the chroniclers wrote about it. Now, however, he brought with him a captive Eleanor, his Brabanter mercenaries, his daughter-in-law Margaret, his youngest children Joanna and John, Robert of Leicester, Hugh of Chester, and possibly Richard's and Geoffrey's betrotheds, Alice and Constance.[110] Henry sent Eleanor to imprisonment at Salisbury Castle, while Margaret, Alice, Constance and the rest of the entourage were sent to Henry's castle at Devizes.[111]

Eleanor's political story, for the time being, was over. She would remain Henry's captive for the next fifteen years. But although Henry denied Eleanor her freedom lest she betray him again, he kept her confined in comfort. Salisbury Castle was a luxurious royal home. Her fellow countryman, the chronicler Richard le Poitevin, declaimed that 'The king of the North has placed you under siege' and, echoing the prophet Isaiah, urged her to 'Shout aloud without restraint; lift up your voice like a trumpet, so that your sons will hear your voice'; but Henry allowed Eleanor no voice. The chronicler concluded, 'For the day approaches when you will be freed by your sons and you will be returned to your own land.'[112] In fact, they were powerless to help their mother and Henry denied them access to her. It is likely that they were not even allowed to write to her, or she to them; if they did correspond, no evidence survives. Eleanor would be more or less absent from the records for at least a decade.

Henry did not go immediately to fight William in the north. Instead, in an extraordinary act during the greatest threat to his rule, Henry turned for Canterbury to do penance for his part in the murder of Thomas Becket. It would be the scene for one of the most dramatic events of Henry's reign.

Henry was not a religious man, although he was a superstitious one. On at least one occasion he sent jewels to a woman as she gave birth, reputed to ease the pain.[113]

Yet superstition could irritate Henry. During the 1150s and 1160s, it became fashionable to read Geoffrey of Monmouth's *Historia*, particularly the fictitious prophecies of Merlin. John Marshal, staunch loyalist to Matilda and then to Henry, and the father of William Marshal, read them, believed he could decipher them, and rashly predicted that when Henry left for the Toulouse campaign, he would never return. Henry, when he found out, was indignant. He excluded John from his favour until 1164.[114] And when Henry visited St David's in Wales on his way to Ireland, Gerald of Wales wrote that a local woman began to harangue Henry about the bishop. Henry did not give her the answer she desired, and she cursed him in Welsh, screaming, 'Avenge us this day, Lechlaver; take vengeance upon this man for our race and kindred.' She was speaking of a prophecy of Merlin's, which claimed that the king of England, having conquered Ireland, would die over Lechlaver, a stone with supposedly magic powers that lay by the church. Henry, having listened to the woman, walked over the stone and proclaimed, 'Who will have faith anymore in Merlin the liar?'[115] It was no accident that Wace omitted Merlin's prophecies when he translated Geoffrey of Monmouth's *History of the Kings of Britain* into French.[116]

As king, and a king consistently preoccupied with display, he was aware of the need to fulfil the conventional notions of piety, which ruled daily life, and he used religion as a tool to power. The chroniclers famously railed against his lack of piety, with Peter of Blois lamenting that Henry stood at all times, even at Mass, where he would often 'doodle'. Henry himself complained that he was so beset by a perpetual stream of petitioners, he had no time even to say a paternoster.[117]

Embroiled in this horrible war with his own wife and children, had Henry found God? It is unlikely. But he did ensure that it looked like it. At Canterbury, Henry publicly played the part of sorrowful penitent. He dismounted and walked through the town from St Dunstan's Church to the cathedral, barefoot and wearing sackcloth. He cut his feet on the stones and they bled. Prior Odo met him at the Altar of the Sword Point in the Martyrdom. William of Newburgh wrote that 'Shedding tears ... he prostrated himself on the ground, and with the utmost humility entreated pardon.'[118] And then:

> The king took off his cloak, and thrust his head and shoulders into one of the openings of St Thomas's tomb ... Then he was flogged, first five strokes of the whip from each of the prelates present and then three lashes from each of the eighty monks. When he had been disciplined and by atonement was reconciled to God, he withdrew his head from the tomb and sat down on the dirty ground with no carpet or cushion under him and he sang psalms and prayers all night, without getting up for any bodily need.[119]

It was a spectacle, and it beguiled Henry's contemporaries.

William of Newburgh dutifully recorded that 'On the following night, in a dream, it was said to a certain venerable old monk of that church, "Hast thou not seen to-day a marvellous miracle of royal humility? Know that the result of those events which are passing around him will shortly declare how much his royal humility had pleased the King of Kings."'[120] Henry, through his theatrical show of contrition, had, his contemporaries believed, absolved himself in the eyes of God.

More practically, by associating himself so quickly with the cult of St Thomas, already spreading like wildfire throughout Europe, he denied his enemies the opportunity to adopt Thomas and his supposed heavenly powers for their own cause.

Henry left Canterbury on 13 July, bound for London. Shortly after his arrival, the chronicler Jordan Fantosme penned an intimate portrait of Henry receiving a messenger in the middle of the night: 'The king had gone into his own room when the messenger came ... [Henry] was leaning on his elbow and sleeping a little, a servant at his feet who scratched them gently; there was no noise nor cry, and nobody spoke there. No harp nor violin was heard at that hour.'[121]

Henry evidently did not like to be woken. William of Newburgh and Jordan Fantosme both left accounts of Henry's chamberlain being unwilling to wake the king.[122] But in both, we see kindness and concern on the part of Henry. He was exhausted, expecting to travel north to continue a long campaign, and evidently unused to being woken. In William of Newburgh's version, his immediate concern was for his friend who had sent the message: Ranulf de Glanville. The king was roused from sleep and asked the man before him, '"Who art thou?" and the messenger replied, "I am the attendant upon Ranulf de Glanville, your faithful liegeman, by whom I have been sent to your highness; and I come to bring good tidings." "Ralph, our friend! Is he well?" asked the king.'[123]

And in Fantosme's poem, Henry, alarmed at being woken, nevertheless says of the messenger, 'He wants help, let him come in.' Henry went on to question him, panicked at what he had to say: 'What news do you bring? Has the king of Scotland entered Richmond? Is Newcastle-on-Tyne, the fortress, seized? Is Odinel de Umfranvile taken or driven out, and all my barons from their lands ejected? Messenger, by thy faith, tell me the truth.'

William the Lion of Scotland had been captured at Alnwick in a surprise attack as he sat down to breakfast without his helmet. His captors killed his horse, which fell on top of William, still alive. He was forced to surrender to Ranulf de Glanville. Henry's major enemy in the north had been dramatically neutralised.

Ranulf de Glanville sent the messenger from Alnwick to London to tell Henry the news. He had travelled non-stop for four days to reach the king.

The king was overjoyed and emotional, saying, 'God be thanked for it, and St Thomas the martyr and all the saints of God!'[124] He apparently wept with relief and joy.[125]

The chroniclers believed that it was his penance for his part in Becket's murder that saved his kingdom for him. One even declared 'divine power' at work in the defeat of William. Even the embittered Gerald of Wales wrote that 'after the penance performed by the pilgrim prince by night at Canterbury, St Thomas, that noble martyr, his anger now appeased by the king's tears and prayers, bestowed his favour upon him'.[126]

William's capture and imprisonment marked the endgame of the Great Revolt. William faced Henry on 24 July at Northampton, and was sent to prison at Caen, and later Falaise.

Henry and his armies now struck the final blows against the rebels in England. His bastard son Geoffrey took part in the action, capturing Roger de Mowbray's castle, Malzeard. On 31 July, Henry accepted the surrender of rebel after rebel at Northampton. When he was reunited with Geoffrey, Henry embraced him, declaring, 'My other sons are the real bastards. This is the only one who's proved himself legitimate!'[127]

He now only had to defeat Louis and his sons by Eleanor.

Henry crossed to France with his prisoner William the Lion, an army of his most loyal friends, Welshmen and Brabanter mercenaries, to relieve Rouen. His enemies fled. Now he pressed to negotiate the peace. A meeting was arranged for 8 September between Henry and Louis at Gisors, and a truce agreed until 29 September – Michaelmas. But as Richard would not heed a peace, and continued to fight his father's forces in Poitou, Henry was forced to bring about Richard's surrender himself. He took an army south and chased Richard around the countryside until he made him cry and beg Henry's forgiveness.

Richard finally met with his father on 23 September, where Henry gave him the kiss of peace. It must have been demeaning, a defining moment in the young Richard's life. He had recently celebrated his seventeenth birthday, on the very day of Henry's abortive meeting with Louis at Gisors.

The Treaty of Montlouis which followed on 30 September marked the formal end of the Great Revolt.

Henry had triumphed while Louis had been humiliated. Diverted from his usual tactic of diplomacy in dealing with the English king, he had allowed himself to be driven by the fervour and anger of the rebels in the misguided belief that he could beat Henry in battle.[128] It had been a grave error.

As Gerald of Wales noted, the Great Revolt had plunged Henry into a perilous position, the outcome of which could easily have been his own defeat. Henry's invincibility had almost been undone through the treatment of, and weakness for, his children:

> A man's enemies are those of his own household, and strife within a family is the very worst of all scourges, his feelings of sorrow and despair were crowned by the fact that even those knights whom he had chosen to guard his bedchamber and into whose hands he had entrusted his life or death, almost nightly turned against him and deserted to his sons, and did not appear in the morning when he looked for them.

This time, however, Henry was favoured by a turn of fortune's wheel: 'Just as at the beginning of the war everyone thought that God's anger had brought this punishment on him, so now this same divine wrath, which nevertheless rejoices in the conversion of a sinner rather than in his ruin, seemed to have been fully placated in due course of time, and to have subsided, giving way to compassion.'[129]

In victory, Henry was generous, at least financially. His proclamation read: 'Our lord the king and all his liegemen and barons are to receive possession of all their lands and castles which they held fifteen days before his sons withdrew from him; and in like manner his liegemen and barons who withdrew from him and followed his sons are to receive possession of their lands which they held fifteen days before they withdrew from him.'[130]

The earl of Leicester was eventually set free, together with his fellow rebels. But the earls in England had been completely crushed, and they no longer held any influence with the king. Henry was perhaps being overly sentimental when, in 1177, it was mooted at the great council that Robert's earldom of Leicester be dismantled, Robert spoke movingly, invoking his father, grandfather and his great-grandfather, all of whom had served Henry and his predecessors so well. 'And when the king heard him speaking so dutifully, he was moved to tenderness, and restored to him all his tenements in their integrity ... save that the king retained in his own hand the castle of Mountsorrel, and the castle of Pacy, which were the only two of all his castles that remained standing.'[131]

William the Lion was also released, but only after Henry's high demands were met – he gained William's fortresses of Roxburgh, Berwick and Edinburgh.[132]

Henri was given two castles in Normandy, and £15,000 per annum from Anjou, on the condition that he accept that John, now seven years old, must be provided for with money and castles out of the lands he would inherit: England, Normandy and Anjou. John's betrothed, Alice of Maurienne, had died; Henry would have to look elsewhere to provide his youngest son with a satisfactory inheritance. Richard was given two properties in Poitiers and half its annual income. Geoffrey received half the annual revenue of Brittany with the caveat that he had to promise to marry Constance, daughter of Conan IV.

A superficial peace was concluded; Gerald of Wales thought it 'more shadowy than real'.[133] Richard and Geoffrey payed homage to their father. The young king wanted to pay homage too, but Henry refused to accept the act from an anointed king.[134]

Henri's, Richard's and Geoffrey's original contentions that they had no power were mostly ignored. The young king had further cause to feel humiliated. Although Henry allowed some autonomy to Richard in Aquitaine and Geoffrey in Brittany, he allowed absolutely no power to Henri. Furthermore the boys came out of the rebellion with their mother locked up, albeit in comfortable surroundings.

Henry's treasurer, Richard FitzNigel, commented wryly on Henry's success: 'So the mighty learned that to wrest the club from the hand of Hercules was no easy task.'[135]

Henry forgave all the major protagonists of the Great Revolt – except for his wife. He blamed Eleanor for orchestrating the rebellion. She was written out of the records. She was not even mentioned at the Treaty of Montlouis. Henry's sons would not forgive him for his treatment of their mother.

X

Henry and Eleanor's marriage had not been a love match. It is unlikely that they felt regret for the shift in their relationship when Eleanor moved south. The nature of their marriage was such that they had not lived together consistently, and on numerous occasions had spent months apart. Eleanor, since the early years of her first marriage, had craved power and influence. Henry had allowed her an opportunity for independence and a return to the land of her birth. If they had once viewed one another romantically, after sixteen years of marriage and eight children, their focus had changed.

Contrary to the historians, filmmakers, playwrights and novelists who for over 800 years have imagined a great romance with Eleanor, Henry had many sexual partners, some noblewomen and some not, and was unfaithful to her throughout their long marriage. Walter Map spoke of the 'creatures of the night' who populated the court; the king was rarely without a sexual partner.

Henry employed whoremasters at his courts; one of them, Ranulf de Broc, aided the murderers of Thomas Becket.[136]

Henry's contemporary Ralph Niger accused him of locking Eleanor up, 'in order that he might more freely indulge his debaucheries', and claimed he took an aphrodisiac, satyrion root, to enhance his sexual prowess.[137]

Others also pronounced Henry a sexual predator. In 1168 Eudo de Porhoët, deposed count of Brittainy, accused Henry of 'incestuously' sleeping with his sister while she was his hostage, and of having a child with her. The liaison, if true, and not the bile of Henry's enemy, was incestuous according to the mores of the day as the girl's mother, Bertha, was the daughter of Maud, an illegitimate daughter of Henry I. She was therefore Henry's cousin. Henry was also reputed to have desired the sister of the earl of Hereford – the 'most beautiful woman in the realm'.[138]

Henry had several illegitimate children and at least one was born before he became king, probably in about 1151. His name was Geoffrey Plantagenet, and he was most likely named after Henry's father. Henry was closer to him than to any of his other children. He eventually created him chancellor of England. Geoffrey would support and comfort his father until the end. Geoffrey's mother, according to Walter Map, was named Ykenai, a 'common wanton (who shrank from no impunity)'.[139] Geoffrey was brought up in Henry's household. If Eleanor complained, we have no record of it.

Henry's other illegitimate children included William Longsword (born around 1167), third earl of Salisbury, son of Ida de Tosny; and Morgan, provost of Beverley and bishop-elect of Durham, most probably born in the mid to late 1170s. Morgan's mother was Nest, a Welsh princess, and she married Ralph Bloet sometime before 1175. Her affair with Henry may have begun before her marriage.[140] Ralph, however, brought Morgan up in his household.

Henry also had an illegitimate daughter, Matilda, born before he married Eleanor. Her mother was called Joan.[141] In the late 1170s Matilda became prioress of Barking Abbey in Essex, replacing Mary, the sister of Thomas Becket, whom Henry had appointed as part of his penance for the archbishop's murder.[142]

Henry fell in love in the late 1160s with Rosamund Clifford, and she is the most famous of his mistresses. Henry's biographer, Wilfred Lewis Warren, thought Rosamund 'the love of his life', and later chroniclers erroneously demonised Eleanor for murdering her.

Gerald of Wales called Henry a 'serial adulterer' before he met Rosamund, but after he imprisoned Eleanor he began to live openly with her. Henry declared his love publicly when he gave a house, the manor of Corfham, to her father Walter Clifford, 'for the love of Rosamund his daughter'. Henry built a beautiful palace for Rosamund, on the site of an old hunting lodge of his grandfather, Henry I, at Woodstock. The palace was called Everswell, and it was built in the style of the palaces of the Norman kingdom in Sicily, with pools, fountains and courtyards.[143] Some historians have argued that Henry, beguiled by his love for Rosamund and the story of Tristan and Iseult, diverted streams at Everswell to recreate the way the lovers sent their secret messages to one another.[144] Its style was unique in northern Europe. But their time together was short. They probably met in the late 1160s, and by 1176 she was dead, possibly of cancer. In her memory, Henry endowed the convent of Godstow, just north of Oxford, where Rosamund's tomb stood, illuminated by candlelight, in front of the great altar.

When Bishop Hugh of Lincoln visited the convent after Henry's death, he was outraged at the position of the tomb, usually a place allotted to saints or royalty – not harlots.[145] He ordered her remains removed from the altar, to the graveyard outside. Hugh's act was cruel for one whom Henry had thought his friend.[146] Henry had defied religious convention to honour the memory of someone he had loved devotedly. The convent and the cemetery were ultimately destroyed by the agents of Henry's descendant, Henry VIII, during the Reformation.

After Rosamund's death, Henry was linked to at least three other women by name. Gerald of Wales believed that in the late 1170s he began a liaison with Louis' daughter Alice, the sister of Margaret, as she waited hopelessly at Henry's court to marry Richard. Alice had been in Henry's care since she was nine years old. Gerald of Wales even claimed that Henry attempted to divorce Eleanor so he could marry her and found a new dynasty.[147] In 1175, when the papal legate arrived in England, Henry sought the opportunity to rid himself of Eleanor. He probably thought of retiring her to Fontevraud Abbey as its abbess, and must have felt he had the tried and tested reason of consanguinity on his side; he and Eleanor were more closely related than Louis and Eleanor had been, and the pope had approved that divorce. While at Winchester for Easter in 1176, Henry reportedly offered Eleanor her freedom in return for retiring from public life.[148] Henry however was to be disappointed. The pope, perhaps swayed by protestation from Eleanor and her sons, refused Henry his divorce. Although Henry did seek to divorce Eleanor in 1175, we do not know if it was to marry Alice.

Henry also had a mistress named Bellebelle in the 1180s – she was evidently an established figure in his life; the pipe roll for 1184 records that when Henry ordered clothes for Eleanor, he ordered clothes for Bellebelle too, 'that various cloaks, hoods and other clothing should be bought for her'.[149] Another shadowy figure linked to Henry romantically is an Annabel de Balliol; we know very little about her.

Did Eleanor care that Henry had many partners, and was serially unfaithful? The chroniclers are silent. A letter she received from Hildegard of Bingen, a Benedictine nun, sometime before 1170, offers an intriguing insight into Eleanor's state of mind during the marriage. Hildegard wrote urging her to be strong, but in reference to which particular event, we do not know: 'Your mind is similar to a wall plunged into a whirlwind of clouds. You look all around, but find no rest. Flee that and remain firm and stable, with God as with men, and God will then help you in all your tribulations.'[150]

Henry and Eleanor did not have a happy marriage, certainly not by 1168 when she moved to Poitiers. Henry did not allow her the power she believed was her due, and he failed her regarding the future of her duchy and Richard's position there. He failed her too with his treatment of the young king, neglecting to groom their eldest son for power, as Eleanor was doing with Richard in Aquitaine. It is almost certain that her motivation to rebel was not sexual jealousy, but a desire to obliterate Henry because he had betrayed her over her duchy and in his treatment of their sons.

The chroniclers who charged her with sexual or jealous motives for her actions during the Great Revolt were unable to ascribe political yearning to a woman as it fell entirely outside their imagination. Eleanor, however, was a politically motivated woman. When she returned to her homeland to govern, it is far more likely that she thought of power and of assuring her children's inheritances than of her husband's sexual partners and bastard children. Eleanor rebelled against Henry because she believed he had left her with no choice. He had reneged on their bargain, denying her real power in her ancestral lands.

Eleanor's part in the rebellion blackened her name for centuries to come. Chroniclers and historians failed to understand the truth of her motivation, instead accusing her of seeking revenge for Henry's affairs, leading to improbable crimes such as the murder of Rosamund. They called her a 'Jezebel' and 'a vindictive woman' to whom 'Henry II had always been a good husband'.[151] For the nineteenth-century French historian Jules Michelet, she was a wicked queen, a 'sorceress' who makes 'a mock of this herd of besotted and submissive males'.[152] And so Eleanor, who in the events surrounding the end of her marriage to Louis and the beginning of her marriage to Henry was accused of sexual lasciviousness, incest and deviancy, was condemned by some later chroniclers and historians of the terrible crime during the Great Revolt of going beyond a woman's natural domain, by venturing into the political sphere.

Henry, however, locked Eleanor away not because he distrusted female power but for practical reasons – she was far too dangerous to be set free. He was convinced that he could control his rebellious nobility, Louis, and his sons, but Eleanor was another matter. She had attempted to rule in Aquitaine alone, and as its rightful duchess commanded power and respect among her nobility. She had incited their sons, Henry's nobility, and even her ex-husband to revolt. If Henry gave Eleanor back her liberty, he had no doubt that she would rebel again, and perhaps succeed. Although Henry had routed his enemies during the revolt, he was aware that luck had been on his side.

Henry the pragmatist refused to risk setting Eleanor free. She would remain Henry's prisoner for the rest of his life.

XI

Henry had been lenient with his sons. But although his public face showed reason and clemency to great acclaim, privately he was in a state of distress. He told the abbot of Bonneville: 'I read in the Old Testament of leaders, kings and even prophets frequently pursuing very harsh vengeance against their enemies … Have I no right to become enraged when anger is a virtue of the spirit and a natural power? By nature I am a son of anger, why then should I not grow angry? God himself becomes angry.'[153]

As far as Henry was concerned, in giving his sons money he had resolved the differences between them. If he truly believed this to be the case, it was arrogant and naive, and ignored the root cause of the problem: He had imprisoned their mother and left Henri with no power; he had granted Richard and Geoffrey a little autonomy, which earned them the ire of their older brother.

Henri, a king without a realm, was still 'at a loss for something to do'.[154] These were turbulent years for the young king. His feelings for his father obviously confused him: he would frequently ignore his father's summonses to join him, or when he did would weep at his feet begging Henry to trust him. Between April 1176 and February 1179 he remained in France, where Louis took every opportunity to foster mistrust between father and son. To supplement his income, and because he enjoyed it and excelled at it, he pursued the tournament circuit in northern France, to great acclaim.

Henry, ever a loving and emotional father, took pride in the young king's success. He 'was happier counting up and admiring his victories, and his father restored in full his possessions that he had taken away. Thus occupied with knightly matters until no glory was lacking to him, he sailed from Wissant and was received with honour by the king his father.'[155]

Henry's feelings were probably guided by more than one motive. While thinking his son incapable of holding real power, he loved him nevertheless, and his joy in Henri's achievements was simply a father revelling in his son's abilities – however frivolous he may have thought them.

But despite the pleasure Henry took in the young king's tournament successes, Henri remained in a state of petulant anger with his father and conducted a rather apathetic war of attrition against him. On 20 April 1176 Henry sent him to aid Richard in Aquitaine, where he was fighting the count of Angoulême and his allies. But Henri delayed. He visited first Louis in Paris, and then Philip of Flanders in Arras, where Philip persuaded him to stay and fight in a tournament near Ressons-sur-Matz, where he did very well.[156] Henri only arrived much later in the summer at the real war, which Richard was winning without any help from his

Thomas Becket appears to a leper in one of the Miracle Windows at Canterbury Cathedral. Almost as soon as Becket's blood pooled around him, miracles attributed to the dead archbishop began to be reported all over the kingdom. Both the monks of Canterbury and Henry harnessed the Becket miracle industry to their own ends.

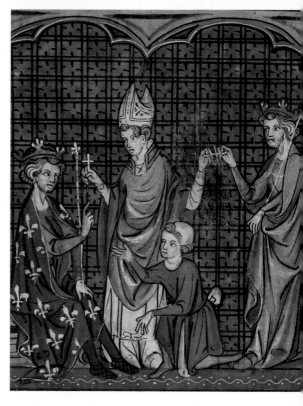

Philip Augustus, son of Louis VII, seated on the left, and Henry (right) taking the cross from an envoy of the pope. In a fatal misjudgement, Henry believed Philip to be a boy-king he could mentor and control.

This mural at the underground chapel of Sainte-Radegonde at Chinon dates from around the turn of the thirteenth century. It is possibly an image of Eleanor being led into captivity by Henry. If so, Henry is likely on the extreme right.

Eleanor gave this rock crystal vase as a wedding gift to Louis. It had most likely been given to her grandfather, Duke William IX, by the Muslim King Imad al-dawla of Saragossa – friendships could exist between people of different faiths. It is on display in the Louvre in Paris.

The charismatic Bernard of Clairvaux roused Christendom when he preached the Second Crusade at Vezelay in 1146. Henry's father, Geoffrey of Anjou, was notable by his absence from the venture; Bernard never forgave him.

In many ways, the life of Frederick Barbarossa (Red Beard), the Holy Roman Emperor, mirrored Henry's own. Frederick drowned in the River Saleph in the summer of 1190, as he travelled to the Latin Kingdom on the Third Crusade.

The crusaders feared the swift horses and lethal arrows of Saladin's army. Unlike their European foes, Saladin's men were not weighed down by heavy armour, could move much faster and shoot more arrows in their lightning raids.

Philip, working with Richard, forced Henry to flee Le Mans, his favourite city, in the summer of 1189. Its loss devastated Henry, who reputedly blamed God, crying, 'I will … deny You what You love best in me, my soul!'

William Marshal, the greatest of Henry's knights, was nearly hanged by Stephen when only five years old. He lived, and served Henry and his family with unsurpassed loyalty for the rest of his life.

Ordeal by fire, depicted in a ninth-century manuscript. In the face of Henry's seismic legal and judicial reforms during his reign, trials by ordeal gradually went out of favour.

Dover Castle: after Louis's surprise visit to Canterbury in 1179, Henry spent a fortune rebuilding it. Ever the generous host, he was embarrassed that he had nowhere suitably regal for Louis to stay.

The first four Plantagenet kings of England: top, left to right – Henry II, in profile, a negative judgement on his kingship; Richard, bellicose, wielding a sword and shield; bottom, left to right – John, crown askew; Henry III, shown face on with his crown firmly on his head – the most positive representation.

Tombs of Eleanor of Aquitaine and Henry II of England at Fontevraud Abbey in the Loire. Eleanor turned Fontevraud into the family mausoleum in the service of Plantagenet power. She designed these magnificent, brilliantly painted *gisants*. In death, Eleanor gives herself something to do: she is shown reading a book.

older brother. Richard, a bitter Henri observed, had genuine power in Aquitaine, something Henri desperately craved, and lacked.

Afterwards, seeking vengeance on Henry for his humiliation, and for coercing him into helping Richard, he took some men into his inner household whom 'his father hated'.[157] Henry still maintained control over much of his son's household.

Crisis followed. Adam of Churchdown, Henri's vice chancellor and one of his father's appointments, wrote to Henry about his son's new intimates. When the young king found out, his response was vicious. He ordered his trial and Adam was condemned to death by a court of Henri's friends. But the bishop of Poitiers interceded: Adam, a clerk, must be judged by the laws of the church. Adam's punishment was commuted to a public beating and imprisonment at Argentan. Henry had to order his son to release Adam and send him to his care.

By the beginning of 1177, Henri's wife Margaret was pregnant, just as Henry was preparing to go to war with Louis once more over the Vexin. The young king sent her to Louis, probably to goad Henry. Henry was livid; if the child was born in the domain of the French king, it would be potentially disastrous for the Angevin succession. Should Margaret give birth to a boy, it was feasible that Henry's grandson and eventual heir would grow up under the sway of his enemy. The baby, baptised William, was born in midsummer, about 19 June. But he died three days later. One chronicler suggests that his birth was premature.[158] Henry, affected by the baby's death perhaps personally and certainly politically, stopped posturing for war and resolved his issues with Louis diplomatically.[159] There is no other record of Margaret being pregnant or giving birth to another child.

The young king spent the next few years at relative peace with his father, busy pursuing the tournament circuit. On 6 August 1178 Henry finally knighted Geoffrey at Woodstock, who then joined his favourite older brother in fighting tournaments. This new closeness between the brothers, coupled with a seismic shift in French politics, would soon precipitate another crisis for Henry.

XII

In the summer of 1179 King Louis had a bad dream, just as his only son and heir lay desperately ill, presumed dying.

Louis' son, Philip, was fourteen years old. Louis had not followed the Capetian tradition of crowning his heir alongside him in his lifetime. There were no candidates for his throne to rival Philip, and perhaps he had not felt the need. However, he had finally decided to do so, prompted by a short illness of his own. The coronation date was set for 15 August – the feast of the Assumption.

Just days before his crowning, Philip went hunting in the woods around Compiègne, north of Paris. Captivated by the thrill of chasing a boar, the prince became lost. It was two days before he was found. Philip was delirious, and Louis feared he would die. When Louis suffered nightmares, he could not rid himself of the image that after all he had gone through to get himself an heir, it had been ultimately fruitless. Should his daughter Margaret give birth to a son, his darkest fears would come true, and his Capetian throne would pass to a Plantagenet.

In Louis' dream, St Thomas appeared, saying, 'Our Lord Jesus Christ sends me as your servant, Thomas the martyr of Canterbury, in order that you should go to Canterbury, if your son is to recover.'[160]

Louis' counsellors, when the French king told them of his plans, were horrified, and they expressed their reservations. But as far as Louis was concerned, he had no choice; he must go to Canterbury. It would be the first time a French king had travelled to England. But before he could visit the tomb to implore Thomas to save his son's life, he was forced to beg his Plantagenet vassal for a huge favour; fuelled by unhappiness and desperation, he wrote to Henry, asking for permission to visit.

It may have confounded Louis that Henry not only extended a warm invitation, but, forsaking sleep, even rode to meet him at Dover. There, Henry

> received him with great honour ... as his most dearly beloved liege lord and friend ... On the following day ... on the vigil of St Bartholomew the Apostle, he escorted him to the tomb of St Thomas the Martyr ... Upon arriving there, Louis ... offered upon the tomb ... a cup of gold, very large and of great value, and gave, for the use of the monks there in the service of God, a hundred tuns of wine, to be received yearly forever at Poissy, in France, entirely at the expense of the king of France.[161]

Henry then escorted Louis to Dover Castle, where they spent the night together. John Gillingham calls Louis' pilgrimage to Canterbury 'the first state visit in English history'.[162]

Louis, however, even in time of huge anxiety was unable to resist a dig at Henry. He brought as a gift the enormous ruby known as the *regale*. It was so large that it was described later as being half the size of a hen's egg. This was the jewel that was eventually plundered by Henry VIII during the Reformation. But for contemporaries, the colour of the jewel – blood red – would have symbolised the blood-drenched nature of St Thomas's martyrdom in the very cathedral where Louis now prayed for his only son's life, accompanied by the perpetrator, Henry.[163]

This would be their last meeting.

Philip duly recovered. But this was Louis' final act in the service of the Capetian dynasty he had tried so diligently to strengthen against Henry's aggression. The journey, as his advisors had feared, wore him out and soon after he returned to Paris, he suffered a stroke which paralysed him on his right side. He could no longer speak or govern. Philip went ahead with his associate coronation, on 1 November 1179, but without his father. He took away Louis' seal and was crowned by his maternal uncle, William, now archbishop of Rheims.

Young Henri and the count of Flanders both played a major role in Philip's lavish ceremony. Henri held the golden crown over his head (to the horror of Ralph of Diceto, who believed it diminished his own regal authority[164]) while the count of Flanders carried the sword of state. Geoffrey attended, and he and Philip became friends. Henry, meanwhile, typically magnanimous and using the occasion to showcase his wealth, sent many expensive gifts and knights in Henri's entourage.

Louis lingered for nearly another year, while Philip acted as de facto king. Louis died on 18 September 1180 and was buried at Barbeau Abbey, south-east of Paris. His epitaph read: 'You who survive him are the successor to his dignity; you diminish his line if you diminish his renown.'[165]

Henry had known Louis for nearly thirty years. Their relationship had been, at best, complicated. Henry had married Louis' ex-wife, fought with him, threatened him, consistently pushed the boundaries of the meaning of 'overlord' and 'vassal', married his son and heir to Louis' daughter, nearly suffered the loss of his empire at Louis' hands, and ultimately, at Canterbury, played the magnanimous host and friend in Louis' darkest days. Roger of Howden believed that Louis had 'always felt hatred for the king of England'.[166] But in the end, Louis may have remembered Henry's kindness to him the last time they met, for Henry did not leave his side as Louis prayed for his son. Henry, doubtless aided by Eleanor's insight, knew this man well.

Henry was arrogant; he believed he knew Philip, now king of France, as well as he had known Louis. But he did not see that Philip, a fifteen-year-old boy to whom he had also shown kindness, and whom he believed he could control, was his adversary. Henry may have intended to be Philip's puppeteer. But Philip had been raised in an atmosphere of 'hatred'; although

Louis may, in his final year, have come to terms with Henry, Philip had not.

Philip used Henry, now the grand old man of Europe, as his mentor. Henry mediated in a family war between Philip on the one side, and his mother and her Blois relatives on the other, 'partly by gentle words and partly by threats.'[167] He aided Philip against the count of Flanders in 1181 and brokered a lasting peace. He acted as Philip's informal advisor.

Henry was flattered and not nearly as wary as he should have been. For Philip, unlike his father, was a natural politician who could play the long game. His mission, concealed from the English king, was not simply to contain the hegemony of Henry FitzEmpress, but to break him and his dynasty altogether, and to make France as great as it had been in the days of Charlemagne. He would turn Henry's sons against him, and they would be Philip's willing accomplices.

XIII

For Gerald of Wales, it appeared that Henry's luck was running out. Henry spent a disastrous Christmas with the young king, Richard and Geoffrey at Caen in 1182:

> Gracious heaven! If such brothers would have regarded the fraternal compact between each other, if they would have looked towards their father with filial affection ... how great, how inestimable, how renowned, how incomparable to all future time would have been the glory of their father and the victory of his offspring! ... For what valour could resist these powers, what kings could stand against these kings, or what kingdoms could successfully oppose such leaders in war?[168]

Earlier that year, in February, Henry had written a new will. His first, written twelve years earlier in response to his sudden frightening illness, detailed how his empire was to be divided on his death. This new will, however, mentioned only religious bequests (specifically 5,000 silver marks each to the Knights Hospitaller and the Knights Templar), perhaps because he believed that he did not need to make clear his wishes again.

Now, as Henry stepped back, allowing Richard autonomy in Aquitaine and Geoffrey in Brittany from 1181 with his marriage to Constance, he commanded them to pay homage to Henri. Geoffrey complied, but Richard refused. He was outraged that he should have to pay homage for Aquitaine to his brother at all, declaring angrily that 'it was not right for him to acknowledge his elder brother as superior by some sort of subjection. Rather, by the law of firstborn sons, the paternal goods were due to his brother, while he, Richard, claimed equal right to legitimate succession to the maternal goods.'[169] Aquitaine was his through right of their mother, and like Eleanor, Richard envisaged it being independent under his rule after Henry's death, and not part of a conglomerate Angevin Empire.

There were further reasons for discontent between the brothers. Richard had seized and fortified the castle of Clairvaux, which Henri declared was his as it lay within Anjou, and not Poitou. Furthermore Henri claimed he wished to protect the barons of Aquitaine against Richard, whom they were complaining about. But Henri was obviously using Richard's seizure of Clairvaux as an excuse; he wanted to cause Richard trouble. Henry was not oblivious to his motives.

The 1182 Christmas gathering should have been joyous. Henry forbade any of his nobility from holding their own Christmas courts, which meant that over a thousand knights flocked to the king's. The family was joined by Henry's daughter Matilda and her husband, Henry the Lion, duke of Saxony, in exile from Germany. Drama, had the Plantagenet royal family needed any more, was provided by William Marshal. The author of *The History of William Marshal* wrote that William had had an adulterous affair with the young king's wife, Margaret. This is not corroborated by any other source, but William was abruptly dismissed from Henri's household in 1182. The argument, if not about an affair, was probably about febrile household rivalry among the young king's intimates.[170] Whatever the source of the conflict, William Marshal arrived at Henry's Christmas court demanding justice.

The occasion was fraught with family quarrels. Although Henry, in a painstaking diplomatic exercise, finally persuaded the bull-headed Richard to pay homage to the young king, Henri – ever capricious – refused to accept it.[171] Henry was furious, and frustrated. Richard, who had a more realistic notion of his brothers' characters than their father, left Henry's emotionally charged Christmas court to prepare for war against the young king and Geoffrey, by building new castles in Poitou and fortifying his existing ones.[172]

Richard was chased by Henri and Geoffrey, albeit separately. Henri had promised his father on 1 January 1183 'that from that day forward, and for all the days of his life, he would keep complete faith with King Henry, as his father and his lord, and always show the honour and service he owed to him'.[173] The spirit of his promise was short-lived. He now roused the rebellious Poitevin nobility to fight against Richard, and accepted the help of a mercenary force sent by Philip, keen to foster hatred between the brothers.

Geoffrey had been sent to Poitou by Henry to gather together the nobility in Aquitaine to hear their concerns. Instead, he betrayed his father by going to Brittany to foment rebellion against him there; then, working closely with Henri, he persuaded the lords of Aquitaine to rebel against Richard and the king. He raised a mercenary army of Brabanters, those 'legions from hell', whose waging of vicious warfare had aided Henry in the Great

Revolt. This time they fought against the king. The young king and Geoffrey together now took their hatred against their father a step further – they tried to kill him.

It cannot have been easy to be the son of Henry FitzEmpress. Henry continued to retain absolute control over every aspect of their lives, including the most intimate: their marriages, and who would populate their inner households. His will could seldom be turned. Yet Henry cloaked this will of steel in an affectionate, emotional and volatile disguise, using anger, tears, manipulation and joy as his weapons against his sons. At times attractive and endearing, it must also have been psychologically draining; it maddened and exasperated Henri and his brothers. In promising them power and then denying them, in exercising such total control, and in not listening to any of them, Henry had pushed them beyond the point of return.

Geoffrey's grievances are more difficult to fathom than the young king's. Perhaps it was greed; Henry had still not given him Nantes and Richmond, part of his inheritance. Perhaps he felt Brittany was too small an inheritance; or possibly he looked to the coming reign as he gambled and threw in his lot with his brother against his father. Roger of Howden put Geoffrey's actions down to a flawed character, calling him a 'son of perdition'. Gerald of Wales was equally damning, saying he was 'overflowing with words, soft as oil, possessed, by his syrupy and persuasive eloquence, of the power of dissolving the seeming indissoluble, able to corrupt two kingdoms with his tongue; of tireless endeavour, a hypocrite in everything, a deceiver and a dissembler'.[174]

In the summer of 1182, dismayed at how much relative power his brothers enjoyed, Henri asked his father once more for Normandy, Anjou or England to rule. When Henry refused, the young king flounced off to Paris with Margaret, to be welcomed by a sympathetic Philip. Here, he announced his intention of going on pilgrimage to Jerusalem. Henry's cousin, Baldwin the leper king, was dying, and perhaps Henri saw an opportunity for himself to rule there. He certainly threatened his father with it. Henry, however, was desperate for him not to go. If he believed that Henri was incapable of governing one of the provinces he was to inherit with his father by his side, how would he possibly cope with the byzantine factionalism of the kingdom of Jerusalem?

Henry instead offered him a pension. But money was obviously not what he sought; Henri was most likely humiliated by the offer. The troubadour poet Bertran de Born, who was a vassal of Richard's, wrote, cruelly, 'Since Sir Henri neither holds nor governs land, let him be King of the Fools! ... he acts like a fool, living this way entirely on an allowance.'[175]

Henri was ultimately landless and, as in 1173, allowed himself to be manipulated by a French king who wished to destroy his father.

Henry, anxious to quell the family feud as quickly as possible, went south to aid Richard against his brothers. Henri and Geoffrey, from inside the fortified city of Limoges, ordered arrows to be shot at the king and Richard. They harmed no one except a knight who stood by Henry. Henry, still unwilling to punish his errant children, pushed for peace talks with the young king and Geoffrey. During the talks, Henry was shot at again. This time the arrow, which would have penetrated his chest and killed him, hit his horse as it reared its head.

Henry cannot have doubted his sons' intentions towards him now, but he allowed himself to be seduced by the young king, who distanced himself from Geoffrey and claimed that he wanted peace. Their men had clearly tried to murder him. Yet he once again forgave his boys, whom he loved, and let himself believe their continued expressions of regret – always followed by betrayal. The horror of yet more treachery by his sons was simply too awful for Henry to contemplate.

Henri now slyly reiterated his vow to take the cross, or go on crusade. In an emotional outburst, Henry begged him not to go:

he used all his endeavours to recall him from this rash vow, asking of him on his knees, and weeping, whether that vow had proceeded from rancour, indignation, poverty, or religious feeling. To this the son made answer, with all kinds of oaths, that he had made the vow solely for the remission of the sins which he had been guilty of towards his father; and added, when he saw his father opposing it and shedding tears, that he would slay himself with his own hands, unless his father should cease to dissuade him from his purpose of assuming the cross ... testified that he ought a long time before that to have assumed the cross ... hoping and trusting that he should be in the more full enjoyment of his father's favour, as he was unwilling to go on the pilgrimage without his favour.[176]

Walter Map remarked how well Henri played his father. He wrote how 'again and again, as I witnessed myself, he was perjured to his father: repeatedly he set snares in his way, and when foiled returned to him, ever the more prone to crime the more clearly he saw that it was impossible not to forgive him'.[177]

This time, most likely to get him out of Aquitaine, Henry agreed. But the situation rapidly deteriorated. Henry sent envoys to treat for peace, but they were massacred, cut down by the young king and Geoffrey's men. Henry was furious; he had finally been pushed too far, and now felt he had no option other than war.

In May he laid siege to Limoges. To fight his war, Henry quickly assembled 'a big army on horse and a great body of knights. They were Normans and men from Anjou, men from Flanders and from Picardy and men from Poitou, and mercenaries of many sorts and many a pennant and banner you would have seen gleaming as it fluttered in the wind. The king rode on in a great fury to meet his sons in Limoges. There were so many tents, pavilions and marquees, that no man could give an account of them, for the king did things there on a very grand scale.'[178]

Geoffrey cannily advised Henri to make peace with William Marshal; they had great need now of his exceptional military skill.[179]

Meanwhile Henri, desperate for cash, began to plunder the surrounding shrines and churches, including Limoges' great abbey of Saint-Martial. He stole goods amounting to 22,000 shillings, and the young king in return gave the monks a charter which amounted to a promissory note.[180] To boot, he also robbed the tomb of St Andemar in Quercy.

Soon after, the young king became seriously ill with dysentery. Roger of Howden wrote that Henri 'was attacked by a severe malady at a village called Martel, not far from ... Limoges. He was first attacked with a fever, and then by a flux of the bowels, which reduced him to the point of death. On seeing that his death was impending, he sent for ... his father.' But Henry did not believe him. He 'dreaded' yet more treachery and 'refused to come to him'.[181] Henry thought it was another ploy, and he feared for his kingship and possibly his life. He could, however, never deny his eldest son. If he would not go in person, he sent instead Bishop Bernard of Agen and Rotrou IV, count of Perche. He dispatched with them a gift for Henri, a sapphire ring – a symbol that he was, once more, forgiven.

The young king, however, was on his deathbed. He made his will, begged his father to take care of his mother and his wife, and asked William Marshal to fulfil his vow to go on pilgrimage to the Holy Land. He put on a hair shirt, put a noose around his neck as a symbol of his treachery to God (and possibly to his father), and asked his friends to move him to a bed covered with ashes in the shape of a cross, with stones for a pillow.[182] A cleric called upon Henri to relinquish his father's ring as it symbolised worldly glory, but he clung desperately to it and refused to let it go. He died on 11 June 1183. He was twenty-eight years old.

Bernard de Reynat, a monk of Grandmont, carried the news to Henry. The monk came upon him sheltering out of the sun in a peasant's hut, near Limoges.[183] At first Henry refused to countenance it. But when other messengers arrived to corroborate the monk's tale, he was compelled to believe. Henry burst into tears, 'threw himself upon the ground, and greatly bewailed his son'. Gerald of Wales painted a portrait of Henry's 'great and immoderate' grief: 'he declared that he had far rather that his son had triumphed over him than that death should have triumphed over his son'.[184] Henry had loved him, despite his numerous betrayals.

But he was forced to put his grief aside. To keep his realms safe, he had to win in Aquitaine and he sent messengers to Richard to finish the siege at Limoges. By 24 June the city fell. Henry, in impotent revenge on the place that had witnessed his ordeal with the young king, ordered its complete demolition, 'not leaving one stone upon another'.[185] Resistance in Aquitaine died with Henri. By July Geoffrey had been forced to make peace with his father.

This latest rebellion was brutal for Henry. He had failed to learn any lessons from the 1173–4 uprisings, with horrific consequences. His heir to England, Normandy and Anjou was dead; Henri's remains were wrapped in the cloth he had been anointed in at his coronation and interred at Rouen Cathedral, as he had wished, among his ancestors.

Henri's death divided the chroniclers. Gerald of Wales, using an account of the young king's virtues to gripe at Henry, compared him to the heroes of the Trojan Wars, Hector and Paris. The biographer of William Marshal, Henri's mentor, likewise lauded him; he was 'the finest of the princes of the earth, be they pagan or Christian'.[186] His mother wished him to be canonised.[187]

Walter Map, however, damned him. He was, he said, blessed with all the gifts of the gods:

fairer than the children of men in stature and in face, richly endowed with eloquence and charm of address, blest with the love and favour of his fellow men, so powerful to persuade that he beguiled almost all his father's liegemen to turn against him … Rich, noble, lovable, eloquent, handsome, gallant, every way attractive, a little lower than the angels – all these gifts he turned to the wrong side, and that mighty man, corrupting his blessings, became a parricide of such baleful soul that his dearest wish was for his father's death … he befouled the whole world with his treasons, a prodigy of unfaith and prodigal of ill, a limpid spring of wickedness, the attractive centre of villainy, a lovely palace of sin, whose realm was full of pleasantness.[188]

Historians have not been kind to Henri. He is remembered as a relentless seeker of fame at tournaments in northern France (banned in England by Henry, who wanted to discourage the meeting of armed men, and anxious to limit the harm to men and horses), narcissistic, immature, incapable of the responsibility of rule – which is why his father never gave him the opportunity. Warren is the most damning: 'He was gracious, benign, affable, courteous, the soul of liberality and generosity. Unfortunately he was also shallow, vain, careless, empty-headed, incompetent, improvident, and irresponsible. These shortcomings, however, were barely noticed by most contemporaries, and seem to have been overlooked even by some who knew him well, beguiled by his fatal charm.'[189]

XIV

In the summer of 1183, Henry may have reflected that he had made some dreadful mistakes. He had alienated Eleanor, and had failed to plan for a viable succession; his plans for a federation among his sons were in tatters. He may have realised that he had brought it all upon himself. But even had he been given to self-reflection, by 1183 it was probably too late to change anything.

Had Henry followed the example of his fellow prince, the Holy Roman Emperor Frederick Barbarossa, things might have turned out very differently. Barbarossa had found himself in a similar situation to Henry in that he had several sons and had had a rich and powerful wife. He, however, handled the succession with aplomb, delegating real power to his sons from an early age and training them for government – in effect, the family business. He treated them with respect in public, and he supported them.[190]

Otto of Sankt-Blasien wrote of Barbarossa's plans for his sons that he 'had them all learn thoroughly to read and write, he acquired huge wealth for them and raised them to important offices, dividing the provinces among them'.[191]

When Barbarossa went on crusade in 1189, he left his eldest surviving son, Heinrich, as regent with full responsibility for the empire. True, he did not have to contend with an Eleanor. His wife Beatrix of Burgundy died as Frederick provided for his eldest sons.[192]

Henry made provision for his sons, but he gave them no real power or autonomy. Much as he loved them, he never had faith that any of them could be his match. He kept them all on a short leash, and they resented him for it. Gerald of Wales imputed motives that were darker still to Henry's behaviour:

> Although he had such distinguished and illustrious sons, one great impediment to his complete happiness was his constant detestation, perhaps with good reason, of those who would succeed him. Since all human prosperity is as short-lived as it is imperfect, Fortune's finely calculated malice saw to it that that which should have been a source of pleasure brought him strife; it brought the knife-edge of danger instead of added security; torment instead of peace, ingratitude instead of strong support, the utmost disquiet and harassment rather than peace and tranquillity.[193]

Revolts of aristocratic and royal sons against fathers, and brothers against brothers, were more common than not. Family warfare was not unknown to Henry, particularly on the Norman side which was particularly murderous. He had fought his brother Geoffrey in the 1150s, his father had fended off revolts by his brother Helias. William the Bastard fought his half-brother Odo, his sons William Rufus and Robert fought one another, his youngest son Henry possibly had William Rufus killed and in turn fought and imprisoned his other brother Robert. And Henry's mother Matilda was fighting her father, Henry I, on his death.[194] The examples were numerous, and have led one historian to identify a 'Norman tradition of family hostility'.[195] Henry's grasp of history was excellent – he would have been only too aware of the consequences of familial strife.

But he chose not to learn the lessons for himself and his own family. By his own actions, Henry had ensured that his son had no proper place in the world. It was a dreadful mistake, and Henry paid a bitter and lasting price through his grief over a beloved dead son.

Act V

Nemesis

My life, when it is written, will read better than it lived.
Henry FitzEmpress, first Plantagenet, a king at twenty-
one, the ablest soldier of an able time. He led men well, he
cared for justice when he could … and ruled, for thirty
years, a state as great as Charlemagne's. He married, out of
love, a woman out of legend. Not in Alexandria or Rome
or Camelot has there been such a queen. She bore him
many children, but no sons. King Henry had no sons.

James Goldman, *The Lion in Winter*

I

In May 1176, the Sicilian ambassador came to Winchester to ask
Henry for his youngest daughter Joanna's hand in marriage for
his master, King William II. Henry agreed.

The following year Walter, the English archbishop of Palermo,
asked his old friend Peter of Blois for a description of Henry. He
was eager to know more about his new queen's father. Peter was
perfectly placed to provide the information. He was at the heart
of Henry's administration, as a letter writer and diplomat. He
knew Henry – now forty-three, and king for twenty-two of his
years – very well.

Peter described a middle-aged man with red hair streaked with grey, balding on top. Henry was of medium height, with a round head and round eyes, which were 'white and plain, while he is of calm spirit; but in anger and disorder of heart they shine like fire and flash in fury'. He was stocky with a leonine face, 'a broad chest and a boxer's arms'. Henry looked like a prizefighter, but an ageing one. Peter did not neglect to describe an ingrowing toenail 'grown into the flesh of his foot' which gave Henry much pain, or an old wound in his leg which troubled him – in August 1174, while negotiating a truce with Hugh Bigod during the Great Revolt, he was kicked in the leg by the horse of Tostes of Saint-Omer, one of the Knights Templar he had made rich.

Peter wrote of Henry's passion for woods and hawking, for dogs, for hunting and exercise, both for enjoyment and to stop him getting fat. He was always on his feet, whether at Mass or in council. Despite his leg wound, Henry never sat, 'unless riding a horse or eating'. Peter talked of Henry's enormous energy, of how exercise preserved 'the lightness of youth'.

Peter's Henry was a man to be admired – constant, passionate, learned, loyal, unstinting in his pursuit of justice and care for his people. 'No one', he said, 'is more cunning in counsel, more fiery in speech, more secure in the midst of dangers, more cautious in fortune, more constant in adversity. Whom once he has esteemed, with difficulty he unloves them; whom once he has hated, with difficulty he receives into the grace of his familiarity.'

Henry was always occupied. Peter penned a portrait of a man whose hands constantly had something in them – a bow, sword, spear or arrow – or a book, 'unless he be in council'. He prized learning in his household: 'Every day is school, in the constant conversation of the most literate and discussion of questions.'

He went on to describe Henry's honesty, his excellent manners, his generosity to the poor, his pursuit of peace. Peter concluded, 'It aims to the peace of his people that he calls councils, that he makes laws, that he makes friendships, that he brings low the proud, that he threatens battles, that he launches terror to the princes ... No one is more mild to the afflicted, no one more friendly to the poor, no one more unbearable to the proud.'[1]

Peter described a near-perfect prince.

In the last years of the 1170s and the early 1180s, Henry was the most powerful ruler in Europe. The king of France, overlord for his continental lands, was a boy-king whom Henry mentored and believed he could influence. Eleanor was imprisoned and, for the present, his boys were calm and his lands enjoyed peace. He had granted Richard and Geoffrey semi-autonomy in Aquitaine and Brittany, while Henri, before his death, busied himself on the tournament circuit. John, Henry's beloved, was still young. Henry was rich, and he had begun his programme of brilliant legal reforms. He was forgiven, at least superficially, for his part in Thomas Becket's murder.

If Henry had died before the young king's rebellion in 1183, he would be remembered very differently. He would number among England's most celebrated monarchs – Henry V, Henry VIII, Elizabeth I, Victoria – and might be considered greater than them all. And what if the young king had not died fighting against his father in the summer of 1183, but instead Henry had perished? It is improbable that Henri would have held his father's massive empire together. Henry's achievements would have appeared stupendous by contrast.

But the final years of Henry's life were marred by the crumbling of his carefully laid plans. The young king's death in such pitiable circumstances, leaving his father broken and guilty, marked the reversal of Henry's luck.

By the end of the decade, Henry was achingly lonely. His dreams of a federation of his sons after his death were in fragments and he was isolated from them; Rosamund, his great love, was dead; Eleanor, from her prison, still managed to incite their sons to hate him. Henry sought solace with court prostitutes whose names we have no record of, amid the ashes of his once glorious kingship.

And worst of all, he had failed to identify his true nemesis until it was too late – King Philip of France.

II

Philip was the long-desired son of Louis, born to his wife Adela of Champagne in August 1165 when Louis was forty-five years old. Gerald of Wales was in the city at the time, and he told how a French woman, celebrating Philip's birth in the streets, spoke to him, crowing, 'we have a king given us by God, through whom *your* kingdom will be destroyed and damned'.[2] The sentiment expressed Gerald's deepest desire to see Henry and his family vanquished by Louis' house; but if true, it was eerily prophetic. The child was named for his uncle, who should have been king, and baptised the day after his birth in the castle's chapel, Saint-Michel-de-la-Place.[3] Louis, and later Philip, would forever attest to the boy's maternal descent from Charlemagne, and his compliant chroniclers called him 'Karolide'.[4]

Louis had reason to rejoice; after nearly twenty years of trying for a male heir by three different wives, and fathering four daughters in the process, he had finally succeeded. A charter of Louis' reflected his relief that a child 'of a more noble sex' had been born to him.[5]

The people of Paris were ecstatic, calling the child '*Dieudonné*' – God-given – ringing bells and lighting candles and fires across the city.

When Philip fell ill aged fourteen, during his hunting trip in 1179, it is no wonder that Louis panicked and visited Canterbury and the shrine of St Thomas to entreat for his son's life. If Philip had died, Henry's heirs might have sat on the Capetian throne. Louis' prayers were answered when Philip recovered. Before Philip fell ill, Louis had planned to have him crowned alongside himself in August 1179. When Louis had a stroke soon after his return from Canterbury, Philip went ahead with the ceremony, without his father. Philip acted as king for a year before his father died, aged sixty, in September 1180.

And what of the Capetian domains inherited by Philip? The royal lands were tiny, and with the exceptions of Berry and Bourges to the south, rarely stretched more than about eighty miles from Paris. The territories under the king's direct control were scattered: from Orléans in the south-west, to Montereau in the south-east, and to Dreux and Mantes in the west, and north towards Soissons. Only these lands owed allegiance to Philip.[6]

Even by 1180, and despite Louis' best efforts, the troubadour Bertran de Born mocked the new monarch, calling him 'the little king of Lesser-Land'.[7] He continued, 'Five duchies has the French crown and, if you count them up, there are three of them missing.'[8] Henry held Aquitaine, Normandy and Brittany, significantly depleting Philip's territory.

Philip, as Louis had been, was surrounded by powerful and potentially hostile magnates. Henry's lands were only forty miles from Paris, while Henry of Champagne's were twenty.[9] Louis VII's France has been called 'the land without a king'. This is not entirely fair; he had some success in bringing his vassals further under his control, and they did attend court more now than in previous reigns. His clever marriage to Adela of Champagne brought an alliance with her powerful brothers, Theobald V of Blois, Henry of Champagne, and Stephen of Sancerre. When Henry's sons rebelled against him, Louis could count on, besides his brothers-in-law, his mighty vassals the counts of Boulogne and Dreux.[10] Other marriages bound new allies to him: his sister Constance's to Raymond of Toulouse, his son's to the niece of the count of Flanders, Isabella of Hainault. It would be a mistake to think of Louis as 'simple-minded'.[11] He deployed the weapons in his kingly arsenal with aplomb. He was more powerful than any of his Capetian predecessors and insisted on homage; it was only

Henry who managed to avoid it. He commissioned magnificent buildings to glorify his kingship and his position with the church – in 1177, a visitor to Paris, observing the building of Notre-Dame, remarked in admiration, 'there will be no church to compete with it on our side of the Alps'.[12] Louis, as much a prince of the twelfth-century renaissance as Henry, fostered the growth of the renowned cathedral schools.

Ralph of Diceto commented that Louis transcended 'the majesty of his predecessors'. Just as Henry used propaganda to promote the glory of his dynasty, so too did Louis; it was Louis who first used the fleur-de-lys as the symbol of France, and who was regarded as the most pious, the 'most Christian' king in Europe.

In the end, Louis was not as rich, as cunning, as broad or as clever as Henry FitzEmpress. He did, however, leave his son and heir a legacy of hatred for his most powerful vassal. He also taught him the lesson that fractures in the Plantagenet family could be exploited to Capetian advantage.

Philip, unlike his father, was not haphazard or opportunistic in his campaign against Henry. He was cool, manipulative and deadly. He was an entirely different kind of adversary.

Philip was still young when he was crowned. He was apparently 'handsome' and could, on occasion, look happy and approachable. A later description, from the Tours chronicler in the 1190s, described him as 'a fine man well-proportioned in stature, with a smiling countenance, bald, a ruddy complexion, inclined to eat and drink well, and sensual'.[13] When he began to rule during his father's lifetime, he was only fourteen years old. Louis, before his stroke, had given his blessing to Philip's marriage to Isabella of Hainault, the niece of the count of Flanders. She was ten years old when they married at Saint-Denis in May 1180; Philip was crowned once more, alongside his bride. The marriage was swiftly followed by a bitter fight to gain control of the new king: ranged on one side, Philip's mother the dowager Queen

Adela and her powerful brothers, Henry count of Champagne, Theobald count of Blois, Stephen count of Sancerre, and William Whitehands, papal legate and the archbishop of Rheims – and on the other, his bride's uncle, the count of Flanders. Philip sided with the charismatic count of Flanders against his mother and her family.

Philip was precocious. He knew his mother's brothers resented his marriage, and he had removed his father's seal as he lay incapacitated, for fear that one of them would take it in a grab for power.[14] When his mother fortified her lands, he did not tread softly. Instead he took them from her. She ran from court to her brother, Theobald.[15] Philip had prevailed in the first political crisis of his reign. He was said to remark, soon afterwards, 'I am only a man, but a man who is king of France.'[16]

It was Henry who was eventually asked to broker a peace by Adela. He was successful, and Philip's maternal family returned to court; he had made it clear, however, that he intended to rule alone. Once they accepted their place, he happily accepted their advice. His uncle William Whitehands was first among his advisors, 'the watchful eye of his councillors, and his right hand in business ... a second king'.[17]

Philip would call on Henry throughout the early 1180s to broker further talks, this time between himself and the count of Flanders, his relationship with whom had grown cold.

This was not Philip's first experience up close to Henry FitzEmpress. They had met before.

Gerald of Wales wrote that Philip first met Henry when he was about seven years old. Gerald, however, described a meeting with Thomas Becket who died in 1170, and therefore Philip would have been five at most. Gerald claimed that Philip sought Henry out, saying, 'On my father's behalf I entreat you, O king, that you would love him more than usual, and being faithful to him, that you would desist from harassing him. For assuredly all may know, that whoever shall presume to molest him in this his old age shall find me, by God's grace, an avenger most hostile to himself when occasion shall offer itself and the time shall come.'[18]

Henry and Philip could not have been more different. Where Henry was superstitious but likely not religious, Philip was pious. Where Henry was open-handed, Philip was mean. And where Henry was magnanimous and kind, Philip was nervous and cold. Unlike Henry, who swore prolifically, Philip abhorred cursing – he fined those of his courtiers who did, or they risked being thrown into the Seine – and had little time for the arts or tournaments.[19] Where Henry respected his Jewish communities, Philip persecuted them and ejected them from his towns.[20] His father Louis had, like Henry, gone above and beyond in protecting his Jewish communities, in spite of dissent from within his own family.

For in May 1171 Louis' son-in-law Theobald of Blois instigated the first blood libel in continental Europe. The Jews of the town were accused of crucifying a Christian child at Passover, and throwing his body into the Loire. Intriguingly, Theobald had a close attachment to a Jewish woman of the town, Pucelina, who tried to intercede to save the community. But Theobald's wife, Alix (Eleanor's and Louis' daughter) was jealous; she was 'cruel ... a Jezebel [who] swayed him, for she hated Dame Pucelina'. She kept Pucelina from Theboald 'for fear she might get him to change his mind'. It was Alix, working with a local priest, who successfully persuaded him to issue the order for the Jews' murder. Over thirty people were burned alive out of a population of about forty. The remnants of the community were saved by a Rabbi Baruch, who raised the £1,000 demanded by Theobald in exchange for their safety.[21]

This attitude was in marked contrast to Louis, who had even put in place a *prepositus judaeorum* (head of the Jewish community).[22] When Philip expelled the Jews from his lands in 1182, Henry welcomed them.

Philip's strategy towards Henry was very different from his father's. Philip was determined to make the Capetian crown as strong as it had been in the days of Charlemagne. It was Philip who, towards the end of the century, turned Paris into the royal capital. He established the treasury and the royal archives, paved the city, built the Louvre Palace, developed Paris as a commercial centre, completed Notre-Dame and ordered a university to be established within the city, building on the flourishing abbey schools.[23] By 1215 Paris was recognised as 'the intellectual capital of the world', and the credit lies with Philip.[24] When he expelled the Jews, he took over their property in the Les Halles area of the city, levelled it, covered it and created a market. This covered area meant that merchants could trade in all weathers, bringing enormous wealth into the city.[25] Philip's reign was marked by the noise, inconvenience and dust of seemingly endless building works.

Philip was convinced that to bring more power to the Crown and for France to prosper, he must break Henry, his mightiest vassal. Philip had watched the interaction between his father and Henry closely. He observed how Henry always got the better of his supposed overlord for his lands on the continent, from the very moment Louis had recognised Henry as duke of Normandy. For Philip it was not just a question of dominance. His victory must be complete and he would show no mercy towards Henry, 'the old beast'. Philip craved both personal vengeance for a father who had given him and the Crown everything, and to succeed where his father had failed.

Once Philip set his sights on a goal, he would pursue it ruthlessly. His brutal marital history was a case in point. Philip tried to divorce his first wife, Isabella of Hainault, when she was still only fourteen. He offered to find her a new husband, but Isabella protested, claiming 'it does not please God that a mortal should enter the bed in which you slept'.[26] Isabella made her unhappiness so public, roaming the streets and churches of Senlis barefoot, that Philip was persuaded to take her back. When she died in 1190, giving birth to stillborn twins, Philip quickly chose another wife. He had only one son, and not a particularly healthy one, and was obliged to marry again. He set his sights on Ingeborg of Denmark, the sister of King Cnut VI. In return, Ingeborg's brother gave Philip 10,000 marks and promised to help him invade England.

But Philip did not like her. She was eighteen when she arrived to marry the twenty-eight-year old king of France. Philip appears to have had a visceral reaction to her. During the coronation ceremony that followed their marriage, he apparently shook uncontrollably. He wanted nothing to do with her; Philip swore that their marriage was never consummated and he immediately petitioned the pope for divorce. But the pope refused, and Ingeborg too would not countenance divorce, claiming the marriage was unbreakable as she had in fact slept with Philip, contrary to his ardent denials. She also refused to enter a convent, which would have been extremely convenient for Philip. In retaliation, he imprisoned her for twenty years, deprived her of an income, and even incarcerated the ambassadors her brother sent to plead for her freedom.

The chroniclers could not make sense of his actions, and some accused Ingeborg of witchcraft. Her effect on him was 'undoubtedly at the instigation of the Devil'.[27] Most, however, simply could not understand, as they found her beautiful and pious. Even if we account for political motivations, Philip's actions still make little sense. One historian suggests that Philip did try to consummate the marriage and failed – hence the whispers of sorcery, which he hoped would persuade the pope to allow him to divorce her.[28] We will never know the reasons for Philip's cruel treatment of this Danish princess. Jim Bradbury, Philip's biographer, speculates that it is possible she 'simply had bad breath'.[29]

Philip's pursuit of a new wife, Agnes of Méran, while still married to Ingeborg in the eyes of Rome, earned the wrath of the pope and nearly all of Christendom. The pope refused to recognise a divorce that Philip's pliant clergy had granted him, and when he married Agnes in June 1196, the pope was outraged and placed France under an interdict. Philip cared nothing for the pope's sanction. He had shown he was prepared to pursue his own interests even at the expense of the happiness and well-being of two of his wives. And if he could be brutal to them, he would – when the time was right – have no compunction in meting out similar treatment towards Henry.

Philip knew he was not yet strong enough to defeat Henry in battle; instead, from the outset of his reign, he began a slow, deliberate war of attrition. If he could not yet destroy Henry militarily, he would flatter and lull him, and use his sons against him, as Louis had done with Henri, Richard and Geoffrey. Philip was nearly eight years old when the Great Revolt began, and he had seen that his father's strategy, to erode the Plantagenet family ties, had nearly worked. It was a good plan, and Philip would carry it out far more consistently and effectively than his father. He was a patient man, with a long-term strategy. He knew how much Henry's boys hated him for his treatment of their mother; he would play on this pitilessly.

III

On the River Epte in the Vexin, on the French side of the river between Gisors and Trie, stood an imposing elm tree.

It was an ancient tree of great height with a glorious crown, and for Henry and his contemporaries it was immersed in symbolism. It signified shelter, dignity, strength and fidelity. It was here, under the protection of this elm marking their borders, that the dukes of Normandy declared their fealty and paid homage to the kings of France. It was here that Henry rode again and again to meet, first with Louis, and then with Philip, to talk peace.[30] And it was on this spot on 6 December 1183, that Philip struck the first blow, compelling his foe to perform homage. Until this time, Henry had always managed to avoid the degradation of the ceremony.

Now, kneeling before Philip he placed his clasped hands between the French king's, and pledged himself entirely to him as his overlord for all his lands 'beyond the sea'.[31] Philip had brought the mighty Henry FitzEmpress to his knees, utterly humiliating him.

What had induced Henry to perform this homage?

When the young king Henri died in June 1183, the war in Aquitaine fizzled out. But his death caused a new and more far-reaching crisis for Henry. Philip used his brother-in-law's death, and the widowed status of his sister, Margaret, to demand that Henry give him back her dowry – the Norman Vexin, and the lands in England and Normandy Henry had promised on her marriage, but never given. Henry was loath to give up either. He refused, deviously telling Philip that he had given those lands designated for Margaret to Eleanor, and he quickly ordered Eleanor out of her prison to make a tour of them in an ostentatious display. He also told Philip that the Vexin was indisputably his; it belonged to Normandy, given by Louis when Henri and Margaret married.

But Philip countered. He demanded that Henry give Margaret a pension, and marry one of his sons to Alice, Margaret's sister and his half-sister. If Henry agreed, whichever son married Alice – Richard or John – would gain the Vexin. Most alarming of all, Philip also demanded that Henry pay homage to him.

Why did Philip suggest that Alice marry Richard *or* John? Alice, in 1183, had been betrothed to Richard for fourteen years, and she had been in Henry's care since she was nine years old. Yet she endured a strange limbo while waiting for Henry to allow Richard to marry her.

Gerald of Wales believed that Henry would not allow the marriage as Alice was his mistress, and he did not want his son to have her. It is possible that they were lovers. One chronicler wrote that Alice had a son by Henry, who did not survive.[32] Gerald claimed too that father and sons had developed 'a great and execrable hatred' for each other, a result of Henry's failed attempt to divorce their mother, supposedly to marry Alice, and that, 'through his heirs begotten of her [Alice], by both his own powers and those of France, he might be able effectually to disinherit his former sons by Eleanor, who had troubled him'.[33]

Whether this was true or not, Philip, wishing to create a rift between Henry and Richard, convinced Richard that it *was* true. Richard continued to believe it, even after his father was dead. Towards the end of the decade, he told Philip that 'I do not reject your sister; but it is impossible for me to marry her, for my father had slept with her and had a son by her.'[34] Richard's vassal, Bertran de Born, claimed that 'Richard doesn't care to have her.'[35]

Philip also made Richard believe that Henry planned to supplant him with John. Richard 'was moved with so great indignation, and the circumstance supplied such cause for hatred, that from that hour he suspected and deeply hated his father, as one who wished to plan his own disinheritance for the sake of a younger son'.[36]

Richard therefore would not marry Alice because he believed she was sleeping with his father; Henry would not allow the marriage because it would give Richard, a son he no longer trusted, too much power.

Henry by necessity had to rethink the succession after Henri's death. He began to move his pieces – his surviving sons – around; he assumed, as he always perhaps somewhat naively did, that they would fall in with his stratagems. Just six weeks before Henry's humiliating exchange with Philip, at the end of September 1183 he demanded that Richard give up Aquitaine to John, and move into his dead brother's place.

There was no discussion, no explanation to Richard of Henry's rationale. To Henry it made perfect sense. He had not provided properly for John, and with the death of Henri his plans of a triumvirate, with brother aiding brother after his death, would still work, with the boon that there would also be a portion for his youngest son. Richard as the eldest would take the young king's role, Geoffrey would remain in Brittany (he had been invested as duke and held it in right of his wife), and John would take Aquitaine.

But Richard did not respond as Henry expected. He had seen how empty his older brother's position had been and he wanted nothing to do with Henry's plan. He asked Henry for three days to consider his offer and to speak with his friends, and then fled court in the middle of the night without telling his father, and rode fast to Poitou. When he arrived, he sent bellicose words back to Henry. He would never give it up. Henry was furious.[37]

At no point did Henry take Richard's feelings into account. Richard had lived in Aquitaine since childhood, where he had been groomed to rule by his mother. Henry, both before and after the revolt, had allowed Richard autonomy here, ever more as he proved himself an able soldier and a capable ruler, unlike Henri. Richard felt deeply his heritage as heir to the dukes of Aquitaine. Now, his refusal to give it up was as much about his antipathy to cede it to a brother who cared nothing for the duchy, as a rebellion against Henry's treatment of Eleanor. Eleanor desired nothing more than for Richard to succeed to an independent Aquitaine. And Richard was determined to grant her wish.

When Philip, at their meeting beneath the ancient elm tree, demanded of Henry that one of his sons marry Alice, Henry could not allow it to be Richard. Richard would be obliged to pay homage to Philip for the Vexin. As such he would have Aquitaine and Normandy in his hands, a huge power base for a son whom Henry did not trust.

Equally, it could not be John. By marrying him to Alice and giving him the Vexin and Normandy, it would incur the wrath of both Richard and Geoffrey – and Henry had no appetite for yet another family fight.[38]

Philip then, in the absence of a marriage, demanded that if Henry wanted to keep the Vexin, he would have to pay him homage.[39] Henry, an anointed king, was left in an excruciating position. He wanted the Vexin. Yet homage was an expression of feudal power, and until now, Henry had always managed to wriggle out of the obligation. He felt it was demeaning for one king to perform homage to another, although he acknowledged that the French king was his overlord for his lands in France.

Louis had never managed to extract the obligation from Henry, except once in 1151 before Henry was crowned, when he came to Paris to pay homage for Normandy. Henry's friend Robert of Torigni even 'found' evidence that the dukes of Normandy were exempt from the act.[40] Similarly the young king had only performed homage before his coronation in 1170, and never after.

But for once, Henry was powerless to resist. He found himself humiliated and on the back foot, a position he was not familiar with. When Philip refused to budge on the Vexin, Henry was left with no choice. If he wanted to keep hold of it, Philip demanded that Henry perform homage for his lands in France.

Had Henry and his sons been united against Philip's power, there is no doubt that Henry would have triumphed. But they were not. And so, under the elm tree, 'Henry king of England swore homage and allegiance ... to Philip king of France, to whom he had never before wished to do homage.'[41] Philip would ensure that this was not a solitary act. He would extract the promise from Henry once more before the decade was out.

IV

Richard had shown Henry his hand when he ran away from his father in the middle of the night, and refused ever to relinquish Aquitaine. When Richard absconded, it marked the beginning of yet another year of war. Henry, when he realised that Richard was immovable, fell into a typical fit of contrived rage. He ordered John, now seventeen years old, to go and fight his brother. It is impossible that this 'order' was anything other than Henry's characteristic bluster, as John, known as Lackland, had no army. But this youngest son, perhaps anxious to prove himself, took his father at his word. He played on Geoffrey's jealousy of Richard, and persuaded him to join him in taking the fight to Aquitaine. Geoffrey did have an army, raised in Brittany, and in August the two of them marched into Poitou. Richard routed them, chasing them back to Brittany, where he annihilated their force.

Henry, exasperated with his warring sons, commanded them all to Westminster in December and forced them to make peace.[42] But it was a token gesture and doubtless there were many heated exchanges that went unreported by the chroniclers.

Henry now resolutely refused to commit to a succession plan. He no longer trusted Richard and Geoffrey, and John was still unproven. After Richard had reacted so violently to Henry's proposal to move him into his dead brother's place, replacing his inheritance of Aquitaine with England, Normandy and Anjou, Henry probably decided to keep his options open. He was reluctant to go to war with Richard to force him out of Aquitaine; coercing him into accepting a different inheritance was not an option.

Instead, he ordered Richard back to Poitou. He sent John to Ireland in the spring of 1185, intending to make him king there. Geoffrey was charged, rather ambiguously, to 'hold' Normandy. Geoffrey may well have believed that Henry intended Normandy, as well as Brittany, for him. It seemed sensible; the dukes of Brittany already accepted the dukes of Normandy as their over-lords.[43] If so, it would make Geoffrey, after Henry's death, immensely powerful. It gave him false hope.

But peace did not endure for long. In April Richard went to war with Geoffrey, and fortified Poitou against his father. Henry was forced to fight Richard to bring him to terms. In May 1185, Henry made Richard a proposal he found impossible to refuse. He forced Richard to relinquish Aquitaine to his mother, threatening that if Richard would not comply, he 'would come in person at the head of a great army to devastate his land'.[44]

In 1182, Henry and Eleanor's eldest daughter, Matilda, had fled with her husband to sanctuary in Normandy. Henry the Lion of Saxony was driven out of his lands by Frederick Barbarossa, when he refused to bring his armies to Frederick's aid as the emperor fought against the Lombard League. Henry offered his daughter and son-in-law a home while he aided the duke in resolving his fight – using diplomacy rather than war – with Barbarossa. The troubadour poet Bertran de Born, lord of Hautefort and a subject of Richard's, was at Henry's Christmas court at Argentan. Richard introduced him to his sister, Matilda, then aged twenty-six. Bertran had written of the qualities of the ideal knight – and his lady: 'Love wants a knightly lover, good with his weapons and generous in serving, sweet-tongued and a great giver, who knows what is right to do and say, out-doors or in, for a man of his potency. He should be amusing company, courtly and pleasing. A lady who lies with a stud like that is clean of all her sins.'[45]

Besotted with his lord's sister, Bertran wrote luridly on her impact on himself and the court. He was stunned by her beauty and called her 'Elena' and 'Lena', both forms of 'Helen', the classical epitome of beauty. He was entranced: 'A frisky, gay Elena attracted me with a sidelong look; I went through a long Lent, but from now on I am at the Thursday of the Last Supper.'[46]

In daydreaming of Matilda, he was saved from the 'boredom' of court. Christmas at Argentan 'nearly killed me, but the noble, lovable and sweet mild face and good companionship of the Saxon lady protected me'.[47]

Whether or not Matilda was aware of Bertran's passion, we do not know.

Far more important, her visit coincided with an increase in her mother's freedom. Henry finally allowed Eleanor to leave her confinement, and mother and daughter spent nearly a year together at Winchester, from June 1184. It was now ten years since the end of the Great Revolt, and perhaps Henry's attitude to his wife had softened. But there were other reasons why he may have granted her more freedom; perhaps he did not want to be embarrassed in front of his daughter; or perhaps Henry, for the first time in a decade, needed Eleanor on his side.

She was with all her sons in November 1184 in London. In May 1185, she crossed to Normandy at Henry's request, and she must have met with Richard here, if not soon after.

Eleanor would doubtless have spoken with Richard, her beloved son, and may well have counselled him to bide his time with his father. Henry was invincible militarily, but he was growing older. Richard would be best advised to wait and see.

And so when Eleanor asked him, at Henry's insistence, for Aquitaine back, he heeded his mother and did so without a fight. He 'returned all Poitou with its castles and fortifications to his mother'.[48] But still Henry, burned by his war with the young king, would not pronounce on his sons' inheritances.

V

While brother fought brother, Henry was busy, fulfilling his role as elder statesman of Europe.

During these years Henry, once more using his generosity and wealth as a display of power, brokered marriages for two of his cousins and erstwhile enemies. He arranged the marriage of Philip, count of Flanders to a Portuguese princess. (The count's first wife, Elizabeth de Vermandois, was Petronilla's daughter and Eleanor's niece; when the count discovered Elizabeth's infidelity, he had her lover beaten to death.)

William the Lion was still unmarried and he approached Henry as his overlord to help him find a wife. In 1184, he hoped to marry Henry's granddaughter, daughter of young Matilda and the duke of Saxony. But the pope refused, citing too close a kinship. Two years later, in 1186, Henry, arranged for his marriage to Ermengarde, daughter of the viscount of Beaumont, and even lent the newly-weds Rosamund's glorious Woodstock palace, Everswell, for their honeymoon. They married on 5 September 1186 and the wedding feast lasted for four days.[49] Henry gave William back Edinburgh Castle, taken after the Great Revolt, as a wedding present. It was a remarkable display of generosity to a former enemy. But Henry would have calculated that it cost him nothing, and bound William to him.

Perhaps the happiest piece of diplomacy Henry undertook was his arbitration in the dispute between his son-in-law Henry of Saxony and Frederick Barbarossa. For the duke of Saxony's exile meant that his daughter Matilda came back to Normandy. She gave birth to a son at Argentan, soon after her arrival in 1182, but the child did not survive. Two years later, she gave birth to a boy at Winchester.[50] Eleanor was with their daughter at the boy's birth. These were pockets of joy for Henry.

To his contemporaries, Henry remained unassailable, a royal 'grand old man'. For a decade, his advice had been sought by fractious kings; in 1177, for example, he was asked to reconcile the warring monarchs of Castile and Navarre.

Philip sought advice from his mighty vassal too. At the beginning of the 1180s, he asked Henry to act as mediator, to resolve the wars between himself and the count of Flanders. He 'adopted the king of England, as if instead of a father, and entirely submitted himself in this matter to his counsel'.[51] Throughout, Philip watched and waited. As he grew in strength, he took what he could from Henry; he learned from him.

Henry's diplomatic efforts during these years were extraordinarily successful. He seemed to have endless perseverance, listening patiently to grievances and offering words of counsel, as he pursued a peaceful resolution between count and king. Henry had acquired a talent for diplomacy. When his mother, in 1167, had entreated him to let Louis have his self-respect and evacuate the town of Andely so Louis could burn it while still keeping his dignity, Henry had listened, and followed her advice. He knew when to be generous and conciliatory, and when to unleash his mercenaries. He understood the need to flatter, and to ensure that all parties retained their dignity. When he paid homage to Philip, Henry had ruled for nearly thirty years, and had seen it all: war from without and within; testing matters requiring the king's justice; disputatious allies; aggrieved enemies and great errors and great shows of penance; and loyal support from some, countered with treachery from others. Over three decades, he had accumulated the wisdom of kings.

Philip had studied his teacher, but while Henry understood weakness and sought to be kind where he could, Philip exploited it remorselessly. He saw the weaknesses in Henry's relationships with his sons and he twisted them to his own advantage. Philip learned from Henry, but he used the knowledge to engineer his rival's defeat.

Philip lulled and beguiled Henry, now in his fifties and perhaps more susceptible to flattery than in his earlier years. Even after Philip's insistence that his vassal perform homage, Henry still did not have his measure. Henry was so used to playing a magnanimous role, using wealth and generosity as an instrument of power, that even after this humiliation, he sent large gifts of game to Philip from his parks in Normandy and Aquitaine, treating him as the junior party.[52]

VI

In January 1185, Patriarch Heraclius of Jerusalem visited Henry to offer him the keys to the Latin Kingdom.

It is hard to overstate the religious and symbolic meaning that the Latin Kingdom of Jerusalem had in the West. In 1099, the forces of the First Crusade captured the Holy Land and Jerusalem, sacred to Christians, Muslims and Jews. It was a bloody endeavour; chroniclers wrote of the warriors of Christ wading ankle-deep through Muslim blood. Three other crusader states were forged at the same time: Edessa, Antioch and Tripoli, and all were ruled over by a Frankish nobility. (Edessa's fall in 1144 precipitated the cataclysmic Second Crusade, when Eleanor's marriage to Louis disintegrated.)

Heraclius was the senior ecclesiastic in the Latin Kingdom. He was also a worldly man, reputedly very handsome, and he kept a mistress, by whom he had at least one child. Nevertheless, on this mission of mercy to Europe he was accompanied by other Levantine luminaries – the masters of the Temple and the Hospital. They carried with them the keys to Jerusalem, the Tower of David and the Holy Sepulchre.

It is 2,300 miles from Jerusalem to Paris, as the crow flies. Heraclius only undertook such a difficult journey because the Latin Kingdom was in dire jeopardy. The king – Baldwin IV, the leper king – was Henry's first cousin. They shared a grandfather, Fulk V of Anjou, who ruled in Jerusalem from 1131 until his death in 1143. He had vacated Anjou in 1128 in favour of his son Geoffrey, so Geoffrey could marry Matilda.

Baldwin IV's regime was weak and his health was poor. By the beginning of the 1180s he was blind, could no longer walk, and was not expected to live long. His aristocracy was riven with infighting just as his adversary, the Ayyubid sultan Salah ad-Din (Saladin), was uniting Muslims against the Christian kingdom. Saladin was ruler of Egypt, Damascus and, since 1183, Aleppo; he was determined to expel the Christian rulers from the Levant. Hopes of support from Constantinople were obliterated when a new regime, antipathetic to the Latin Kingdom, took power there.[53] Baldwin's heir was his five-year-old nephew, also named Baldwin. A weak and divided regime under a child ruler would be no match for Saladin's encroaching power. The Latin Kingdom needed financial and military help, and King Baldwin sent Heraclius to Europe to secure it.

Heraclius first met with Pope Lucius III at Verona in September 1184, who issued a crusade bull. Heraclius arrived in Paris in January 1185, where he offered Philip the keys to Jerusalem. But Philip wanted neither to be king nor to lead an expensive expedition, and so the patriarch departed for England to try his luck with Henry.

They met on 29 January at Reading. Heraclius knelt before Henry and offered him the keys to the Latin Kingdom. He asked Henry to come and save them.

Henry, ever emotional, apparently cried when Heraclius told him of the perilous situation of the Franks in the East. But although Henry had repeatedly promised to go on crusade, it was merely an exercise in propaganda. It had no appeal for him. Even Louis had not believed that he ever intended to go, complaining about it in 1168.[54] Although both Henry and the young king had talked of their wish to make pilgrimage to Compostela, neither had gone. The young king had wanted to go on crusade to Jerusalem; he never did, although from his deathbed he sent William Marshal to take his cross to Jerusalem, and fulfil his vow for him.[55] William, having given his promise, did go, at enormous personal expense. He did not return to Europe for almost two years.

Henry had made repeated promises to go. He levied a crusading tax in 1166; he intimated to Archbishop Frederick of Tyre that he would go in 1170, and then tearfully excused himself after Becket's murder;[56] he promised the pope at Avranches in 1172 as part of his penance for Becket's murder; in 1177 at the Treaty of Nonancourt, he and Louis swore to go together. But he never did. Instead, to avoid the obligation but to retain influence in the East, he kept sending money to the Latin Kingdom.[57]

Once the funds arrived, however, no one could touch Henry's financial reserves, as they were guarded by the orders of the Knights Templar and the Knights Hospitaller.[58] Since 1172, as a part of his public display of penance for Thomas Becket's death, Henry had transferred money to his account in Jerusalem every year. By 1187, it was thought to be worth 30,000 silver marks, a tremendous amount of money. To put it in perspective, on Henry's death Richard found 100,000 silver marks in his father's treasury.[59] Henry's revolutionary administrative reforms brought huge revenue to the Crown, and Richard would benefit. The money in Jerusalem gave Henry enormous political leverage, and it led even Gerald of Wales to call him 'the chief support of the Holy Land'.[60] The patriarch was motivated to ask for Henry's help not least because he was so rich in the East. Baldwin IV and Heraclius wanted Henry to use his account for the defence of the Holy Land. The easiest way to do it would be to invite Henry to become king.

Henry, although he put on a good display, was aware of Heraclius's motives. Gerald of Wales recorded a conversation he had with Henry while hunting with him and his son-in-law, the duke of Saxony, at Clarendon. Gerald saw nothing but honour and glory for Henry in the patriarch's visit. But Henry replied, 'If the patriarch or any others come to us, they seek their own advantage rather than ours … The clergy may well call us to arms and peril, since they themselves will receive no blows in the fray nor shoulder any burdens that they can avoid.'[61] Henry, Gerald could see, had no intention of going.

Even had Henry desired to go, it was impossible. His sons were battling, he did not trust them, and he had not yet decided on the succession.

However, Henry duly summoned his magnates and William the Lion to London on 10 March to discuss the patriarch's offer. The assembly was fittingly gathered at the house of the knights of St John of Jerusalem at Clerkenwell. Here, Henry asked the convocation a question: should he leave his kingdom to rule the Latin Kingdom in Jerusalem? The question was couched to make it impossible for his barons to answer 'yes'. They responded as Henry doubtless wanted, that it was better that he 'should govern his kingdom with due care and protect it from the intrusion of foreigners and from external enemies, than that he should in his own person seek the preservation of the easterners'.[62]

Heraclius tried everything he could to induce Henry to come, even emotional blackmail in the form of a visit to Becket's tomb. Henry, although he continued to be polite, remained firm. Instead, both he and Philip promised assistance in the form of money and men to fight.

Heraclius had failed and was forlorn. He told Henry, 'We want a prince, not money. From everywhere we receive money, but no prince ... We want a prince who needs money, not money which needs a prince.'[63] He asked if instead Henry would send one of his sons. But Henry refused. He did not want his eastern account to be spent.[64] Bitterly, Heraclius lamented a dynasty that refused to help him; no wonder, for they were 'descended from the Devil'. He chastised Henry for his failure to help them.[65] Henry, though, was determined to hang on to his money in the East, despite the patriarch's pleas.

VII

Meanwhile, Henry had made sporadic attempts to provide for John, since his fateful betrothal to Alice, the Maurienne heiress, and the promise of the young king's castles in 1173. After John's heiress died, Henry had to look elsewhere. When Henry's loyal uncle Reginald of Cornwall died, Henry disinherited Reginald's three daughters and gave his property over to John – vast estates in Wales, Normandy and England.[66]

Reginald had always supported Henry. He fought for his half-sister Matilda, and after Henry made peace with Stephen and left for Normandy, Reginald stayed in England in 1153 to protect his nephew's interests. During the Becket dispute, Reginald remained utterly loyal to Henry. He fought to guard England for his nephew during the Great Revolt. With Richard de Lucy and Robert earl of Leicester, Reginald formed one of a triumvirate of intimates closest to Henry. Yet despite Reginald's unimpeachable loyalty, Henry was ruthless where his sons' inheritances were concerned.

Reginald's property was not enough, however, for the legitimate son of a king, and a favourite legitimate son to boot. In 1176, had Henry found a new heiress to marry John, Isabella of Gloucester, and in doing so he disinherited her sisters.

In 1185 John, now eighteen, was desperate to answer Heraclius's call to go to Jerusalem but Henry was reluctant. He did not want John to spend the money from his eastern treasury.[67] Instead, Henry sent John to Ireland with an army to claim his kingdom. Henry had conquered Ireland thirteen years earlier, partly to remove himself from England and Normandy until the furore over Becket's death calmed down. By 1177, he had already designated Ireland to John, asking the pope to grant him a crown. He even commissioned a sword for his son that resembled the legendary Tristan's – the famous Curtana – to add the mystique of Celtic legend to his coronation regalia.[68] Just as Tristan had fought the wicked Irish giant Morholt, so John would triumph.

Ireland offered a convenient solution to get John an inheritance, and out of the way. It should have been easy; Ireland was already conquered. But it was an utter disaster.

John and his force put in at Waterford on 25 April. They were met by several Irish chiefs, who immediately submitted to John's authority. The expedition should have been a walkover. These lords were 'disposed to be peaceable' and 'came to congratulate him as their new lord, and receive him with the kiss of peace'. But John was disrespectful of Irish rights and customs. He parcelled out their lands among his men. Gerald of Wales, who accompanied John's expedition as a clerk, wrote that 'our new-comers and Normans not only treated them with contempt and derision, but even rudely pulled them by their beards, which the Irishmen wore full and long'.[69]

Hugh de Lacy, justiciar of Ireland, possibly incited the kings of Limerick, Connaught, and Cork to fight against John. When John returned to England in September, shrouded in failure, he blamed Hugh and complained bitterly to Henry. Both Gerald of Wales and Roger of Howden, however, held John responsible. As John was too mean to pay his troops, they defected to the Irish, already incensed with him for trampling on their land rights and disrespecting their customs.

In July 1186 an Irish assassin, possibly in the employ of the king of Tethba, seeking vengeance for the death of his son by Anglo-Norman soldiers, cut off Hugh de Lacy's head.[70]

Henry was on the brink of sending John back to try once more, when a momentous family event stopped him.[71]

VIII

On 10 March 1186, Henry and Philip met once again under the elm tree at Gisors to discuss the Vexin. Alice remained in Henry's custody, and with no marriage to Richard in sight, Philip demanded a resolution.

Despite the knotty issue of the Vexin, however, relations between Henry and Philip were superficially excellent. Henry had mediated several times in Philip's ongoing battles with the count of Flanders, using both soldiers and diplomacy to aid the French king. Philip continued to treat Henry as his revered mentor. Henry was ill in November 1185, and it was Philip who visited him at Belveir and kept him company.[72]

The matter at the March meeting was resolved amicably. Henry agreed to pay Margaret a pension, and he promised that Alice would be married to Richard. Henry was still livid with Richard, and continued to refuse to make his succession plans clear; after all, his sons had given him no reason to trust them and he feared he would be vulnerable should he pronounce on the succession. But Henry realised the importance of Philip believing that Richard was his heir. He obfuscated, and Philip was (for now) satisfied. At the end of the meeting, Philip said that he would not again bring up the Vexin 'against the king of England, nor against Richard his son, nor against their heirs'.[73]

If Philip was mollified, Henry's legitimate son Geoffrey was dismayed. He believed that Henry had made his decision; Richard would inherit the greater part of their father's kingdom, and Geoffrey felt sidelined. His father had dangled a kingdom in front of him, and just as swiftly removed it. Geoffrey, incensed, now allied himself to a very accommodating Philip.

This marked the beginning of a new phase in Henry and Philip's relationship.

Geoffrey courted Philip in Paris, who honoured him with the position of seneschal of France. The two apparently became very close, although whether their relationship was warmed by real liking, or simply a shared antipathy towards Henry, it is impossible to say. As he sought to create divisions within Henry's family, Philip was able to achieve something his father never had: he made Henry's sons feel genuine affection for him.

Gerald of Wales believed Geoffrey incited both Philip and 'the whole of that realm' against Henry, and that he and Philip were scheming to raise a massive force against Henry, which would induce such 'disquietude as [Henry] had never before experienced'.[74]

But before the army to destroy Henry had materialised, in August 1186 Geoffrey fell ill and died. His illness may have been the result of wounds sustained in a tournament, or a bowel complaint, or a fever – the chroniclers differ. Philip was apparently in utter despair; he even tried to throw himself into Geoffrey's grave, but he was restrained by his courtiers.[75] Philip's show of grief, however, was likely a charade; like Henry, whom Philip had been observing keenly for years, he too could project strong emotional responses to manipulate. Philip would have known that his reaction to Geoffrey's death would be reported back to Henry, and would cause him pain.

For the troubadour poet Bertran de Born, Geoffrey's crimes were of a more earthy nature; for, 'he does not know how to please the ladies'.[76]

Geoffrey had been duplicitous and had betrayed his father. Yet Henry's grief was 'beyond all grief which had ever been; for there never was sorrow like his sorrow: for this affliction, following upon it, again awakened the grief for his former son, which time had laid to rest'.[77]

To compound Henry's heartache, his relationship with Philip suddenly – and to Henry, inexplicably – disintegrated. It is likely that Philip now believed himself strong enough to confront him.

Philip insisted that Henry give up the wardship of Geoffrey's two young daughters to him, and relinquish Brittany to the French crown. Brittany was a fief of the Norman dukes, yet Philip postured and claimed it for France.

Henry countered by swiftly betrothing Constance, Geoffrey's widow, to his cousin Ranulf de Blundeville, earl of Chester and viscount of the Avranchin. Henry probably did not take Constance's feelings into consideration. The dates of the marriage vary between accounts, but she was possibly still pregnant with Geoffrey's child when she was told of the match. Geoffrey's posthumous son, Arthur, was born on Easter Day – 29 March – 1187, at Nantes.

The marriage was, by all accounts, extremely unhappy, a reminder of the absolute control Henry exerted over his family's lives. Constance's chosen name for her child was an attempt to assert her authority and her independence. She called him Arthur, after the legendary king the Bretons supposed to be their ancestor, in defiance of her father-in-law, who wanted the boy christened Henry.

William of Newburgh recorded the hopes for Breton independence that Constance and her people invested in this baby:

> The king, his grandfather, who had ordered that the child be given his own name, was opposed by the Bretons, and by solemn acclamation the child was named Arthur when he was held over the sacred font. Thus the Bretons, who are said to have been long waiting for an imaginary Arthur, are now raising up one who is quite real, and they do so in great hope, in accordance with the opinion that certain prophets express in their long and celebrated Arthurian legends.[78]

Philip also demanded that Richard and his armies leave Toulouse. If Henry did not comply, he said, he would invade Normandy.

Richard had invaded Toulouse in April 1186, at the command of his father. Raymond had taken advantage of the young king's uprising in Aquitaine three years earlier to capture some castles in Quercy. Henry, who in 1186 had time to turn his attention to the matter, 'entrusted to his son Richard unlimited funds, bidding him go and subdue his enemies under him'.[79] In the summer, Raymond asked Philip for aid against the Angevins. Philip, who wanted influence in the south and a strengthening of Capetian kingship, felt compelled to agree to help his vassal.

In May 1187 Philip moved an army into Berry, a contested land between the kings of France and the dukes of Aquitaine. Henry also moved a large force in, putting his illegitimate son Geoffrey at the head of a quarter of his army. Philip realised that he was not yet ready to take on the mighty Henry FitzEmpress, and war between the kings did not break out. Eventually a two-year truce was negotiated.[80] It is likely that Philip was testing his strength.

Why did Philip choose this moment to turn on the man he had called his mentor? The problem of the Vexin was not going away, and Philip could see that Henry would continue to do nothing to facilitate the marriage of Richard and Alice. Philip was a proud man, who felt that Henry's inaction tarnished his authority. Philip was also growing stronger: he had become richer, implicitly more powerful, and his wife had given birth to a son. Despite having tried, briefly, in 1184 to divorce Isabella, they had repaired the marriage enough for her to conceive and give birth – to the future Louis VIII – in September 1187. She would die only three years later.

Diplomacy had won, for now. But something happened during the negotiations that would eventually lose everything for Henry. Philip had previously managed to enchant both the young king and Geoffrey. Now he set his sights on Richard. He sent the count of Flanders to speak to Richard:

> Many of us believe that you are acting extremely foolishly and ill-advisedly in bearing arms against your lord the king of France. Think of the future: why should he be well disposed towards you, or confirm you in your expectations? Do not despise his youth: he may be young in years, but he has a mature mind, is far-seeing and determined in what he does ... How splendid and useful it would be if you had the grace and favour of your lord.[81]

Richard capitulated to the charismatic count; he went to Paris and fell under Philip's spell, as his brothers had done before him.

Following in his father's footsteps, Philip did his utmost to undermine Henry in Richard's eyes. With his gift for identifying and exploiting an opponent's psychological weak spot, Philip persuaded Richard that the succession was by no means secure, and that Henry favoured John over himself. Philip was charming when he wished to be, and very persuasive. Richard was beguiled, and Gerald of Wales reported that 'every day they ate from the same dish, and at night the bed did not separate them. The king of France loved him as his own soul and their mutual love was so great that the lord king of England was stupefied by its vehemence.'[82]

Richard left Paris for Chinon and equipped himself with arms and money. Then he fortified his castles. Henry begged him to return, and he did. Perhaps Richard believed that his father had softened and was ready to name him his successor. He 'submitted to his father in all things, and was penitent for having yielded to the evil counsels of those who strove to sow discord between them'.[83]

Henry had the opportunity to heal the breach with Richard by naming him his heir. But he still feared giving too much away, anxious that if he did, Richard would rise against him again. Henry, the lonely tyrant, had manoeuvred himself into a position with no easy way out.

IX

With Philip whispering in his ear, Richard asked Henry to make a decision. Richard was desperate to go on crusade. The patriarch's fears were realised when Saladin united the disparate forces of Islam in a jihad against the Latin Kingdom, reaching its climax at the battle of Hattin on 4 July 1187. Saladin was aided in his struggle by the vicious factionalism and infighting that plagued the Latin Kingdom, with the Frankish nobility scrabbling for power. A Muslim chronicler commented that the Franks' 'unity was disrupted and their cohesion broken. This was one of the most important factors that brought about the conquest of their territories.'[84]

Baldwin IV's young nephew and heir, Baldwin V, had died the previous year, in 1186. He had been king of Jerusalem for just over a year. The throne now passed to his mother, Sibylla. But Sibylla's second husband Guy of Lusignan, a vassal of Richard's, was extremely unpopular among some of the Latin nobility. William of Tyre reflected their views when he wrote that he had 'neither the knowledge nor the ability to govern the kingdom'.[85] Sibylla's brother had not liked him, chiefly because he believed him to be incompetent, and possibly because Guy and Sibylla were lovers before Baldwin had consented to their marriage. To mollify the nobility, she promised to divorce him before she was crowned, with the stipulation that once queen, she would be free to choose her own husband.[86]

The patriarch Heraclius duly crowned the now-divorced Sibylla at the Church of the Holy Sepulchre. She then did something that nobody expected. With an eye for drama, and the crown now on her head, she declared to the flabbergasted nobility and clergy, 'I Sibylla choose as king and husband, my husband: Guy of Lusignan who was my husband. I know him to be a man of prowess and honour, well able, with God's aid, to rule his people. I know too that while he is alive I can have no other husband for, as the Scripture says, "Those whom God has joined together, let no man put asunder."' Sibylla then crowned Guy king of Jerusalem.[87]

But King Guy had mighty enemies. Among them was Count Raymond of Tripoli, a powerful Latin nobleman who contested his right to wear the crown. Years earlier, Raymond had earned the hatred of the Grand Master of the Knights Templar, Gerard of Ridefort. The story of how Gerard became a Templar was one of pique and vengeance. As a young man, Gerard was betrothed to a woman named Lucia, daughter of the deceased lord of Botron. Raymond was her guardian. When Plebanus, a wealthy Pisan merchant, asked Raymond if he would give Lucia in marriage to his nephew, Raymond disregarded the betrothal and agreed. The merchant's proposal was too tempting to resist: he offered to give Raymond Lucia's weight in gold. She weighed around sixty-three kilograms, and the marriage was secured for a payment of 10,000 bezants. His marriage prospects shattered, Gerard joined the Knights Templar. He never forgot the slight.[88] Now Gerard supported King Guy against the power of Count Raymond. For Gerard, it was personal.

To meet Saladin's army, King Guy and his fractious nobility had agreed a plan. Just days before, Saladin had besieged Count Raymond's wife in Tiberias, in the hope that Guy, as his overlord, would lead his armies to save her – Raymond, in a recent volte-face, had pledged his homage to Guy, against the increasing threat of Saladin. This would have been an extremely foolhardy move, and both Guy and Saladin knew it. To reach Tiberias, twenty-five miles distant, meant crossing a desert with very little access to water other than the supplies his men could carry. They would also leave themselves exposed to raiders from Saladin's armies. It was risky, and Guy was persuaded by Count Raymond not to do it. The count argued cogently that if Saladin 'takes Tiberias he will not be able to stay there and when he has left it and gone away we will retake it; for if he chooses to stay there he will be unable to keep his army together, for they will not put up for long with being kept away from their homes and families'.[89] He evidently trusted in Saladin's famous impeccable manners, convinced his wife would not be harmed. It was decided. They would stay where they were, and prepare to meet Saladin's forces.

But in the middle of the night, Gerard of Ridefort, driven by his hatred for Raymond, stole into the king's tent and persuaded Guy to undertake the march. He destroyed in Guy's mind the precarious peace he had made with Raymond. Gerard counselled the king to 'not trust the advice of the count for he is a traitor, and you well know that he has no love for you and wants you to be put to shame and to lose the kingdom ... let us move off immediately and go and defeat Saladin'.[90] Guy determined no longer to listen to the man who had been his enemy, and now he accepted the Templar's advice. They would cross the plain. Gerard's long-nursed antipathy and desire for vengeance against a fellow Frank led the armies of Christendom to disaster. In the process, Henry would lose all his money in the East.

Saladin's army stood at roughly 20,000 men, including about 12,000 men on horseback, and the Christians, under the command of King Guy, at 16,000.[91] The Christians threw everything they had at this battle, moving nearly all their men from their towns and castles to fight. Saladin was equally determined to drive the Christians out of the Middle East. 'We should confront all the enemy forces with all the forces of Islam,' he declared, 'for it is foolish to dissipate this concentration of troops without striking a tremendous blow in the holy war.'[92]

King Guy led his men towards Tiberias, despite their protests at his sudden change of plan. But they found themselves surrounded by Saladin's forces, cut off from any water in high summer. As they fought, the desperately thirsty men could see Lake Tiberias in the distance. Of Guy's Christian army, the Muslim chronicler Beha ad-Din said 'They were closely beset as in a noose, while still marching on as though being driven to a death that they could see before them, convinced of their doom and destruction and themselves aware that the following day they would be visiting their graves.'[93]

The next day, 4 July, Guy and his army tried to run for Lake Tiberias. It was tantalisingly close, shimmering only six miles away, offering them hope of fresh water. But Saladin tormented them. He did not engage them in the early morning, but waited until the midday heat when they were even more tired and demoralised. His soldiers, who had a plentiful supply of water, banged their drums relentlessly and burned the grass so the fire and smoke scorched the Franks' throats and exacerbated their thirst. The Christian infantry scattered, and a last-ditch attempt to murder Saladin failed. Count Raymond and his men escaped through the Muslim lines. Saladin's son shouted in triumph, '"We have beaten them!", but he [Saladin] replied, "Be quiet! We have not beaten them until that tent falls." As he spoke Guy's tent crumpled. The sultan dismounted, prostrated himself in thanks to God almighty and wept for joy.'[94]

Saladin had obliterated the chaotic Christian army. He captured King Guy and the most holy relic of the Latin Kingdom – the True Cross, supposedly the remains of the cross Jesus was crucified upon.[95] It was utterly demoralising: a chronicler of the Latin Kingdom recorded how 'in one moment, all the glory of the kingdom of Jerusalem passed from it'. Saladin ordered Sufi holy men to behead the 200 Knights Templar and Knights Hospitaller held prisoner. These holy men were not trained assassins, and they botched the executions, subjecting their victims to excruciating pain before they died. Those who were not killed were sold into slavery. Only King Guy, and the Grand Master of the Knights Templar, Gerard of Ridefort, were spared. Guy, afforded the hospitality due to a monarch, was even given a cold drink before Saladin sent him to prison at Nablus.[96] After the battle, Saladin swiftly took the major cities of the Latin Kingdom – Tiberias, Acre, Nazareth, Caesarea and Jaffa. Jerusalem was lost in October; not even the will of the patriarch, who led its defence alongside Queen Sibylla, could withstand Saladin's forces. They had very few soldiers to help them; all had been mustered for the battle at Hattin. They were forced to come to terms with Saladin, offering him the keys to the city at the beginning of October.

* * *

Pope Urban III, when he discovered Jerusalem was lost, died, apparently of shock, on 20 October. Now no more than a handful of fortified coastal citadels, including Tyre, and Kerak, east of the Dead Sea, held out against Saladin. Henry learned of the annihilation in November, when Peter of Blois wrote to him from

Rome; Richard, desperate to go on crusade, was the first western European prince to take the cross.[97]

He did so in secret, without telling his father. But despite the desperate situation in the East, Richard was loath to leave England without a formal acknowledgement from Henry, naming him his heir.

Henry, when he found out, was not pleased. Richard begged to be allowed to go on crusade at peace, in the knowledge that his future was assured, but Henry sidestepped his request. Instead, he suggested that they go 'on crusade together'. Hedging his options, Henry still refused to pronounce on the succession, although he did now relent and promise to pay for Richard's crusade, presumably out of his eastern account. It is feasible that Henry had no intention of doing so. It is also possible that he encouraged three counts – Geoffrey de Lusignan, Geoffrey de Rancon, and the count of Angoulême – to revolt, to keep Richard busy.[98]

Richard dutifully subdued the rebellious counts, and then found himself immersed in another war with Raymond of Toulouse. When Richard reached the outskirts of Toulouse, having taken seventeen castles on the way, Raymond panicked and asked Philip to intervene.

Philip did not want to alienate Richard, but equally he wanted to show himself capable of acting in the interests of his vassal, Count Raymond. When diplomacy with Richard failed, Philip blamed Henry, and demanded that he bring Richard to heel. If not, he would break their truce. Henry, according to Roger of Howden, attempted to curb Richard in Toulouse, but failed. So, in July 1188 Philip acted on his threat and invaded the contested borderland of Berry.

In a rare act of accord, Henry and Richard worked together. Henry had been busy in England preparing to go on crusade, having in January 1188 made a joint promise with Philip in response to the archbishop of Tyre's impassioned sermon on the desperate situation in the East. It is even possible that this time he was serious.[99] But there was a major impediment: he no longer had any money in his eastern account. Patriarch Heraclius had understood that Henry would not come until it was too late. He, together with Gerard of Ridefort, stole most of Henry's money to fund the final push against Saladin. The Chronicle of Tyre recalled that King Guy and Gerard of Ridefort 'opened the treasure of the lord king of England and gave stipends to all who could carry a bow or a lance into battle'.[100]

The remains of Henry's account were drained by the Knights Hospitaller to pay for the defence of Tyre and to ransom impoverished Christians, forced to flee Jerusalem after Saladin's conquest. When Henry heard that the battle was lost and his money spent, he was 'speechless for four days'.[101]

Left without money for crusade, he levied the unpopular 'Saladin tithe' to pay for it. It was a harsh tax, amounting to 10 per cent on all income and 'movable goods'.[102] Henry's Jewish communities were even harder hit by the tax, forced to pay 25 per cent. It may have raised as much as £70,000.

X

Putting his crusading plans to one side, Henry crossed the Channel in a gale. He landed at Barfleur on 11 July.[103] He gathered a large army at Alençon, supplemented by a host of Welsh mercenaries.[104] Richard meanwhile marched north and devastated Berry. Philip responded in kind: ordering his army into Normandy, he embarked on a blistering campaign, burning and capturing towns and castles. His men took prisoner forty of Henry's knights.[105]

Old and weary, Henry did not march to meet Philip's force. Instead, he attempted diplomacy. His envoys were William Marshal and John, bishop of Evreux. But Philip resisted diplomatic overtures, and so Henry once more went to war, using the combined forces of an army raised in Normandy and the Welsh mercenaries. His army met with Richard's at Mantes, and then they separated, Richard attacking Berry, and Henry, Damville. Henry's men even attacked Philip's gardens at Saint-Clair.[106]

Philip may himself have been ready to fight Henry. But he quickly discovered that his barons were unwilling, citing lack of appetite for warfare against Christians during a time of crisis in the Holy Land. Neither did he have enough money to pay his mercenaries. Instead he had no option but to treat for peace.

They met at Gisors in August, but they could not agree terms. Henry was tired; he wanted a lasting peace, whereas Philip's requirements were far more ephemeral. He meant to battle Henry again at the earliest opportunity. When they failed to reach an accord, Philip vented his frustration on the ancient elm tree. On 1 September, he ordered it hacked down.

William le Breton believed that Philip attacked the tree because Henry sheltered under it on a hot August day, while Philip was left in the sun. But Philip was only too aware of its symbolism. The tree was encircled with an iron ring, put there by the king of England, and inscribed with the words that if the tree be lost, the king would lose his domains.[107] Henry, enraged, left the conference and, on the advice of William Marshal, ravaged Philip's lands as far as Mantes. William apparently told the king:

Listen to me, sire. Philip has divided and disbanded his troops. I advise you to disperse your men too, but to give them secret orders to reassemble at a given time and place. From there they are to launch a *chevauchée* [a raiding method that involved burning the enemy's lands] into the territory of the king of France. If this is done in force, prudently and promptly, then he will find he has to suffer far greater damage than the loss of one elm. This will be a better and a finer deed.

Henry agreed, replying, 'By God's eyes, Marshal, you are most courteous and have given me good advice. I shall do exactly as you suggest.'[108]

Even at this advanced stage, Henry might have triumphed. He and Richard had shown through their recent rout of Philip that they could work well together. If Henry had now spoken with Richard, and assured him that he would succeed him, he might still have avoided the course of events that were to follow; but he did not.

Richard determined to force the situation. At a conference on 7 October at Châtillon, he sabotaged his father. To Henry's amazement, Richard publicly told Philip that he would accept his judgement concerning his battle with the count of Toulouse. Richard's explanation was 'so that there may be peace between the kings'.[109] In truth, he despaired that Henry would ever trust him enough to designate him his successor. Believing that his father intended to betray him in favour of John, Richard sought out Philip, attempting 'to soften the mind of the French king, that in him he might find some solace if his father should fail him'.[110]

Philip may have made known to Richard the rumours that Henry had encouraged the three counts to revolt to keep him from crusade. Richard was proud, and likely felt immense frustration at his father's control over his life. More pointedly still, whether true or not, Philip played on Richard's fears that Henry planned to supplant him with John.

Henry's relationship with John was certainly easier than his relationship with Richard. But John had never risen in rebellion against him. Henry was reluctant to name either legitimate son his successor, as he realised what a huge mistake he had made in naming Henri so early. Neither of his sons presented an attractive option. John's behaviour in Ireland was atrocious, and Richard's military prowess was accompanied by a gratuitous brutality that may have alarmed Henry, a far more subtle ruler. Henry may have secretly desired to name his illegitimate son Geoffrey his successor. But the days when an illegitimate son could succeed were fast disappearing.

Henry took the worst possible course: paralysed by indecision, he did nothing.

Richard, however, needed resolution. On 18 November 1188, at Bonmoulins near Alençon, he organised yet another peace summit. But this conference was a trap set for Henry by Richard and Philip. They were now working together to render Henry obsolete.

When he saw that Richard and Philip had arrived at Bonmoulins together, Henry was disconcerted. The atmosphere was uncomfortable, but both sides remained calm. By the third day, however, the situation deteriorated, with some knights growing hostile and drawing their swords. Philip demanded that Richard marry Alice immediately, and that Henry acknowledge Richard as his heir by having his magnates swear allegiance to him. But Henry could not do it. He either said nothing or was evasive – the sources differ.

Richard, believing that Henry might disinherit him in favour of John, angrily proclaimed that 'I can only take as true what previously seemed incredible'. He unbuckled his sword and threw himself down before Philip, prostrating himself in homage to the French king as his overlord for Normandy, Anjou, Maine, Berry and his recent gains in Toulouse.[111] Richard asked for Philip's help against his father, that he 'not be deprived of his legal due'.

Pandemonium ensued; Richard and Henry left separately, without saying a word to one another.

Richard was lost to him, as Henri and Geoffrey had been, seduced by the soothing promises of the king of France. Philip had been relentless in his courtship, and Richard was susceptible because he believed that Henry had failed him.

But still, Henry attempted to reconcile with Richard, begging him to come back. Henry fell ill and temporary truces were made, and broken. Philip believed that Henry was lying about his sickness, and, together with Richard, they ravaged Henry's lands on the French–Norman border. Henry, Richard and Philip met again, at Easter: another disaster. The pope now intervened, dispatching his legate, Cardinal John of Agnani, to negotiate a peace. His real purpose, though, was to salvage the crusade; and this time it looked as if it would work. Henry, 'sick to death of war', was prepared to negotiate.

At La Ferté-Bernard, the site of the meeting and just twenty-five miles from Henry's Angevin capital Le Mans, Philip listed his demands: Alice would be married to Richard, Henry would assure Richard of his inheritance, and John would take the cross. Henry refused to consent.

Instead he suggested that Alice marry John.[112] After all, Philip had proposed in the past that Alice marry *one* of Henry's sons. But it was too late; the accord between Philip and Richard rendered Henry's offer unacceptable. Philip saw in Richard a future ruler he could manipulate. He did not know John at all and it suited him that Richard succeed Henry. He declined Henry's offer, and they left the conference 'mutually displeased'.[113]

The papal legate was desperate to find a solution, and threatened to place France under an interdict unless Philip agreed terms. But Philip said he cared nothing for the threat as 'it was not the duty of the Church of Rome to punish the kingdom of France by its sentence or in any other manner, if the king of France should think fit to punish any vassals of his who had shown themselves undeserving, and rebellious against his sway'. Philip was resolute; now he had the strength, he was determined to break Henry. Shamelessly, Philip accused the legate of being in Henry's pay.[114]

The peace conference had failed. Henry went to Le Mans, the city of his birth. Philip and Richard, however, did not return to the border; instead they attacked La Ferté-Bernard, and then took in quick succession the castles of Montfort, Beaumont and

Balim as they steadily made their way towards their quarry at Le Mans. On 12 June, they reached Henry.

Stephen de Tours, Henry's seneschal in Anjou, ordered his men to set fire to the suburbs of the city to halt Philip and Richard.[115] And they did. But the wind changed, and Le Mans itself began to burn.

Henry fled with 700 knights. He was 'in a state of desperation ... for he had promised the inhabitants [of Le Mans] that he would not forsake them'.[116]

Henry's flight was marked by violent skirmishes between the two armies, and Richard was surprised by a rearguard force of his father's army, led by William Marshal.[117] William had the opportunity to kill Richard, but he did not take it. As he came at him with a lance, Richard reportedly said, 'By God's legs, do not kill me, Marshal. That would be wrong. I am unarmed.' 'No, let the Devil kill you,' said William, 'for I won't.' Instead, he killed Richard's horse with his lance.[118]

When Henry was about two miles outside his burning capital, he paused on top of a hill to look back at the city. Gerald of Wales wrote of Henry's anguish as he watched Le Mans burn. Henry, if Gerald is to be believed, was a broken man. He blamed God for taking his beloved city, crying, 'O God, since You have taken away from me the city that I loved most on earth, the city where I was born and bred, the city where my father is buried, I will repay You as best I can. I will deny You what You love best in me, my soul!'[119]

Henry and his men turned away and charged north towards the safety of Alençon and, beyond it, a heavily fortified Normandy. But Henry suddenly changed his mind. Instead of racing for the safety of the north, he turned south towards Chinon, over 120 miles away. It was potentially a suicidal journey.

Henry did not want to put his men in danger. The countryside was riddled with Philip's people and capture was likely. Instead he sent Geoffrey, his beloved bastard son, with his men to safety in Alençon. Geoffrey had remained, fighting alongside Henry throughout the crisis. In 1182, Henry had rewarded his affection and his loyalty, making him Chancellor of England. We may imagine that Geoffrey would not have left his father's side without a fight. But Henry prevailed.

Henry and a small force evaded Philip's men by travelling away from the major routes, taking instead a slow course through the forests. His route was so tortuous that he travelled nearly 200 miles to reach Chinon. He was desperately ill. Henry had come to Chinon to die; he had lost the will to fight his son any longer.

Philip and Richard attacked Maine, with great success. Most castles and cities surrendered without a fight.[120] Henry knew he was beaten. When Tours fell, he agreed to meet with Philip and Richard, and he rode to Ballan, just outside Tours, on 4 July 1189. The meeting cost Henry a great deal. He was in such pain that even Philip noticed, and offered him his cloak so that he could sit on the ground. But Henry preferred to stay on his horse, supported by his men, and asked to hear what Philip wanted from him.[121]

Philip demanded nothing less than Henry's complete submission. Henry was required to 'place himself under the control and at the will of the king of France'.[122] He was then obliged to pay homage to Philip for a second time. Alice was to be turned over to a person of Richard's choosing, and Richard would marry her when he returned from crusade. Richard was to receive the oath of fealty from all Henry's subjects. Henry was to pay Philip 20,000 silver marks. Henry was to relinquish to Philip and Richard the cities of Le Mans and Tours, and Château Loire. Some of Henry's castles were to be handed over as surety. Henry was forced to promise to go on crusade with Philip and Richard, departing from Vézelay at Lent the following year. Henry agreed to it all.

The weather was as dramatic as the scene. A summer storm rolled in, apparently out of a cloudless sky, and Roger of Howden wrote that a thunderbolt fell between Henry and Philip. To seal his obligations, Henry was to give the kiss of peace to Richard. As Richard bent down to his father to receive it, Henry whispered in his ear, 'God grant that I may not die until I have had my revenge on you.'[123]

Henry was so weak that he was taken back to Chinon in a litter. He asked for a list of the names of those of his men who had deserted him for Richard and Philip. His companions begged him not to read the list, but he insisted. Henry may have believed that he could not be brought any lower. But he was. For John's name headed the list. It is likely that John, looking to the future and seeing how Henry had been vanquished by Philip and Richard, decided to abandon him. It was grim treatment of a father who loved him so. According to Gerald of Wales, Henry lamented, 'Is it true that John, dear to me as my own heart, whom I have loved above all my sons, and for the sake of whose advancement I have endured all these evils, is it true that he has deserted me?'

Henry gave Geoffrey, who had returned to his father to comfort him, his seal engraved with a leopard, and a sapphire ring.[124]

His final wish was that Geoffrey become bishop of Winchester or archbishop of York.[125] Henry then turned his face to the wall, declaring that he no longer cared for himself, or for anything in this world.[126] His last words were reputedly, 'O the shame of a conquered king! O shame!'[127]

* * *

If Gerald of Wales's story was true, and Henry did commission a mural at Winchester towards the end of the 1170s, he may have reflected that the eaglets, including 'the youngest ... whom I embrace with so much affection, will sometime in the end insult me more grievously and more dangerously than any of the others'.[128] His sons had indeed destroyed their father.

Henry willed himself to die; he did so, on 6 July 1189. He was fifty-six years old. He had been defeated by the man he had failed to recognise as his enemy – in Bertran de Born's phrase, the 'little king of Lesser-Land'.

Richard had not believed that his father was dying, thinking it a ruse to the end. Gerald of Wales even reported that when Richard went back to the French court, he regaled the company with how he had triumphed over his father.[129] He was not with him when he died. It was William Marshal who brought Richard the news.

Henry's daughter Matilda died just days before her father, at the end of June. But she died in Germany, and it is unlikely that Henry knew.

Roger of Howden wrote that in death, his servants stripped Henry of his clothes and jewels.[130]

Henry's body was carried down from Chinon Castle and taken to Fontevraud; as the party left Chinon, Richard finally came. He then accompanied his father's body to Fontevraud and had him buried in the Choir of the Nuns.[131] He was silent and still beside his father's dead body, as it waited for burial. Roger of Howden wrote that blood streamed from Henry's nostrils as Richard approached.[132]

At Fontevraud, Richard rewarded William Marshal and his half-brother Geoffrey for remaining loyal to Henry. He forgave William for the attempt on his life outside Le Mans, and allowed him to marry the rich heiress Henry had promised him months earlier, Isabel de Clare, the daughter of Strongbow, making him earl of Pembroke. William Marshal, after years of service to Eleanor, the young king and Henry, and despite his 'moaning' to Henry about his poverty, was finally rich.[133] Geoffrey gave up the seal of England to Richard, and Richard in turn promised to confirm him as archbishop of York, fulfilling their father's last wishes.

Gerald of Wales believed that the choice of Fontevraud as Henry's resting place was Eleanor's, as vengeance for Henry wishing to divorce her and confine her there as a nun in 1175. But this is unlikely; although one of Richard's first acts as king was to free his mother, she was still in England, far from Fontevraud. Henry had desired to be buried instead at Grandmont, an order of which he was extremely fond and to which he had donated a great deal of money. Fontevraud was probably chosen because it was so near to Chinon. The summer was extremely hot, and Henry's body had to be buried quickly. William Marshal and Geoffrey made the funeral arrangements.[134]

The arc of Henry's story was interpreted by contemporaries as one of magnificent promise, which hubris had turned to dust. Gerald of Wales wrote of Henry at the end of his life: 'If he had turned to serve Him [God], he would have been without equal among the princes of this world in the large number of natural gifts with which he was endowed'.[135]

Towards the end of many classical tragic dramas, the protagonist-king who has been struck by catastrophe is left glimpsing self-knowledge; he is overwhelmed by catharsis and sorrow. This king, however, displayed no remorse, nor did he ever acknowledge that it was his own errors of judgement that destroyed him. Henry believed that he was always right and that his family would follow him, regardless. That, in the end, was his undoing – and his tragedy.

EPILOGUE

The descendants of King Henry must bear the curse
pronounced in Holy Scripture: 'The multiplied brood
of the wicked shall not thrive ... The children of adulterers
shall be rooted out.' The present king of France [Philip]
will avenge the memory of his virtuous father, King Louis,
upon the children of the faithless wife [Eleanor]
who left him to unite with his enemy.

Bishop Hugh of Lincoln on his deathbed, 1200

Neither Henry nor his contemporaries called his conglomerate of lands an 'empire'. The word is a nineteenth-century construct. Henry referred to his territories as 'our kingdom and everything subject to our rule wherever it may be'.[1] Henry was not in the lucky position of the French kings. He did not inherit a kingdom ruled over by one of God's anointed, whose monarchs, from Philip, could claim descent from a figure of legend such as Charlemagne and thus command a natural pivot for allegiance and respect. Instead Henry's was a hotchpotch of lands, which included a kingdom, but also comprised duchies for which he owed allegiance to a weak overlord. Henry only held these lands through incomparable speed and a brute force of will.

Henry's demise coincided with the ascendency of his enemy and nemesis, Philip, whose real nature Henry realised only when it was too late. Had Philip encountered a Henry of twenty-one years old, a Henry at the peak of his powers when he became king of England and was lord of much of France, instead of a man pitifully broken by his sons' betrayals, what happened next might have been very different.

After Henry's death, Richard freed his mother. Eleanor was about sixty-seven years old and the next fifteen years were the most politically active of her life.

Henry had sidelined her, but her sons did not make the same mistake. In return, she now embraced the notion of Henry's 'Plantagenet Empire', and with Richard monarch, even the assimilation of her beloved Aquitaine. It was only with Henry's death that she was free to promote the interests of his regime. Her successes were impressive, and it was during these years of activity that Eleanor was finally allowed to flourish. What might this remarkable woman have done for Henry, had he allowed her autonomy?

She was the linchpin of government during Richard's reign, and he put absolute authority into her hands. When he embarked on the Third Crusade, Eleanor was 'entrusted with the power of acting as regent by her son. Indeed, he issued instructions to the princes of the realm, almost in the style of a general edict, that the queen's word should be law in all matters. To make up for his many excesses, [Richard] took care to show his mother all the honour that he could, that by obedience to his mother he should atone for the offences committed against his father.'[2] She held 'queenly courts' and embarked on diplomatic missions that crisscrossed Europe.

Eleanor was finally popular, enormously so, and was praised for her compassion. Richard of Devizes described the scene when she encountered the desperate poverty of some of her subjects living under the care of the bishop of Ely: 'Wherever she went, men with women and children ... weeping and pitiful ... with bare feet, unwashed clothes, and unkempt hair came before her ... There was no need for an interpreter ... they spoke through their tears.'[3] Eleanor immediately arranged for their relief, sending messages to the bishop that 'compelled him to revoke the sentence'.[4]

She was instrumental in negotiating Richard's marriage to Berengaria of Navarre, and in 1191, went to fetch the bride and bring her to him at Messina. Despite his marriage, Eleanor took precedence over Berengaria, as she would over John's second wife, Isabella of Angoulême. And when Richard was captured by Duke Leopold of Austria on his way back from crusade at the end of 1192, it was Eleanor who raised the extortionate ransom of £100,000, consisting of 24 million silver pennies, and who went to Germany to negotiate his release.[5]

The chroniclers, for the most part, abandoned their antipathy to this now elderly woman. The rumours of incest, sexual deviancy and unqueenly conduct were forsaken in favour of paeans of admiration. She was 'beautiful yet virtuous, powerful yet gentle, humble yet keen-witted, qualities which are most rarely found in a woman, who ... had two kings as husbands and two kings as sons, still tireless in all labours, at whose ability her age might marvel'.[6]

Richard's relationship with Philip swiftly disintegrated in the aftermath of his father's death. While Richard was in captivity, Philip, acting with John, tried to pay the Holy Roman Emperor to keep him. It was Eleanor's diplomacy that saved him.

From 1194 and Richard's release, Eleanor entered semi-retirement at Fontevraud, but she never ceased to work, and continued to visit her capital, Poitiers. She enjoyed the company of family members she had never met, or those she had not seen for many years. A daughter of Alix, Eleanor's youngest child by Louis, resided at Fontevraud as a nun during Eleanor's time there; we have no record that Eleanor had met this granddaughter before. She would later become abbess there.[7]

Richard was shot by a crossbow on 26 March 1199 at the siege of Chalus, just as he had negotiated a five-year truce with Philip. He ignored the claims of his nephew, Arthur of Brittany, and on his deathbed he named John his heir. Eleanor may have influenced his decision. Richard's magnates were reluctant to name Arthur, as he was so young, and Eleanor may have been equally reluctant because his mother, Constance, would hold power through a regency. William Marshal, now in service to Richard, added his voice to John's claim – he believed Arthur to be too far under Philip's influence. John raced for Fontevraud from Brittany where he had been visiting Arthur, to claim his kingdom. Eleanor may have written to ask him to come. Richard died just days later, on 6 April. Eleanor accompanied his body 130 miles north for burial at Fontevraud. Bishop Hugh of Lincoln said Mass over Richard's body, on Palm Sunday, and Eleanor remembered her beloved boy in a grant of £100 in Poitevin money for the soul of 'that mighty man King Richard'.[8]

Eleanor's youngest daughter Joanna joined her mother soon after Richard's death, fleeing from a rebellion in Toulouse. She was pregnant. After her husband William II of Sicily had died in 1189, and with no son to act as regent for, Richard soon found her another husband. He toyed with the idea of marrying her to Saladin's brother, Saphadin, or Malik ad-Adil (it is doubtful he was serious), but married her instead to Raymond VI of Toulouse in 1196. Raymond was the son of Henry's slippery, sometime adversary, Raymond V. The following year Joanna gave birth to a son, the future Raymond VII of Toulouse. He would be her only surviving child.

Soon after Richard's funeral, Joanna fell desperately ill. She died in September 1199 during childbirth by ceasarean section, just five months after Richard. She had chosen to be buried next to him at Fontevraud, dressed as a nun. Eleanor now had only two children living – John, and young Eleanor, queen of Castile.

When John became king, Eleanor was equally integral to his government. She knew what this youngest son of hers was. While Richard had been the prisoner of the emperor, she had written to the pope, admitting that John was 'killing the people of the prisoner's kingdom with the sword … ravaging the land with fires'.[9] Yet he was her son, and Richard's legitimate heir. She did everything in her power to support him, particularly against the claims of her Breton grandson, Arthur, who was completely in thrall to Philip. As John went north after Richard's death to secure Normandy, Eleanor went west to punish the Angevins who had come out for Arthur. John was duly crowned king of England on 25 May 1199. In 1200, aged about seventy-eight years old, as part of a peace treaty with France, she crossed the Alps to collect her granddaughter Blanca of Castile (young Eleanor's daughter) as a bride for Philip's son, the future Louis VIII. In France, Blanca became known as Blanche.

Eleanor attempted to retire to the peace and seclusion of Fontevraud two years later, but John could not rule without her. His catastrophic policies led to the loss of Anjou, Brittany, Maine, Touraine and Normandy. By the time she died, all that was left to John of his father's mighty empire in France were the duchy of Aquitaine and the county of Poitou. John lost these, too, to Philip, soon after his mother's death. Only a small rump remained.

John's nephew Arthur disappeared in 1203. From infancy, Arthur had been a pawn in Plantagenet and French power politics, used by Richard, John and Philip alike. Resurfacing in France, Philip betrothed him to his six-year-old daughter Marie, knighted him in July at Gournay as 'Arthur, duke of Brittany and Aquitaine, count of Anjou and Maine', and sent him to invade Poitou.[10] Philip had given Arthur John's lands, although he would have to fight his uncle for them. But it was Eleanor, about eighty years old, who was forced to leave Fontevraud to defend them. When she found herself trapped by Arthur at Mirebeau Castle, she sent word to John; in one of the only successful campaigns of his life, he embodied the spirit of Henry and marched his men from Le Mans, covering a hundred miles in two days. He lifted the siege and freed Eleanor. Arthur was now his captive; by the beginning of April 1203 Arthur was dead, most likely at John's hands. He probably set upon the boy at Rouen, hit him with a large stone and threw his body into the Seine.[11] John sent a letter to Eleanor alluding to the death.[12]

How Eleanor felt about her son murdering her grandson is not recorded. But this gruesome act blackened his name. The thirteenth-century chronicler Matthew Paris was harsh in his condemnation: 'Black as is hell, John's presence there makes it blacker still.' After Arthur's death, John's position in France unravelled. Many Angevin and Norman noblemen who had supported him were disgusted by Arthur's murder, and at John's appalling treatment of his prisoners.

Later in the year, John lost Normandy to Philip; on 6 March 1204 Richard's supposedly impregnable fortress, Château Gaillard, fell too, leaving Philip a clear path to Rouen. He took the city just weeks later. Philip now held the colossal riches of Normandy in his hands. By August, the French king was in Poitiers, and soon after he made plans to invade England. On 27 July 1214, at the battle of Bouvines in northern France, with a coalition army led by his nephew Otto IV, the Holy Roman Emperor, John finally lost most of his lands in France to Philip. Philip's victory against the Plantagenets was now complete. Within a generation the wheel of fortune had turned; Philip had humiliated Henry's heir and was now the strongest monarch in Europe.

Philip tripled his possessions in the process. In 1215, John was forced to submit to his barons' Great Charter – or Magna Carta – which severely curtailed the king's rights. 'The road from Bouvines to Runnymede was a short one.'[13] But once his barons realised that John had no intention of keeping the promises he had made when he signed the charter, some asked Prince Louis of

France to invade England, in right of his wife Blanche of Castile – Henry's granddaughter. John died of dysentery on 19 October 1216, in the midst of the French invasion of 1216–17.

For his contemporaries, John was untrustworthy, 'for his heart is soft and cowardly'.[14] Henry's best-beloved legitimate son would be remembered as the worst king in English history.

It was Philip's heir, the future Louis VIII, who ruled briefly in London, before he was driven out by William Marshal. Marshal, now aged about seventy and ever in service to his Plantagenet masters, fought to protect the interests of John's young son and heir, Henry III. He was only nine years old when Marshal made him king, the first minor to be crowned king of England. (The only remarkable feature of this grandson's kingship was that he reigned for such a long time, fifty-six years; Henry III was consigned by Dante to 'the limbo of ineffectual souls'.[15])

In a brilliant piece of propaganda, Eleanor turned Fontevraud into the final resting place of the Plantagenets. Eleanor had been pivotal to the reigns of both Richard and John, and it was therefore in her interests to perpetuate Henry's Plantagenet Empire. Fontevraud became the family mausoleum, a symbol of Plantagenet power. By 1199 Eleanor, regardless of any antipathy that may have remained towards Henry, could, in service to Plantagenet propaganda, refer to him as her 'revered husband … of good memory', in a charter to the abbey.[16] Henry, Richard, Eleanor and her daughter-in-law Isabella of Angoulême are all commemorated with splendid tomb effigies. Her grandson, Raymond VII of Toulouse, was also buried here and the remnants of his portrait may still be seen at Fontevraud today. This grandson would be remembered for his involvement in the Albigensian crusade, his supposed sympathies for the Cathars, and his excommunication by Rome. When his only daughter died, childless, Toulouse too was subsumed by the French crown.

Eleanor commissioned Henry's and Richard's tombs together when Richard died in 1199. She may have designed her own effigy. In death, she gives herself something to do; she is depicted reading a book.[17]

Eleanor died on 31 March 1204, nearly fifteen years after Henry. She had chosen to be buried next to her favourite son Richard, rather than the husband who had betrayed her by denying her power. Richard would be the last king of England to be buried at Fontevraud; from 1204 it was in French hands, and although the hearts of both John and Henry III were interred there, English monarchs would now be buried in England, most at Westminster, or at William the Bastard's fortress of Windsor.

It was Henry's and Eleanor's granddaughter, Blanche, married into the Capetian royal family, who would become Philip's protégée. She would learn statecraft from Philip, as he had studied and learned from Henry. After her husband Louis VIII's death, acting as regent for her young son Louis IX, she continued his work in bringing the French barons firmly under royal control, successfully fighting off a bid for power from Philip's son, Philip Hurepel, child of the only one of his three wives he had loved, Agnes of Méran.

Hugh of Lincoln, as he lay dying prophesied the fall of his masters – England's ruling dynasty, the Plantagenets; his words turned out to be strangely prescient.

Henry II had, for over forty years, endured a ceaseless round of battle and diplomacy to build and hold an empire. He had amazed his contemporaries, was their 'Alexander of the West'. But Henry, perhaps in the belief that heroes were born and not made, did not train any of his sons to succeed him. And within only twenty-five years of his death – the Capetian mission to remove Angevin power from France now complete – Henry's glorious empire was gone.

TIMELINE

Henry's life	Year	Henry's times
William the Bastard, duke of Normandy, conquers England.	1066	
	1095	Launch of the First Crusade.
	1098	The first two crusader states, the County of Edessa and the Principality of Antioch, are established.
	1099	Jerusalem is captured for Christendom by crusader armies; founding of the Order of the Knights Hospitaller.
William's third son is crowned King Henry I of England.	1100	
Matilda, Henry I's daughter, departs for Germany, and marriage to Heinrich V.	1110	
	1111	Heinrich V is crowned Holy Roman Emperor; Heinrich V appoints Adalbert as archbishop of Mainz, a disastrous decision repeated by a king fifty years later.
The *White Ship* sails.	1120	Probable birth of Thomas Becket; founding of the Order of the Knights Templar.
	1122	Probable birth of Eleanor of Aquitaine.

Matilda returns to England after Heinrich's death.	1126	
Henry I's magnates swear oaths to uphold Matilda's queenship on her father's death.	1127	
Matilda marries Geoffrey of Anjou.	1128	Geoffrey's father, Fulk V, departs for Jerusalem and marriage to Queen Melisende.
	1130	A Norman kingdom is established in Sicily and southern Italy.
Birth of Henry, eldest son of Matilda and Geoffrey of Anjou, at Le Mans.	1133	
Death of Henry I.	1135	
Matilda's first cousin, Stephen, seizes the throne and is crowned king of England.	1136	
	1137	Following the death of William X of Aquitaine, Eleanor becomes duchess in her own right; death of Louis the Fat (VI) of France; Louis VII marries Eleanor – they are crowned king and queen of France.
Matilda lands in England, precipitating civil war.	1139	Theobald of Bec is consecrated archbishop of Canterbury.
	1140	Peter Abelard leaves Paris.
	1141	Louis invades Toulouse in Eleanor's name.
Nine-year-old Henry is brought to England by his uncle, Robert of Gloucester.	1142	
Henry is recalled to Normandy by Geoffrey.	1144	Completion of the cathedral of Saint-Denis by Abbot Suger; Nur-ad-Din captures the crusader state of Edessa; first blood libel accusation against the Jews – in England.

	1146 Bernard of Clairvaux preaches the Second Crusade.
Henry, aged fourteen, lands in England, to fight for his mother's cause.	1147 Louis VII, accompanied by Eleanor, embarks on Second Crusade.
Henry is knighted by his uncle, David King of Scots.	1149 Eleanor and Louis VII arrive back in Paris from Second Crusade.
Henry is pronounced 'duke' of Normandy by his father.	1150 Adelard of Bath dedicates his work *De opera astrolapsus* to Henry.
Henry meets Eleanor of Aquitaine in Paris; death of Geoffrey of Anjou – Henry is now duke of Normandy, lord of Anjou, Touraine and Maine; possible birth year of Henry's eldest illegitimate son, Geoffrey Plantagenet.	1151 Abbot Suger, Louis' friend and advisor, dies.
Henry marries Eleanor, adding Aquitaine to his domains; Henry is briefly at war with Louis and his allies.	1152 Louis divorces Eleanor of Aquitaine.
Birth of William, Eleanor and Henry's eldest child; Henry meets Thomas Becket; civil war ends, with Stephen recognising Henry as his heir.	1153 Death of Eustace; death of Bernard of Clairvaux.
Death of Stephen; Henry is crowned King Henry II of England.	1154 Englishman Nicholas Breakspear is elected Pope Adrian IV; Louis marries Constance of Castile.
Birth of Henri, Henry and Eleanor's second child; Henry appoints Becket as chancellor of England.	1155
Louis recognises Henry as count of Anjou; death of young William; birth of Matilda, Henry and Eleanor's eldest daughter; Henry fights his brother, Geoffrey FitzEmpress.	1156

Birth of Richard – the future 'Lionheart' – to Henry and Eleanor.	**1157**	
Death of Henry's brother, Geoffrey FitzEmpress; Eleanor gives birth to Henry's legitimate son, Geoffrey; Becket travels to Paris to negotiate the marriage of young Henri to the French princess, Margaret.	**1158**	
Henry invades Toulouse in Eleanor's name, with Thomas Becket fighting alongside him.	**1159**	Papal schism follows the death of Pope Adrian IV – dual election in Rome of Alexander III, and antipope Victor IV.
Marriage of young Henri to Margaret of France.	**1160**	Louis marries Adela of Blois-Champagne within weeks of Constance's death; Bishop Henry of Blois commissions the Winchester Bible.
Birth of young Eleanor to Henry and Eleanor.	**1161**	Death of Theobald, archbishop of Canterbury; Pope Alexander canonises Edward the Confessor.
Young Henri enters the household of Thomas Becket; Becket is consecrated archbishop of Canterbury.	**1162**	Frederick Barbarossa invades Italy in support of Victor IV – Alexander III flees to France, and refuge with Louis.
	1163	St Edward the Confessor's remains moved to a shrine within Westminster Abbey.
Henry issues the 'Constitutions of Clarendon'; death of Henry's brother, William FitzEmpress; Thomas Becket flees to France.	**1164**	
Birth of Joanna, Henry and Eleanor's youngest daughter.	**1165**	Birth of Louis VII's only son, Philip Augustus.

Birth of John – later King John – Henry and Eleanor's youngest child; Henry issues an inquest into knights' service; Henry calls the assize of Clarendon; Henry betrothes his legitimate son Geoffrey to Constance, heiress to Brittany, and takes control of the duchy; Thomas Becket excommunicates those associated with drawing up the Constitutions of Clarendon.	**1166**	
Possible birth year of Henry's illegitimate son, William Longsword; death of Henry's mother, Matilda; Henry prohibits his citizens from studying in Paris – many students in exile gather at Oxford.	**1167**	
Eleanor settles in Aquitaine; young Matilda marries Henry the Lion of Saxony.	**1168**	
Young Geoffrey invested as duke of Brittany; Henry and Louis make peace at Montmirail.	**1169**	
Henry, seriously ill, makes his first will; coronation of Henri as king in his father's lifetime; Henry orders the Inquest of the Sheriffs; Thomas Becket is murdered.	**1170**	
Henry campaigns in Ireland.	**1171**	Louis' son-in-law, Theobald of Blois, instigates the first blood libel in continental Europe.

Henry does penance at Avranches Cathedral for Becket's death; Henry begins to send an annual sum of money to his Jerusalem account; Richard invested as duke of Aquitaine; young Henri is re-crowned, alongside his wife, Margaret.	1172	
The Great Revolt – Eleanor and sons ally with Louis and many of the great magnates of France and the Anglo-Norman realm against Henry; Henry captures and imprisons Eleanor.	1173	Pope Alexander III canonises Thomas Becket.
Henry does penance at Canterbury; young Eleanor marries into the Castilian royal family; Henry puts down the Great Revolt.	1174	Pope Alexander III canonises Bernard of Clairvaux.
Henry unsuccessfully lobbies the pope to divorce Eleanor.	1175	
Henry calls the assize of Northampton – his justices are regularly touring the country; Joanna marries King William 'the Good' of Sicily; possible year of the death of Henry's favourite mistress, Rosamund Clifford.	1176	
Henry, the international statesman, mediates in a dispute between the kings of Castile and Aragon; the Welsh princes pay homage to Henry as their overlord.	1177	
Henry knights his legitimate son, Geoffrey.	1178	
Louis visits the shrine of St Thomas at Canterbury.	1179	Third Lateran Council in Rome; Philip Augustus recovers from a near-fatal illness.

Henry initiates huge building works at Dover Castle; Henry appoints Ranulf de Glanville his chief justiciar.	1180	Death of Louis VII, and accession of Philip Augustus.
Henry brokers a peace between Philip and the count of Flanders; Geoffrey marries Constance of Brittany.	1181	
Henry's eldest daughter, Matilda of Saxony, flees with her husband to sanctuary in Henry's domains; Geoffrey Plantagenet is made chancellor of England.	1182	Philip expels the Jews from his lands.
Henri and Geoffrey of Brittany rebel against Henry; death of Henri the Young King; Henry pays homage to Philip.	1183	Salah ad-Din (Saladin) conquers Aleppo.
Eleanor is allowed some limited freedoms; Henry issues his assize of the forest.	1184	Pope Lucius III issues a crusade bull.
John embarks for Ireland; Patriarch Heraclius of Jerusalem offers Henry the keys to the Latin Kingdom.	1185	
Death of Geoffrey, duke of Brittany.	1186	Death of Baldwin V of Jerusalem – his mother Sibylla is crowned queen, ruling with husband Guy of Lusignan.
Henry's Jerusalem account is drained, without his knowledge.	1187	Philip's wife Isabella gives birth to the future Louis VIII; Saladin defeats the armies of Christendom at Hattin.
Henry at war with Philip and Richard; Henry levies the Saladin Tithe to raise funds for a crusade.	1188	Gerald of Wales gives a lecture to the masters at Oxford.

	1189	
Henry dies; Richard takes the throne, and Eleanor is freed.		Completion of the *Treatise on the Laws and Customs of the Realm of England*, traditionally attributed to Ranulf de Glanville; death of Joanna's husband, William II of Sicily; death of young Matilda.

NOTES

Prologue

1. W. L. Warren, *Henry II* (University of California Press, 1973), p. 560.

Act I – The Bargain

1. Judith A. Green, *Henry I* (CUP, 2009), p. 165.
2. Ibid., p. 166.
3. Ibid., p. 165.
4. Wace, *Roman de Rou*, ed. A. J. Holden (Société des Anciens Textes Français, 1970–3), line 10, p. 219.
5. Green, p. 167.
6. William of Malmesbury, *Gesta regum Anglorum*, I, p. 758.
7. Green, p. 164, cites Victoria Chandler, 'The Wreck of the *White Ship*: A Mass Murder Revealed?', in D. J. Kagay and L. J. Andrew Villalon (eds), *The Final Argument: The Imprint of Violence on Society in Medieval and Early Modern Europe* (Boydell Press, 1998).
8. See Green for a full analysis of Henry I's actions towards the daughters of his illegitimate daughter Juliana.
9. John Le Patourel, *The Norman Empire* (Clarendon Press, 1976), pp. 175–6.
10. Marjorie Chibnall, *The Empress Matilda: Queen Consort, Queen Mother and Lady of the English* (Wiley, 1991), p. 7, cites *The Anglo Saxon Chronicle* and *The Ecclesiastical History of Orderic Vitalis*.
11. Ibid., p. 8.
12. Ibid., p. 11, cites Eadmer, *Eadmeri Historia Novorum in Anglia*, ed. M. Rule (Rolls Series, 1884), p. 127.
13. Judith Green suggests that the marriage may have been arranged some time before William's death; this would account for the speed with which it took place; Green, pp. 168–9.
14. Green, p. 170, cites Hildebert of Lavardin's letters to Adeliza, where he consoled her on her childless state. Hildebert of Lavardin, *Letters*, in J. P. Migne (ed.), *Patrologia Latina*, 221 vols (Paris, 1844–64), CLXXI, cols 135–312, no. 18.
15. Green, pp. 170, 187.
16. Marjorie Chibnall, 'Matilda (1102–1167)', *Oxford Dictionary of National Biography* (OUP, 2004).
17. Chibnall, *The Empress Matilda*, p. 15.
18. Ibid., p. 24.
19. Ibid., p. 25, cites *Chronique des ducs de Normandie par Benôit*, ed. Carin Fahlin, II, pp. 604–6.

335

20. Heinrich was crowned Holy Roman Emperor at St Peter's in Rome in 1111, by Pope Paschal II. Whether or not Matilda was crowned by the pope too, as she later claimed, is uncertain. Nevertheless, she would maintain that she had been for the rest of her life.

21. Chibnall, *The Empress Matilda*, p. 26, cites *Anonymi Chronica Imperatorum Heinrico V dedicata*, eds F. J. Schmale and I. Schmale-Ott (*Ausgewählte Quellen zur deutschen Geschichte des Mittelalters*, 1972), p. 262 (tr. Chibnall).

22. Karl Leyser, *Communications and Power in Medieval Europe: The Gregorian Revolution and Beyond* (Continuum, 1994), cites Orderic Vitalis, *Historia Ecclesiastica* XI, V, p. 200 (tr. Leyser).

23. Ibid., p. 40, cites Hermann, *Liber de Restaurliiatione*, *MGH SS*, XIV, p. 282.

24. See Chibnall, *The Empress Matilda*, p. 33.

25. Ibid., p. 38.

26. Matilda's sister-in-law, Matilda of Anjou, entered Fontevraud Abbey following the death of William Atheling. She eventually became its abbess.

27. Some sources suggest that William the Conqueror intended to deny Robert his entire inheritance, but was persuaded by the archbishop of Rouen that he should inherit Normandy, while William Rufus had England. Robert probably expected to inherit all his father's possessions.

28. Legend blamed the demise of Philip IV's (Philip le Bel) dynasty on his execution of the Grand Master of the Knights Templar, Jacques de Molay, who, as he burned to death on a scaffold outside Notre-Dame in March 1314, apparently cursed the king and his dynasty. Philip was dead within the year, his eldest son Louis X two years later, his next son Philip V by 1322, and finally Charles IV by 1328. They all died leaving only daughters. The throne of France then passed to their cousin, Philip of Valois.

29. William of Malmesbury, *Historia Novella*, ed. K. R. Potter (1955), p. 18.

30. David Crouch, *The Reign of King Stephen* (Routledge, 2013), p. 18.

31. Henry, like his father William, typically wore his crown at the three great Church festivals, Christmas, Whitsun and Easter. See P. E. Schramm, *The History of the Coronation* (Clarendon Press, 1937), p. 32.

32. William of Malmesbury, *Historia Novella*, pp. 6–8. It is possible that another oath was sworn to Matilda the following year, at the Easter court on 29 April 1128. See John of Worcester, although he is the only chronicler to mention it.

33. Chibnall, *The Empress Matilda*, p. 55.

34. Ibid. Chibnall's translation from Migne (ed.), CLXXI, cols 291–2.

35. Michael Clanchy, *England and its Rulers* (OUP, 1983), p. 72, cites the author of *The Anglo-Saxon Chronicle* in H. Rothwell (ed.), *English Historical Documents 1189–1327* (Methuen, 1975), II, p. 195.

36. Chibnall, *The Empress Matilda*, p. 54. Charles the Good of Flanders was murdered at the church of St Donatian in Bruges.

37. Kathryn Dutton, 'Geoffrey, Count of Anjou and Duke of Normandy, 1129–51', unpublished PhD thesis (University of Glasgow, 2011), p. 28.

38. Dutton cites the *Regesta pontificum Romanorum*, ed. Philip Jaffe, 2 vols (Leipzig, 1956), I, p. 833.

39. Dutton, 'Geoffrey', p. 29.

40. Chibnall, *The Empress Matilda*, p. 57.
41. John Gillingham, 'Love, Marriage and Politics in the Twelfth Century', in J. L. Nelson (ed.), *Richard Coeur de Lion in History and Myth, King's College Medieval Studies 7* (King's College London, 1992).
42. Josèphe Chartrou-Charbonnel, *L'Anjou de 1109 à 1151: Foulque de Jérusalem et Geoffroi Plantagenêt* (Paris, c.1928), pp. 36–7.
43. Chibnall, *The Empress Matilda*, p. 58, cites *The Chronicle of Henry of Huntingdon: The History of England, From the Invasion of Julius Caesar to the Accession of Henry II*, ed. and tr. Thomas Forester (H. G. Bohn, 1853), p. 252; William of Malmesbury, *Historia Novella*, p. 10.
44. Chibnall, *The Empress Matilda*, p. 61.
45. Roger of Howden, *Chronica*, ed. William Stubbs (Rolls Series, 1868–71), I, pp. 186–7. Quoted in Chibnall, *The Empress Matilda*, p. 60.
46. *The Chronicle of Henry of Huntingdon*, p. 253.
47. Chibnall, *The Empress Matilda*, cites Roger of Howden, *Chronica*, I, pp. 186–7.
48. Ibid., cites Robert of Torigni, *Interpolations*, pp. 304–5.
49. Dutton, 'Geoffrey', p. 38, cites Robert of Torigni, I, pp. 195–6.
50. Ibid., cites Orderic Vitalis, VI, pp. 444–5.
51. Ibid., p. 146, cites *Actus pontificum Cenomannis in urbe degentium*, eds G. Busson et al. (Le Mans, 1902), pp. 432–3.
52. Ibid., p. 39.
53. William of Malmesbury, *Historia Novella*, p. 13.
54. Crouch, *King Stephen*, p. 30, points out that William of Malmesbury's source was probably Robert of Gloucester, Matilda's half-brother, and after 1138, her staunch supporter.
55. *Gesta Stephani*, pp. 10–12.
56. *Historia Pontificalis*, p. 85.
57. *Gesta Stephani* pp. 12–15, quoted in Chibnall, p. 65.
58. Kate Norgate, 'Robert Earl of Gloucester', *Dictionary of National Biography* (OUP, 1900). See also F. M. Powicke, 'Gerald of Wales', in *The Christian life in the Middle Ages and Other Essays* (OUP, 1935), pp. 107–29.
59. David Crouch, 'Robert, first earl of Gloucester', *Dictionary of National Biography* (OUP, 2006).
60. Ibid., cites William of Malmesbury and Simeon of Durham.
61. Crouch, *King Stephen*, p. 31.
62. W. L. Warren, *Henry II* (University of California Press, 1973), p. 15, cites *The Chronicle of Henry of Huntingdon*, p. 245.
63. William of Malmesbury, *Historia Novella*, p. 5.
64. 1 Chronicles 16:22.
65. Chibnall, *The Empress Matilda*, p. 66, cites Orderic Vitalis, vi, pp. 448–9, 454–5.
66. Dutton, 'Geoffrey', p. 41.
67. Chibnall, *The Empress Matilda*, p. 67.
68. Walter Map, p. 475.
69. Dutton, 'Geoffrey', p. 48.
70. Kate Norgate, *Robert Earl of Gloucester: A Short Biography* (Shamrock Eden Publishing, 2011).
71. Chibnall, *The Empress Matilda*, p. 84.
72. Edmund King, 'Brian fitz Count (c.1090–c.1149)', *Oxford Dictionary of National Biography* (OUP, 2004), cites the *Gesta Stephani*.
73. Sharon Penman, *When Christ and his Saints Slept* (Michael Joseph, 1994). See also Nesta Pain, *Empress Matilda: Uncrowned Queen of England* (Weidenfeld & Nicolson, 1978).

74. King, 'Brian fitz Count (c.1090–c.1149)'.
75. John of Salisbury, *Historia pontificalis*, p. 84.
76. Chibnall, *The Empress Matilda*, p. 88.
77. Ibid., p. 89, cites William of Malmesbury, *Historia Novella*, p. 42.
78. Ibid., p. 90, cites William of Malmesbury, *Historia Novella*, p. 40.
79. *Gesta Stephani*, pp. 10–11.
80. Edmund King, 'Stephen (c.1092–1154)', *Oxford Dictionary of National Biography* (OUP, 2004, online edn, September 2010).
81. William of Malmesbury, *Historia Novella*, p. 123.
82. Ibid., p. 71.
83. Ibid., p. 72.
84. Ibid., pp. 72–4, quoted in Chibnall, *The Empress Matilda*, p. 117.
85. Gervase of Canterbury, I, pp. 123, 125.
86. Kathryn Dutton, 'Angevin Comital Children', in C. P. Lewis (ed.), *Proceedings of the Battle Conference* (Boydell Press, 2009).
87. The American academic Charles Homer Haskins coined the phrase in 1927 in his book *The Renaissance of the Twelfth Century*.
88. William was repeating a phrase ascribed to Henry's ancestor, Fulk II (942–60), when speaking of the king of France. The phrase also appears in John of Marmoutier's eulogy to Geoffrey, praising his wisdom and learning, and in John of Salisbury's *Policraticus*.
89. Richard of Poitiers, quoted in Charles Burnett, 'The Education of Henry II', in *The Introduction of Arabic Learning into England* (British Library, 1997).
90. Ibid.
91. John Gillingham, *The English in the Twelfth Century* (Boydell Press, 2000), pp. 19–40.
92. Martin Aurell, 'Henry II and Arthurian Legend', in Christopher Harper-Bill and Nicholas Vincent (eds), *Henry II: New Interpretations* (Boydell Press, 2007), p. 368, cites Tatlock, *Legendary History*, p. 426.
93. Marjorie Chibnall, *The Normans* (Wiley, 2000), p. 152.
94. Gervase of Canterbury, I, pp. 123, 125.
95. Chibnall, *The Empress Matilda*, p. 112, cites *Regesta*, III, no. 635.
96. Ibid., p. 117.
97. Walter Map, *Courtiers' Trifles*.
98. Edmund King, 'The Accession of Henry II', in Harper-Bill and Vincent (eds), p. 24.
99. Dutton, 'Angevin Comital Children', pp. 34–5.
100. Dutton, 'Geoffrey', p. 104.
101. Norgate, 'Robert Earl of Gloucester'.
102. Dutton, 'Geoffrey', p. 208.
103. Jim Bradbury, 'Geoffrey V of Anjou, Count and Knight', in Christopher Harper-Bill and Ruth Harvey (eds), *Ideals and Practice of Medieval Knighthood, Vol. III* (Boydell Press, 1990), p. 22, cites *Chronique des ducs de Normandie et des rois d'Angleterre*, eds C. Fahlin and S. Sandquist, 4 vols (Lund, 1951–79); *Chroniques des comtes d'Anjou et des seigneurs d'Amboise*, eds L. Halphen and R. Poupardin (Paris, 1913); *Chroniques des églises d'Anjou*, eds P. Marchegay and E. Mabille (Paris, 1869).
104. Dutton, 'Geoffrey', p. 13.
105. Burnett, 'The Education of Henry II'.
106. Ibid.
107. Suzanne Conklin Akbari, 'Between Diaspora and Conquest', in Jeffrey Jerome Cohen (ed.), *Cultural Diversity in the British Middle Ages* (Palgrave Macmillan, 2008), p. 29, cites William of Conches, *Dragmaticon* 6.2.22 tr. Italo Ronca, pp. 164–5.

108. John of Salisbury was quoting Bernard of Clairvaux, *The Metalogicon*, pp. 1159–60.
109. Charles Burnett, 'Bath, Adelard of (*b.* in or before 1080?, *d.* in or after 1150)', *Oxford Dictionary of National Biography* (OUP, 2004).
110. Burnett, 'The Education of Henry II', p. 32.
111. Ibid., pp. 44–5, cites *De opera astrolapsus*, ed. Dickey, pp. 168–70.
112. *Gesta Stephani*, p. 123.
113. A. L. Poole, 'Henry Plantagenet's Early Visits to England', *English Historical Review*, vol. 47, no. 187 (July 1932), 447–52.
114. *Gesta Stephani*, pp. 210–11.
115. Chibnall, *The Empress Matilda*, p. 88.
116. *Gesta Stephani*, p. 134.
117. Chibnall, *The Empress Matilda*, p. 63, cites *Gesta Stephani*, pp. 10–11, 118–21.
118. Ibid., p. 97, cites Bernard, *Sancti Bernardi Opera*, eds J. Leclercq, C. H. Talbot and H. M. Rochais, 9 vols (Rome, 1957–77), VIII, pp. 297–8 (Ep. 354); William of Malmesbury, *Historia Novella*, p. 56.
119. Warren, p. 32, cites *Recueil des Actes de Henry II*, I, p. 13.
120. Crouch, *King Stephen*, p. 240, cites *Earldom of Gloucester Charters*, ed. Robert B. Patterson (OUP, 1973), p. 97.
121. *Letters of Arnulf of Lisieux*, ed. Frank Barlow (RHS, 1939), pp. 6–7, no. 4.
122. Warren, p. 36.
123. *Gesta Stephani*, p. 214. The author of the *Gesta* was almost certainly either the bishop of Bath, or one of his circle. Some historians believe that the last part of the *Gesta*, so supportive of Henry, was written by a different author. See Jim Bradbury, *Stephen and Matilda* (The History Press, 2005).
124. Crouch, *King Stephen*, p. 244, cites John of Hexham, p. 323.
125. Warren, p. 37, cites *Gesta Stephani*, p. 145.
126. John of Worcester, *Chronicle of Worcester*, ed. J. R. H. Weaver (OUP, 1908).
127. William of Malmesbury, *Historia Novella*, p. 36.
128. Emilie Amt, *The Accession of Henry II in England* (Boydell & Brewer, 1983), p. 142.
129. *Gesta Stephani*, pp. 154–7.
130. *The Chronicle of Henry of Huntingdon*, p. 273.
131. Amt, *Accession of Henry II*, p. 31, cites *Landboc sive Registrum Monasterii Beatae Mariae Virginis et Sancti Cenhelmi de Winchelcumba*, ed. David Royce (Exeter, 1892), I, p. 81.
132. Amt, *Accession of Henry II*, p. 31.
133. Ibid.
134. Cited by Christopher Hibbert, *The English: A Social History 1066–1945* (Grafton, 1987), p. 138.
135. Bradbury, *Stephen and Matilda*.
136. Amt, *Accession of Henry II*, p. 46.
137. William FitzStephen, in *Materials for the History of Thomas Becket*, ed. James Craigie Robertson (Longman, 1885), pp. 47–9.
138. Bradbury, 'Geoffrey V of Anjou, Count and Knight', p. 31.
139. *The Letters of St Bernard of Clairvaux*, tr. Bruno Scott James (Sutton Publishing, 1998). Letter 252 to Pope Innocent, on behalf of Arnulf, bishop-elect of Lisieux.
140. David Crouch, 'King Stephen and Northern France', in P. Dalton and G. J. White (eds), *King Stephen's Reign (1135–1154)* (Boydell Press, 2008), p. 54.
141. Chartrou, p. 73, cites Robert of Torigni, I, p. 254.
142. Ibid., p. 74, cites Geoffroi de Clairvaux, *Vita Sancti Bernardi* (*Sancti Bernardi Opera*, 1690 edn, col. 1135).

143. Edmund King, *King Stephen* (Yale University Press, 2010), pp. 262–3, 265.

144. Robert of Torigni, I, p. 255.

145. Jane Martindale, 'Eleanor of Aquitaine', in Nelson (ed.), cites Bernard de Ventadour, *Chansons d'Amour*, ed. and tr. M. Lazar (King's College Centre for Late Antique and Medieval Studies, 1966).

146. Richard Barber, 'Eleanor of Aquitaine and the Media', in Catherine Léglu and Marcus Bull (eds), *The World of Eleanor of Aquitaine: Literature and Society in Southern France between the Eleventh and Thirteenth Centuries* (Boydell Press, 2005), pp. 13–27.

147. Ralph V. Turner, *Eleanor of Aquitaine* (Yale University Press, 2009), p. 13.

148. Martindale, p. 29.

149. Georges Duby, *France in the Middle Ages, 987–1460* (Wiley, 1983), p. 28.

150. Ibid., p. 29.

151. Ibid., p. 27.

152. Turner, *Eleanor of Aquitaine*, p. 18.

153. Ibid.

154. Ibid., p. 19, cites *Geoffrey de Vigeois, Receuil des historiens des Gaules et de la France*, eds Léopold Delisle et al., 24 vols (Paris, 1738–1904), XII, p. 430.

155. From a collection of thirteenth-century troubadour songs, cited by ibid., p. 20.

156. Elizabeth A. R. Brown, 'Eleanor of Aquitaine Reconsidered: The Woman and her Seasons', in Bonnie Wheeler and John C. Parsons (eds), *Eleanor of Aquitaine: Lord and Lady* (Palgrave Macmillan, 2003).

157. Martindale, p. 28.

158. Map, p. 441.

159. Jim Bradbury, *Philip Augustus* (Routledge, 1997), p. 3, cites Suger, *Vie de Louis VI, le Gros*, ed. H. Waquet.

160. Turner, *Eleanor of Aquitaine*, cites Bernard Suger, *Deeds of Louis the Fat*, trs Richard C. Cusimano and John Moorhead (Catholic University of America Press, 1992), p. 157.

161. Ibid., p. 19.

162. George T. Beech, 'The Eleanor of Aquitaine Vase', in Wheeler and Parsons (eds), p. 373.

163. Jim Bradbury, *The Capetians: Kings of France 987–1328* (London, 2007), p. 148.

164. Ibid.

165. J. M. Roberts, *The Penguin History of Europe* (Penguin, 1997), p. 125.

166. Charlemagne had eleven children – five sons and six daughters – with five different wives. By the time he died, Louis the Pious was his only son still alive. Had his brothers survived, Charlemagne would undoubtedly have divided his empire.

167. Bradbury, *Philip Augustus*, p. 7.

168. Ibid., p. 6, cites Ordericus Vitalis, *Historia Ecclesiastica*, 6:490.

169. James A. Brundage, 'The Canon Law of Divorce', in Wheeler and Parsons (eds), p. 214.

170. Ibid., cites Bernard of Clairvaux, Epistola 224, in Bernard, *Sancti Bernardi Opera* 8:93 [91–3].

171. *The Letters of John of Salisbury Vol. 2*, eds W. J. Millor, H. E. Butler and C. N. L. Brooke (Clarendon Press, 1986), pp. 52–3.

172. Ibid.

173. David Bell, *A Saint in the Sun: Praising Saint Bernard in the France of Louis XIV*. Today Vitry-le-Brûlé is known as Vitry-en-Perthois.

174. Turner, *Eleanor of Aquitaine*, p. 68.

175. Jim Bradbury, *The Capetians* (Bloomsbury, 2007), p. 157, cites Robert of Torigni, IV, p. 164.

176. Brown, 'Eleanor of Aquitaine Reconsidered: The Woman and her Seasons', in Wheeler and Parsons (eds), p. 7.

177. Michael R. Evans, *Inventing Eleanor: The Medieval and Post-Medieval Image of Eleanor of Aquitaine* (Bloomsbury, 2016), p. 25, cites William of Newburgh, *The History of English Affairs*, eds and trs P. G. Walsh and M. J. Kennedy, 2 vols (Liverpool University Press, 1998), I, p. 128.

178. The term 'black legend' to describe Eleanor was coined in 2003 by Martin Aurell, professor of medieval history at the University of Poitiers and director of the Centre d'Études Supérieures de Civilisation Médiévale.

179. Jacques Le Goff, 'Le Moyen Age', *L'Express*, 11 July 2002.

180. Turner, *Eleanor of Aquitaine*, p. 81.

181. Jonathan Phillips, *The Second Crusade: Extending the Frontiers of Christendom* (Yale University Press, 2007), p. 197, cites Otto of Friesing.

182. Ibid., p. 199.

183. Jonathan Phillips, *The Crusades: 1095–1204* (Pearson, 2002), p. 201, cites William of Tyre, *A History of Deeds Done Beyond the Sea*, trs E. A. Babcock and A. C. Krey (New York, 1943), 'Historia rerum', pp. 751–2, tr. 2.177.

184. Turner, *Eleanor of Aquitaine*, p. 85.

185. Ibid., p. 86.

186. Turner, Ralph V., 'Eleanor of Aquitaine, Twelfth-Century English Chroniclers and her "Black Legend"', *Nottingham Medieval Studies*, vol. 52 (2008).

187. Turner, *Eleanor of Aquitaine*, p. 87.

188. Phillips, *Second Crusade*, p. 208, cites William of Tyre, p. 754, tr. 2.180.

189. Ibid., p. 209.

190. Ibid., cites William of Tyre, p. 755, tr. 2.180.

191. James A. Brundage, 'The Canon Law of Divorce in the Mid-Twelfth Century', in Wheeler and Parsons (eds), cites John of Salisbury, *Historia pontificalis*, c. 23 (tr. Chibnall, p. 53).

192. Phillips, *Second Crusade*, p. 210.

193. Peggy McCracken, 'Scandalizing Desire: Eleanor of Aquitaine and the Chroniclers', in Wheeler and Parsons (eds), p. 248, cites John of Salisbury, *Historia pontificalis*, pp. 52–3.

194. Ibid., p. 249, cites translation from William of Tyre, p. 752, tr. 2.180.

195. Turner, *Eleanor of Aquitaine*, p. 92, cites Gerald of Wales, *Opera*, 1:299, bk 3, ch. 27, tr. Joseph Stevenson (1858).

196. Ibid., cites Ruth Harvey, *The Troubadour Marcabru and Love* (Westfield Publications in Medieval Studies, 1989), p. 133, citing *The Chronicle of Richard of Devizes*, ed. John. T. Appleby (Thomas Nelson & Sons, 1963), pp. 25–6.

197. Phillips, *Second Crusade*, p. 26, cites Suger, 'Epistolai', in Migne (ed.), CLXXXVI, col. 1378.

198. Ibid., cites William of Tyre, p. 755, tr. 2.180–1.

199. Jonathan Phillips, *Holy Warriors: A Modern History of the Crusades* (Bodley Head, 2009), cites Ibn al-Qalanisi, *Damascus Chronicles of the Crusades*, pp. 291–2.

200. Turner, *Eleanor of Aquitaine*, p. 96.

201. Brundage, cites John of Salisbury, *Historia pontificalis*, c. 29 (tr. Chibnall, p. 4).

202. Bradbury, *The Capetians*, cites John of Salisbury, *Historia pontificalis*, pp. 61–2.

203. Gillingham, 'Love, Marriage and Politics in the Twelfth Century', p. 234.

204. *The History of William of Newburgh*, in *The Church Historians of England*, ed. and tr. Joseph Stevenson, 5 vols (London, 1853–8), V, p. 442.

205. Map, pp. 474–6.

206. McCracken, p. 250, cites Helinand de Froidmont, *Chronicon*, in Migne (ed.), CCXII, cols 1057–5.

207. Martindale, p. 42, cites Alfred Richard, *Histoire des comtes de Poitou* (A. Picard, 1903), II, p. 457.

208. Norgate cites Peter de Langtoft, ed. Thomas Wright (Rolls Series, 1866–8), I, p. 466.

209. Martin Aurell, *The Plantagenet Empire 1154–1224*, tr. David Crouch (Routledge, 2007), p. 187. Aurell cites John of Marmoutier, *Historia Gaufride*, p. 224; William of Newburgh, *Historia rerum Anglicarum*, ed. R. Howlett (London, 1884–9), I, p. 105.

210. John of Marmoutier.

211. Dutton, 'Geoffrey', p. 147, cites John of Marmoutier, p. 224.

212. Warren, p. 42.

213. Ralph V. Turner, 'Eleanor of Aquitaine and her Children: An Inquiry into Medieval Family Attachment', *Journal of Medieval History*, vol. 14 (1988), 323. It is possible, although we have no evidence, that they met their mother when she was at Poitiers sometime between 1170 and 1173, and again in 1191 as Eleanor travelled through Champagne to pay Richard's ransom.

214. Brundage, p. 218.

215. Ibid.

216. Turner, *Eleanor of Aquitaine*, p. 114.

217. Martindale, p. 31.

218. Cited in Turner, *Eleanor of Aquitaine*, p. 114.

219. Richard le Poitevin, cited by Ffiona Swabey, *Eleanor of Aquitaine, Courtly Love, and the*
Troubadours (Greenwood Press, 2004), p. 127.

220. Cited by John Gillingham, 'War and Chivalry in the History of William the Marshal', in Nelson (ed.), p. 235.

221. Warren, p. 47, cites Robert of Torigni, pp. 169–70, and Gervase of Canterbury, I, pp. 149–50.

222. Ibid., p. 49, cites William of Newburgh and Robert of Torigni.

Act II – Triumph

1. *The Chronicle of Henry of Huntingdon: The History of England, From the Invasion of Julius Caesar to the Accession of Henry II*, ed. and tr. Thomas Forester (H. G. Bohn, 1853), p. 289.

2. Ibid.

3. William of Newburgh, *Historia rerum Anglicarum*, ed. R. Howlett (London, 1884–9), I, p. 114.

4. Edmund King, 'The Accession of Henry II', in Christopher Harper-Bill and Nicholas Vincent (eds), *Henry II: New Interpretations* (Boydell Press, 2007), p. 26, cites *Gesta Stephani: The Deeds of Stephen*, ed. K. R. Potter (London, 1955), pp. 234–5.

5. Ibid., p. 24, cites Gervase of Canterbury, I, pp. 152–3.

6. W. L. Warren, *Henry II* (University of California Press, 1973), p. 50.

7. *Gesta Stephani*, p. 157.

8. Emilie Amt, *The Accession of Henry II in England* (Boydell & Brewer, 1983), p. 14, cites ibid., pp. 238–9.

9. Robert of Torigni, p. 174.

10. King, p. 30, cites *Gesta Stephani*, pp. 238–9.

11. Stephen's biographer David Crouch believes that Eustace was suffering from food poisoning. David Crouch, *The Reign of King Stephen* (Routledge, 2013), p. 270.

12. *The Chronicle of Henry of Huntingdon*, p. 293.
13. *The History of William of Newburgh*, in *The Church Historians of England*, ed. and tr. Joseph Stevenson, 5 vols (London, 1853–8), p. 441.
14. Amt, p. 16.
15. Thomas K. Keefe, 'Henry II (1133–1189)', *Oxford Dictionary of National Biography* (OUP, 2004, online edn, January 2008); Warren, p. 52.
16. King, p. 30.
17. Ibid.
18. Ibid., p. 33.
19. Ibid., cites *Gesta Stephani*, pp. 240–1.
20. Ibid., cites *John of Hexham*, p. 331.
21. Ibid., p. 37, cites *The Chronicle of Henry of Huntingdon*, pp. 770–3.
22. Amt, p. 19, cites Gervase of Canterbury, I, pp. 157–8; William of Newburgh, ed. Stevenson, I, p. 91.
23. Ibid., p. 87, cites Gervase of Canterbury, II, p. 73.
24. Cited in Ralph V. Turner, *Eleanor of Aquitaine* (Yale University Press, 2009), p. 117.
25. *The Chronicle of Henry of Huntingdon*, p. 296.
26. Amt, p. 21.
27. William of Malmesbury, *Historia Novella*, ed. K. R. Potter (1955), p. 16.
28. *The Chronicle of Henry of Huntingdon*, p. 296.
29. William of Newburgh, ed. Howlett, I, p. 434.
30. *The Chronicle of Henry of Huntingdon*, p. 296.
31. A. W. Clapham, *English Romanesque Architecture after the Conquest* (1934), p. 2.
32. *Gesta Stephani*, p. 159.
33. *The Letters of John of Salisbury Vol. 1*, eds and trs W. J. Millor, H. E. Butler and C. N. L. Brooke (Clarendon Press, 1955), p. 161.
34. Elisabeth Van Houts, 'The Emperor's Robe: Thomas Becket and Angevin Political Culture', *Proceedings of the Battle Conference 2014*. Matilda brought two diadems with her to England from Germany after the death of her first husband.
35. Marjorie Chibnall, *The Empress Matilda: Queen Consort, Queen Mother and Lady of the English* (Wiley, 1991), p. 189.
36. Eleanor had been crowned and anointed at Bordeaux in 1137 as Louis' consort, which is why she may not have been anointed again.
37. Amt, p. 21.
38. William of Newburgh, ed. Stevenson, IV, part II, p. 444.
39. Warren, p. 262, cites William Stubbs (ed.), *Select Charters* (Clarendon Press, 1870), p. 158.
40. Nicholas Vincent, 'The pilgrimages of the Angevin kings of England 1154–1272', in Colin Morris and Peter Roberts (eds), *Pilgrimage: The English Experience from Becket to Bunyan* (CUP, 2002), pp. 12–46.
41. Martin Aurell, *The Plantagenet Empire 1154–1224*, tr. David Crouch (Routledge, 2007), p. 27.
42. Karl Leyser, 'Frederick Barbarossa, Henry II and the Hand of St James', *English Historical Review*, vol. 90, no. 356 (1975), 481–506.
43. Ibid., cites *Gesta Frederici*, III, c. 8, p. 406 (tr. Karl Leyser).
44. Aurell, *Plantagenet Empire*, p. 27, cites Otto of Freising, *Gesta Frederici*, III, 7, p. 406.
45. King, p. 44.
46. Warren, p. 266.
47. John Hudson, 'Nigel (c.1100–1169)', *Oxford Dictionary of National Biography* (OUP, 2004).
48. John Hudson, 'Richard FitzNigel', *Oxford Dictionary of National Biography* (OUP, 2004).

49. M. T. Clanchy, *From Memory to Written Record* (London, 1979).

50. Warren, p. 271.

51. Gerald of Wales, *Opera*, eds J. S. Brewer, James F. Dimock and George F. Warner (CUP, 2012), III, p. 28.

52. Michael Clanchy, *England and its Rulers* (Oxford, 1983), p. 77.

53. For an unsurpassable assessment of the period, see Clanchy, *From Memory to Written Record.*

54. King, p. 44.

55. Turner, *Eleanor of Aquitaine*, pp. 151–2.

56. Jane Martindale, 'Eleanor, suo jure duchess of Aquitaine (*c.*1122–1204)', *Oxford Dictionary of National Biography* (OUP, 2004).

57. Turner, *Eleanor of Aquitaine*, p. 162.

58. Ibid., p. 154.

59. Ibid., p. 155.

60. Nicholas Vincent, 'The Court of Henry II', in Harper-Bill and Vincent (eds), p. 289. Professor Vincent has led pioneering research into the Acta of Henry II and I am extremely grateful to him for sharing his unpublished research with me.

61. John Hudson, 'Ilchester, Richard of (*d.* 1188)', *Oxford Dictionary of National Biography* (OUP, 2004).

62. Vincent, 'The Court of Henry II'.

63. Ibid.

64. Aurell, *Plantagenet Empire*, p. 53.

65. D. J. A. Matthew, 'Thomas Brown (*d.* 1180)', *Oxford Dictionary of National Biography* (OUP, 2004).

66. Frank Barlow, 'Simon of Apulia (*d.* 1223)', *Oxford Dictionary of National Biography* (OUP, 2007).

67. *The Chronicle of Battle Abbey*, pp. 160–1.

68. King cites John of Salisbury's *Entheticus de Dogmate Philosophorum*, I, p. 197.

69. William of Newburgh, ed. Howlett, I, pp. 103–4.

70. Warren, p. 60.

71. Ibid., pp. 60–1.

72. Ibid., p. 56.

73. Aurell, *Plantagenet Empire*, p. 50, cites Orderic Vitalis.

74. Ibid., p. 53.

75. Vincent, 'The Court of Henry II', p. 308.

76. *The Chronicle of Richard of Devizes*, ed. John. T. Appleby (Thomas Nelson & Sons, 1963), p. 65.

77. Warren, p. 143, cites Ralph of Diceto, *Radulfi de Diceto Decani Lundoniensis Opera Historica*, ed. William Stubbs, 2 vols (Rolls Series, 1876), I, p. 416.

78. British Museum exhibition, 2016: *Sicily: Culture and Conquest.*

79. Ibid.

80. Suzanne Conklin Akbari, 'Between Diaspora and Conquest', in Jeffrey Jerome Cohen (ed.), *Cultural Diversity in the British Middle Ages* (Palgrave Macmillan, 2008), p. 30, cites Petrus Alfonsi, Epistola, pp. 175–6.

81. R. W. Southern, 'The place of England in the twelfth-century renaissance', *History*, XLV (1960), 201–16.

82. Rôn Barqây, *A History of Jewish Gynaecological Texts in the Middle Ages* (Brill, 1999).

83. Turner, *Eleanor of Aquitaine*, p. 173.

84. Adrian IV died in 1159.

85. Jane E. Sayers, 'Adrian IV (*d.* 1159)', *Oxford Dictionary of National Biography* (OUP, 2004).

86. Aurell, *Plantagenet Empire*, p. 13, cites Antonia Gransden, *Historical Writing in England c.550 to c.1307* (Routledge & Kegan Paul, 1974), p. 210.

87. John Gillingham, 'The Cultivation of History, Legend and Courtesy at the Court of Henry II', in Ruth Kennedy and Simon Meecham-Jones (eds), *Writers of the Reign of Henry II* (Palgrave Macmillan, 2006), p. 28.

88. Turner, *Eleanor of Aquitaine*, p. 168.
89. Ibid., p. 170. At the beginning of the thirteenth century, Layamon, a priest, translated the *Brut* into English, and it was he who made the claim for the dedication to Eleanor.
90. Peter Dronke, 'Peter of Blois and Poetry at the Court of Henry II', *Medieval Studies*, 38 (1976), 207.
91. John Charles Fox, 'Marie de France', *English Historical Review*, vol. 25, no. 98 (1910), 303–6. Aurell, *Plantagenet Empire*, p. 162, cites Chrétien de Troyes, *Eric et Enide*, l. 6636, 'Henry II and Arthurian Legend', p. 379.
92. Martin Aurell, 'Henry II and Arthurian Legend', in Harper-Bill and Vincent (eds), p. 375.
93. Ibid., p. 369.
94. Ibid., p. 371. Aurell cites Layamon, the English priest who translated Wace's work into Middle English, for the source of the dedication.
95. Ibid., p. 382. See also Aurell, *Plantagenet Empire*, p. 158. Joseph of Exeter compared Henry to Hector.
96. Aurell, *Plantagenet Empire*, p. 288, cites Gerald of Wales, *On the Instruction of Princes*, in *Opera*, VIII, pp. 126–8.
97. Clanchy, *England and its Rulers*, p. 168, cites *A Mirror for Fools*, tr. J. H. Mosley (University of Notre Dame Press, 1963), p. 39.
98. G. A. Loud, 'The Kingdom of Sicily and the Kingdom of England, 1066–1266', *Journal of the Historical Association*, vol. 88, issue 292 (October 2003).
99. Clanchy, *England and its Rulers*, p. 175.
100. Ibid.
101. Ibid., p. 176.
102. Ibid.
103. Rodney M. Thomson, 'England and the Twelfth-Century Renaissance', *Past & Present*, no. 101 (1983), 3–21, cites N. R. Ker, *English Manuscripts in the Century after the Norman Conquest* (OUP, 1960), p. 1.
104. Ibid., p. 7.
105. Southern, 'The place of England in the twelfth-century renaissance'.
106. William Rothwell, 'Language and Government in Medieval England', *Zeitschrift für französische Sprache und Literatur*, vol. 93, no. 3 (1983), 258–70.
107. Ibid.
108. Scholarship is divided, and some historians have dated the poem as late as the beginning of the fourteenth century.
109. Akbari, p. 32.
110. Peter of Blois, *Epistolae*, no. 66, col. 197.
111. Walter Map, *Courtiers' Trifles*, p. 1.
112. Herbert of Bosham, in J. P. Migne (ed.), *Patrologia Latina*, 221 vols (Paris, 1844–64), XC, col. 1322.
113. Ralph of Diceto, I, p. 351.
114. Vincent, 'The Court of Henry II', p. 294.
115. Warren, p. 210, cites Peter of Blois, Epistola 14, in Migne (ed.), CCVII, pp. 48–9.
116. Southern, p. 212, cites Peter of Blois, Epistola 14, in Migne (ed.), CCVII, pp. 48–9.
117. Map, p. 9.
118. Ibid.
119. John Southworth, *Fools and Jesters at the English Court* (The History Press, 2003), p. 39.
120. *Chronicle of Battle Abbey*, pp. 156–7.
121. William of Newburgh, ed. Howlett, I, p. 280.
122. *Chronicle of Battle Abbey*, p. 187.
123. Aurell, *Plantagenet Empire*, p. 98. The canon of Rodez made this claim, although he was writing in the thirteenth century.
124. Jordan Fantosme, *Jordan Fantosme's Chronicle*, ed. and tr. R. C. Johnston (OUP, 1981).

125. *Materials for the History of Thomas Becket*, ed. James Craigie Robertson (Longman, 1885), VI, p. 72.

126. Gerald of Wales, *The Conquest of Ireland*, eds and trs A. B. Scott and F. X. Martin (Dublin, 1971), p. 91.

127. *Magna Vita*, pp. 115–16.

128. Map, p. 103. John Gillingham's translation, 'The Cultivation of History, Legend and Courtesy', p. 40.

129. Map, p. 487.

130. Southworth, p. 35.

131. Map, p. 485.

132. Gerald of Wales, *Conquest of Ireland*, pp. 128–9.

133. Warren, pp. 272–3, cites *Dialogus de Scaccario*, p. 2.

134. Amt, p. 169.

135. Ibid., p. 191.

136. Ibid., p. 174.

137. Edmund King, *England 1175– 1425* (Routledge & Kegan Paul, 1979), pp. 44–9.

138. *History of the King's Works*, I, p. 59.

139. Amt, p. 183, cites J. H. Round, *Feudal England* (S. Sonnenschein, 1895), pp. 219–22.

140. Ibid. Amt points out that for that year, scutage was also collected as 'dona', another military tax.

141. Vincent, 'The Court of Henry II', p. 300.

142. Pipe roll 23, Henry II, p. 95.

143. Warren, p. 270, cites pipe roll 30, Henry II, 37, 82, 97, 105, 101.

144. Vincent, 'The Court of Henry II', p. 301.

145. Warren, p. 271, cites pipe roll 22, Henry II, 100.

146. Vincent, 'The Court of Henry II', cites Gerald of Wales, *Opera*, VIII, pp. 305–6.

147. Cecil Roth, *A History of the Jews in England* (Clarendon Press, 1978), p. 16.

148. Ibid.

149. Leviticus 25:36.

150. This charter is now lost. Roth, p. 6.

151. Ibid., p. 9.

152. Roth, p. 10, cites William of Newburgh, ed. Howlett, I, p. 280.

153. Ibid., p. 12.

154. Ibid.

155. It was not until the reign of Henry's grandson Henry III that we find a Master of the King's Works. *The History of the King's Works*, ed. H. M. Colvin (HMSO, 1963), I, p. 64.

156. John Gillingham, 'The King and his Castle: How Henry II Rebuilt his Reputation', *BBC History Magazine*, March 2011.

157. *History of the King's Works*, I, p. 65.

158. Warren, p. 234.

159. *History of the King's Works*, I, p. 69. Henry spent more on his castle defences during this period than at any other time during his reign.

160. John D. Hosler, *Henry II: A Medieval Soldier at War, 1147– 1189* (Brill, 2007), p. 183.

161. Roger of Howden, *Gesta Regis Henrici Secundi*, ed. William Stubbs (Rolls Series, 1867), I, p. 127.

162. *History of the King's Works*, I, p. 69.

163. Lindy Grant, 'Le patronage architectural d'Henri II et de son entourage', *Cahiers de civilisation médiévale. 37e année (n° 145–146)* (January–June 1994).

164. Jonathan Phillips, *Holy Warriors: A Modern History of the Crusades* (Bodley Head, 2009), p. 115, cites William of Tyre, *A History of Deeds Done Beyond the Sea*, trs E. A. Babcock and A. C. Krey (New York, 1943), 'Historia rerum', p. 417, tr. 2.398.

165. Christopher Hibbert, *The English: A Social History 1066– 1945* (Grafton, 1987), p. 158.

166. Grant.

167. Nicholas Vincent, 'The Great Lost Library of England's Medieval Kings? Royal Use and

Ownership of Books, 1066–1300', in Kathleen Doyle and Scot McEndrick (eds), *1000 Years of Royal Books and Manuscripts* (University of Chicago Press, 2014).

168. Grant.

169. *History of the King's Works*, I, pp. 87–8.

170. Warren, p. 465, cites William of Newburgh, ed. Howlett, I, p. 140.

171. Ibid., cites William FitzStephen, in *Materials for the History of Thomas Becket*, ed. Robertson, III, pp. 45–6.

172. Herbert of Bosham, in Migne (ed.), III, p. 266.

173. Paul Brand, 'Henry II and the Creation of the English Common Law', in Harper-Bill and Vincent (eds), p. 78.

174. Map, p. 477.

175. *The Chronicle of Battle Abbey*, ed. and tr. E. Searle (Clarendon Press, 1980), p. 311.

176. Map, p. 477.

177. Ibid., p. 509.

178. Roger of Howden on the Assize of Clarendon, 1166, *Gesta Regis Henrici Secundi*, I, p. 107.

179. Warren, p. 324, cites Van Caenegem, *Royal Writs*, 461, no. 95.

180. William of Newburgh, ed. Howlett, I, p. 102.

181. Brand, 'Henry II and the Creation of the English Common Law', p. 93.

182. Migne (ed.), CCVII, cols 48–9.

183. Brand, 'Henry II and the Creation of the English Common Law', p. 81, cites *The Anglo-Saxon Chronicle*, eds Dorothy Whitelock, D. X. Douglas and S. I. Tucker (London, 1965), p. 191.

184. Warren, p. 331.

185. Weber, cited in Clanchy, *From Memory to Written Record*.

186. Ralph V. Turner, *Judges, Administrators and the Common Law in Angevin England* (Hambledon Press, 1994), cites H. G. Richardson and G. O. Sayles, *Law and Legislations from Aethelberht to Magna Carta*, p. 11.

187. Roger of Howden, *Chronica*, ed. William Stubbs (Rolls Series, 1868–71), II, p. 215.

188. Glanville, *Tractatus de legibus et consuetudinibus regni Angliæ*, XII, p. 6.

189. Warren, pp. 317–18.

190. Ibid.

191. Paul Brand, 'Anstey, Richard of (c.1137–1194/5)', *Oxford Dictionary of National Biography* (OUP, 2006).

192. Glanville, XIII, pp. 33, 167–8. Warren, p. 340, points out that the names and dates, in italics, were changeable according to circumstance.

193. Warren, p. 288, cites Stubbs (ed.), *Select Charters*, pp. 175–8.

194. Ibid., p. 321.

195. Ibid., p. 341.

196. Brand, 'Henry II and the Creation of the English Common Law', p. 221.

197. See Warren, p. 341, n. 2.

198. Ibid., p. 355.

199. Ibid., p. 356, cites Glanville, XIV, p. 171.

200. Ibid., p. 333, cites *Battle Abbey*, p. 106.

201. See Warren, p. 342.

202. Assize of Northampton, clause 4; Warren, p. 343, cites Stubbs (ed.), *Select Charters*, pp. 179–80.

203. Nick Barratt, 'Finance and the Economy in the Reign of Henry II', in Harper-Bill and Vincent (eds), pp. 242–56.

204. Brand, 'Henry II and the Creation of the English Common Law', p. 237.

205. Ibid., p. 221.

206. Gerald of Wales, *Conquest of Ireland*, pp. 302–3.

207. Wace, *Roman de Rou*, ed. A.J. Holden (Anciens Textes, 2011), vv. 35–6, I, p. 4.

208. William of Newburgh, ed. Stevenson, p. 440.
209. William of Newburgh, *The History of English Affairs*, eds and trs P. G. Walsh and M. J. Kennedy (2 vols, Oxford, 1988–2001), II, pp 30–1.
210. Warren, p. 66.
211. Hosler, p. 163. He suggests that these numbers are exaggerated.
212. Amt, p.183.
213. Hosler, p. 153.
214. Ibid., p. 59.
215. John Gillingham, 'The Angevin Empire', in J. L. Nelson (ed.), *Richard Coeur de Lion in History and Myth, King's College Medieval Studies 7* (King's College London, 1992). In the event that England and France be at war, the count of Flanders was obliged to provide the French king with twenty knights; the English king would still receive his 1,000 men.
216. Ibid., p. 164.
217. Ibid., cites *The Chronicle of Melrose*, eds A. O. Anderson and M. O. Anderson (London, 1936).
218. Ibid., p. 29.
219. William of Newburgh, ed. Stevenson, p. 552.
220. For a full discussion, see Acts Four and Five.
221. Turner, *Eleanor of Aquitaine*, p. 129.
222. Michael Evans cites examples of Eleanor's contemporaries Matilda of Scotland, Ermangarde, vicountess of Narbonne, and Eleanor's eldest daughter by Louis, Marie of Champagne, as being far more active patrons.
223. Aurell, 'Henry II and Arthurian Legend', p. 365, cites Lejeune, 'Rôle littéraire de la famille d'Aliénor d'Aquitaine', p. 5.
224. Elizabeth A. R. Brown, 'Eleanor of Aquitaine Reconsidered', in Bonnie Wheeler and John C. Parsons (eds), *Eleanor of Aquitaine: Lord and Lady* (Palgrave Macmillan, 2003), p. 2. Historians have erroneously repeated as fact Andreas Capellanus' twelfth-century satirical work *De amore*.
225. Ralph V. Turner, 'Eleanor of Aquitaine and her Children: An Inquiry into Medieval Family Attachment', *Journal of Medieval History*, vol. 14 (1988), 323.
226. Ibid.
227. Ibid.
228. Kathryn Dutton, 'Geoffrey, Count of Anjou and Duke of Normandy, 1129–51', unpublished PhD thesis (University of Glasgow, 2011), p. 161.
229. Aurell, *Plantagenet Empire*, p. 43.
230. Turner, 'Eleanor of Aquitaine and her Children'.
231. Marie Lovatt, 'Geoffrey (1151?–1212)', *Oxford Dictionary of National Biography* (OUP, 2004, online edn, October 2007).
232. Ibid.

Act III – Pariah

1. Frank Barlow, 'Thomas Becket (1120?–1170)', *Oxford Dictionary of National Biography* (OUP, 2004).
2. Anne Duggan, *Thomas Becket* (Hodder Education, 2004), p. 12.
3. Ibid., p. 14, cites *Thomas Saga*, I, p. 28.
4. Ibid., p. 16, cites William FitzStephen, *Life of St Thomas*, tr. Michael Staunton, p. 48.
5. Ibid., p. 21, cites John of Salisbury, *Letters*, I, no. 28.
6. Ibid.
7. William FitzStephen in *Materials for the History of Thomas Becket*, ed. James Craigie Robertson (Longman, 1885), III, pp. 17–26.

8. Ibid.
9. Ibid.
10. John D. Hosler, *Henry II: A Medieval Soldier at War, 1147–1189* (Brill, 2007), p. 163.
11. Duggan cites FitzStephen, *Life of St Thomas*, pp. 34–5.
12. Ibid.
13. L. A. Finke and M. B. Schichtman, *Cinematic Illuminations: The Middle Ages on Film* (Johns Hopkins University Press, 2010), p. 97.
14. Duggan, p. 22, cites FitzStephen, *Life of St Thomas*, pp. 34–5.
15. W. L. Warren, *Henry II* (University of California Press, 1973), p. 404, cites Eadmer, *Historia Novorum*, pp. 9, 10.
16. R. W. Southern, 'Anselm [St Anselm] (*c.*1033–1109)', *Oxford Dictionary of National Biography* (OUP, 2004).
17. Ibid.
18. Warren, p. 112.
19. Ibid., p. 412, cites Anselm, *Opera*, IV, pp. 126–9, letter no. 223.
20. *The Letters of John of Salisbury Vol. 1*, eds and trs W. J. Millor, H. E. Butler and C. N. L. Brooke (Clarendon Press, 1955), no. 116, p. 190.
21. Ibid.
22. Duggan, *Thomas Becket*, p. 23, cites Herbert of Bosham, tr. Michael Staunton, p. 181.
23. FitzStephen, *Life of St Thomas*.
24. Duggan, *Thomas Becket*, p. 23.
25. Ibid., pp. 23–34, cites Edward Grim (one of Becket's biographers), pp. 366–7.
26. Ibid., cites FitzStephen, *Life of St Thomas*.
27. Ibid., p. 38, cites William of Canterbury, p. 12.
28. Thomas K. Keefe, 'Henry II (1133–1189)', *Oxford Dictionary of National Biography* (OUP, 2004, online edn, January 2008), cites Robertson and Sheppard, 2.373–4.
29. Duggan, *Thomas Becket*, p. 39, cites *Letters of John of Salisbury*, I, p. 16.
30. FitzStephen, *Life of St Thomas*.
31. Christopher Hibbert, *The English: A Social History 1066–1945* (Grafton, 1987), p. 40, cites John R. H. Moorman, *Church Life in England in the Thirteenth Century* (CUP, 1945), p. 89.
32. Warren, p. 466, cites Herbert of Bosham, *Materials for the History of Thomas Becket*, III, p. 266.
33. Duggan, *Thomas Becket*, p. 40.
34. Warren, p. 466, cites Knowles, *The Episcopal Colleagues of Thomas Becket*, pp. 56–7.
35. Ibid., p. 470, cites Herbert of Bosham, III, pp. 273–5.
36. Duggan, *Thomas Becket*, p. 40.
37. Ibid.
38. Ibid.
39. Frank Barlow, 'Roger de Pont l'Évêque (*c.*1115–1181)', *Oxford Dictionary of National Biography* (OUP, 2004).
40. Ibid.
41. *The Correspondence of Thomas Becket*, ed. and tr. Anne Duggan, I, p. 41, letter 17, Archbishop Thomas of Canterbury to Pope Alexander.
42. Ibid., I, p. 49, letter 19, Pope Alexander to Archbishop Thomas of Canterbury.
43. Stubbs, *Select Charters*, pp. 163–4.
44. Duggan, *Thomas Becket*, p. 44, cites FitzStephen, *Life of St Thomas*, p. 48.
45. Gilbert Foliot, *Letters and Charters*, no. 170, pp. 233–4.
46. Duggan, *Thomas Becket*, p. 77, cites FitzStephen, *Life of St Thomas*, p. 65.
47. Ibid., cites FitzStephen, *Life of St Thomas*, pp. 67–8.
48. Ibid., pp. 82–3, cites *Materials for the History of Thomas Becket*, V, no. 71, October 1164.
49. Ian Robinson, *The Papacy, 1073–1198: Continuity and Innovation* (CUP, 1990), p. 83.

50. Duggan, *Thomas Becket*, p. 93, cites *The Correspondence of Thomas Becket*, I, no. 37.
51. Gervase of Canterbury, pp. 332–3.
52. Duggan, *Thomas Becket*, p. 97.
53. Marjorie Chibnall, *The Empress Matilda: Queen Consort, Queen Mother and Lady of the English* (Wiley, 1991), p. 169.
54. Kathryn Dutton, 'Geoffrey, Count of Anjou and Duke of Normandy, 1129–51', unpublished PhD thesis (University of Glasgow, 2011), p. 17.
55. Martin Aurell, 'Henry II and Arthurian Legend', in Christopher Harper-Bill and Nicholas Vincent (eds), *Henry II: New Interpretations* (Boydell Press, 2007), p. 380.
56. Chibnall, p. 191, cites Geoffrey of Vigeois.
57. Ibid., p. 194, cites Ralph of Diceto, *Radulfi de Diceto Decani Lundoniensis Opera Historica*, ed. William Stubbs, 2 vols (Rolls Series, 1876), II, pp. 15–18.
58. Michael R. Evans, *Inventing Eleanor: The Medieval and Post-Medieval Image of Eleanor of Aquitaine* (Bloomsbury, 2016), p. 22.
59. *The Letters of John of Salisbury Vol. 2*, eds W. J. Millor, H. E. Butler and C. N. L. Brooke (Clarendon Press, 1979), no. 168, to Bartholomew, bishop of Exeter, June 1166.
60. Ibid., no. 272, to Baldwin of Exeter, April/May 1168. Dr Charles Burnett believes there may have been something in Henry's threat, in the light of the pleasure he took in Arabic learning. See Charles Burnett, 'The Education of Henry II', in *The Introduction of Arabic Learning into England* (British Library, 1997).
61. Duggan, *Thomas Becket*, p. 116, cites *The Correspondence of Thomas Becket*, I, no. 82.
62. Ibid.
63. Warren, p. 504, cites *Materials for the History of Thomas Becket*, Epistolae, V, p. 270.
64. Martin Aurell, *The Plantagenet Empire 1154–1224*, tr. David Crouch (Routledge, 2007), p. 248.
65. Duggan, *Thomas Becket*, p. 184, cites *The Correspondence of Thomas Becket*, II, no. 300.
66. *The Correspondence of Thomas Becket*, p. 1333.
67. Duggan, *Thomas Becket*, p. 204.
68. Warren, p. 509, cites John of Salisbury to Bartholomew, bishop of Exeter, *Materials for the History of Thomas Becket*, Epistolae, V, p. 381.
69. Nicholas Vincent, 'The Murderers of Thomas Becket', in Natalie Fryde and Dirk Reitz (eds), *Bischofsmord im Mittelalter/The Murder of Bishops in the Middle Ages* (Vandenhoeck & Ruprecht, 2003), p. 228.
70. Ibid.
71. Duggan, *Thomas Becket*, p. 210, cites Benedict of Peterborough, *Materials for the History of Thomas Becket*.
72. Ibid., p. 212.
73. *Materials for the History of Thomas Becket*, III, p. 142.
74. Peterborough's account, p. 204, in Michael Staunton.
75. Arnulf of Lisieux, *Letters*, pp. 122–3.
76. Roger of Howden, *Gesta Regis Henrici Secundi*, ed. William Stubbs (Rolls Series, 1867), I, pp. 14–15.
77. Roger of Howden, *Chronica*, ed. William Stubbs (Rolls Series, 1868–71), II, pp. 22–5.
78. Vincent, p. 253.
79. Ibid., cites *Materials for the History of Thomas Becket*, VIII, no. 746, pp. 457–8.
80. Ibid., p. 262.
81. William of Newburgh, *Historia rerum Anglicarum*, ed. R. Howlett (London, 1884–9), p. 167.

82. Hosler, p. 164.
83. Anne Duggan, '*Ne in dubium*: The Official Record of Henry II's Reconciliation at Avranches, 21 May, 1172', *English Historical Review*, vol. 115, no. 462 (2000), 643–58.
84. Warren, p. 534, cites *Materials for the History of Thomas Becket*, Epistolae, VIII, p. 521.
85. *History of the King's Works*, vol. 1, p. 63.
86. Charles Freeman, *Holy Bones, Holy Dust* (Yale University Press, 2011), p. 7.
87. Ibid., cites Jonathan Sumption, *Pilgrimage: An Image of Medieval Religion* (Faber & Faber, 1975), p. 155.

Act IV – Rebellion

1. Richard le Poitevin bemoaning Eleanor's imprisonment after the failed rebellion. Quoted by Ffiona Swabey, *Eleanor of Aquitaine, Courtly Love and the Troubadours* (Greenwood Press, 2004), p. 127; Matthew Strickland, *Henry the Young King* (Yale University Press, 2016), p. 135, cites Jean Flori, *Eleanor of Aquitaine* (Edinburgh University Press, 2007), pp. 111–12.
2. *The History of the King's Works*, ed. H. M. Colvin (HMSO, 1963), I, p. 67.
3. Gerald of Wales, *On the Instruction of Princes*.
4. Ralph V. Turner, *Eleanor of Aquitaine* (Yale University Press, 2009), p. 176, cites A. J. Holden, S. Gregory and D. Crouch (eds), *History of William Marshal* (Anglo-Norman Text Society, 2003), lines 1566–80.
5. Ibid., p. 182.
6. Ibid., p. 141. Henry's conquest of Brittany led to the subjugation of Duke Conan, and the betrothal of Conan's daughter Constance to young Geoffrey. In winning a war, Henry had gained one of his sons a dukedom. Eleanor however was unable to subdue the nobility of Maine and Brittany, and Henry was compelled to come and assert his own authority to quash revolt.
7. Marie Hivergneaux, 'Queen Eleanor and Aquitaine, 1137–1189', in Bonnie Wheeler and John C. Parsons (eds), *Eleanor of Aquitaine: Lord and Lady* (Palgrave Macmillan, 2003), p. 67.
8. Turner, *Eleanor of Aquitaine*, p. 183, cites Gervase of Canterbury, I, p. 267.
9. Ibid.
10. Ibid., p. 143.
11. Ibid., p. 186, cites *History of William Marshal*, lines 1908–22.
12. Ibid., p. 188.
13. Hivergneaux, p. 67.
14. Turner, *Eleanor of Aquitaine*, cites *Geoffrey de Vigeois, Recueil des historiens des Gaules et de la France*, eds Léopold Delisle et al., 24 vols (Paris, 1738–1904), XII, p. 442.
15. Ibid., p. 186.
16. Ibid., p. 191.
17. Ibid.
18. Hivergneaux, p. 69.
19. Turner, *Eleanor of Aquitaine*, p. 163.
20. *The History of William of Newburgh*, in *The Church Historians of England*, ed. and tr. Joseph Stevenson, 5 vols (London, 1853–8), p. 552.
21. Gerald of Wales, *The Conquest of Ireland*, eds and trs A. B. Scott and F. X. Martin (Dublin, 1971), quoted in Turner, *Eleanor of Aquitaine*, p. 207.
22. Geoffrey was invested as duke at Rennes Cathedral in May 1169. Here, ten-year-old Geoffrey received homage from some of the Breton barons resigned to his marriage to their duchess.
23. Turner, *Eleanor of Aquitaine*, p. 213.

24. W. L. Warren, *Henry II* (University of California Press, 1973), p. 111.
25. Warren, p. 595.
26. Martin Aurell, *The Plantagenet Empire 1154–1224*, tr. David Crouch (Routledge, 2007), p. 6, cites Walter Map, *Courtiers' Trifles*, IV, 13, p. 370.
27. Ralph V. Turner, 'Eleanor of Aquitaine and her Children: An Inquiry into Medieval Family Attachment', *Journal of Medieval History*, vol. 14 (1988).
28. Strickland, *Henry the Young King*, p. 2, cites Gervase of Tilbury, *Otia Imperialia*, eds and trs S. E. Banks and J. W. Binns (Oxford, 2002), pp. 486–7.
29. Warren, p. 77.
30. Ibid., cites Robert of Torigni, 196–7.
31. Turner, *Eleanor of Aquitaine*, p. 136.
32. Lindsay Diggelmann, 'Marriage as Tactical Response: Henry II and the Royal Wedding of 1160', *HER*, vol. 119.
33. Diggelmann cites Lambert, pp. 517–18.
34. Diggelmann cites Newburgh, *Chronicles*, p. 159.
35. Diggelmann cites and translates Roger of Howden, *Gesta Regis Henrici Secundi*, ed. William Stubbs (Rolls Series, 1867), I, p. 218.
36. Warren, p. 90.
37. Diggelmann cites Roger of Howden, *Gesta Regis Henrici Secundi*, I, p. 218.
38. Matthew Strickland, 'On the Instruction of a Prince: The Upbringing of Henry, the Young King', in Christopher Harper-Bill and Nicholas Vincent (eds), *Henry II: New Interpretations* (Boydell Press, 2007), p. 191, cites William FitzStephen, *Vita Sancti Thomae Cantuarensis Archiepiscopi et Martyris*, in *Materials for the History of Thomas Becket*, ed. James Craigie Robertson (Longman, 1885), II, p. 22.
39. Strickland, *Henry the Young King*, p. 32.
40. Ibid., p. 47.
41. Ibid., p. 48, cites Edward Grim (Becket's biographer), *Materials for the History of Thomas Becket*, II, p. 366.
42. Ibid., cites *The Letters of John of Salisbury, Vol. 2*, eds W. J. Millor, H. E. Butler and C. N. L. Brooke (Clarendon Press, 1979), pp. 10–11.
43. Ibid., p. 53.
44. William FitzJohn, one of Henry's *familiaris*, or an intimate of the royal household, was an itinerant justice – see ibid., p. 60.
45. See ibid., p. 90.
46. Ibid., p. 91, cites Jordan Fantosme, II, p. 12.
47. Strickland, 'On the Instruction of a Prince: The Upbringing of Henry, the Young King', p. 205.
48. Strickland, *Henry the Young King*, p. 116.
49. Ibid.
50. Ibid., p. 124, cites Roger of Howden, *Gesta Regis Henrici Secundi*, I, p. 177.
51. Ibid., p. 129, cites *Brut y Tywysogion or the Chronicle of the Princes*, ed. T. Jones (Peniarth MS. 20 Version), p. 69. His few surviving acta, or charters, show that even his grants were merely confirmations of his father's grants. Charters offer a fascinating insight into aristocratic activity and power. Although Henri died young, by the time of his death at twenty-eight years old, he had produced only forty charters, and many of these simply affirmed his father's charters. In contrast Frederick Barbarossa's eldest son Heinrich produced eighty surviving charters up until the comparable age of twenty-four

when his father left on crusade, and we have 3,000 charters of Henry II's that have survived. Henri was allowed to do very little. In marked contrast, Barbarossa actively groomed his eldest son and designated heir for government, and he acted as his father's regent and ruled in fact as well as name. See Strickland, 'On the Instruction of a Prince: The Upbringing of Henry, the Young King'.

52. Strickland, *Henry the Young King*, p.13.
53. Ibid.
54. Fantosme II, pp. 21–2, 17–20, quoted in ibid., p. 124.
55. Warren, p. 118, cites Geoffrey de Vigeois, II, p. 319.
56. The Toulouse campaign was the first significant defeat of Henry's career, which happened when Louis, his overlord for his lands in France, placed himself in the city.
57. Louis had four brothers and one sister. Two of his brothers belonged to the church and as such did not have legitimate offspring. His remaining brothers, Robert count of Dreux and Peter lord of Courtenay, only produced sons later. Peter's eldest son was probably not born before 1159.
58. Jim Bradbury, *The Capetians* (Bloomsbury, 2007), p. 162.
59. Warren, p. 105, cites Robert of Torigni, p. 229.
60. Mark Gregory Pegg, *A Most Holy War*, p. 51.
61. Ibid., cites *Geoffrey de Vigeois, Recueil des historiens des Gaules et de la France*, eds Léopold Delisle et al., 24 vols (Paris, 1738–1904), XVI, pp. 158–9.
62. Strickland, 'On the Instruction of a Prince: The Upbringing of Henry, the Young King', p. 194.
63. Strickland, *Henry the Young King*, p. 126, cites Fantosme, II, pp. 81–2.

64. John D. Hosler, *Henry II: A Medieval Soldier at War, 1147–1189* (Brill, 2007), p. 196.
65. Strickland, *Henry the Young King*, p. 128, cites Robert of Torigni, pp. 255–6.
66. Ibid.
67. Ibid., p. 131, cites *The Chronicle of Melrose*, eds A. O. Anderson and M. O. Anderson (London, 1936), p. 40.
68. William of Newburgh, ed. Stevenson, p. 484.
69. Ibid.
70. Gerald of Wales, *Opera*, eds J. S. Brewer, James F. Dimock and George F. Warner (CUP, 2012), VIII, p. 165.
71. Strickland, *Henry the Young King*, p. 135, cites Peter of Blois, *Epistolae*, no. 154, in J. P. Migne (ed.), *Patrologia Latina*, 221 vols (Paris, 1844–64), CCVII, cols 448–9.
72. Ibid., p. 135, cites Peter of Blois, *Epistolae*, no. 154; tr. Flori, p. 108.
73. See Elizabeth A. R. Brown, 'Eleanor of Aquitaine Reconsidered' for a discussion of various historians' views as to who the figures in the wall painting represent. The other contemporary images of Eleanor are her various seals, her tomb effigy at Fontevraud, and the stained-glass window commissioned by Henry and Eleanor at Poitiers cathedral. It must be remembered that there was no sense of portraiture in the medieval period; images were types rather than attempts to portray the individual.
74. Gerald of Wales, *Conquest of Ireland*, pp. 121–2.
75. Philip's wife Elizabeth de Vermandois was Eleanor's niece, daughter of Petronilla and Raoul de Vermandois.
76. For a full list of the young king's allies and his promises to them, see Hosler, pp. 196–8.

77. Strickland, *Henry the Young King*, p. 154.
78. *The Chronicle of Battle Abbey*, ed. and tr. E. Searle (Clarendon Press, 1980), pp. 274–5.
79. Aurell, *Plantagenet Empire*, p. 37, cites *The Annals of St Aubin of Angers*, p. 16.
80. Warren, p. 123.
81. Ibid., p. 124, cites Ralph of Diceto, *Radulfi de Diceto Decani Lundoniensis Opera Historica*, ed. William Stubbs, 2 vols (Rolls Series, 1876), I, p. 371.
82. Ibid., cites Robert of Torigni, p. 251.
83. William of Newburgh, ed. Stevenson, p. 553.
84. Roger of Howden, *Annals*, p. 369; Aquitaine was barely involved in the revolt. The action never went further south than Saintes, south of La Rochelle.
85. Hosler, p. 76.
86. For a full account, see ibid., pp. 195–219.
87. Hosler, p. 201, cites William of Newburgh, *Historia rerum Anglicarum*, ed. R. Howlett (London, 1884–9), I, p. 183; Fantosme, p. 71.
88. Hosler, pp. 202–3.
89. Ibid., p. 204, cites *The History of the Norman People: Wace's Roman de Rou*, tr. G. S. Burgess (Boydell Press, 2004), p. 4.
90. Ibid., p. 205.
91. Fantosme, pp. 130–40.
92. Hosler, p. 229, cites Roger of Howden, *Gesta Regis Henrici Secundi*, II, p. 33.
93. William of Newburgh, ed. Stevenson, p. 485. Henry was grateful to the Jewish moneylenders for their support. After the battles were won, he reaffirmed their exemption from tax in his lands in France, and throughout England. See Strickland, *Henry the Young King*, p. 198.
94. Hosler, p. 122, cites J. Boussare, 'Les mercenaires au xii siècle: Henry II Plantagenet et les origines de l'armée de métier', *Bibliothèque de l'école des Chartres*, vol. 106 (1945–6).
95. Hosler, p. 144, cites Roger of Howden, *Chronica*, ed. William Stubbs (Rolls Series, 1868–71), II, p. 51.
96. William of Newburgh, ed. Stevenson, p. 487.
97. Ibid., p. 488.
98. Hosler cites Roger of Howden, *Chronica*, II, pp. 53–4.
99. Henry did not appoint another co-justiciar on Robert third earl of Leicester's death. From 1168, Richard de Lucy was Henry's sole justiciar in England.
100. John Beeler, *Warfare in Feudal Europe, 730–1200* (Cornell University Press, 1971), p. 105.
101. Hosler, p. 210.
102. Fantosme, p. 950.
103. Hosler, p. 147.
104. Beeler, p. 105.
105. Fantosme, pp. 100–9.
106. Ibid., pp. 110–20.
107. Roger of Howden, *Annals*, p. 377.
108. Warren, p. 134, cites Gervase of Canterbury, I, pp. 147–8; Ralph of Diceto, I, p. 381.
109. Warren, p. 127, notes that none of the chroniclers recorded Henry's secret trip; it is only seen in pipe roll 19, Henry II, 33. Warren also notes that Henry's ship the *Esnecca* travelled to England at least four times during the first year of the conflict, carrying valuables.
110. Turner, *Eleanor of Aquitaine*, p. 231.
111. Ibid.
112. Ibid., p. 232, cites Richard Barber, 'Eleanor of Aquitaine and the Media', in Catherine Léglu and Marcus Bull (eds), *The World of Eleanor of Aquitaine: Literature and Society in Southern France between the Eleventh and*

Thirteenth Centuries (Boydell Press, 2005), pp. 22–3.

113. Nicholas Vincent, 'The Great Lost Library of England's Medieval Kings? Royal Use and Ownership of Books, 1066–1300', in Kathleen Doyle and Scot McEndrick (eds), *1000 Years of Royal Books and Manuscripts* (University of Chicago Press, 2014), p. 5.

114. Ralph of Diceto, I, p. 308.

115. Gerald of Wales, *Conquest of Ireland*, p. 106, cited in Barbara Lynne McCauley, 'Giraldus "Silvester" of Wales and his "Prophetic History Of Ireland": Merlin's role in the *Expugnatio Hibernica*', *Quondam et Futurus*, vol. 3, no. 4 (Winter 1993), 41–62.

116. Martin Aurell, 'Henry II and Arthurian Legend', in Harper-Bill and Vincent (eds), p. 391.

117. Peter of Blois, letter of 1177 to Walter, archbishop of Palermo. See also Peter of Blois, imagining a conversation between Henry and the abbot of Bonneval, in Migne (ed.), CCVII, col. 975.

118. William of Newburgh, ed. Stevenson, p. 494.

119. Garnier of Pont-Sainte-Maxence, cited in Danny Danziger and John Gillingham, *1215: The Year of Magna Carta* (Hodder & Stoughton, 2003).

120. William of Newburgh, ed. Stevenson, p. 494.

121. Fantosme, p. 91.

122. William of Newburgh, ed. Stevenson, p. 494; Fantosme, p. 91.

123. William of Newburgh, ed. Stevenson, p. 494.

124. Fantosme, p. 93.

125. William of Newburgh, ed. Stevenson, p. 495.

126. Gerald of Wales, *On the Instruction of Princes*, p. 123.

127. Marie Lovatt, 'Geoffrey (1151?– 1212)', *Oxford Dictionary of National Biography* (OUP, 2004, online edn, October 2007), cites Gerald of Wales, *Opera*, IV, p. 368.

128. Jean Dunbabin, 'Henry II and Louis VII', in Harper-Bill and Vincent (eds), p. 61.

129. Gerald of Wales, *On the Instruction of Princes*, p. 123.

130. Warren, p. 138.

131. Ibid., p. 366, cites Roger of Howden, *Gesta Regis Henrici Secundi*, I, pp. 133–4.

132. William of Newburgh, ed. Stevenson, p. 499.

133. Gerald of Wales, *Opera*, VIII, p. 165.

134. Roger of Howden, *Chronica*, I, p. 216.

135. Warren, p. 136, cites *Dialogus de Scaccario* ('Dialogue Concerning the Exchequer'), p. 76.

136. Nicholas Vincent, 'The Court of Henry II', in Harper-Bill and Vincent (eds).

137. Ralph Niger, *Radulfi Nigri Chronica*, ed. R. Anstruther (Reprint, New York, 1967), II, p. 175.

138. Chris Given-Wilson and Alice Curteis, *The Royal Bastards of Medieval England* (Routledge & Kegan Paul, 1984), p. 100.

139. Map, p. 479.

140. David Crouch, 'Nest Bloet (d. 1224/5)', *Oxford Dictionary of National Biography* (OUP, 2004, online edn, January 2008).

141. Aurell, *Plantagenet Empire*, p. 137.

142. Turner, *Eleanor of Aquitaine*, p. 110.

143. *History of the King's Works*, I, p. 84.

144. Aurell, 'Henry II and Arthurian Legend', p. 375.

145. Nicholas Vincent, 'The pilgrimages of the Angevin kings of England 1154–1272', in Colin Morris and Peter Roberts (eds), *Pilgrimage: The English Experience from Becket to Bunyan* (CUP, 2002), p. 41.

146. Hugh's biographer, Adam of Eynsham, recorded that there existed huge affection between Hugh and Henry, so much so that some believed Hugh was Henry's son. It is unlikely.

147. Warren, p. 601, cites Gerald of Wales, *Opera*, I, pp. 256–7.

148. Turner, *Eleanor of Aquitaine*, p. 234.

149. Given-Wilson and Curteis, p. 100.

150. Turner, *Eleanor of Aquitaine*, p. 130, cites Joan M. Ferrante, 'Correspondent: "Blessed is the Speech of Your Mouth"', in Barbara Newman (ed.), *Voice of the Living Light: Hildegard of Bingen and Her World* (Berkeley, 1998), p. 94.

151. Michael R. Evans, *Inventing Eleanor: the Medieval and Post-Medieval Image of Eleanor of Aquitaine* (Bloomsbury, 2016), p. 50, cites F. Guizot, *The History of England from the Earliest Times to the Accession of Queen Victoria*, 2 vols (London, 1882), and J. Michelet, *Histoire de France*, 7 vols (Paris, 1833–42).

152. Ibid., p. 51, cites J. Michelet, *Satanism and Witchcraft: A Study in Medieval Superstition*, tr. A. R. Allison (New York, 1939).

153. Strickland, *Henry the Young King*, p. 206, cites Peter of Blois' record of the conversation, 'Dialogus inter regem Henricum secundem et abbatem Bonevallis', ed. R. B. C Huygens, *Revue Bénédictine*, vol. 68 (1958), 87–112.

154. Fantosme, II, pp. 21–2.

155. Strickland, 'On the Instruction of a Prince: The Upbringing of Henry, the Young King', cites Ralph of Diceto, I, p. 428.

156. Ibid.

157. Ibid., cites Roger of Howden, *Gesta Regis Henrici Secundi*, I, p. 114.

158. Roger of Howden, *Gesta Regis Henrici Secundi*, I, p. 177.

159. Strickland, *Henry the Young King*, p. 237.

160. Jim Bradbury, *Philip Augustus* (Bloomsbury, 1997), cites Roger of Howden, *Gesta Regis Henrici Secundi*, I, pp. 240–3.

161. Roger of Howden, *Annals*, I, pp. 516–17.

162. John Gillingham, 'The King and his Castle: How Henry II Rebuilt his Reputation', *BBC History Magazine*, March 2011.

163. Vincent, 'The Great Lost Library of England's Medieval Kings?'.

164. Warren, p. 609, cites Ralph of Diceto, I, pp. 438–9.

165. Bradbury, *Philip Augustus*, p. 39, cites Robert of Torigni.

166. Roger of Howden, *Gesta Regis Henrici Secundi*, I, p. 34.

167. Roger of Howden, *Annals*, I, p. 520.

168. Gerald of Wales, *On the Instruction of Princes*.

169. Strickland, *Henry the Young King*, p. 284, cites Ralph of Diceto, II, pp. 18–19.

170. For a full analysis see ibid., pp. 278–9.

171. Warren, p. 588, cites Roger of Howden, *Gesta Regis Henrici Secundi*, I, p. 292.

172. Ibid., p. 589, cites Roger of Howden, *Gesta Regis Henrici Secundi*, I, p. 292.

173. Strickland, *Henry the Young King*, p. 285, cites Roger of Howden, *Gesta Regis Henrici Secundi*, I, p. 294.

174. Warren, p. 592, cites Gerald of Wales, *Opera*, VIII, pp. 177–9.

175. *The Poems of the Troubadour Bertran de Born*, eds and trs William D. Padden, Tilde Sankovitch and Patricia H. Stäblein (California, 1986), p. 186.

176. Roger of Howden, *Annals*, II, p. 24.

177. Map, p. 283.

178. Strickland, *Henry the Young King*, p. 295, cites the *History of William Marshal*, II, pp. 6371–82.

179. Warren, p. 593.
180. Strickland, *Henry the Young King*, p. 300.
181. Roger of Howden, *Annals*, II, p. 26.
182. Strickland, *Henry the Young King*, p. 307.
183. Ibid., p. 310.
184. Gerald of Wales, *On the Instruction of Princes*, II, pp. 149–50.
185. Ibid., cites Roger of Howden, *Gesta Regis Henrici Secundi*, I, pp. 302–3.
186. Strickland, 'On the Instruction of a Prince: The Upbringing of Henry, the Young King', cites *History of William Marshal*, I, pp. 1956–8.
187. Strickland, *Henry the Young King*, p. 314, argues that Eleanor led the move, but it came to nothing.
188. Map, p. 281.
189. Warren, p. 580.
190. Alheydis Plassmann, 'The King and His Sons: Henry II's and Frederick Barbarossa's Succession Strategies Compared', Battle Conference 2013, no. 35.
191. Ibid., cites *Ottonis de Sancto Blasio Chronica*, ed. Adolf Hofmeister (MGH Scriptores rerum Germanicarum [47], 1912), chs. 21, 30, 31.
192. Ibid.
193. Gerald of Wales, *Conquest of Ireland*, pp. 131–3.
194. Bernard S. Bachrach, 'Henry II and the Angevin Tradition of Family Hostility', *Albion: A Quarterly Journal Concerned with British Studies*, vol. 16, no. 2 (Summer 1984), 111–30.
195. Turner, 'Eleanor of Aquitaine and her Children', p. 330.

Act V – Nemesis

1. Peter of Blois, *Epistolae*, no. 66, col. 197.
2. Gerald of Wales, *Opera*, eds J. S. Brewer, James F. Dimock and George F. Warner (CUP, 2012), VIII, pp. 292–3.
3. Jim Bradbury, *Philip Augustus* (Routledge, 1997), p. 2.
4. Ibid., p. 4.
5. Ibid., p. 3.
6. Ibid., p. 36.
7. *The Poems of the Troubadour Bertran de Born*, eds and trs William D. Padden, Tilde Sankovitch and Patricia H. Stäblein (California, 1986), p. 114.
8. Michael Clanchy, *England and its Rulers* (London, 1989), p. 115, cites *Anthology of Troubadour Lyric Poetry*, ed. A. R. Press (Edinburgh University Press, 1971), p. 163.
9. Bradbury, p. 47.
10. Ibid.
11. Bradbury cites Alexander Cartellieri, *Philipp II*, 2 vols (Leipzig, 1899–1921), I, p. 2.
12. Bradbury cites Robert of Torigni in William of Newburgh, *Historia rerum Anglicarum*, ed. R. Howlett (London, 1884–9), p. 127.
13. Bradbury cites 'Chronique du chanonie de Tours', in *Recueil des historiens des Gaules et de la France*, eds Léopold Delisle et al., 24 vols (Paris, 1869–1904), XVIII, p. 304.
14. Bradbury, p. 42.
15. Ibid.
16. Ibid., cites 'Historia regum Francorum', in Delisle et al. (eds), XVII, p. 425.
17. Bradbury cites Baldwin, p. 32; Delisle et al. (eds), I, no. 109, p. 137.
18. Gerald of Wales, *On the Instruction of Princes*, p. 217.
19. Bradbury, p. 167.
20. Ibid., p. 171.
21. Ephraim Ben Jacob of Bonn, in Marc Saperstein and Jacob Rader Marcus, *The Jews in Christian Europe: A Source Book, 315–1791* (University of Pittsburgh Press, 2015).
22. Jim Bradbury, *The Capetians* (Bloomsbury, 2007), p. 148.

23. Ibid., p. 171.
24. Maurice Druon, *The History of Paris, from Caesar to St Louis* (Hart-Davis, 1969), p. 75.
25. Bradbury, p. 69.
26. Ibid., cites Giselbert of Mons, pp. 152–4.
27. Ibid., p. 177, cites Rigord, *Œuvres de Rigord et de Guillaume le Breton, historiens de Philippe-Auguste*, ed. Henri-François Delaborde (Librairie Renouard, 1882), p. 24.
28. Ibid., cites J. W. Baldwin, *The Government of Philip Augustus* (University of California Press, 1986), p. 83.
29. Ibid., p. 179.
30. Martin Aurell, *The Plantagenet Empire 1154–1224*, tr. David Crouch (Routledge, 2007), p. 125. In *Chansons de geste*, an elm tree marked a border.
31. John Gillingham, 'Doing Homage to the King of France', in Christopher Harper-Bill and Nicholas Vincent (eds), *Henry II: New Interpretations* (Boydell Press, 2007). Gillingham argues that 1183 was the first time that Henry paid homage. He paid homage to Louis only once, for Normandy in 1151, before he was crowned king of England.
32. W. L. Warren, *Henry II* (University of California Press, 1973), cites *The Chronicle of Meaux* (Rolls Series, 1866–8), I, p. 256.
33. Gerald of Wales, *On the Instruction of Princes*, pp. 183–4.
34. Roger of Howden, *Gesta Regis Henrici Secundi*, ed. William Stubbs (Rolls Series, 1867), I, p. 159.
35. *The Poems of the Troubadour Bertran de Born*, p. 380.
36. Gerald of Wales, *On the Instruction of Princes*, pp. 183–4.
37. Roger of Howden, *Gesta Regis Henrici Secundi*, I, p. 308.
38. Gillingham, 'Doing Homage', p. 80.
39. Ibid.
40. Aurell, *Plantagenet Empire*, p. 265.
41. Roger of Howden, *Gesta Regis Henrici Secundi*, I, p. 306.
42. Ibid., I, p. 177.
43. Warren, p. 597.
44. Ralph V. Turner, *Eleanor of Aquitaine* (Yale University Press, 2009), p. 249, cites Roger of Howden, *Gesta Regis Henrici Secundi*, I, pp. 337–8.
45. *The Poems of the Troubadour Bertran de Born*, p. 342.
46. Ibid., p. 160.
47. Ibid., p. 164.
48. Turner, p. 249, cites Roger of Howden, *Gesta Regis Henrici Secundi*, I, pp. 337–8.
49. Warren, p. 604, cites Roger of Howden, *Gesta Regis Henrici Secundi*, I, p. 350.
50. Roger of Howden, *Annals*, II, p. 32.
51. Gerald of Wales, *On the Instruction of Princes*.
52. Gillingham, 'Doing Homage', p. 74.
53. Jonathan Phillips, *The Crusades: 1095–1204* (Pearson, 2002), p. 157.
54. *The Letters of John of Salisbury Vol. 2*, eds W. J. Millor, H. E. Butler and C. N. L. Brooke (Clarendon Press, 1979), no. 272, p. 569.
55. Nicholas Vincent, 'The pilgrimages of the Angevin kings of England 1154–1272', in Colin Morris and Peter Roberts (eds), *Pilgrimage: The English Experience from Becket to Bunyan* (CUP, 2002), p. 18.
56. Jonathan Phillips, *Holy Warriors: A Modern History of the Crusades* (Bodley Head, 2009), p. 112.
57. Hans Eberhard Mayer, 'Henry II of England and the Holy Land', *English Historical Review*, vol. 97, no. 385 (October 1982), 721–39.
58. The Knights Templar and the Knights Hospitaller were founded

in 1120 and c.1099 respectively, and emerged into organisations charged with the defence of the Holy Land for Christians.

59. Mayer cites Gerald of Wales, *Expugnatio Hibernica*, in *Opera*, eds J. S. Brewer et al. (Rolls Series 21, 1861–91), V, p. 304.

60. Mayer, p. 724.

61. Gerald of Wales, *On the Instruction of Princes*, III, pp. 295–6, cited in Aurell, *Plantagenet Empire*, pp. 86–8.

62. Warren, pp. 604–5, cites Ralph of Diceto, *Radulfi de Diceto Decani Lundoniensis Opera Historica*, ed. William Stubbs, 2 vols (Rolls Series, 1876), II, pp. 33–4.

63. Mayer cites Gerald of Wales, *Opera*, VIII, p. 208.

64. Ibid., p. 733.

65. During the early weeks of Heraclius's visit, he consecrated Temple Church in London.

66. Matthew Strickland, *Henry the Young King* (Yale University Press, 2016), p. 212.

67. Mayer, p. 733.

68. Martin Aurell, 'Henry II and Arthurian Legend', in Harper-Bill and Vincent (eds), p. 373.

69. Gerald of Wales, *The Conquest of Ireland*, eds and trs A. B. Scott and F. X. Martin (Dublin, 1978), pp. 77–8.

70. Roger of Howden, *Annals*, p. 56.

71. Warren, p. 599.

72. Ibid., p. 609.

73. Roger of Howden, *Gesta Regis Henrici Secundi*, I, pp. 343–4.

74. Gerald of Wales, *On the Instruction of Princes*, p. 151.

75. Ibid.

76. *The Poems of the Troubadour Bertran de Born*, p. 228.

77. Gerald of Wales, *On the Instruction of Princes*, p. 151.

78. Aurell, 'Henry II and Arthurian Legend', p. 387, cites William of Newburgh, ed. Howlett, I, pp. 14–18.

79. Warren, p. 614, cites Roger of Howden, *Gesta Regis Henrici Secundi*, I, p. 36.

80. Gervase of Canterbury, I, pp. 369–73.

81. Warren, p. 617, cites Gervase of Canterbury, I, pp. 370–1.

82. Ibid., cites Gerald of Wales, *Opera*, VIII, pp. 232–3.

83. Roger of Howden, *Gesta Regis Henrici Secundi*, II, p. 9.

84. Phillips, *Holy Warriors*, cites Ibn al-Athir, *Chronicles, Part 2*, pp. 315–16.

85. Ibid.

86. Sibylla's first husband, and her son Baldwin V's father, was William of Montferrat. He died before Baldwin was born.

87. John Gillingham, 'Love, Marriage and Politics in the Twelfth Century', in J. L. Nelson (ed.), *Richard Coeur de Lion in History and Myth, King's College Medieval Studies 7* (King's College London, 1992), p. 245, cites Roger of Howden, *Gesta Regis Henrici Secundi*, II, pp. 315–16.

88. Phillips, *The Crusades*, p. 132.

89. Phillips, *Holy Warriors*, cites Ibn al-Athir, *Chronicles, Part 2*, p. 321.

90. Ibid., cites 'Old French Continuation of William of Tyre', pp. 38–9.

91. Ibid., p. 126.

92. Ibid., cites Ibn al-Athir, tr. Gabriele, 1969: 119.

93. Phillips, *The Crusades*, cites Beha ad-Din, tr. Richards, 2001: 73.

94. Phillips, *Holy Warriors*, cites Ibn al-Athir, *Chronicles, Part 2*, p. 323.

95. Phillips, *The Crusades*, p. 134.

96. Ibid., p. 136. Guy was offered iced sherbert.

97. Mayer, p. 735.

98. John Gillingham, 'Richard I (1157–1199)', *Oxford Dictionary of National Biography* (OUP, 2004, online edn, October 2009).

99. Frederick Barbarossa also responded to the call to save the Latin Kingdom, and embarked on his second pilgrimage to Jerusalem, setting off in May 1189. He died however just over a year later, drowning in the River Göksu in Asia Minor on 10 June 1190, before he could reach his destination.

100. Mayer, p. 736.

101. Ibid., cites Gervase of Canterbury, I, p. 389.

102. Despite its unpopularity, William of Newburgh recorded that this was the first time Henry had imposed such a heavy tax on England or his continental possessions.

103. Warren, p. 619, cites Gervase of Canterbury, I, pp. 432–3.

104. John D. Hosler, *Henry II: A Medieval Soldier at War, 1147–1189* (Brill, 2007), p. 156.

105. Ibid.

106. Ibid.

107. Aurell, *Plantagenet Empire*, p. 125.

108. John Gillingham, 'War and Chivalry in the Middle Ages', in Nelson (ed.), p. 233, cites *L'Histoire de Guillaume le Maréchal*, lines 7782–852.

109. Warren, p. 620, cites Roger of Howden, *Gesta Regis Henrici Secundi*, II, p. 50.

110. Ibid., p. 620, cites Gervase of Canterbury, I, p. 435.

111. Ibid., p. 621, cites Gervase of Canterbury, I, p. 435.

112. Roger of Howden, *Annals*, I, p. 107.

113. Ibid.

114. Ibid.

115. Ibid., pp. 106–7.

116. Ibid.

117. Warren, p. 623.

118. John Gillingham, *Richard I* (Yale University Press, 2002), pp. 98–9, cites *L'Histoire de Guillaume le Maréchal*, lines 8831–50.

119. Gerald of Wales, *On the Instruction of Princes*, p. 215.

120. Tours was an exception; the city remained loyal to Henry, until Philip broke its defences by bringing in his siege engines. It fell on 3 July.

121. Warren, p. 625.

122. Roger of Howden, *Annals*, I, p. 109.

123. Warren, p. 626, cites Gerald of Wales, *Opera*, VIII, p. 296.

124. Marie Lovatt, 'Geoffrey (1151?–1212)', *Oxford Dictionary of National Biography* (OUP, 2004, online edn, October 2007).

125. One of Richard's first acts was to confirm his half-brother Geoffrey as archbishop of York.

126. Gerald of Wales, *On the Instruction of Princes*, VIII, p. 221.

127. Ibid., p. 297.

128. Ibid.

129. Gillingham, *Richard I*, p. 99.

130. Roger of Howden, *Annals*, I, p. 111.

131. Ibid.

132. Roger of Howden, *Chronica*, ed. William Stubbs (Rolls Series, 1868–71), II, p. 366.

133. As far as Henry was concerned, William Marshal was forever asking him for money. In 1188, in exchange for his military service, Henry promised him a wealthy honour, dictating to the scribe, 'you have ever so often moaned to me that I have bestowed on you a small fee'. See Strickland, p. 128; Nicholas Vincent, 'William Marshal, King Henry II and the Honour of Chateauroux', in *Archives*, 35 (2000), 1–15.

134. Turner, p. 254.

135. Gerald of Wales, *The Conquest of Ireland*, p. 133.

Epilogue

1. Karl Leyser, 'Frederick Barbarossa, Henry II and the Hand of St James', *English Historical Review*, vol. 90, no. 456 (1975), 481–506.

2. Ralph V. Turner, *Eleanor of Aquitaine* (Yale University Press, 2009), p. 258, cites Ralph of Diceto, *Radulfi de Diceto Decani Lundoniensis Opera Historica*, ed. William Stubbs, 2 vols (Rolls Series, 1876), II, p. 67.

3. Jane Martindale, 'Eleanor of Aquitaine', in J. L. Nelson (ed.), *Richard Coeur de Lion in History and Myth, King's College Medieval Studies 7* (King's College London, 1992), p. 49, cites *The Chronicle of Richard of Devizes*, ed. John. T. Appleby (Thomas Nelson & Sons, 1963), p. 59.

4. Martindale, p. 49.

5. Edmund King, *England 1175–1425* (Routledge & Kegan Paul, 1979), p. 69.

6. *The Chronicle of Richard of Devizes*, p. 25.

7. Turner, p. 277.

8. Ibid., p. 278. Eleanor also remembered Henry, young Henri, Geoffrey and Matilda of Saxony in this grant, as was fitting.

9. Ibid., p. 280, cites Anne Crawford (ed.), *Letters of the Queens of England* (The History Press, 2002), p. 40.

10. Michael Jones, 'Arthur, duke of Brittany (1187–1203)', *Oxford Dictionary of National Biography* (OUP, 2004), cites A. Teulet et al. (eds), *Layettes du trésor des chartes*, 5 vols (Paris, 1863–1909), I, p. 647.

11. Ibid., cites the Margam annals and the *Phlippidos* of Guillaume le Breton.

12. Turner, p. 29.

13. D. A. Carpenter, *The Minority of Henry III* (University of California Press, 1990), p. 9, cites Sir James Holt, *The Northerners: A Study in the Reign of King John* (OUP, 1992), p. 100.

14. John Gillingham, 'Magna Carta and Royal Government', in Nelson (ed.), p. 206, cites the troubadour Bertran de Born the younger.

15. When Henry III signed the Treaty of Paris in 1258, he acknowledged the loss of most of England's possessions in France.

16. Martindale refers to a charter of Eleanor's confirming an annual grant of £100 to the nuns of Fontevraud, made soon after Richard's death.

17. Lindy Grant, 'Aspects of the Architectural Patronage of the Family of the Counts of Anjou in the Twelfth Century', in John McNeill and Daniel Prigent (eds), *Anjou: Medieval Art, Architecture and Archaeology* (Maney Publications, 2003), p. 102. Today, Eleanor's effigy is next to Henry's. Fontevraud was sacked during the French Revolution and the tombs were moved from the choir, and later placed in the nave.

BIBLIOGRAPHY

Primary Sources
Adam of Eynsham, *Magna Vita Sancti Hugonis*, eds C. N. L. Brooke, D.
    Greenway and M. Winterbottom (Oxford, 1985)
The Anglo-Saxon Chronicle, in *The Church Historians of England*, tr. Joseph
    Stevenson, 5 vols (London, 1853–8)
The Life of St Anselm, ed. and tr. R. W. Southern (London, 1962)
Arnulf of Lisieux, *The Letters of Arnulf of Lisieux*, ed. Frank Barlow (London,
    1939)
Becket, Thomas, *The Correspondence of Thomas Becket*, ed. and tr. Anne
    Duggan, 2 vols (Oxford, 2000)
Becket, Thomas, *Materials for the History of Thomas Becket*, eds J. C.
    Robertson and J. B. Sheppard (Rolls Series, 1875–85)
Bernard of Clairvaux, *St Bernard of Clairvaux: The Story of his life as recorded
    in the Vita Prima Bernardi by certain of his contemporaries, William of St
    Thierry, Arnold of Bonnevaux, Geoffrey and Philip of Clairvaux, and Odo of
    Deuil*, tr. Geoffrey Webb and Adrian Walker (London, 1960)
Bernard of Clairvaux, *The Letters of Saint Bernard of Clairvaux*, tr. Bruno Scott
    James (London, 1953)
Bertran de Born, *The Poems of the Troubadour Bertran de Born*, eds and trs
    William D. Padden, Tilde Sankovitch and Patricia H. Stäblein (Berkeley, 1986)
The Brut, or the Chronicles of England, ed. F. W. D. Brie, 2 vols (London, 1906–8)
Catalogue des actes de Philippe Auguste, ed. Léopold Delisle (Paris, 1856)
Chrétien de Troyes: *Arthurian Romances*, tr. D. D. R. Owen (London, 1987)
The Chronicle of Battle Abbey, ed. Eleanor Searle (Oxford, 1980)
The Chronicle of Ernoul and the Continuations of William of Tyre, ed. M. R.
    Morgan (Oxford, 1973)
The Chronicle of Meaux, ed. E. A. Bond, 3 vols (Rolls Series, 1866–8)
Chronicles of the Reigns of Stephen, Henry II, and Richard I, ed. Richard
    Howlett (Rolls Series, 1885–90)
Eadmer's History of Recent Events in England: Historia Novorum in Anglia, tr.
    Geoffrey Bosanquet (London, 1964)
Etienne de Rouen, *Draco Normannicus*, ed. R. Howlett, in *Chronicles of the
    Reigns of Stephen, Henry II, and Richard I*, 4 vols (Rolls Series, 1884–9)
Eyton, R. W., *Court, Household, and Itinerary of King Henry II* (London, 1878)
FitzNigel, Richard, *Diologus de Scaccario*, eds C. Johnson, F. E. L. Carter and
    D. E. Greenway (Oxford, 1983)

Bibliography

FitzStephen, William, *A Description of London*, tr. H. E. Butler, Historical Association Pamphlets 93 and 94 (1934)

FitzStephen, William, 'The Life of Thomas Becket', in G. W. Greenaway (ed. and tr.), *The Life and Death of Thomas Becket, Chancellor of England and Archbishop of Canterbury* (London, 1961)

FitzStephen, William, *Materials for a History of Becket*, ed. J. C. Robertson (Rolls Series, 1875–85)

Foliot, Gilbert, *The Letters and Charters of Gilbert Foliot*, eds Z. N. Brooke, A. Morey and C. N. L. Brooke (London, 1967)

Historia Gaufredi ducis Normannorum et comitis Andegavorum, in *Chronique des comtes d'Anjou et des Seigneurs d'Amboise*, eds L. Halphen and R. Poupardin (Paris, 1913)

Geoffrey of Monmouth, *Historia regum Britanniae: The History of the Kings of Britain*, eds and trs A. Griscom and R. E. Jones (New York, 1929)

Geoffrey de Vigeois, *Chronica Gaufredi Coenobitae Monasterii S. Martialis Lemovicensis ac Prioris Vosciensis Coenobbi: La Chronique de Geoffre, prieur de Vigeois*, in *Recueil des historiens des Gaules et de la France*, eds Léopold Delisle et al., 24 vols (Paris, 1738–1904)

Gerald of Wales, *The Autobiography of Giraldus Cambrensis*, ed. and tr. H. E. Butler (London, 1937)

Gerald of Wales, *The Conquest of Ireland*, eds and trs A. B. Scott and F. X. Martin (Dublin, 1971)

Gerald of Wales, *Giraldus Cambrensis Concerning the Instruction of Princes*, in *The Church Historians of England*, tr. Joseph Stevenson, 5 vols (London, 1853–8)

Gerald of Wales, *Giraldi Cambrensis Opera*, eds J. S. Brewer, James F. Dimock and George F. Warner, 8 vols (Rolls Series 21, 1861–91)

Gerald of Wales, *The Historical Works of Giraldus Cambrensis: Containing the Topography of Ireland and the History of the Conquest of Ireland*, tr. Thomas Forester (London, 1863).

Gerald of Wales, *The Itinerary through Wales and the Description of Wales*, tr. R. C. Hoare, ed. T. Wright (London, 1887)

Gerald of Wales, *De Principis Instructione Liber*, in G. F. Warner (ed.), *Giraldi Cambrensis Opera*, vol. 8 (Rolls Series 21, 1861–91)

Gervase of Canterbury, *The Historical Works of Gervase of Canterbury*, ed. William Stubbs (London, 1879–80)

Gervase of Canterbury, *The History of the Archbishops of Canterbury by Gervase, Monk of Canterbury*, in *The Church Historians of England*, tr. Joseph Stevenson, 5 vols (London, 1853–8)

Gesta Regis Henrici Secundi Benedicti Abbatis, The Chronicle of the Reigns of Henry II and Richard I, known commonly under the name of Benedict of Peterborough, ed. W. Stubbs, 2 vols (Rolls Series, 1867)

Gesta Stephani, eds K. R. Potter and R. H. C. Davis (Oxford, 1976)

The Treatise on the Laws and Customs of the Realm of England, Commonly Called Glanvill, edited with introduction, notes and translation by G. D. G. Hall, with 'A Guide to Further Reading' by M. T. Clanchy (Oxford, 1993)

The Great Rolls of the Pipe (Pipe Roll Society, 1884–)

The Great Rolls of the Pipe for the First Year of the Reign of King Henry II, in *The Red Book of the Exchequer*, vol. 2, ed. H. Hall, 3 vols (Rolls Series, 1896)

The Great Rolls of the Pipe for the Second, Third and Fourth Years of the Reign of King Henry II, 1155–1158, ed. J. Hunter (London, 1844)

The Great Rolls of the Pipe of the Reign of Henry the Second, 5th–34th Years, 30 vols (Pipe Roll Society, 1884–1925)

The Great Roll of the Pipe for the Thirty-Third Year of the Reign of King Henry the Second, AD 1186–7, ed. J. H. Round (Pipe Roll Society, London, 1915)

History of King Henry the First, in *The Church Historians of England*, tr. Joseph Stevenson, 5 vols (London, 1853–8)

Henry of Huntingdon, *The Chronicle of Henry of Huntingdon: The History of England, From the Invasion of Julius Caesar to the Accession of Henry II*, ed. and tr. Thomas Forester (London, 1853)

Henry of Huntingdon, *Historia Anglorum*, ed. and tr. Diana Greenway (Oxford, 1996)

Ingulph's Chronicle of the Abbey of Croyland: with the Continuations by Peter of Blois and Anonymous Writers, tr. H. T. Riley (London, 1908)

The Jews of Angevin England: Documents and Records: from Latin and Hebrew Sources, Printed and Manuscripts, for the First Time Collected and Translated, ed. Joseph Jacobs (London, 1993)

Jocelin of Brakelond, *The Chronicle of Jocelin of Brakelond*, ed. Sir Ernest Clarke (London, 1903)

The Chronicles of John and Richard of Hexham, in *The Church Historians of England*, tr. Joseph Stevenson, 5 vols (London, 1853–8)

John of Salisbury, *Historia Pontificalis*, ed. Marjorie Chibnall (Nelson, 1956)

John of Salisbury, *The Letters of John of Salisbury Vol. 1: The Early Letters (1153–1161)*, eds W. J. Millor and H. E. Butler, revised C. N. L Brooke (Oxford, 1955)

John of Salisbury, *The Letters of John of Salisbury Vol. 2: The Later Letters (1163–1180)*, eds W. J. Millor and C. N. L. Brooke (Oxford, 1979)

John of Salisbury, *The Metalogicon*, ed. and tr. Daniel D. McGary (Berkeley, 1955)

John of Salisbury, *Policraticus*, ed. and tr. Cory J. Nedeman (Cambridge, 1990)

John of Worcester, *The Chronicle of John of Worcester, 1118–1140*, ed. J. R. H. Weaver (Oxford, 1908)

Jordan Fantosme, *Chronicle*, in *Chronicle of the Reigns of Stephen, Henry II and Richard I*, ed. Richard Howlett (Rolls Series, 1890)

Jordan Fantosme, *Jordan Fantosme's Chronicle*, ed. and tr. R. C. Johnston (Oxford, 1981)

Marshal, William, *L'Histoire de Guillaume le Maréchal*, ed. P. Meyer, 3 vols (Paris, 1891–1901)

Marshal, William, *History of William Marshal, Vol. 1*, eds A. J. Holden, S. Gregory and D. Crouch (London, 2002)

Orderic Vitalis, *The Ecclesiastical History*, ed. Marjorie Chibnall (Oxford, 1969–80)

Peter of Blois, *The Later Letters of Peter of Blois*, ed. E. Revell (Oxford, 1993)

Peter of Blois, *Petri Blensis Archidiaconi Opera Omnia*, ed. J. A. Giles, 4 vols (Oxford, 1846–7)

Pierre de Langtoft, *The Chronicle of Pierre de Langtoft*, ed. T. Wright (London, 1866–8)

Pipe Rolls of the Exchequer of Normandy: for the Reign of Henry II, 1180 and 1184: Printed from the Originals in the National Archives, ed. V. Moss (London, 2004)

Ralph of Diceto, *Radulfi De Diceto decani Lundoniensis Opera Historica: the Historical Works of Master Ralph de Diceto, Dean of London*, ed. W. Stubbs, 2 vols (Rolls Series, 1876)

Bibliography

Ralph Niger, *Radulfi Nigri Chronica: The Chronicles of Ralph Niger*, ed. Robert Anstruther, in *Publications for the Members of the Caxton Society* (Reprint, New York, 1967)

Recueil des Actes de Henry II, Roi d'Angleterre et Duc de Normandie, eds L. Delisle and E. Berger, 4 vols (Paris, 1909–27)

The Red Book of the Exchequer, ed. H. Hall (London, 1896)

Richard of Devizes, *The Chronicle of Richard of Devizes*, ed. John T. Appleby (London, 1963)

Richard of Devizes, *Richard of Devizes*, in *The Church Historians of England*, tr. Joseph Stevenson, 5 vols (London, 1853–8)

Richard le Poitevin, *Ex Chronico*, in *Recueil des historiens des Gaules et de la France*, eds Léopold Delisle et al., 24 vols (Paris, 1738–1904)

Robert of Torigni, *Chronicle*, in *Chronicle of the Reigns of Stephen, Henry II and Richard I*, ed. Richard Howlett (Rolls Series, 1890)

Roger of Howden, *The Annals of Roger of Hoveden, Comprising the History of England and of Other Countries of Europe from A. D. 732 to A. D. 1201*, ed. and tr. Henry T. Riley, 2 vols (London, 1853)

Roger of Howden, *Chronica Magistri Rogeri de Houedene*, ed. William Stubbs (Rolls Series, 1868–71)

The Acts of Stephen, King of England, and Duke of Normandy, in *The Church Historians of England*, tr. Joseph Stevenson, 5 vols (London, 1853–8)

Abbot Suger, *Vie de Louis VI le Gros par Suger, suivie de l'histoire du roi Louis VII: Historia Ludovici VII*, ed. A. Molinier (Paris, 1887)

Wace, *The History of the Norman People: Wace's Roman de Rou*, tr. G. S. Burgess (Woodbridge, 2004)

Wace, *Le Roman de Brut de Wace*, ed. Ivor Arnold (Paris, 1938–40)

Walter Map, *De Nugis Curialium: Courtiers' Trifles*, eds M. R. James, C. N. L. Brooke and R. A. B. Mynors (Oxford, 1983)

The Gesta Normanorum Ducum of William of Jumièges, Orderic Vitalis, and Robert of Torigni, ed. and tr. E. M. C. Van Houts, 2 vols (Oxford, 1992–5)

William of Malmesbury, *Historia Novella*, ed. K. R. Potter (London, 1955)

William of Malmesbury, *The History of the Kings of England, and of his Own Times*, in *The Church Historians of England*, tr. Joseph Stevenson, 5 vols (London, 1853–8)

William of Newburgh, *Historia Rerum Anglicarum*, in *Chronicles of the Reigns of Stephen, Henry II, and Richard I*, vols I–II, ed. Richard Howlett (Rolls Series, 1885)

William of Newburgh, *The History of English Affairs*, eds and trs P. G. Walsh and M. J. Kennedy, 2 vols (Oxford, 1988–2001)

The History of William of Newburgh, in *The Church Historians of England*, tr. Joseph Stevenson, 5 vols (London, 1853–8)

Secondary Sources
Amt, Emilie, *The Accession of Henry II in England: Royal Government Restored 1149–1159* (Woodbridge, 1993)

Amt, Emilie, 'The Meaning of Waste in the Early Pipe Rolls of Henry II', *Economic History Review*, vol. 44 (2) (1991)

Aurell, Martin, 'Aliénor d'Aquitaine (1124–1204) et ses historiens: la destruction d'un mythe?', in J. Paviot and J. Verger (eds), *guerre, pouvoir et noblesse au Moyen Âge. Mélanges en l'honneur de Philippe Contamine* (Paris, 2003)

Aurell, Martin, 'Henry II and Arthurian Legend', in Christopher Harper-Bill and Nicholas Vincent (eds), *Henry II: New Interpretations* (Woodbridge, 2007)

Aurell, Martin, *The Plantagenet Empire 1154–1224*, tr. David Crouch (London, 2007)

Bachrach, Bernard S., 'Henry II and the Angevin Tradition of Family Hostility', *Albion*, vol. 16 (1 July 1984)

Baldwin, John W., *Masters, Princes and Merchants: The Social Views of Peter the Chanter and his Circle*, 2 vols (Princeton, 1970)

Barber, Richard, 'Eleanor of Aquitaine and the Media', in Catherine Léglu and Marcus Bull (eds), *The World of Eleanor of Aquitaine: Literature and Society in Southern France between the Eleventh and Thirteenth Centuries* (Woodbridge, 2005)

Barber, Richard, *King Arthur, Hero and Legend* (Woodbridge, 1986)

Barlow, Frank, 'Roger of Howden', *English Historical Review*, vol. 65 (1 July 1950)

Barlow, Frank, 'Roger de Pont l'Évêque (c.1115–1181)', *Oxford Dictionary of National Biography* (Oxford, 2004)

Barlow, Frank, 'Thomas Becket (1120?–1170)', *Oxford Dictionary of National Biography* (Oxford, 2004)

Barqây, Ron, *A History of Jewish Gynaecological Texts in the Middle Ages* (Leiden, 1998)

Barrett, Nick, 'Finance and the Economy in the Reign of Henry II', in Christopher Harper-Bill and Nicholas Vincent (eds), *Henry II: New Interpretations* (Woodbridge, 2007)

Bartlett, Robert, *England under The Norman and Angevin Kings, 1075–1225* (Oxford, 2003)

Bartlett, Robert, *Gerald of Wales, 1146–1223* (Oxford, 1982)

Bartlett, Robert, *Gerald of Wales: A Voice of the Middle Ages* (Stroud, 2006)

Bates, David, *The Normans and Empire: the Ford Lectures Delivered in the University of Oxford during Hilary Term 2010* (Oxford, 2013)

Beech, George, 'The Eleanor of Aquitaine Vase', in Bonnie Wheeler and John C. Parsons (eds), *Eleanor of Aquitaine: Lord and Lady* (London, 2002)

Beeler, John, *Warfare in England 1066–1189* (New York, 1966)

Beeler, John, *Warfare in Feudal Europe, 730–1200* (Ithaca, 1971)

Bell, David, *A Saint in the Sun: Praising St Bernard in the France of Louis XIV* (Collegeville, 2017)

Benham, J. E. M., 'Anglo-French Peace Conferences in the Twelfth Century', in Marjorie Chibnall, Christopher Harper-Bill, John Gillingham, C. P. Lewis, David Bates and Elisabeth Van Houts (eds), *Proceedings of the Battle Conference on Anglo-Norman Studies* (XXVII) (Woodbridge, 1978–)

Biancalana, Joseph, 'For Want of Justice: Legal Reforms of Henry II', *Columbia Law Review*, vol. 88, no. 3 (1988)

Bigelow, Melville Madison, *Placita Anglo-Normannica: Law Cases from William I to Richard I Preserved in Historical Records [1066–1195]* (London, 1879)

Blomme, Yves, *Anjou Gothique* (Paris, 1998)

Boorman, Julia, '*Nisi feceris* under Henry II', in Marjorie Chibnall, Christopher Harper-Bill, John Gillingham, C. P. Lewis, David Bates and Elisabeth Van Houts (eds), *Proceedings of the Battle Conference on Anglo-Norman Studies* (XXIV) (Woodbridge, 1978–)

Bradbury, Jim, *The Capetians: Kings of France, 987–1328* (London, 2007)

Bradbury, Jim, 'Geoffrey V of Anjou, Count and Knight', in C. Harper-Bill and R. Harvey (eds), *The Ideals and Practice of Medieval Knighthood III* (Woodbridge, 1990)

Bradbury, Jim, *The Medieval Siege* (Woodbridge, 1992)

Bradbury, Jim, *Philip Augustus: King of France 1180–1223* (London, 1998)

Bradbury, Jim, *Stephen and Matilda: The Civil War of 1139–53* (Stroud, 1996)

Brand, Paul, 'Henry II and the Creation of the English Common Law', in Christopher Harper-Bill and Nicholas Vincent (eds), *Henry II: New Interpretations* (Woodbridge, 2007)

Brand, Paul, *The Making of the Common Law* (London, 1992)

Brand, Paul, and Joshua Getzler (eds), *Judges and Judging in the History of the Common Law and Civil Law: From Antiquity to Modern Times* (Cambridge, 2012)

Brett, Martin, and David A. Woodman (eds), *The Long Twelfth-Century View of the Anglo-Saxon Past* (Ashgate, 2015)

Brittain Bouchard, Constance, 'Eleanor's Divorce from Louis VII: The Uses of Consanguinity', in Bonnie Wheeler and John C. Parsons (eds), *Eleanor of Aquitaine: Lord and Lady* (London, 2002)

Brooke, Christopher, *The Twelfth Century Renaissance* (London, 1969)

Brooke, Z. N. and C. N. L. Brooke, 'Henry II, Duke of Normandy', *English Historical Review*, vol. 61 (1946)

Brown, Elizabeth A. R., 'Eleanor of Aquitaine, Parent, Queen and Duchess', in William Kibler (ed.), *Eleanor of Aquitaine: Patron and Politician* (London, 1976)

Brown, Elizabeth A. R., 'Eleanor of Aquitaine Reconsidered: The Woman and her Seasons', in Bonnie Wheeler and John C. Parsons (eds), *Eleanor of Aquitaine: Lord and Lady* (London, 2002)

Brundage, James, 'The Canon Law of Divorce in the Mid-Twelfth Century: Louis VII c. Eleanor of Aquitaine', in Bonnie Wheeler and John C. Parsons (eds), *Eleanor of Aquitaine: Lord and Lady* (London, 2002)

Bull, Marcus, 'Criticism of Henry II's Expedition to Ireland in William of Canterbury's Miracles of St Thomas Becket', *Journal of Medieval History*, vol. 33 (1 June 2007)

Bullón-Fernández, María, *England and Iberia in the Middle Ages Twelfth–Fifteenth Centuries: Cultural, Literary, and Political Exchanges* (New York, 2007)

Bullough, D. A. and R. L. Storey (eds), *The Study of Medieval Records: Essays in Honour of Kathleen Major* (Oxford, 1971)

Burgess, Glyn S., *The Lais of Marie de France: Text and Context* (Manchester, 1987)

Burnett, Charles, 'Bath, Adelard of (*b.* in or before 1080?, *d.* in or after 1150)', *Oxford Dictionary of National Biography* (Oxford, 2004)

Burnett, Charles, *The Introduction of Arabic Learning into England* (London, 1997)

Carpenter, D. A., 'Abbot Ralph of Coggeshall's Account of the Last Years of King Richard and the First Years of King John', *English Historical Review*, vol. 113 (November 1998)

Carpenter, D. A., *The Minority of Henry III* (London, 1990)

Caviness, Madeline, 'Anchoress, Abbess, and Queen: Donors and Patrons or Intercessors and Matrons?', in J. H. McCash (ed), *The Cultural Patronage of Medieval Women* (Atlanta, 1996)

Cazel, Fred A., 'The Tax of 1185 in Aid of the Holy Land', *Speculum*, vol. 30 (1 July 1955)

Chandler, Victoria, 'The Wreck of the White Ship: A Mass Murder Revealed?', in D. J. Kagay and L. J. Andrew Villalon (eds), *The Final Argument: The*

Imprint of Violence on Society in Medieval and Early Modern Europe (Woodbridge, 1998)

Chartrou, Josèph, *L'Anjou de 1109 à 1151, Folque de Jérusalem et Geoffroi Plantagenêt* (Paris, 1928)

Cheney, Mary, 'The Compromise of Avranches of 1172 and the Spread of Canon Law in England', *English Historical Review*, vol. 56 (1 April 1941)

Chibnall, Marjorie, *The Ecclesiastical History of Orderic Vitalis* (Oxford, 1969–80)

Chibnall, Marjorie, *The Empress Matilda: Queen Consort, Queen Mother and Lady of the English* (Oxford, 1991)

Chibnall, Marjorie, *The Normans* (Oxford, 2000)

Chibnall, Marjorie, *The World of Orderic Vitalis* (Oxford, 1984)

Church, S. D. (ed.), *King John: New Interpretations* (Woodbridge, 1999)

Clanchy, Michael, *England and its Rulers 1066–1272: Foreign Lordship and National Identity* (London, 1989)

Clanchy, M. T., *From Memory to Written Record* (London, 1979)

Clapham, A. W., *English Romanesque Architecture after the Conquest* (Oxford, 1934)

Cohen, Jeffrey Jerome (ed.), *Cultural Diversity in the British Middle Ages: Archipelago, Island, England* (London, 2008)

Colvin, Howard (general ed.), *The History of the King's Works*, vol. 1 (London, 1963–82)

Cotts, John D., 'Peter of Blois and the Problem of the "Court"', in Marjorie Chibnall, Christopher Harper-Bill, John Gillingham, C. P. Lewis, David Bates and Elisabeth Van Houts (eds), *Proceedings of the Battle Conference on Anglo-Norman Studies* (XXVII) (Woodbridge, 1978–)

Crouch, David, *The Birth of Nobility: Constructing Aristocracy in England and France, 900–1300* (London, 2005)

Crouch, David, *The English Aristocracy, 1070–1272: A Social Transformation* (New Haven, 2011)

Crouch, David, *The Reign of King Stephen 1135–1154* (London, 2000)

Crouch, David, *William Marshal: Court, Career and Chivalry in the Angevin Empire, 1147–1219* (London, 1990)

D'Avray, David, *Dissolving Royal Marriages: A Documentary History, 860–1660* (Cambridge, 2014)

Dalton, Paul, and David Luscombe, *Rulership and Rebellion in the Anglo-Norman World, c.1066–c.1216: Essays in Honour of Professor Edmund King* (Ashgate, 2015)

Dalton, P, and White, G. J. (eds), *King Stephen's Reign (1135–1154)* (Woodbridge, 2008)

Danziger, Danny, and John Gillingham, *1215: The Year of Magna Carta* (London, 2003)

Davidson, Roberta, 'The "Reel" Arthur: Politics and Truth Claims in Camelot, Excalibur, and King Arthur', *Arthuriana*, vol. 17 (1 July 2007)

Davies, R. R., *The First English Empire: Power and Identities in the British Isles, 1093–1343* (Oxford, 2000)

Davis, H. W. C., C. Johnson and H. A. Cronne (eds), *Regesta Regum Anglo-Normannorum: 1066–1154*, 1 (Oxford, 1913–70)

De Hauvilla, Johannes, *Architrenius*, ed. and tr. Winthorp Wetherbee (Cambridge, 1994)

Diggelmann, Lindsay, 'Marriage as Tactical Response: Henry II and the Royal Wedding of 1160', *English Historical Review*, vol. 119 (2004)

Doyle, Kathleen, and Scot McKendrick (eds), *1000 Years of Royal Books and Manuscripts* (London, 2013)

Dronke, Peter, 'Peter of Blois and Poetry at the Court of Henry II', *Medieval Studies*, 38 (1976)

Druon, M., *The History of Paris, from Caesar to St Louis* (London, 1969)

Duby, Georges, *France in the Middle Ages 987–1460* (Oxford, 1991)

Duffy, Seán, 'Henry II and England's Insular Neighbours', in Christopher Harper-Bill and Nicholas Vincent (eds), *Henry II: New Interpretations* (Woodbridge, 2007)

Duggan, Anne J, 'Henry II, the English Church and the Papacy, 1154–76', in Christopher Harper-Bill and Nicholas Vincent (eds), *Henry II: New Interpretations* (Woodbridge, 2007)

Duggan, Anne '*Ne in dubium*: The Official Record of Henry II's Reconciliation at Avranches, 21 May, 1172', *English Historical Review*, vol. 115, no. 462 (2000)

Duggan, Anne, *Thomas Becket* (London, 2004)

Dunbabin, Jean, *France in the Making: 843–1180* (Oxford, 1985)

Dunbabin, Jean, 'Henry II and Louis VII', in Christopher Harper-Bill and Nicholas Vincent (eds), *Henry II: New Interpretations* (Woodbridge, 2007)

Dutton, Kathryn, '*Ad Erudiendum Tradidit*: The Upbringing of Angevin Comital Children', in Marjorie Chibnall, Christopher Harper-Bill, John Gillingham, C. P. Lewis, David Bates and Elisabeth Van Houts (eds), *Proceedings of the Battle Conference on Anglo-Norman Studies* (XXXII) (Woodbridge, 1978–)

Dutton, Kathryn, 'Geoffrey, Count of Anjou and Duke of Normandy, 1129–51', unpublished PhD thesis (University of Glasgow, 2011)

Earenfight, Theresa (2009) *The King's Other Body: Maria of Castile and the Crown of Aragon* (Pittsburgh, 2010)

Evans, Michael, *Inventing Eleanor: The Medieval and Post-Medieval Image of Eleanor of Aquitaine* (London, 2014)

Evergates, T. (ed.), *Aristocratic Women in Medieval France* (Philadelphia, 1999)

Facinger, Marion, 'A Study of Medieval Queenship: Capetian France (987–1237)', in W. M. Bowsky (ed.), *Studies in Medieval and Renaissance History, Vol. 5* (Lincoln, Nebr., 1968)

Fawtier, Robert, *The Capetian Kings of France: Monarchy and Nation, 987–1328*, trs Lionel Butler and R. J. Adam (London, 1960)

Finke, L. A. and M. B. Schichtman, *Cinematic Illuminations: The Middle Ages on Film* (Baltimore, 2010)

Flori, Jean, *Eleanor of Aquitaine: Queen and Rebel* (Edinburgh, 2007)

Gameson, Richard, and Henrietta Leyser (eds), *Belief and Culture in the Middle Ages: Studies Presented to Henry Mayr-Harting* (Oxford, 2001)

Ganshof, F. L., *Feudalism*, tr. Philip Grierson (London, 1952)

Gibbon, E., *The History of the Decline and Fall of the Roman Empire*, ed. F. Fernandez-Armesto, 8 vols (London, 1989)

Gillingham, John, *The Angevin Empire* (Oxford, 2001)

Gillingham, John, 'Conquering Kings: Some Twelfth Century Reflections on Henry II and Richard I', in *The English in the Twelfth Century: Imperialism, National Identity and Political Values* (Woodbridge, 2000)

Gillingham, John, 'The Cultivation of History, Legend, and Courtesy at the Court of Henry II', in Ruth Kennedy and Simon Meecham-Jones (eds), *Writers of the Reign of Henry II: Twelve Essays* (London, 2006)

Gillingham, John, 'Doing Homage to the King of France', in Christopher Harper-Bill and Nicholas Vincent (eds), *Henry II: New Interpretations* (Woodbridge, 2007)

Gillingham, John, *The English in the Twelfth Century: Imperialism, National Identity and Political Values* (Woodbridge, 2000)

Gillingham, John, 'The Historian as Judge: William of Newburgh and Hubert Walter', *English Historical Review*, vol. 119 (2004)

Gillingham, John, 'The King and his Castle: How Henry II Rebuilt his Reputation', *BBC History Magazine* (March 2011).

Gillingham, John, 'The Meetings of the Kings of France and England 1066–1204', in D. Crouch and K. Thompson (eds), *Normandy and its Neighbours 900–1250* (Brepols, 2011)

Gillingham, John, *Richard Coeur de Lion: Kingship, Chivalry and War in the Twelfth Century* (London, 1994)

Gillingham, John, *Richard I* (New Haven, 1999)

Given-Wilson, Chris, and Alice Curteis, *The Royal Bastards of Medieval England* (London, 1984)

Goodall, John, *The English Castle, 1066–1650* (New Haven, 2011)

Grant, Lindy, *Architecture and Society in Normandy c.1120–c.1270* (New Haven, 2005)

Grant, Lindy, 'Le patronage architectural d'Henri II et de son entourage', *Cahiers de civilisation médiévale. 37e année (n° 145–146)* (January–June 1994)

Green, Judith, *The Aristocracy of Norman England* (Cambridge, 1997)

Green, Judith, *Henry I: King of England and Duke of Normandy* (Cambridge, 2006)

Harper-Bill, C., and R. Harvey (eds), *The Ideals and Practice of Medieval Knighthood III: Papers from the Fourth Strawberry Hill Conference 1988* (London, 1990)

Harper-Bill, Christopher, and Nicholas Vincent (eds), *Henry II: New Interpretations* (Woodbridge, 2007)

Haseldine, Julian, 'Thomas Becket: Martyr, Saint – and Friend?', *Belief and Culture in the Middle Ages: Studies Presented to Henry Mayr-Harting* (Oxford, 2001)

Haskins, Charles H., 'Adelard of Bath and Henry Plantagenet', *English Historical Review*, vol. 28 (1913)

Haskins, Charles H., 'England and Sicily in the Twelfth Century', *English Historical Review*, vol. 26 (1911)

Haskins, Charles Homer, 'Henry II as a patron of literature', in A. G. Little and F. M. Powicke (eds), *Essays in Medieval History Presented to T. F. Tout* (Manchester, 1925)

Haskins, Charles H., 'The Inquest of 1171 in the Avranchin', *English Historical Review*, vol. 26 (1911)

Haskins, Charles Homer, *The Renaissance of the Twelfth Century* (Cambridge, Mass., 1927)

Hibbert, Christopher, *The English: A Social History, 1066–1945* (London, 1987)

Hivergneaux, Marie, 'Autour d'Aliénor d'Aquitaine: Entourage et Pouvoir au Prisme des Chartes (1137–1187)', in *Plantagenêts et Capétiens* (Paris, 2006)

Hivergneaux, Marie, 'Queen Eleanor and Aquitaine, 1137–1189', in Bonnie Wheeler and John C. Parsons (eds), *Eleanor of Aquitaine: Lord and Lady* (London, 2002)

Hollister, Warren C. (ed.), *Anglo-Norman Political Culture and the 12th Century Renaissance* (Woodbridge, 1997)

Hollister, Warren, and Thomas Keefe, 'The Making of the Angevin Empire', *Journal of British Studies*, vol. 12, no. 2 (1 May 1973)

Hosler, John, *Henry II: A Medieval Soldier at War* (Leiden, 2007)

Jenks, Susanne, Jonathan Rose and Christopher Whittick (eds), *Laws, Lawyers and Texts: Studies in Medieval Legal History in Honour of Paul Brand* (Leiden, 2012)

Joliffe, C. F., 'The Camera Regis under Henry II', *English Historical Review*, vol. 681 (January 1953)

Joliffe, John, *Angevin Kingship* (London, 1963)

Jones, Colin, *Paris: Biography of a City* (London, 2004)

Jones, Thomas M., 'Henry II in Drama: Changing Historical Outlooks', *Comparative Drama*, vol. 12, no. 4 (1 December 1978)

Jordan, Erin, *Women, Power and Religious Patronage in the Middle Ages* (New York, 2006)

Keefe, Thomas, *Feudal Assessments and the Political Community under Henry II and his Sons* (Berkeley, 1983)

Keefe, Thomas, 'Geoffrey Plantagenet's Will and the Angevin Succession', *Albion*, vol. 6 (3) (1 October 1974)

Keefe, Thomas, 'King Henry II and the Earls: The Pipe Roll Evidence', *Albion*, vol. 13 (3) (1 October 1981)

Kelly, Amy, *Eleanor of Aquitaine and the Four Kings* (Cambridge, Mass., 1950)

Kennedy, Ruth, and Simon Meecham-Jones (eds), *Writers of the Reign of Henry II: Twelve Essays* (London, 2006)

Kerr, Berenice, *Religious Life for Women c.1100–c.1350: Fontevraud in England* (Oxford, 1999)

Kibler, William (ed.), *Eleanor of Aquitaine: Patron and Politician* (Austin, 1976)

King, Edmund, 'The Accession of Henry II', in Christopher Harper-Bill and Nicholas Vincent (eds), *Henry II: New Interpretations* (Woodbridge, 2007)

King, Edmund, *England 1175–1425* (London, 1979)

King, Edmund, *King Stephen* (New Haven, 2010)

Kinoshita, Sharon, and Peggy McCracken, *Marie de France: A Critical Companion* (Woodbridge, 2012)

Lees, Beatrice, 'The Letters of Queen Eleanor of Aquitaine to Pope Celestine III', *English Historical Review*, vol. 21 (1906)

Le Patourel, John, 'The Norman Conquest, 1066, 1106, 1154?', in Marjorie Chibnall, Christopher Harper-Bill, John Gillingham, C. P. Lewis, David Bates and Elisabeth Van Houts (eds), *Proceedings of the Battle Conference on Anglo-Norman Studies* (XII) (Woodbridge, 1978–)

Le Patourel, John, *The Norman Empire* (Oxford, 1997)

Lewis, Andrew W., 'The Birth and Childhood of King John', in Bonnie Wheeler and John C. Parsons (eds), *Eleanor of Aquitaine: Lord and Lady* (London, 2002)

Lewis, Andrew W., 'Six Charters of Henry II and his Family for the Monastery of Dalon', *English Historical Review*, vol. 110 (June 1995)

Leyser, Karl, *Communications and Power in Medieval Europe: The Gregorian Revolution and Beyond* (London, 1994)

Leyser, Karl, 'Frederick Barbarossa, Henry II and the Hand of St James', *English Historical Review*, vol. 901 (July 1975)

Loud, G. A. 'The Kingdom of Sicily and the Kingdom of England, 1066–1266', *Journal of the Historical Association*, vol. 88, issue 292 (October 2003)

Lunt, W. E., 'The Text of the Ordinance of 1184 Concerning an Aid for the Holy Land', *English Historical Review*, vol. 37 (1922)

McCauley, Barbara Lynne, 'Geraldus "Silvester" of Wales and his "Prophetic History Of Ireland": Merlin's Role in the *Expugnatio Hibernica*', *Quondam et Futurus*, vol. 3, no. 4 (Winter 1993)

McCracken, Peggy, 'Scandalizing Desire: Eleanor of Aquitaine and the Chroniclers', in Bonnie Wheeler and John C. Parsons (eds), *Eleanor of Aquitaine: Lord and Lady* (London, 2002)

McNeill, John, and Daniel Prigent (eds), *Anjou: Medieval Art, Architecture and Archaeology* (London, 2003)

Maréchal, Chantal A. (ed.), *In Quest of Marie de France: A Twelfth-Century Poet* (New York, 1992)

Martin, Therese, 'The Art of a Reigning Queen as Dynastic Propaganda in Twelfth-Century Spain', *Speculum*, vol. 80, no. 4 (October 2005)

Martindale, Jane, 'Eleanor of Aquitaine', in Janet Nelson (ed.), *Richard Coeur de Lion in History and Myth* (London, 1992)

Martindale, Jane (2002) 'Eleanor of Aquitaine and a "Queenly Court"', in Bonnie Wheeler and John C. Parsons (eds), *Eleanor of Aquitaine: Lord and Lady* (London, 2002)

Mayer, Hans Eberhard, 'Henry II of England and the Holy Land', *English Historical Review*, vol. 97, no. 385 (October 1982)

Mayer, Hans Eberhard, 'Latins, Muslims and Greeks in the Latin Kingdom of Jerusalem', *History*, vol. 63 (June 1978)

Mayhew, N. J., 'Money and Prices in England from Henry II to Edward III', *Agricultural History Review*, vol. 35, no. 2 (1987)

Meade, Marion, *Eleanor of Aquitaine: A Biography* (London, 1977)

Miller, Edward, and John Hatcher, *Medieval England: Towns, Commerce and Crafts 1086–1348* (London, 1995)

Morris, Colin, and Peter Roberts, *Pilgrimage: The English Experience from Becket to Bunyan* (Cambridge, 2002)

Morris, Marc, *King John: Treachery, Tyranny and the Road to Magna Carta* (London, 2015)

Mortimer, Richard, 'The Charters of Henry II: What are the Criteria for Authenticity?', in Marjorie Chibnall, Christopher Harper-Bill, John Gillingham, C. P. Lewis, David Bates and Elisabeth Van Houts (eds), *Proceedings of the Battle Conference on Anglo-Norman Studies* (XII) (Woodbridge, 1978–)

Mullally, Evelyn, 'The Reciprocal Loyalty of Eleanor of Aquitaine and William Marshal', in Bonnie Wheeler and John C. Parsons (eds), *Eleanor of Aquitaine: Lord and Lady* (London, 2002)

Mullet, Jacques, *L'art roman de l'ancien Anjou* (Paris, 1984)

Myhill, Henry, *The Loire Valley: Plantagenet and Valois* (London, 1978)

Nolan, Kathleen, 'The Queen's Choice: Eleanor of Aquitaine and the Tombs at Fontevraud', in Bonnie Wheeler and John C. Parsons (eds), *Eleanor of Aquitaine: Lord and Lady* (London, 2002)

Nolan, Kathleen, *Queens in Stone and Silver: The Creation of a Visual Imagery of Queenship in Capetian France* (New York, 2009)

Norgate, Kate, *England under the Angevin Kings*, 2 vols (London, 1887)

Norgate, Kate, 'Robert, Earl of Gloucester', *Dictionary of National Biography* (1900)

Norwich, John Julius, *The Kingdom in the Sun* (London, 1970)

Orme, Nicholas, *From Childhood to Chivalry: The Education of the English Kings and Aristocracy* (London, 1984)

Owen, D. D. R., *Eleanor of Aquitaine: Queen and Legend* (Oxford, 1993)

Pain, Nesta, *Empress Matilda, Uncrowned Queen of England* (London, 1978)

Painter, Sidney, 'The Lords of Lusignan in the Eleventh and Twelfth Centuries', *Speculum* vol. 32, no. 1 (January 1957)

Paterson, L. M., *The World of the Troubadours: Medieval Occitan Society c.1100–c.1300* (Cambridge, 1993)

Pegg, Mark Gregory, *A Most Holy War: The Albigensian Crusade and the Battle for Christendom* (Oxford, 2008)

Peltzer, Jörg, 'The Angevin Kings and Canon Law: Episcopal Elections and the Loss of Normandy', in Marjorie Chibnall, Christopher Harper-Bill, John Gillingham, C. P. Lewis, David Bates and Elisabeth Van Houts (eds), *Proceedings of the Battle Conference on Anglo-Norman Studies* (XXVII) (Woodbridge, 1978–)

Peltzer, Jörg, 'Henry II and the Norman Bishops', *English Historical Review*, vol. 119 (2004)

Petzhold, Andreas, *Romanesque Art* (London, 1995)

Phillips, Jonathan, *The Crusades: 1095–1204* (London, 2002)

Phillips, Jonathan, *Holy Warriors: A Modern History of the Crusades* (Bodley Head, 2009)

Phillips, Jonathan, *The Second Crusade: Extending the Frontiers of Christendom* (New Haven, 2007)

Plain, Nancy, *Eleanor of Aquitaine and the High Middle Ages* (London, 2005)

Plant, J. S, 'The Tardy Adoption of the Plantagenet Surname', *Nomina*, 30 (2007)

Plassmann, Alheydis, 'The King and his Sons: Henry II's and Frederick Barbarossa's Succession Strategies Compared', *Battle Conference 2013* (no. 35)

Poole, A. L., 'Henry Plantagenet's Early Visits to England', *English Historical Review*, vol. 47 (1 July 1932)

Poole, Reginald L., 'The Dates of Henry II's Charters', *English Historical Review*, vol. 23 (1 January 1908)

Poole, Reginald L., 'Henry II, Duke of Normandy', *English Historical Review*, vol. 42 (1 October 1927)

Power, Daniel, 'Henry, Duke of the Normans', in Christopher Harper-Bill and Nicholas Vincent (eds), *Henry II: New Interpretations* (Woodbridge, 2007)

Power, Daniel, *The Norman Frontier in the Twelfth and Early Thirteenth Centuries* (Cambridge, 2004)

Powicke, F. M. (ed.), *The Christian Life in the Middle Ages and Other Essays* (Oxford, 1968)

Reuter, Timothy (ed.), *Warriors and Churchmen: Essays Presented to Karl Leyser* (London, 1992)

Richardson, H. G., *The English Jewry under Angevin Kings* (London, 1960)

Roberts, J. M., *History of Europe* (London, 1997)

Robinson, Ian, *The Papacy, 1073–1198: Continuity and Innovation* (Cambridge, 1990)

Rothwell, William, 'Language and Government in Medieval England', *Zeitschrift für Französische Sprache und Literatur*, vol. 93, no. 3 (1983)

Runciman, S., *A History of the Crusades* (Cambridge, 1951–4)

Saperstein, Marc, and Jacob Rader Marcus (eds), *The Jews in Christian Europe: A Source Book, 315–1791* (Pittsburgh, 2015)

Scholz, Bernhard W., 'The Canonization of Edward the Confessor', *Speculum*, vol. 36 (1 January 1961)

Schramm, Percy Ernst, *A History of the English Coronation* (Oxford, 1937)

Selwood, Dominic, *Knights of the Cloister: Templars and Hospitallers in Central-Southern Occitania*, c. 1100–c. 1300 (Boydell Press, 2002)

Short, Ian, 'Literary Culture at the Court of Henry II', in Christopher Harper-Bill and Nicholas Vincent (eds), *Henry II: New Interpretations* (Woodbridge, 2007)

Shuttleworth, John, *Fools and Jesters at the English Court* (Stroud, 1998)

Simmons, Loraine N., 'The Abbey Church at Fontevraud in the Later Twelfth Century: Anxiety, Authority and Architecture in the Female Spiritual Life', *Gesta*, vol. 31 (1 January 1992)

Skinner, P. (ed.), *Jews in Medieval Britain: Historical, Literary and Archaeological Perspectives* (Woodbridge, 2003)

Smith, R. J., 'Henry II's Heir: The Acta and Seal of Henry the Young King, 1170–83', *English Historical Review*, vol. 116 (2001)

Southern, R. W., *The Making of the Middle Ages* (London, 1953)

Southern, R. W., 'The Place of England in the Twelfth-Century Renaissance', *History*, vol. 45, no. 155 (1960)

Southern, R. W., *Saint Anselm and his Biographer: A Study of Monastic Life and Thought 1059–c.1130* (Cambridge, 1963)

Staunton, Michael (tr. and annotated), *The Lives of Thomas Becket* (Manchester, 2001)

Staunton, Michael, 'Thomas Becket's Conversion', in Marjorie Chibnall, Christopher Harper-Bill, John Gillingham, C. P. Lewis, David Bates, Elisabeth Van Houts (eds), *Proceedings of the Battle Conference on Anglo-Norman Studies* (XXI) (Woodbridge, 1978–)

Strickland, Matthew, 'On the Instruction of a Prince: The Upbringing of Henry, the Young King', in Christopher Harper-Bill and Nicholas Vincent (eds), *Henry II: New Interpretations* (Woodbridge, 2007)

Strickland, Matthew, *Henry the Young King* (New Haven, 2016)

Swabey, Ffiona, *Eleanor of Aquitaine, Courtly Love, and the Troubadours* (Santa Barbara, 2004)

Thomson, Rodney M., 'England and the Twelfth Century Renaissance', *Past and Present*, issue 1011 (November 1983)

Turner, Ralph V., *Eleanor of Aquitaine* (New Haven, 2009)

Turner, Ralph V., 'Eleanor of Aquitaine, Twelfth-Century English Chroniclers and her "Black Legend"', *Nottingham Medieval Studies*, vol. 52 (2008)

Turner, Ralph V., 'Eleanor of Aquitaine and her Children: An Inquiry into Medieval Family Attachment', *Journal of Medieval History*, vol. 14 (1998)

Turner, Ralph V., 'Eleanor of Aquitaine in the Governments of Her Sons Richard and John', in Bonnie Wheeler and John C. Parsons (eds), *Eleanor of Aquitaine: Lord and Lady* (London, 2002)

Turner, Ralph V., *Men Raised from the Dust: Administrative Service and Upward Mobility in Angevin England* (Philadelphia, 1988)

Turner, Ralph V., 'The Problem of Survival for the Angevin "Empire": Henry II's and His Sons' Vision versus Late Twelfth-Century Realities', *American Historical Review*, vol. 100 (1 February 1995)

Van Houts, Elisabeth, 'Normandy's View of the Anglo-Saxon Past in the Twelfth Century', in Martin Brett and David A. Woodman (eds), *The Long Twelfth-Century View of the Anglo-Saxon Past* (Ashgate, 2015)

Bibliography

Vincent, Nicholas (ed.), *Acta of Henry II and Richard I pt. 2: A Supplementary Handlist of Documents Surviving in the Original Repositories in the United Kingdom, France, Ireland, Belgium and the USA* (Kew, 1996)

Vincent, Nicholas, 'The Court of Henry II', in Christopher Harper-Bill and Nicholas Vincent (eds), *Henry II: New Interpretations* (Woodbridge, 2007)

Vincent, Nicholas, 'The Great Lost Library of England's Medieval Kings? Royal Use and Ownership of Books, 1066–1272', in Kathleen Doyle and Scot McEndrick (eds), *1000 Years of Royal Books and Manuscripts* (London, 2013)

Vincent, Nicholas, 'Henry II and the Historians', in Christopher Harper-Bill and Nicholas Vincent (eds), *Henry II: New Interpretations* (Woodbridge, 2007)

Vincent, Nicholas, 'King Henry II and the Monks of Battle: The Battle Chronicle Unmasked', *Belief and Culture in the Middle Ages: Studies Presented to Henry Mayr-Harting* (Oxford, 2001)

Vincent, Nicholas, *Magna Carta: A Very Short Introduction* (Oxford, 2012)

Vincent, Nicholas, 'The Murderers of Thomas Becket', in Natalie Fryde and Dirk Reitz (eds), *Bischofsmord im Mittelalter/The Murder of Bishops in the Middle Ages* (Göttingen, 2003)

Vincent, Nicholas, 'The pilgrimages of the Angevin kings of England 1154–1272', in Colin Morris and Peter Roberts (eds), *Pilgrimage: The English Experience from Becket to Bunyan* (Cambridge, 2002)

Vincent, Nicholas (ed.), *Records, Administration and Aristocratic Society in the Anglo-Norman Realm: Papers Commemorating the 800th Anniversary of King John's Loss of Normandy* (Woodbridge, 2009)

Vincent, Nicholas, 'The Strange Case of the Missing Biographies: The Lives of the Plantagenet Kings of England, 1154–1272', in *Writing Medieval Biography, 750–1250: Essays in Honour of Frank Barlow* (Woodbridge, 2006)

Vincent, Nicholas, 'The Use and Abuse of Anglo-Saxon Charters by the Kings of England, 1100–1300', in Martin Brett and David A. Woodman (eds), *The Long Twelfth-Century View of the Anglo-Saxon Past* (Ashgate, 2015)

Vincent, Nicholas, 'Warin and Henry FitzGerald, the King's Chamberlains: the Origins of the FitzGeralds Revisited', in Marjorie Chibnall, Christopher Harper-Bill, John Gillingham, C. P. Lewis, David Bates and Elisabeth Van Houts (eds), *Proceedings of the Battle Conference on Anglo-Norman Studies (XXI)* (Woodbridge, 1978–)

Vollrath, Hanna, 'Was Thomas Becket Chaste? Understanding Episodes in the Becket Lives', in Marjorie Chibnall, Christopher Harper-Bill, John Gillingham, C. P. Lewis, David Bates, Elisabeth Van Houts (eds), *Proceedings of the Battle Conference on Anglo-Norman Studies (XXVII)* (Woodbridge, 1978–)

Von Moschzisker, Robert, 'The Historic Origin of Trial by Jury', *University of Pennsylvania Law Review and American Law Register*, vol. 70 (1 November 1921)

Warren, W. L, *Henry II* (Berkeley, 1973)

Warren, W. L, *King John* (London, 1961)

Webb, Clement Charles Julian, *John of Salisbury* (London, 1932)

Whalen, Logan E. (ed.), *A Companion to Marie de France* (Leiden, 2011)

Wheeler, Bonnie, and John C. Parsons (eds), *Eleanor of Aquitaine: Lord and Lady* (London, 2002)

Wilks, Michael (ed.), *The World of John of Salisbury* (Oxford, 1984)

ACKNOWLEDGEMENTS

I would like to thank my agent Vivienne Schuster for believing in me and in this project. She has always been my champion and I am incredibly grateful to her. I also thank Felicity Blunt, who took up the cause of Henry when Vivienne retired, for approaching this book with equal enthusiasm.

I could not have wished for a more encouraging and knowledgeable editor than Arabella Pike at William Collins. My huge thanks to her and all of her team.

I am indebted to the many professional and amateur historians who have been so generous with their time and research while I was writing this book. Special thanks to Nicholas Vincent, for sharing his unpublished archival research on the Acta of Henry II with me. Thanks too, in no particular order, to Patrick Bade, Marc Morris, David d'Avray, Zoé Wozniak-Queffélec, John Julius Norwich, Andrew Hadfield, Stanley Wells, Rina Wolfson, Bruce Thompson, Richard Plant, Laura Profitt, Fran Spalter, Dominic Selwood, David Bell and Benjamin Sheward. My thanks to the incredible staff at the London Library.

My talented friends and family deserve my enormous gratitude. They have all been typically yet unfailingly generous. I am grateful to my mother, Trudy Gold, for helping me to place Henry within the context of Jewish history. My sister, Tanya Gold, always kept me on the path. Peter Leach presented the

Plantagenet family to me as a modern family business. My god-father Raymond Levine guided me through the complexities of Henry and the law, and my brother-in-law, Andrew Watts, offered his invaluable insights into twelfth-century Latin.

Above all I thank my husband, Phil Rubenstein, a superb writer and editor, and my first reader. This book was the result of a conversation on the cliffs in Cornwall with him, and it would not have happened without his energy, his insight and his encouragement. Our sons, Asher and Jake, and our nephew, Arthur, showed the most extraordinary understanding and patience as I disappeared into the twelfth century for the best part of four years. Thank you, my brilliant boys. And finally to Jerry Gotel, who was passionate about Henry, for introducing me to *The Lion in Winter*. Jerry did not live to see the publication of this book; we will miss him always.

Claudia Gold,
London, March 2018

ILLUSTRATIONS

Fourteenth-century manuscript showing Henry I on his throne, grieving for the loss of his only legitimate son, and the hundreds besides him who died on the *White Ship* in 1120. (British Library, London, UK/© British Library Board. All Rights Reserved/Bridgeman Images)

Enamel effigy of Henry's father, Geoffrey Plantagenet, Count of Anjou. Henry spared no expense commemorating a father he admired and loved. (Musée de Tesse, Le Mans, France/Bridgeman Images)

Matilda, Henry's mother, from the late-fourteenth-century *Golden Book of St Albans*. She was accused of being a 'virago'. Failing to win the English crown for herself, Matilda devoted herself to her son's cause. (British Library, London, UK/© British Library Board. All Rights Reserved/Bridgeman Images)

The hand of St James, one of the twelve apostles, on display at St Peter's Church, Marlow. (Photo By RDImages/Epics/Getty Images)

Eleanor of Aquitaine's wedding to Louis VII of France. The marriage was a disaster, and she later complained that Louis was 'more monk than man'. (Getty Images)

King Stephen, the charming and chivalrous favourite of his uncle, Henry I; he stole the throne from his first cousin Matilda – in spite of his pledges of loyalty to her. (© National Portrait Gallery, London)

Henry's face on a coin, curly hair topped by a crown made up of five pearls, issued after 1180. (Courtesy of www.HallsHammeredCoins.com)

Henry and Eleanor's eldest surviving son, Henri – the Young King. He was crowned alongside his father in 1170, but he had absolutely no power. Henry did not think his son capable of ruling his empire when he died. (Granger Historical Picture Archive/Alamy Stock Photo)

Pilgrims at Edward the Confessor's shrine. Henry successfully petitioned the pope to have his ancestor canonised, to glorify his own regime. (British Library, London, UK/© British Library Board. All Rights Reserved/Bridgeman Images)

Fascinated by design, Henry himself commissioned the intriguing octagonal Byzantine-Romanesque-style kitchen, or smokehouse, at Fontevraud Abbey. (Geoffrey Taunton/Alamy Stock Photo)

In an impressive display of wealth and power, Henry and Eleanor rebuilt Poitiers cathedral, some time after John was born in 1166. Here, they may be seen offering up the window; their four sons are in the background. (akg-images/Paul M.R. Maeyaert)

King Henry II seated on his throne, arguing with Thomas Becket. (British Library, London, UK/© British Library Board. All Rights Reserved/Bridgeman Images)

Murder of Thomas Becket, from the fifteenth-century *St Albans Chronicle*. (Lambeth Palace Library, London/Bridgeman Images)

Thomas Becket appears to a leper in one of the Miracle Windows at Canterbury cathedral. (Granger Historical Picture Archive/Alamy Stock Photo)

Philip Augustus, son of Louis VII, seated on the left, receiving an envoy of the pope. The illustration, from the fourteenth-century *Grandes Chroniques de France*, shows Philip and Henry (right) taking the cross. (British Library, London, UK/© British Library Board. All Rights Reserved/Bridgeman Images)

This mural at the underground chapel of Sainte-Radegonde at
Chinon dates from around the turn of the thirteenth century.
(Roger-Viollet/Topfoto)

Eleanor gave this rock crystal vase as a wedding gift to Louis. It
had most likely been given to her grandfather, Duke William IX,
by the Muslim King Imad al-dawla of Saragossa – friendships
could exist between people of different faiths. It is on display in
the Louvre in Paris. (Jacqueline Guillot/akg-images)

The charismatic Bernard of Clairvaux roused Christendom
when he preached the Second Crusade at Vezelay in 1146.
Henry's father, Geoffrey of Anjou, was notable by his absence
from the venture; Bernard never forgave him. (Signol,
Emile (1804–92)/Château de Versailles, France/Bridgeman
Images)

In many ways, the life of Frederick Barbarossa (Red Beard), the
Holy Roman Emperor, mirrored Henry's own. Frederick
drowned in the River Saleph in the summer of 1190, as he
travelled to the Latin Kingdom on the Third Crusade. (Private
Collection/© Look and Learn/Elgar Collection/Bridgeman
Images)

The crusaders feared the swift horses and lethal arrows of Saladin's
army. Illustration from the fourteenth-century *Le Roman de
Godefroi de Bouillon*. (Bibliothèque Nationale, Paris, France/
Bridgeman Images)

Philip, working with Richard, forced Henry to flee Le Mans, his
favourite city, in the summer of 1189. Its loss devastated Henry,
who reputedly blamed God, crying, 'I will … deny You what
You love best in me, my soul!' (Granger Historical Picture
Archive/Alamy Stock Photo)

William Marshal, the greatest of Henry's knights, was nearly
hanged by Stephen when only five years old. He lived, and
served Henry and his family with unsurpassed loyalty for the
rest of his life. (English School/Temple Church, London, UK/
Bridgeman Images)

Ordeal by fire, depicted in a ninth-century manuscript. In the face of his seismic judicial reforms, trials by ordeal gradually went out of favour during Henry's reign. (Bibliotheque Nationale, Paris, France/Archives Charmet/Bridgeman Images)

Dover Castle: Henry spent a fortune rebuilding it after Louis's surprise visit to Canterbury in 1179. Ever the generous host, he was embarrassed that he had nowhere suitably regal for Louis to stay. (Granger/Bridgeman Images)

The first four Plantagenet kings of England: Henry II, in profile, a negative judgement on his kingship; Richard, bellicose, wielding a sword and shield; John, crown askew; Henry III, shown face on with his crown firmly on his head – the most positive representation. (British Library, London, UK/© British Library Board. All Rights Reserved/Bridgeman Images)

Tombs of Eleanor of Aquitaine and Henry II of England at Fontevraud Abbey in the Loire. Eleanor turned Fontevraud into the family mausoleum in the service of Plantagenet power. She designed these magnificent, brilliantly painted *gisants*. In death, Eleanor gives herself something to do: she is shown reading a book. (Brian Harris/Alamy Stock Photo)

INDEX